EMILY DAVIES AND GIRTON COLLEGE

A volume in the Hyperion reprint series

PIONEERS OF THE WOMAN'S MOVEMENT

EMILY DAVIES

From a drawing by Annabella Mason, 1851

EMILY DAVIES
AND GIRTON COLLEGE

by

Barbara Stephen

HYPERION PRESS, INC.
Westport, Connecticut

Published in 1927 by Constable & Co., Ltd., London
Hyperion reprint edition 1976
Library of Congress Catalog Number 75-644
ISBN 0-88355-282-5
Printed in the United States of America

Library of Congress Cataloging in Publication Data

Stephen, Barbara Nightingale, Lady.
  Emily Davies and Girton College.

  (Pioneers of the woman's movement)
  Reprint of the 1927 ed. published by Constable, London.
  Bibliography: p.
  Includes index.
  1. Davies, Emily, 1830-1921. 2. Cambridge. University.
Girton College. I. Title.
LF797.G54D33   1976   370'.92'4 [B]   75-644
ISBN 0-88355-282-5

PREFACE

I WISH to thank the members of Miss Emily Davies' family who have entrusted me with the task of writing her life, and have placed her papers and much helpful information at my disposal. I must also express my thanks to the representatives of George Eliot, Professor Henry Sidgwick, Viscount Bryce, Sir Thomas Dyke Acland, and Sir John Seeley, for permission to publish extracts from letters ; to the London School of Economics, for leave to quote some letters from Madame Bodichon and Miss Davies to Miss Helen Taylor, now in their library ; to the Council of Girton College, for leave to refer to minute books and papers at Girton ; and to a number of former students of Girton for helpful information, among whom I must specially name Dame Louisa Lumsden, Mrs. Townshend, Miss Maynard, Mrs. Higgs, Miss Dove, and Miss Ridding. Dr. Louisa Garrett Anderson has kindly allowed me to use letters from her mother which throw light on the careers of both Miss Davies and Mrs. Garrett Anderson, and has given me some interesting details.

It will be noticed that there are very few letters from Madame Bodichon in the book. George Eliot told her she was " a vilely uncertain correspondent," and certainly not many of her letters seem to have survived. I am the more grateful to those who have helped me to fill the gap, especially to Madame Bodichon's nephew, Mr. Valentine Leigh Smith, of Scalands, who has allowed me to use various papers, including letters from Miss Davies, Miss Metcalfe, and Lady Stanley of Alderley ; and to Mrs. Benjamin Leigh Smith, who has lent me copies of letters from George Eliot. I must also express my thanks to Madame Bodichon's friend Miss Gertrude Jekyll, to Miss Hope Malleson, Mrs. Belloc Lowndes, and Mrs. Ayrton Gould, for much valuable information. I wish it were possible to do more than record my gratitude to Madame Belloc, and to Mrs. Hertha Ayrton, from both of whom I received many interesting particulars, shortly before their deaths.

Limitations of space make it impossible to thank all the friends who have helped me with information, suggestions, and criticisms, but I may be allowed to mention Mrs. James Adam, Mrs. Oliver Strachey, Miss B. A. Clough, late Principal of Newnham College, and Miss Hermia Durham. Mrs. Vaughan Nash and my husband, Sir Harry Stephen, have read the proofs.

In the Biographical Index will be found particulars, which could not conveniently be given in the text, as to some of the persons mentioned. These particulars, not always easily accessible, will, it is hoped, be useful to readers who are young enough to have only a vague knowledge of certain personages of importance in a past generation.

BARBARA STEPHEN.

July, 1926.

CONTENTS

CONTENTS

CONTENTS

ix

CONTENTS

LIST OF ILLUSTRATIONS

CHAPTER I

Introduction

" I have no hesitation in declaring my full belief in the inferiority
of woman, nor that she brought it upon herself. . . . Woman was
created as a helpmeet for man . . . but when the test came, whether
the two human beings would pay allegiance to God or to the Tempter,
it was the woman who was the first to fail. . . . Thence her punishment of physical weakness and subordination. . . ."

—*Womankind*, by C. M. YONGE.

MISS EMILY DAVIES left among her papers a memorandum expressing her wishes as to a memoir of herself. " I should object," she wrote, " to anything
of an intimate personal nature, and there are not materials for
it, but I think it reasonable that some information should be
available as to the founders of Girton College. . . . It might be
well to combine in such a sketch some account of Madame
Bodichon, of whom there is not, so far as I know, any permanent
record in existence." An attempt has accordingly been made
in this memoir to give some account of Miss Davies, Madame
Bodichon, and the other founders of Girton ; of the novel,
almost revolutionary work which they accomplished in various
fields ; and of the eventful history of the College during its
earlier years.

The foundation of Girton was an educational experiment of the
boldest kind, but it was even more. It was a step, and a very
important one, in the movement which led to a revolution in the
position of women. In this movement, Miss Davies was a
pioneer and a leader ; and in order to arrive at a fair estimate
of the work which she accomplished, both educational and
political, some attempt must first be made to give a brief sketch

of the condition of society which drove her and her friends to devote themselves to this work.

Closely associated with Miss Davies' life in different ways were two distinguished women, Barbara Leigh Smith (Madame Bodichon), the elder friend already taking a leading part in the inception of the women's movement when Emily Davies came to London ; and Elizabeth Garrett (Mrs. Garrett Anderson), the young student who, at Miss Davies' suggestion and with her earnest and constant co-operation, contrived to get a medical education in London and an English qualification to practise medicine, the first woman to do so. No life has been written of either, or is likely to be written, and the space which will be given to their share in the story will probably not be grudged by readers interested in the main subject.

Miss Davies was brought up within the close restrictions accepted as proper for girls at that time, but she was born a " feminist " (to use the phraseology of a later day), and it was through native force of character that she was able to break away from the conventional grooves and strike out her own line. In all that concerned women, she was a revolutionary ; in all else, a conservative. Her contemporaries did not think of her as a revolutionary. As Dame Louisa Lumsden has said of her, " She had a strong sense of order and law and a considerable power of organization, and from this sense of order she had a reverence for outward conformity and a certain contempt for what she might have called, one's own particular little heresies." When a new departure appealed to her sense of justice, as it did in the case of women, while she was fearless and venturous in supporting it, she was always most careful to avoid anything that might needlessly shock the conventions of the day. " Her dainty little figure and smiling face," writes Mrs. Townshend, one of the first students of Girton, " were most misleading. They concealed untiring energy, a will of iron, and a very clear and definite set of opinions. . . . She was a person of single aim who looked neither to the right hand nor to the left." For the sake of that aim she was prepared to sacrifice herself, and she expected as much of those who worked with her. Intensity of feeling, and a certain limitation of sympathies, caused her to have strong antipathies as well as warm friendships ; but no one could fail

2

to recognize her devotion to her aims, and the power and originality of her character. Although it so fell out that the foundation of a College became the main work of her life, she was herself neither a scholar nor a student. Yet her native abilities, combined as they were with courage, caution, and forethought, might have earned her the rank of statesman in another field, or even that of general ; it is constantly noticeable that she thought of life as a battle, and of herself as leading an attack upon hostile forces. Her outstanding service to the cause of women lies in this, that it is largely owing to her that women are now admitted to share in the common stock of learning ; and that there is no field of thought, research, or teaching from which, as women, they are excluded. In her youth, it was accepted as a matter of course that the intellectual powers of women were strictly limited and could only be profitably exercised on certain subjects. Many people, even among those who were most eager for the improvement of women's education, wanted to see it developed on special lines of its own, apart from men. This could only have meant limitation and therefore inferiority ; and there would have been a great loss to men and women alike, from the perpetuation of a system which cut women off both from the direct influence of the old universities, and from the possibility of taking a part in the common effort.

With Mrs. Garrett Anderson, as with Miss Davies, the dominant passion was to set women free from unnecessary limitations, and to open to them every possible opportunity for using their faculties and developing their powers. A delightful impression is given of her in a letter of 1870, from Mrs. Russell Gurney. " Dear Goddess of Health," she writes, " you brought in with you such a fresh current of health and vigour last Tuesday that you took away my cold, and I perceived a *radiance* for some time afterwards." Mrs. Anderson's sister, Dame Millicent Garrett Fawcett, has written of her " deep fund of natural human affection and almost maternal feeling " towards her younger brothers and sisters. But to a woman of her strong and aspiring character, it was impossible to stay at home in a large family circle, happy though it was, where she was not really needed. She longed to be of use in a wider field, and she chose the medical profession as a means to this end. Her career proved—and proof was needed—that a woman could be capable not only of persevering through a long and severe course of study, but of combining success in an arduous profession with the happy life of a married woman with a family.

Like Miss Davies and Mrs. Garrett Anderson, Madame Bodichon was a woman of intense convictions, endowed with strong cheerful common sense. Unlike them, she had a childhood and youth very different from that of most girls of her time. It was largely owing to this that she was extraordinarily modern in her outlook ; she seemed to have been born two generations too soon. She was early allowed to have an unusual degree of personal independence, was well educated, and could count many reformers, social and political, among the friends of her family. These advantages were heightened by her personal qualities. She was very handsome and attractive, and her generous character, overflowing with life and vigour, made her greatly beloved. These were no small advantages to so unpopular a cause as that of women's rights, and her influence was of great value ; with her independence and originality (unwomanly as these qualities were then considered), she drew many friends to the cause, and her generous sympathy and frank enthusiasm were an inspiration to her fellow-workers on the same thorny path.

The revolution which these three friends helped to initiate has been so complete that some effort of the imagination is needed in order to understand the state of things which prevailed in their youth. The " deconsideration " of women, as Madame Bodichon called it, was due to the state of the law and of public opinion. Exclusion from the Parliamentary franchise was scarcely perceived to be a hardship at a time when the franchise was exercised by only a small proportion of men. It was the laws relating to property and marriage which were chiefly felt as oppressive to women. A single woman could have control over her own property equal to that of a man ; directly she married, she ceased to have any property at all ; whether earned or inherited by her, all belonged to her husband. She had no independent power of making a will, entering into a contract, or bringing an action ; her signature was not valid without that of her husband. " The existing law is a relic of slavery," said Sir George Jessel (Master of the Rolls, and one of the greatest lawyers of his time) in the House of Commons, in 1869 ; " the law of slavery, whether Roman or English—for we once had slaves and slave laws in England—gave to the master of a slave the important rights of flogging and imprisoning him. A slave could not possess property of his own and could not make contracts except for his master's benefit, and the master alone could sue for an injury to the slave ; while the only liability of the master was that he must not let his slave starve. This is exactly the position of the wife under the English law." As in the case of master and slave, the husband alone could sue for an injury to his wife ; though from force of circumstances, if injury there were, it was more likely to come from the husband himself than from anyone else. Divorce or separation could only be obtained by those who were rich enough to afford two legal actions and a private Act of Parliament ; and the fact that a woman had no money of her own was alone enough, as a rule, to make it impossible for her to take action against her husband, who, on the other hand, might use any money he had acquired through marrying his wife to bring an action against her. The husband, moreover, had full control over the children, and the wife could do nothing even to protect them against a bad husband. These facts were tragically exemplified in Mrs. Norton's famous case, on which we find the following comment in the *North British Review* :

" In this unhappy instance, all the evils of the existing laws, as they affect women, find apt illustration. . . . It is obvious, that so long as the dissolution of the marriage contract is almost an impossibility, and the marriage contract is what it is, the larger and more important section of the women of England must be legal nonentities. That the effect of this is to limit the aspirations, to paralyse the energies, and to demoralize the characters of women, is not to be denied. . . . To retain and preserve a condition of independence, it is necessary that they should abide in a state of singleness, which is more or less a state of reproach." [1]

Among rich families, the hardships of the law were generally mitigated by means of settlements, which secured some inde-

[1] *The Non-existence of Women*, in the *North British Review*, August, 1855. See Biographical Index, p. 368.

pendent property even to married women. Among people who could not afford settlements, or neglected them, there was much silent suffering. But the laws were supported by public opinion. As the *Saturday Review* remarked : " No woman ought to be encouraged in the belief that she has separate interests or separate duties. God and Nature have merged her existence in that of her husband." [1]

There were economic as well as social forces at work which pressed even more heavily on women than did the marriage laws. It was commonly supposed that every woman had a man to support her, but the facts were proving to be out of harmony with this comfortable belief. Miss Davies was born in 1830, that is to say, about half-way between the end of the Napoleonic wars in 1815 and the repeal of the Corn Laws in 1848. This period was one of commercial and financial troubles, which were felt with especial force by those women of the middle class whose husbands and fathers lost their livelihood. The financial collapse of 1826 has been described by Harriet Martineau with the vivid words of an eye-witness :

" There are some now of the most comfortable middle-class order who cannot think of that year without bitter pain. They saw many parents grow white-haired in a week's time ; lovers parted on the eve of marriage ; light-hearted girls sent forth from the shelter of home, to learn to endure the destiny of the governess or sempstress ; governesses, too old for a new station, going actually into the workhouse ; rural gentry quitting their lands ; and whole families standing as bare under the storm as Lear and his strange companions on the heath." [2]

The Martineaus were among the many who were ruined ; but the daughters, though left destitute, were exceptional in having been well educated and brought up in the expectation that they might have to work for a living. Most women had no such equipment for the battle of life, and their case was made pecu-

---

[1] *Saturday Review*, February 14, 1857.

[2] *History of the Thirty Years' Peace*, by Harriet Martineau, II, 21–22. Harriet Martineau's *Autobiography*, I, 128, *et seq.* Harriet was delighted to find that ruin brought her " the blessing of a wholly new freedom. I, who had been obliged to write before breakfast, or in some private way, had henceforth liberty to do my own work in my own way, for we had lost our gentility."

liarly hard by the social conventions which made it impossible for them to do anything for themselves. Though marriage was accepted as the natural provision for girls, public opinion, while it had a romantic prejudice against *mariages de convenance*, laid no obligation on parents to provide for their daughters either by endowment or by education, which indeed was severely discouraged. Middle-class women left with no means of support had no course open to them but to become governesses or " needle-women," doing the work now done by sewing machines. Both these employments were naturally overstocked, and the women who entered upon them, uneducated except in habits of dependence, while they could command only starvation wages, were condemned by public opinion as demeaning themselves by earning anything at all. To become a governess, as described even by the sober and reserved Miss Austen, was to " retire from all the pleasures of life, of rational intercourse, equal society, peace and hope, to penance and mortification for ever." [1]

The hard case of women thrown on their own resources passed almost unnoticed, except for a few voices crying in the wilderness, such as Harriet Martineau's. So late as 1868, we find an enlightened and philanthropic man of business, Mr. W. R. Greg, laying down the axiom that " the essentials of a woman's being " are those fulfilled /by domestic servants, namely " *they are supported by, and they minister to, men.*" [2] This was the text of a whole tribe of books written mostly by women, for the special benefit of women—*The English Maiden, The Feminine Soul, The Mental and Moral Dignity of Woman, Womankind* (by Miss Charlotte Yonge), and a multitude of others. The most popular writer of this stamp was perhaps Mrs. William Ellis, whose " elegant and instructive volumes," *The Women of England, The Wives of England, The Daughters of England, The Mothers of England*, were greeted with a chorus of praise. These admonishers of women unite in preaching inferiority, self-repression, patience, and resignation. " It is the privilege of a married woman," writes Mrs. Ellis, " to be able to show, by the most delicate attentions, how much she feels her husband's superiority

[1] *Emma*, Chap. XX. See also Chap. XXXV.
[2] Article on *Why are Women Redundant?* in *Social and Literary Judgments*, by W. R. Greg, 1868. (The italics are Mr. Greg's.)

7

to herself, not by mere personal services . . . but by a respectful deference to his opinion, a willingly imposed silence when he speaks." Even " a highly gifted woman " must not " exhibit the least disposition to presume upon such gifts," for fear of raising her husband's " jealousy of her importance." She will gain his confidence by " a respectful deportment, and a complying disposition." After this, it is perhaps not surprising to learn that " All women . . . should be prepared for discovering faults in men, as they are for beholding spots in the sun, or clouds in the summer sky." Mrs. Ellis nevertheless could speak as a woman of sense, as may be seen from the following :

" Much allowance should be made for the peculiar mode of education by which men are trained for the world. From their early childhood, girls are accustomed to fill an inferior place, to give up, to fall back, to be as nothing in comparison with their brothers ; while boys, on the other hand, have to suffer all the disadvantages in after-life, of having had their precocious selfishness encouraged, from the time when they first began to feel the dignity of superior power, and the triumph of occupying a superior place. Men who have been thus educated by foolish and indulgent mothers ; who have been placed at public schools, where the influence, the character, and the very name of woman was a by-word for contempt ; who have been afterwards associated with sisters who were capricious, ignorant, and vain —such men are very unjustly blamed for being selfish, domineering, and tyrannical to the other sex. In fact, how should they be otherwise ? " [1]

George Osborne and his son were, in fact, the complement of Amelia Sedley. There were many other writers like Mrs. Ellis, who saw the evil, but could find no way of remedying it but that of preaching to women that they must submit, and try to make themselves useful in trifles. Mrs. A. G. Penny, in *The Afternoon of Unmarried Life*,[2] feels " how drooping and embittered is the life of many women " who have " no harmless mode of doing active service," and suggests that " there is always some unrelished occupation that may devolve upon a willing coadjutor ; in default of every other, the dullest branch of family

[1] *The Wives of England*, Chap. III (published in 1843).
[2] Published in 1858. Cf. *Domestic Life*, in *Temple Bar*, February, 1862.

correspondence will often be gladly conceded. . . . If these uncoveted parts of family business are pleasantly accepted, and if, when done, no thanks or gratitude is expected . . . I will answer for it that they will help to make the doer happy." Mrs. John Sandford tells us, in *Woman in her Social and Domestic Character*,[1] that woman must be religious. " She needs solace and occupation, and religion affords her both." When " her nuptial wardrobe becomes obsolete," religion will " relieve the monotony of domestic life. . . . It is the domesticating tendency of religion that especially prepossesses men in its favour, and makes them, even if indifferent to it themselves, desire it, at least, in their nearest female relations."

To religion, then, women were expected to turn for " solace and occupation " ; but their religion was apt to become rather a torturing of conscience than a solace, for it could find no practical outlet, since activity and independence were denied them. There is plenty of evidence of the mental struggles of women suffering from the weariness of a vacant, listless life. " We fast mentally, scourge ourselves morally, use the intellectual hair shirt," writes Miss Nightingale, " in order to subdue that perpetual day-dreaming which is so dangerous." [2] A book in which she tried to find help and comfort, *Passages from the Life of a Daughter at Home*, by Sarah Stephen, gives a picture of a young woman's life at that time, in a family of girls, where the duties of housekeeping, entertaining visitors, and waiting on their invalid mother, are fully provided for. One daughter alone has absolutely nothing to do ; she tries to occupy herself with study, but " a general murmur " arises when she leaves the family circle in the drawing-room ; she tries to teach in the village school, but this is forbidden by her mother.[3] At last, she learns to find peace and even

[1] Published in 1833.

[2] Cf. *Woman in her Social and Domestic Character*, by Mrs. John Sandford, p. 147. " Young women . . . have often so much leisure to indulge in reveries and ecstasies. . . . It is so distressing to see a young woman sighing and weeping, and dreaming away her existence."

[3] Cf. *Thoughts on Self-Culture*, by Miss Shirreff and Mrs. Grey, I, 409, for a description of the " petty domestic oppressions " which kept women dependent. Daughters at home were expected to spend their days all in the same room (and families were large in those days). Often they could make no engagements of their own, and could not even

happiness in little things, through submission to the will of God. The "will of God," the "laws of Nature," were constantly and complacently quoted as the foundation on which the submission of women, and their restriction to "little things," were based.

It must not be supposed that there was any "anti-feminism" in this. The position of women was far too securely founded in physical and intellectual inferiority for any such thought to arise. So late as 1867, only two years before the foundation of Girton, we find in the *Athenæum* a review—and a very favourable review—of Dr. Sophia Jex-Blake's book, *A Visit to some American Schools and Colleges*, in which the following passage occurs :

" Just as parents are awakening to the importance of physical education for the slight frames and delicate limbs of their girls, *whom no perseverance in calisthenic operations can ever endow with the muscles of an athlete*, so are they becoming more anxious to increase by wholesome processes of culture the intellectual talents with which Nature has endowed the same children, *whom no course of study would qualify to win the first places of a tripos or class list.*" [1]

Women were not wanting, even among those not specially known as advocates of women's rights, who saw the fallacy and chafed under the restrictions. Madame Mohl, a clever and intensely social woman, the happy centre of a *salon* in Paris, observed that " what girls ought to learn is, not Latin, but how to live ; but how are they to learn this ? Always watched, always kept in leading strings, they are . . . children at thirty. . . . It is not the fault of nature, but that of men, who require of them only one virtue, and the proof of this is that that one quality only goes by the name of virtue in women." Mrs. Somerville has recorded in her charming *Memoirs* that she was annoyed that her " turn for reading was so much disapproved of, and thought it unjust that women should have been given a desire for knowledge if it were wrong to acquire it." In the letters

order a book they wanted from the bookseller. " Careful repressive influence " was advocated by Miss Yonge (*Womankind*, p. 12) as the proper system for teaching girls refinement.

[1] The *Athenæum*, July 20, 1867. (The italics are mine.)

of Caroline Frances Cornwallis we read : " When the condition of my sex is righted, a woman may perhaps contribute what God has given her of talent, to a good purpose without calling forth coarse jests and offensive expressions, and then the world will get civilized the faster, because it will have the use of *all* the intellect which its Creator has turned loose in it." Miss Cornwallis published a book, which attracted much notice and praise, on *Philosophical Theories and Philosophical Experience* —" by a Pariah "—a word which aptly described the feelings of women of unusual powers.

At the same time, the average woman, while accepting her lot without complaint as part of the normal state of affairs, was deteriorating for want of occupation. " Women," said Florence Nightingale, " are revived by practical reality," by " a full and interesting life, with training constantly kept up to the occupation, and occupation constantly testing the training." Before the industrial revolution, this life had been theirs, within the strict limits of the home where their many industries were carried on. " The regular routine of business, where so much was done at home, was really a perpetual amusement," writes Mrs. Smith (Miss Grant of Rothiemurchus) in the *Memoirs of a Highland Lady.* " I used to wonder when travellers asked my mother if she did not find her life dull." This was written in 1812. Further south, women were already beginning to lose these occupations. Madame de la Tour du Pin, during her exile in the time of the Terror, was struck by the excellent organization in England by means of which tradesmen's carts delivered the necessaries of life at her door in Richmond.[1] It was becoming unnecessary for women to spin and weave at home, to make bread, butter, preserves, candles, and other necessaries ; and nothing arose to take the place of these duties. Among the unfortunate results were, that working men's wives and daughters went into factories, and among women of the richer classes a habit of idleness was established, and a false standard of gentility. Instead of being useful members of the household as they had once been, they had to fill up their time with aimless fancy work and accomplishments, such as playing the piano and making wax flowers.

[1] *Journal d'une Femme de Cinquante Ans*, Vol. II, pp. 180–1 (date 1798). An interesting passage, too long for quotation.

They had lost their economic value and gained nothing in its place. Activities outside the house were hindered by the impossibility of going about unchaperoned (a relic of rougher days), as well as by difficulties of communication. Women went little out of doors, and practically never alone. Intellectual pursuits were checked by the disapproval of public opinion, and by want of education. Miscellaneous learning by heart, with fancy work and playing the piano,[1] formed the staple of a girl's education. The Miss Bertrams of Mansfield Park may be cited as fair specimens of a type which prevailed till well on in the nineteenth century. " How long ago is it, Aunt, since we used to repeat the chronological order of the kings of England, with the dates of their accession, and most of the principal events of their reigns ? " " Yes," added the other, " and of the Roman Emperors as low as Severus ; besides a great deal of the heathen mythology, and all the metals, semi-metals, planets, and distinguished philosophers." The lessons, such as they were, were to be dropped as soon as the Miss Bertrams were seventeen, and they would never again bestow a thought on the semi-metals and distinguished philosophers. Side by side with Maria and Julia Bertram, there existed Fanny Price and Anne Elliott ; but they were choice spirits, and their intellectual tastes and occupations were in both cases the almost accidental result of encouragement from a friend ; the average is clearly represented by Maria and Julia.

Mansfield Park appeared in 1814 ; and Ethel May's lessons, described in *The Daisy Chain*, published in 1856, were of the same kind as the Miss Bertrams'. Forty years had brought no improvement in the " chaos of laborious trifling." [2] Girls' schools, with a few exceptions, were conducted with an equal lack of intelligence and progress, with the additional drawback that the pupils were often injured in health through over-

---

[1] Much time was spent on this, usually the only form of " music " included in a girl's education, the chief aim being to produce brilliant mechanical execution. In Trollope's *Miss Mackenzie* we hear of girls practising on four pianos in one room, all of them out of tune ; and this seems to have been a common method.

[2] *Thoughts on Self-Culture*, by Miss Shirreff and Mrs. Grey (1856), Vol. II, p. 113.

work and want of air and exercise.[1] About half-way through the century, economic pressure and the fashion for philanthropy brought into existence an institution which was to be the source of better things. The Governesses' Benevolent Institution, founded in 1843, came to the help of distressed governesses with loans, annuities, and asylums for the aged ; [2] but it was soon found that these measures of alleviation were quite inadequate. On the initiative of the Rev. David Laing and Miss Murray (one of Queen Victoria's maids of honour), steps were taken to establish a college for Governesses where women could qualify themselves for the profession of teaching, and pass examinations which would help them to command more reasonable salaries. In this way was founded in 1848 Queen's College, Harley Street, which produced those great pioneers of the reformation in girls' schools, Miss Beale and Miss Buss.[3] Bedford College was founded a year later. In the beginning, these colleges were practically equivalent to what would now be called secondary schools ; little more was possible at a time when women were not only unprepared, but were generally held, even by enlightened people, to be mentally disqualified for higher education. A few intellectual women contrived in spite of everything to attain to a real degree of cultivation, but though individuals such as Elizabeth Barrett Browning, " George Eliot," and Florence Nightingale won respect and admiration, it is no exaggeration of language to say that the popular idea of a well educated woman was, that she was a ridiculous monster.

The average middle-class woman, therefore, while expecting to depend upon a husband, was not educated to be a companion to him in his pursuits, intellectual or otherwise ; nor was she taught anything of domestic management. It is hardly surprising to find, in the words of the *Saturday Review*, that though

---

[1] Report of Schools Enquiry Commission of 1864, Vol. I, Chap. VI. See also Reports of Assistant Commissioners in Vols. VII and IX. An amusing description of a fashionable boarding school in 1836–8 is given in the *Life of Frances Power Cobbe by Herself*, Chap. III.

[2] Martineau, *History of the Thirty Years' Peace*, Vol. IV, p. 217 ; the *Englishwoman's Journal*, Vol. I, No. 1, March, 1858 ; and subsequent volumes, *passim*.

[3] See *The First College Open to Women*, ed. by Mrs. Alec Tweedie, 1898.

" her one object in life, her whole being's aim and end is to marry," yet " even the alarming scarcity of marriageable men is not so serious an evil as their growing disinclination to marry." [1] Mr. W. R. Greg, in the article already quoted, throws some light upon this. " Thousands of men find it perfectly feasible to combine all the freedom, luxury, and self-indulgence of a bachelor's career with the pleasures of female society. . . . While the *monde* has been deteriorating, the *demi-monde* has been improving ; as the one has grown stupider and costlier, the other has grown more attractive, more decorous, and more easy. . . . As long as men are fond of female society, and yet hate to be bored "—so long will they frequent the *demi-monde*.

This is plain speaking, and we find plenty of confirmation of it elsewhere. Readers of Disraeli's *Life* will remember the famous compliment which so delighted Mrs. Disraeli : " Why, my dear, you are more like a mistress than a wife ! " This puts it in a nutshell. " Is it not a pity," asks Anthony Trollope, " that people who are bright and clever should so often be exceedingly improper ? and that those who are never improper should so often be dull and stupid ? " [2] As Bishop Creighton wrote :

> " But alas, it is seldom or never
> These two hit it off as they should.
> The good are so harsh to the clever,
> And the clever so rude to the good."

Anyone who reads the old issues of *Punch* will notice what a great improvement has taken place in the popular view of women since the earlier part of the nineteenth century. That there has been a complete change of tone will be seen from the following passage, taken as one example among many which in the present day would seem meaningless :

> " Can you read or write amid the yells of a nursery ?
> Can you wait any given time for breakfast ?
> Can you cut your old friends ?
> Can you stand being contradicted in the face of all reason ?

---

[1] *Saturday Review*, January 12, 1867.
[2] *Barchester Towers*, Chap. XXIII.

Can you keep your temper when you are not listened to ?
In a word, young Sir, have you the patience of Job ?
If you can lay your hand upon your heart and answer ' Yes,'
Take out your licence and marry—not else." [1]

A similar picture of married life is drawn in *Mrs. Caudle's
Curtain Lectures*, a series by Douglas Jerrold, which appeared
in *Punch* in 1845. Mrs. Caudle was treated as comic " copy."
A modern reader can see her only as the victim of nervous exhaus-
tion from incessant and unrelieved family cares ; but the writer
did not perceive what married life might be for an ignorant
and inexperienced girl, without the education or the practical
experience which could enable her to manage her numerous
children and household.[2] In exposing the ignorance of women
and their want of self-control he wrote without malice. *Punch*
in fact prided himself on his benevolence towards women ; he
laughed at them partly as Mr. Bennett, in *Pride and Prejudice*,
laughed at his wife, because " her ignorance and folly contributed
to his amusement " ; partly as a cheerful way of administering a
lecture.[3] *Punch's* campaign against the crinoline and other
fashions might have met with more success but for the cries of
ridicule and disgust which met any attempt at change, cries in
which Mr. Punch himself was often inconsistent enough to join.
The " Bloomers " of the fifties, like the now forgotten " divided

[1] *Punch*, Vol. VIII (Jan. to June, 1845), p. 32.
[2] *How to " Finish " a Daughter* (*Punch*, 1852, Vol. XXIII, p. 161)
illustrates this aptly, but is too long to be quoted here. " The Caudle
Lectures did more than any series of papers for the universal popularity
of *Punch*," writes Mr. Spielmann (*The History of Punch*, p. 291). The
author was surprised and disturbed on receiving a protest from " an
aggrieved matron." But the Lectures continued to appear, were trans-
lated into " nearly every Continental language and were transferred to
the stage both in London and in the provinces."
[3] Cf. *Punch*, December 25, 1869, " *The Liberator of the Ladies*. It
has ever been the aim of Mr. Punch to elevate woman as well as man.
To this end he has directed pen and pencil to the special exposure of
the peculiarities which distinguish silly from sensible women to deri-
sion." Women are improving under this treatment, and will soon be
emancipated, owing to Mr. Punch's efforts.
The *Saturday Review* used women as " copy " in a less kindly spirit,
e.g. in the series of articles on *The Girl of the Period*, beginning on
March 14, 1868.

skirt " of a later day, in spite of absurdities, were, after all, serious attempts to introduce a more simple and healthy style of dress. Active exercise was impossible, and even walking was difficult, when a woman was expected to carry the weight of a number of petticoats [1] under a voluminous yet tightly fitting dress with long skirts trailing on the ground. The fashions were not only inconvenient but injurious to health. " Women, mostly, are always ailing," says *Punch* [2] ; if a man were tightlaced like a young lady, " he would be afflicted with indigestion ; he would grow peevish, fretful, melancholy, be always moaning and sighing, and taking sal volatile, and would pass much of his time lounging on a sofa." A medical authority, Dr. E. J. Tilt, writing in 1852, states that " mothers in high life unfortunately exist " who stint their girls in food and exercise lest they should look " strong and ruddy," and therefore unladylike ; girls, he observes, are not taught how to manage their health, for " it is contended that women should know as little as possible about this delicate subject." [3]

" Those women who do not marry," writes Dr. Tilt, " should not be left as they are now, generally speaking, without any resources for the mind to fall back upon, to the great detriment of the bodily health." Public opinion, though beginning to show some advance, was by no means unanimous as to this, and it is hard to say who received the larger share of blame, those women who, as the *Saturday Review* [4] observed, wrapped themselves in their indolence and were perfectly satisfied with their lot, or those who tried to find something to do. " Work," says Anthony Trollope, " is a grand thing—the grandest thing we have ; but work is not picturesque, graceful and in itself alluring. . . . I for one would not wish to throw any heavier share of it on to a woman's shoulders. . . . Say that by advocating the rights of women, philanthropists succeed in apportioning more work to their share, will they eat more, wear better clothes, lie softer,

[1] Miss Nightingale once told the writer that she used to wear five petticoats.

[2] *Punch*, September 18, 1869. Cf. *The Wives of England*, by Mrs. Ellis, Chap. VIII ; and *Recreation*, by G. J. Romanes, in the *Nineteenth Century*, September, 1879.

[3] *Elements of Health and Principles of Female Hygiene*, by E. J. Tilt, M.D. (1852).

[4] *Saturday Review*, March 28, 1868.

and have altogether more of the fruits of work than they do now ? " [1] Here the women who are forced to support themselves, and those who might want " the grandest thing we have " for its own sake, are alike ignored. In the same way, exceptional women who happened to have work of their own often could not understand what it was that others wanted. Queen Victoria " could not bear women mixing in politics " ; [2] and when the women's movement began to gain ground, she expressed her views with her usual vigour :

" The Queen is most anxious to enlist every one who can speak or write to join in checking this mad, wicked folly of ' Woman's Rights,' with all its attendant horrors, on which her poor feeble sex is bent, forgetting every sense of womanly feeling and propriety. . . . It is a subject which makes the Queen so furious that she cannot contain herself. . . . Woman would become the most hateful, heartless, and disgusting of human beings were she allowed to unsex herself ; and where would be the protection which man was intended to give the weaker sex ? The Queen is sure that Mrs. Martin agrees with her." [3]

Mrs. Martin, one of the most admired actresses of her day, led a life full of hard work and success ; and the Queen of course was the only woman in England whose rights included the right to work in the service of her country. As she wrote to her uncle, the king of the Belgians, she did " regular, hard, but to *me delightful* " work, with her Ministers. " It is to me the *greatest pleasure* to do my duty for my country and my people, and no fatigue, however great, will be burdensome to me if it is for the welfare of the nation." [4] The Queen, a thorough believer in the heaven-sent beneficence of family tyranny, did not know what it was to be forbidden to be public spirited. Others were equally inconsistent. Ordinary women could only exercise their tra-

[1] Trollope, *North America*, Chap. XVIII, *The Rights of Women.*
[2] *The Girlhood of Queen Victoria*, II, 229.
[3] *Queen Victoria as I knew Her*, by Sir Theodore Martin, K.C.B., K.C.V.O., pp. 69-70.
[4] *The Letters of Queen Victoria*, June 25, 1837. She was conscious of some inconsistency : " We women are not *made* for governing—and if we are good women, we must *dislike* these masculine occupations ; but there are times which force one to take *interest* in them *mal gré bon gré*, and *I* do, of course, *intensely* " (Letter of February 3, 1852).

ditional virtues on the smallest possible scale and in the most
personal way ; yet they were constantly exhorted and appealed
to as the upholders of the highest morality and the loftiest ideals,
and reproached for their failure to rise to the heights required of
them.   Mrs. Carlyle wrote of Tennyson : " Alfred is dreadfully
embarrassed with women alone—for he entertains at one and the
same moment a feeling of almost adoration for them, and an
ineffable contempt !   Adoration, I suppose, for what they *might
be*—contempt for what they *are* ! " [1]   Women were bewildered
by the praise and the blame which were alternately lavished on
them, and by the impossibility of persuading the world to take
them seriously when they made any attempts to better their lives.

It may seem that an unduly depressing picture has been drawn
of the world into which Miss Davies and her friends were born.
There were of course happy exceptions, families where women
were not only treated considerately, but well educated and encouraged to use their powers.   But any attentive reader of the newspapers, biographies, and novels of the time will find the general
level, the average view of women, to be as here described.

[1] Jane Welsh Carlyle, *Letters to her Family*, 1839–63, p. 230.

CHAPTER II

Miss Davies' Early Life. 1830-1857

MISS DAVIES' father, the Rev. John Davies, was born in 1795 at Llandewi Brefy in Cardiganshire. He was the son of James Davies, a farmer, who on losing his wife emigrated to America, leaving his only son to be brought up in Wales by a maternal uncle, Mr. Richards. The boy early showed an intellectual bent ; on account of his classical attainments he was known in the neighbourhood as " Horace bach "—little Horace. He became, as recorded in his diary, " at 13 a tutor in a respectable family, and at 14 an usher in a school." An entry in an old manuscript book, made when he was seventeen—" Beginning to be good at two o'clock in the afternoon of Monday the 24th February, 1812 "—seems to show that he was already acquiring the Evangelical habit of self-examination which he practised zealously in later life. He speaks in his diary of " the natural vehemence, pride, and impetuosity " of his character. Together with these qualities, he had a strong tendency to scornful incredulity. His daughter used to say that on hearing a good story his usual remark was : " I don't believe a word of it." His opinions of Popery, as also of atheism, were expressed in forcible language ; he relieved his feelings by writing in the margin of Hume's *Essays*—" vile sarcastic sophist—impious blasphemer " ; and Cardinal Manning, whom he knew as Archdeacon of Chichester, " showed the cloven hoof." Mr. Davies was fond of writing verses, and a poem by him on the Restoration of the Jews was praised by the old poet William Hayley (afterwards his neighbour in Sussex) as " a very animated composition, that promised greater productions in maturer life." The greater productions did not make their appearance, but he

19

had a natural gift of expression, and was a forcible and effective speaker of a rhetorical type.

In 1815, at the age of twenty, John Davies went to Queen's College, Cambridge, at that time a centre of Evangelical influence. On leaving Cambridge, from which University he received the degrees of B.D. (1831) and D.D. (1844), Mr. Davies took orders, and became Vicar of St. Pancras, Chichester. Here he made the acquaintance of his future wife, Mary, daughter of a retired man of business, Mr. John Hopkinson, formerly of Derby. They were married in 1823, and set up a boarding school for boys in a house in Chichester, where their two eldest children were born, Mary Jane in 1824, and John Llewelyn in 1826. For some reason not clearly explained, in 1827 Mr. Davies moved his whole establishment to Southampton, where they remained about three years. While continuing to carry on the school, he was occupied with literary work. In 1828 he published an elaborate philosophical treatise entitled *An Estimate of the Human Mind*, and about the same time *Splendid Sins*, a pamphlet against Sabbath breaking by people of high rank, which he used to say was the only publication of his that ever " sold wildly." At Southampton were born two more children, William Stephen in 1828, and Sarah Emily, the subject of this memoir, in 1830.

About this time, Mr. Davies became a candidate for the Professorship of Moral and Political Philosophy in the newly founded University of London. His application was supported by Zachary Macaulay, Dr. Thomas Chalmers, Michael Maurice (the father of F. D. Maurice) and other evangelicals ; but he found that the stipend of £300 a year was not to be guaranteed, as he had expected, and he felt himself obliged to withdraw his candidature. Mrs. Davies recorded her feelings on the occasion in her journal.

" My carnal heart would certainly have preferred London and the honour and fame which I anticipated that my dear husband would gain, but at the same time I felt fully aware that the situation was a very dangerous one to our spiritual interests, and this made me anxious that we should not stir a step without the Lord's guidance and feeling conscious that we were in the path of duty. May the Lord make this as well as all other events to work together for good."

Instead of moving to London, therefore, they returned to

Chichester in the summer of 1830. The school was established there again, and Mr. Davies became busy with a new book, *The Ordinances of Religion Practically Illustrated and Applied.* In 1832 their fifth and youngest child, Henry Barton, was born. Unfortunately they were soon obliged to move again. Mr. Davies had been overworking for some years past, and he now found it necessary to give up the school. For about six years they led an unsettled life, moving about in search of health. A year spent at Avranches in Normandy seemed beneficial, but it proved impossible for him to resume his work. Early in 1838 they settled at Ashling, four miles from Chichester, where Mrs. Davies' parents were still living. Emily Davies was now eight years old, and her earliest connected recollections date from this time. In her *Family Chronicle*, a fragment of autobiography compiled at the request of her youngest nephew when she was seventy-five, she described their life at Ashling as follows :

" During these years of retirement,[1] my father taught the two boys, and I did some lessons with my mother or Jane. From twelve to one every day we all took a regular walk, which was greatly disliked. It was a great satisfaction that we were occasionally exempted on account of the muddiness of the roads. After tea, at 5 or 5.30 p.m. we had reading aloud, *en famille*. The only book that I remember certainly was Rollin's *History*, but I think we also had *Paradise Lost*. . . . I remember our holding a Missionary Meeting (for play). . . . There were occasional expeditions to Chichester, four miles off, to see my grandparents, and for shopping, and for music lessons for Jane."

Milton and Rollin seem rather stiff reading for a child of eight but the older children (the eldest, Jane, was now fourteen) would be more able to follow, while Emily no doubt sat quietly by and picked up what she could. Amusements were few ; out-of-door games were little practised in those days, and other entertainments were strictly limited in evangelical circles. Even Sir Walter Scott's novels were not read by the Davies'. Theatres (even if they had been accessible), and cards were absolutely forbidden. The children however had playmates and friends in the neigh-

[1] They were at Ashling for rather less than two years, but no doubt the time seemed much longer in Miss Davies' recollections of her childhood.

bourhood, and visits were paid from time to time to friends, principally to a family of Quaker extraction, the Hacks, who lived at this time near Chichester but moved later to Torquay. Mrs. Hack was very fond of Jane and Emily. After a visit paid in 1837 she wrote to thank Mrs. Davies " for the portion we have had of your interesting children—much too small, I assure you. . . . You were regretting Jane's want of order and neatness. We think her very much improved in both respects. She is never likely to have *my sweet* Emily's precision, but there is no fear of her not being quite respectable in that department of female excellence. . . . Her treatment of Emily was beautiful."

The Davies were on terms of intimacy with the Bishop of Chichester, Dr. Maltby, as well as with the evangelical clergy of the neighbourhood. " The Evangelical clergy," writes Miss Davies, " formed a clerical meeting, to which Mr. (afterwards Cardinal) Manning belonged. They met from time to time at each other's houses, and I can remember on one of these occasions hearing Mr. Manning say to my mother in the passage of the house as he was taking his leave—I don't know how it is, Mrs. Davies, but your husband and I are like cat and dog, whenever we meet, we differ ! " When Manning published his sermon, *The Rule of Faith*, Dr. Davies attacked it in a pamphlet to which Manning replied privately ; but a friendly feeling remained between them, for Dr. Davies, some nine years later, sent a new edition of his *Estimate of the Human Mind* to his antagonist, and received a kindly and even affectionate letter of thanks.

The period of rest and quiet at Ashling restored Dr. Davies' health, and in November, 1839, he was able to accept the living of Gateshead, offered to him by his friend Dr. Maltby, now become Bishop of Durham. Early in the following year, the family removed thither ; the railway had not yet reached so far north, and the last stage of their journey was performed by coach from York. Gateshead was a large parish, with a population of about 15,000. The Rectory, which was to be their home for the next twenty-two years, was a roomy house, with a large garden and shrubbery, and a meadow in which the children played cricket and made hay. The gardener had charge of a pony and phæton. Indoors there were only two maids. " This meant, of course," writes Miss Davies, " that we were not much waited upon and did a good deal for ourselves. I do not remember that we took much part in the cooking, though my mother may have done a little. The *menus* were very simple. At breakfast, coffee, bread and butter, and cold meat ; at dinner at 1 o'clock, or 1.30, a joint and two vegetables, and some simple pudding. The parents used to adjourn to the Library for about half an hour and take wine together there. Tea at 6 p.m. consisted of tea, bread and butter, and dry toast ; and after Prayers at 9 p.m., there was a slight supper in the Library, of milk porridge, or bread and milk. My father sat in the library, the others in the dining-room or schoolroom. The drawing-room was only used for company. Our muslins, i.e. collars and cuffs, etc., were washed at home, and my mother, Jane and I did the ironing, about once a month, in a store-room in the basement. . . . We did mending also, but not much of dressmaking or millinery." The family accounts were kept by Mrs. Davies, who, as her daughter records, " used to hand to my father a half-sovereign at a time for his personal use, which I believe consisted mainly in making small gifts to the people whom he visited."

The gardener, George Lister, described by Miss Davies as " a very clever and cultivated Scotchman," was a person of some importance in the lives of the children. " During all the early years at Gateshead," she writes, " Lister and his wife were our constant companions. He was a Conservative in politics. I remember his telling me, when I was playing at being a candidate for Parliament, that the way to succeed was ' to have civil and religious liberty always on your tongue.' " It was evidently Lister who turned her attention to political questions. In 1841, Emily and William (the brother next above her in age) started weekly newspapers of their own, neatly and laboriously written in narrow columns imitating the real thing. Emily's paper, the *Herald*, contained advertisements, Parliamentary and Foreign Intelligence, Reviews, and correspondence. Lister was an occasional contributor, dictating advertisements to the young journalist while he cleaned the knives and boots. A good deal of space was given to Parliamentary Intelligence, where we find that Emily was a whole-hearted supporter of Sir Robert Peel and Conservative principles. The paper contained also many denunciations against Popery and Tractarianism, no doubt in imitation of the talk heard at home on questions of the day. Advertisements for curates make it a condition that they must be sound evangelical clergymen ; and a sermon by Dr. Davies is favourably noticed. " This excellent sermon," writes the preacher's daughter, aged eleven, " is particularly salutary just now as from the great spreading of Puseyite opinions at this time the cautions contained in it concerning those errors are peculiarly necessary." An advertisement for a governess for Emily herself deserves to be quoted :

" Wanted, a Governess in a gentleman's family. The lady who is to fill this situation must be a person of great firmness and determination, as the young lady who is to be the object of her care is rather inclined to be self-willed. Phrenologically speaking she has the organ of self-esteem rather largely developed and it will require the utmost care on the part of her governess to prevent this organ from being unduly developed. The lady who is to fill this situation must be a person well skilled in the languages and sciences, as Miss D. is ambitious to excel all her contemporaries in these departments of knowledge. The salary proportioned to her success in the management of her pupil. *Address, M. D., Gateshead.*" [1]

The self-examination inculcated by evangelical parents had apparently made Emily conscious of her ambitions as well as of other qualities. A letter written in later life shows that she felt herself to have inherited what her father described as the " natural vehemence " of his character :

(*Miss Davies to Mr. Tomkinson.*)

August 5, 1868.

" It is very good of you to suggest the heat of the weather as an apology for my hasty speaking, but everybody else was reasonable and polite, though it *was* hot. The real explanation, or excuse, is that the rest were pure English and therefore to be expected always to behave properly. If you have read Matthew Arnold, you will understand that the unfortunate people who are made up of an ill-assorted compound of Celtic and Anglo-Saxon blood, are by the nature of their constitution continually impelled to say and do what they are sorry for afterwards."

The advertisement for a governess for herself shows the alertness of mind which also she probably inherited from her father.

[1] The *Herald*, October 6, 1841. *M. D.* was her mother, Mary Davies.

Her mother knew of her intellectual ambitions. In an affectionate and sensible letter to Emily, who was for a time alone at home with her father, while her mother and Jane were paying visits, Mrs. Davies gives her some small commissions to do—exercises in responsibility for a girl of twelve—and adds : " I am delighted to receive your letters. . . . I am glad to hear you intend to be such a proficient in the various branches of education by the time I return. I shall hope to find you *grown* in everything good. Above all, my own dear Emily, remember that ' one thing is needful.' Be watchful over yourself and pray to be enabled to overcome your most besetting sins. Then you will indeed grow in that which is the most important of all things."

A few years later, Emily started another newspaper, the *North of England Record*, named after the evangelical organ, the *Record*. This was written, with more zeal than accuracy, in a variety of languages—English, French, Italian, German, and Latin. She had had but little teaching. At nine years old she went for a few months to a small day school for girls ; and later she and Jane had lessons in French and Italian from a French master, and in music. Otherwise she was chiefly taught by her mother and Jane. " Our education," she writes in the *Family Chronicle*, " answered to the description of that of clergymen's daughters generally, given by Mark Pattison in his evidence before one of the Education Commissions. Do they go to school ? No. Do they have governesses at home ? No. They have lessons and get on as they can.[1] (I write from memory.) I learnt a little Latin for my own pleasure, simply because the boys were doing it, but I think this had ceased before we reached Gateshead. William and I used to do what were then called Themes, i.e. bits of English composition, once a week, looked over by my father, and the practice was no doubt very useful." It was probably to her father's teaching that she owed the power, most useful to her in later life, of expressing herself in writing with clearness and force.

Meanwhile, her brothers' education was being pursued on the usual lines. One of Dr. Davies' curates took pupils, among

[1] The reference is to Mark Pattison's evidence before the Schools Enquiry Commission of 1864 (Report of the Commission, Vol. V, May, 1866)

whom were the three Davies boys. Llewelyn, aged sixteen, went in 1842 to school at Repton, and in 1844 to Trinity College, Cambridge. William followed him at Repton and the University. Henry went to school at Rugby, and was afterwards articled to a solicitor at Doncaster. In 1848 Llewelyn took a first class in the Classical Tripos and a second in Mathematics. He remained at Cambridge for a time, taking pupils. The brothers were now of course generally away from home, and the sisters continued to lead a busy but desultory life, picking up what education they could, helping their mother, and paying visits. In 1846 Emily went to the Hacks at Torquay, to be bridesmaid at their niece's wedding, and stayed on with them for six months. A visit of this length was no unusual event in a girl's life. There was no regular plan of education to suffer interruption ; and the difficulty and expense of journeys, increased by the need of an escort, made a short visit hardly worth while.

In 1848 the society of Gateshead was enlarged by the arrival of Mr. and Mrs. Crow, who came to settle there with their family—an event which proved to be of great importance in Miss Davies' life. Mr. Crow, a business man, had several daughters who were educated at a well-known school kept by the Miss Brownings at Blackheath. The elder girls were great readers, and found many interests in common with the Davies'. The second daughter, Jane Crow, was the same age as Emily, and the two became close friends. This brought about an acquaintance with Jane's schoolfellow Elizabeth Garrett (afterwards Mrs. Garrett Anderson). Miss Garrett visited the Crows for the first time in 1854, and a few years later she and Jane Crow and Emily were bridesmaids at the wedding of the youngest Miss Crow, Annie, to Mr. T. Austin. The three bridesmaids were destined to be lifelong allies and fellow-workers in the women's movement. There was as yet no thought of this ; but Miss Davies and Miss Garrett made friends on the occasion of the wedding, and afterwards corresponded with each other.

In 1851 there came a pleasant break in the home routine. Dr. and Mrs. Davies with their two daughters went abroad, and spent some months at Geneva. Emily was then just twenty-one. " It was a stimulating time," she wrote afterwards, " as besides taking lessons in languages, we saw much of the leading

Swiss pastors and their friends and families. . . . From Geneva we ascended Mont Salève, and also made an expedition to Chamonix, accompanied by Llewelyn's friends, Mr. and Mrs. Sheppard. We returned by the Rhine, reaching home on August 5th." A characteristic record, showing her interest in the people they met, rather than in the scenes they visited.

Later in the year they had a visit from Miss Hannah Mason and her sister Annabella, granddaughters of Dr. Davies' old friend Lady Grey, mother of Sir George Grey of Fallodon. Annabella, as Miss Davies notes, " used to take likenesses, and our albums contain sketches of Jane, William, and myself." The drawing of Emily, reproduced as the frontispiece, is the only portrait extant of her in her youth.

In the winter of 1851 Llewelyn was ordained, and went to London as curate of St. Anne's, Limehouse. A little later he became vicar of St. Mark's, Whitechapel, and in 1856 he was appointed to the Rectory of Christ Church, Marylebone, a large parish including a dense and poor population. On going to London, he was soon attracted by the social and educational movement which drew its inspiration from Frederick Denison Maurice, whose theological views he also accepted.[1] " Christian Socialism " and Maurice's distinctive doctrines were foreign to the atmosphere of Gateshead Rectory, and as may be imagined, some distress was felt there. To Emily, who followed her brother in his admiration for Maurice, the new developments were full of interest. Though she was throughout life a faithful daughter of the Church of England, the evangelical teaching of her youth seems to have had no special attraction for her. Her own aspirations, together with admiration for her brother, drew her with him along new paths.

These new paths soon led towards the question which was to be peculiarly her own ; and when the time came for her to take up the women's question and work at it on her own lines, her brother gave her his unfailing sympathy and support. His interest in the education of women found practical expression in connection with Queen's College, Harley Street, where Mr. Maurice was Principal from 1851 till 1853, and later for many

[1] Some account of Mr. Llewelyn Davies may be found in the *Contemporary Review*, June, 1916.

years Professor of History. Maurice's teaching and influence counted for much in its success. The College, which had been founded with the special object of improving the status of governesses, proved to be the first step towards a general improvement in the education of women. It performed a most valuable and necessary pioneer work in providing a solid education for girls, and thus leading on to higher education. Mr. Llewelyn Davies, who had worked with Maurice in connection with the co-operative movement, and was afterwards to take part with him in founding the Working Men's College, threw himself into the novel scheme for the education of women, and was Principal of Queen's College from 1873 till 1886. Through him, his sister Emily was for the first time brought into contact with people whose plans for social reform included some effort to improve the position and education of women.

Emily's interest was strongly stirred by the new developments of her brother's life in London, but for some years troubles at home prevented her from taking any part in them. In 1855 Jane developed symptoms of lung disease, and was ordered to go south. In the following year, Henry had a similar breakdown in health. It was arranged that he should go to Algiers, and Jane with Emily to Torquay. After three years of illness and anxiety, Jane died there on January 17, 1858. Shortly afterwards, alarming accounts were received of Henry's health, and it was arranged that Emily, with her friend Jane Crow, should join him in Algiers. Llewelyn travelled with them, and stayed a short time. To Emily fell the task of bringing the invalid home to England, where he died in the following summer. These troubles were followed by another. William, after taking orders, had gone as a naval chaplain to the Crimea in 1855. He was invalided home, but afterwards served in a similar post at Devonport, whence he went to China. From China came the news of his death in October, 1858.

These three deaths in the course of one year left Emily as the only daughter in a home overshadowed with sorrow, just when a fresh interest had arisen to attract her to London. Of this interest she became aware through a friendship formed in Algiers with Miss Leigh Smith and her sister Madame Bodichon.

" On my return to Gateshead I went back to parish work, but tried to combine with it some effort in another direction. After making acquaintance at Algiers with Annie Leigh Smith (Madame Bodichon's sister)—the first person I had ever met who sympathized with my feeling of resentment at the subjection of women—I corresponded with her and she introduced me to others of the same circle and kept me up to what was going on. In 1858 the first organized movement on behalf of women was set on foot. The first number of the *Englishwoman's Journal* appeared in March." [1]

This movement was the beginning of the efforts made by women to raise their own position. Before going on to describe it, something may be said as to Miss Davies' " feeling of resentment at the subjection of women." In these words we have the earliest recorded expression of her views, which she seems to have evolved for herself.[2] She had not apparently read anything in the way of feminist literature. She kept a record, with extracts, of her reading, from which it appears that she read conscientiously on a variety of miscellaneous subjects ; but there is no mention of Mary Wollstonecraft, whose *Vindication of the Rights of Women* would indeed scarcely have been allowed to enter the Rectory. Miss Davies' feminist views were formed as the result of her own experience and observation. She perceived that it was the common lot of girls like herself to stay at home and pick up such education and occupations as they could, while great pains were taken to send their brothers to public schools and Universities, and to launch them in professions. Some passages in her writings have a flavour of personal feeling in them which may show what was thought by a clever, vigorous, active-minded girl, observant of the world around her :

" Probably only women who have laboured under it can understand the weight of discouragement produced by being perpetually told that, as women, nothing much is ever to be expected of them, and it is not worth their while to exert themselves—that they can write lively letters, full of graphic description and homely touches, but that anything like original research or profound learning is not for them to think of—that whatever they do they must not interest themselves, except in a second-hand and shallow way, in the pursuits

---

[1] *Family Chronicle*, p. 159.
[2] Cf. *What I Remember*, by Dame Millicent Garrett Fawcett, pp. 39–41.

of men, for in such pursuits they must always expect to fail. Women who have lived in the atmosphere produced by such teaching know how it stifles and chills ; how hard it is to work courageously through it. Every effort to improve the education of women which assumes that they may, without reprehensible ambition, study the same subjects as their brothers and be measured by the same standards does something towards lifting them out of the state of listless despair of themselves into which so many fall." [1]

" I understand that when a youth goes into an office, he is not expected to wait about all day, on the chance of something turning up. He is not told that he will find something to do, if he really wishes it, or that he is to look about him, and watch for opportunities of making himself useful. He has his appointed post, his own desk and his stool, and regular work cut out for him. And when he has learned the business, he receives a salary, and is recognized as doing work of appreciable importance. As a rule, there is not the same order in the conduct of household business, so far as the young ladies are concerned. It is usual for the whole family to congregate in one room, every one carrying on her individual occupation in suspense, so to speak, liable at any moment to be called off from it for something else, trifling or important, as the case may be. Naturally enough, these half-occupied people prey upon each other." [2]

This reads like an echo from *Passages in the Life of a Daughter at Home*. As the Rector's daughter, however, Miss Davies had more scope for an active life than the heroine of that book, as she was expected to occupy herself with district visiting, Sunday-school teaching, and the like. Through parish work, she made the acquaintance of a schoolmistress, Miss Isabella Fedden, who became her intimate friend. Through Miss Fedden she saw something of other teachers and schools, whereby she learned much that was of value to her later. " I remember," she writes in the *Family Chronicle*, " making some attempts at getting to know lower middle-class people, and as one means of doing so I got leave to teach something, I think Arithmetic, in a small private girls' school." These occupations were, as she records, " interspersed with somewhat varied reading." She worked by herself

---

[1] *Special Systems of Education for Women.* Reprinted in *Thoughts on Some Questions relating to Women*, from *The London Student*, 1868.

[2] *Home and the Higher Education*, 1878, reprinted in *Thoughts on Some Questions relating to Women*.

at Greek and French, and at one time attended a singing class. In such pursuits she passed her time at home. Occasional visits to her brother in London enabled her to pursue her acquaintance with the Leigh Smiths and their friends, and to take some part in the new movement on behalf of women. Of that movement, one of the chief organizers was Barbara Leigh Smith (Madame Bodichon) ; and here it will be convenient to introduce some account of Madame Bodichon, in accordance with the wish expressed by Miss Davies.

CHAPTER III

Madame Bodichon and the Birth of the Women's Movement. 1827–1857

MADAME BODICHON, when she made Miss Davies' acquaintance, had already been active for some years in working for the welfare of women. Born in 1827, at Watlington in Sussex, she was the eldest child of Benjamin Leigh Smith. To her grandfather, William Smith, M.P. for Norwich, she owed much in her character and circumstances. He was the head of a firm of merchant grocers (now Messrs. Travers & Sons) established in Cannon Street since the seventeenth century; and he was an ardent supporter of the abolition of slavery, the removal of religious disabilities, and the introduction of Parliamentary Reform. Although a Unitarian, he was on terms of affectionate intimacy with Wilberforce, Clarkson, and other members of the "Clapham Sect." He was a man of many friends and interests, and of a cheerful, kindly and vigorous temper. For about forty-six years he sat in the House of Commons, representing Norwich from 1802 till his retirement in 1830. Norwich had an interesting society of its own, including various people of intellectual distinction, particularly among the Martineau and Taylor families. The Norwich school of painters was flourishing at this time; William Smith was the patron of Cotman, and of Opie, who painted his portrait and Mrs. Smith's; and he acquired a fine collection of pictures of various schools, of both old and modern masters.[1] He was

---

[1] A manuscript catalogue shows that the collection included two pictures by Reynolds (*Mrs. Siddons as the Tragic Muse*, and *Ariadne*); three by Rembrandt (*Head of a Rabbi, Rembrandt's Mother*, and *The Mill*); and many pictures by Dutch masters.

BARBARA LEIGH SMITH (MME. BODICHON)

From a photograph by Disdéri, Paris

Commissioner of Roads and Bridges, and in this capacity travelled much, often with his wife and older children (he had a
family of ten). The love of travel, artistic tastes, an interest in
philanthropy, with religious and political connections of a liberal
character—these were the chief elements of the atmosphere into
which his children were born.

Mr. Smith's eldest son, Benjamin (Madame Bodichon's father),
succeeded his father as member for Norwich, which he represented from 1841 till 1847. He added his grandmother's maiden
name of Leigh to his surname, acquired property in Sussex, and
lived at Mountfield, near Battle, often staying at Hastings. His
wife, Anne Longden, died young, leaving him with a family of
five children (three girls and two boys), when Barbara, the eldest
(afterwards Madame Bodichon), was only seven. Their aunt
Julia, Mr. Leigh Smith's youngest sister, befriended the family,
and through her they knew some remarkable women of an older
generation, such as Mrs. Howitt, Mrs. Somerville, Mrs. Opie,
and Harriet Martineau, with whom Julia Smith was very intimate. One of Julia's chief interests was education—she was
active about village schools, and took part in the foundation of
Bedford College, where in 1849 she and her niece Barbara
entered themselves as students.[1] Mrs. Howitt gives us a
glimpse of the Leigh Smiths, of whom she saw something
during a visit to Hastings in 1845.

" The father is the member for Norwich, a good Radical and par-
tisan of Free Trade and the abolition of the Corn Laws. Objecting
to schools, he keeps his children at home, and their knowledge is
gained by reading. They have masters, it is true, and then the young
people are left very much to pursue their own course of study. The
result is good ; and as to affection and amiability, I never saw more
beautiful evidences of it. There are five children, the oldest about
twenty-two, the youngest eleven. They have carriages and horses at
their command ; and their buoyant frames and bright clear com-
plexions show how sound is their health.

" Every year their father takes them out a journey. He has had a

---

[1] Madame Bodichon was a " member" of Bedford College from
1869 till her death. She bequeathed £1,000 and some of her pictures
to the College, where the " Bodichon Studio " has been named after
her.

large carriage built like an omnibus, in which they and their servants can travel, and in it, with four horses, they make long journeys. This year they were in Ireland, and next year I expect they will go into Italy. Their father dotes on them. They take with them books and sketching materials ; and they have every advantage which can be obtained for them, whether at home or abroad." [1]

The three girls were all fond of painting, and had lessons from good masters, among whom was William Hunt, senior. Their grandfather on one occasion took Barbara to visit Turner in his studio. The management of the household was thrown upon Barbara at an early age, owing to her mother's death, and she was thus brought into close companionship with her father, and saw much of his political friends, especially at his London house, No. 5, Blandford Square. Among their friends were Cobden and his family ; W. J. Fox, the Radical member for Oldham, and his daughter Mrs. Bridell Fox, who was a painter ; and Mr. Parkes, whose daughter, Miss Bessie Rayner Parkes,[2] became a close friend of Barbara's. The two had lessons together as children, and as young women their interest in social questions was awakened by the movement for the repeal of the Corn Laws.[3]

Mr. Leigh Smith held the unusual opinion that daughters should have an equal provision with sons. He did not adopt the ordinary plan of paying his daughters' bills and giving them an occasional present, but when Barbara came of age in 1848 he gave her an allowance of £300 a year. Money was to her, as she wrote in one of her pamphlets,[4] " a power to do good . . . a responsibility which we must accept." We can gather how she liked to spend hers ; " if you get money," she writes, " you gain a power of sending a child to school, of buying a good book to give to the ignorant, of sending a sick person to a good climate, etc." Generosity was the keynote of her character, and she enjoyed the hospitality which she had the power of exercising. At Scalands, near Robertsbridge, she built a small

---

[1] Mary Howitt, *Autobiography*, Vol. II, p. 34.
[2] Afterwards Madame Belloc.
[3] See an article by Madame Belloc on Madame Bodichon, the *Englishwoman's Review*, July 15, 1891.
[4] *Women and Work*, published in 1857.

house of red brick, in the style of an old Sussex cottage—probably one of the earliest attempts to introduce a more beautiful kind of domestic architecture in place of the devastating ugliness which held sway before the time of William Morris. Among her early visitors here were D. G. Rossetti and Miss Siddal, in 1854, when " the indefatigable and invaluable Barbara," as Rossetti calls her, was trying to help them with plans for the benefit of Miss Siddal's health.[1]

Freedom and responsibility, and the sympathy of her elders, encouraged Barbara's natural feeling of public spirit, and enabled her to do things which were then unusual and unconventional with a remarkable absence of self-consciousness. As a friend wrote of her, she was " grandly innocent and simple." She had none of the painful struggles with conscientious scruples and conventions which made it hard for other women (such as her cousin Florence Nightingale, who was brought up in a much more conventional home) to follow their bent. Another cousin, Mrs. Albert Dicey, in recalling a long visit which first made her well acquainted with Barbara, describes her aptly : " I had till that year never come across any woman who was so much of a *citizen*."

Treating her money as a power to do good, one of the first uses to which Barbara put it was educational. In the absence of any State system of education, there was of course a great need of schools, and a tempting field open for experiments. The Birkbeck schools, recently founded by the Utilitarian William Ellis, attracted Barbara's interest, and with her friend Miss Elizabeth Whitehead (afterwards Mrs. F. Malleson) she made herself well acquainted with their work. They found the teaching most efficient. The chief aim was to make the pupils intelligent, self-reliant, and thrifty future citizens. " Everything presented to their minds was to be investigated, known, apprised ; they were purposely never brought to the limits of the *unknowable* ; they were never allowed to pause in reverence in view of those limits. They were tacitly permitted to believe that their industry, economy and moral rectitude would attain for them in life all that was worth possessing." [2] Barbara and Miss Whitehead saw that the

---

[1] *Memoir of D. G. Rossetti*, by W. M. Rossetti, II, 128.

[2] The quotations are from an article by Mrs. Malleson in the *Journal of Education*, September 1, 1886.

result was to encourage " a negation of reverence and imagination," and they felt that something better was needed. It was difficult to find anyone among professional teachers who would share their views, and Miss Whitehead at Barbara's request determined to train herself for the work. Training colleges were then unknown, so Miss Whitehead evolved for herself a course of educational reading, combined with practical work in the best primary schools then in London. The Portman Hall School was at length started in hired rooms in a poor neighbourhood near Edgware Road, and not far from the Leigh Smiths' house in Blandford Square. In its curriculum and general arrangements it was extraordinarily modern, in many ways resembling the High Schools started about twenty years later. The equipment was exceptionally good, including well-chosen pictures, maps and diagrams—things rarely seen in schools in those days. As for text-books in arithmetic and the like, Miss Whitehead had to work out her own with infinite labour. The curriculum, which was planned in a happy state of freedom from examinations, included the usual elementary subjects, as well as composition, geography, and (most unusual at that time) the rudiments of physiology and hygiene. There were no corporal punishments and very few of any kind. Punctual and early attendance was encouraged by the pleasure of Saturday visits to museums and picture galleries. Singing was rarely taught in schools, but in this one, " much prominence was given to singing as a moral agent, and the singing lesson was usually the second in order of the morning's work, and under its influence the children went to their severer exercises in a cheerful state of mind." The boys and girls of the neighbouring tradespeople and artisans attended the school, as well as the children of professional men. Miss Whitehead's own younger sisters were among the pupils, and for a time a son of Garibaldi's was taught there. The school received children belonging to all denominations, including Roman Catholics, Jews, and pupils from families of advanced free thought. This mixture of sexes, classes and creeds was most unusual, but it gave rise to no difficulty. Moral teaching, on the broadest lines, exercised a penetrating influence on the whole school. As an old pupil expressed it, " the children were really educated rather than merely taught."

The school was a remarkable piece of pioneer work, especially for two young women, both under thirty. The two friends were in close sympathy ; Barbara constantly visited the school and kept in touch with the work, and Miss Whitehead's practical ability and enthusiasm made it a great success. Unfortunately she broke down in health after a year or two, but she had established the school on the desired lines, and after her marriage to Mr. F. R. Malleson, she kept in touch with it, acting as " inspector." The pupils paid a nominal fee of sixpence a week, but the main cost was borne by Barbara and her friends. Among the volunteers who helped in the teaching were Barbara's two sisters, her friend Eliza Fox, and Miss Octavia Hill. Miss Hill suggested that her sister Miranda should become a regular teacher in the school. " You know," she wrote to her, " I do not think the absence of all religious teaching a sufficient reason for disapproval, to counterbalance the immense good which I consider they are doing there, especially as the teacher and three of the monitors are earnest believers in Our Lord. . . . You would find Madame Bodichon and Mrs. Malleson delightful people to work under." Miss Miranda Hill consulted Mr. F. D. Maurice, and on his advice declined to join the staff. Both the Miss Hills, however, afterwards taught in the Working Women's College, an unsectarian institution founded in 1864 by Mr. Maurice and Mrs. Malleson. Barbara was not so much " unsectarian " as quite inattentive to sects and divisions of all sorts. " If anyone asks you what I am," she said to a friend, " say that I'm a Sanitarian " —a true word, for she cared for the health of both body and mind.[1]

A frequent visitor to the Portman Hall School was George Eliot, with whom Barbara had become acquainted in 1852 through their common friend Miss Parkes. She was at that time unknown to fame, and was beginning her literary career in London as

[1] An interesting account of a school on similar lines, carried on by the Rev. F. V. Thornton, in Hampshire, may be found in the Report of the Schools Enquiry Commission of 1864. Owing to the want of organization and publicity which prevailed as regards education generally, these excellent schools remained as isolated experiments, working in ignorance of each other's existence, and leading to no permanent results.

37

assistant editor of the *Westminster Review*. The acquaintance
soon became a close friendship. It is said that when she was
hesitating over the step which was to unite her life with George
Lewes's, she consulted Barbara, who replied that she could not
advise her, but would stand by her faithfully whatever the event.
Barbara was as good as her word, and the friendship was of
special value to George Eliot, whose circumstances made it
difficult for her to have women friends. " I will not call you
friend," she wrote to Barbara. " I will rather call you by some
name that I am not obliged to associate with evaporated professions and petty egoism. I will call you only Barbara, the
name I must always associate with a true large heart." [1] George
Eliot's literary and introspective life was very unlike Barbara's,
whose sincerity and energy, as she said, brought " a little draught
of pure air " into her world. " One always gets good," she wrote,
" from Barbara's healthy practical life." Her heroine Romola
was in outward appearance drawn from Barbara, and the description in Chapter V indicates something in her personality which
made her seem at times rather formidable. " Refinement of
brow and nostril " was counterbalanced " by a full though firm
mouth and powerful chin, which gave an expression of proud
tenacity and latent impetuousness. . . . Her queenly step was
the simple action of her tall, finely-wrought frame." When *Adam
Bede* was published in 1859, Barbara was the first to recognize
the unknown author, though she had read only extracts from
reviews. " God bless you, dearest Barbara," wrote George
Eliot, " for your love and sympathy." Barbara's gaiety and
vitality were delightful to her friends—" a jolly fellow," Rossetti
called her.

> " Dear Barbara, your cheerful spirit
> Never needs a stick to stir it,"

wrote her father, in some doggerel verses.

As George Eliot said, Barbara's life was " full of joyful work."
It was too full, and she suffered from the clash of interests. " It
is my duty to be an artist," she wrote to Mrs. Malleson after her
marriage. " I should like to give all I had to schools, and earn
my own living by painting. . . . There are so many people I

---

[1] From an unpublished letter of George Eliot's.

love and want to see ! I do wish I had three immortal lives. I would spend one only with my Eugène, and the other two for art and social life." Other interests were so strong as to prevent her from making the most of her artistic gifts, but she worked hard at her painting. She was well acquainted with Daubigny, who often visited her, and with Corot, who took her into his studio as a pupil for a time. Her opportunities for learning of course were exceptional. The ordinary private teaching available for ladies was poor in quality, and there was almost nothing else to be had.[1] In 1858 there was only one life class in London open to ladies ; " nor," we are told, " is the practice of landscape art much easier to a woman unless she have a very determined will and very thick boots. Long hours of exposure to sun and wind are inevitable, and free access to nature for months at a time, and a courageous exercise of personal independence." [2] Barbara, who loved the open air [3] and was not afraid of wearing thick boots, worked a great deal out of doors, as well as in her studio. Her friend Eliza Fox started a co-operative evening class for ladies, for drawing from life from an undraped model. The class excited much comment, and some Academicians who became interested promised to help in getting women admitted to the Royal Academy Schools.[4] Soon after, Miss Laura Herford, encouraged by Sir Charles Eastlake (President of the Royal Academy), applied for admission. Her application was supported by a Petition, which was sent in 1858 to every Academician, signed by a number of

[1] Ruskin, drawing his conclusions, like most people, from facts, without considering their causes, declared that " no woman could paint " —an opinion which he recanted on seeing the work of Elizabeth Thomson and Francesca Alexander (*Ruskin on Pictures*, Vol. II, p. 262).

[2] *On the Adoption of Professional Life by Women*, in the *Englishwoman's Review*, September, 1858, pp. 4–6. Thick boots seem to have been regarded as especially unladylike. See a review of *Unprotected Females in Norway*, in the *Saturday Review* (Aug. 1, 1851), where " hobnail shoes " are declared to be " articles of doubtful femininity."

[3] Sometimes her friends thought her love of fresh air was carried too far. Rossetti, when staying at Scalands in 1870, wrote to William Allingham : " Barbara does not indulge in bell-pulls. What she does affect is any amount of thorough draught."

[4] See *English Female Artists*, by Ellen Clayton, 1876 ; *Women in English Life*, by Georgiana Hill, II, 165 ; the *Englishwoman's Journal*, March, 1861, p. 71.

ladies, among whom were Barbara Leigh Smith and her two sisters. The Schools were opened to women students in 1861. The Academy had not admitted any woman to membership since the days of Mary Moser and Angelica Kauffmann, though pictures by women artists were not excluded from its exhibitions. The Old and the New Water Colour Societies admitted a few "lady associates," but these societies were closed to exhibitors who were not either members or associates. It was therefore not easy for a woman to exhibit her work, unless she could afford to hire a gallery. In 1856 the Society of Female Artists was formed to meet this difficulty.[1] It was hardly to be expected that their exhibitions would be very high in quality, but it was something that they could be held at all, and that the exhibitors should feel the stimulus and discipline of public criticism. Barbara Leigh Smith sent her work to these exhibitions, and often had special shows of her pictures at other galleries, and in her own house.

Meanwhile, as quite a young woman, Miss Leigh Smith had become actively interested in the question of the position of married women, which the sensation caused by Mrs. Norton's troubles had brought into public notice. In 1854 she drew up and published *A Brief Summary, in Plain Language, of the Most Important Laws concerning Women*. This excellent little pamphlet was widely circulated and attracted much attention. Her friend Mr. Matthew Davenport Hill, Q.C., Recorder of Birmingham, helped her in composing it with his criticism and encouragement. Mr. Davenport Hill was one of the originators of the Law Amendment Society—a Society founded in 1844, to further the movement for law reform, a movement both scientific and philanthropic in its aims. Among the members of the Society were various friends of the Leigh Smiths, including Lord Brougham, Mr. Serjeant Manning, and Mr. Hastings, who was its Secretary. Through Miss Leigh Smith's exertions, the Society was induced to take up the question of the position of married women, and to refer it to their Committee on Personal Laws. After careful investigation the Committee presented a Report,[2] drafted by Sir Erskine

[1] See the *Englishwoman's Journal*, May, 1858.

[2] An outline of the proposals embodied in the Report, with a notice of the petitions being circulated, is given in the revised edition of Miss Leigh Smith's *Brief Summary*, issued in 1856.

Perry, recommending that a married woman should own property as if she were a *feme sole*, and should have the power of making a will. The Committee thought at first that they could confine the remedy proposed to hard cases, but they were forced to the conclusion that justice could be done to married women in no other way than by giving them a power over their own property equal to that which the husband has over his. The Law Amendment Society arranged for a public meeting to discuss the question, with Sir John Pakington in the chair. The meeting, which was crowded, was attended by Lord Denman, Sir Erskine Perry, M.P., Mr. Monckton Milnes, M.P., Mr. M. Davenport Hill, Q.C., Mr. Serjeant Manning ; and, as the Law Amendment Society's *Journal* records, " a large number of ladies were also present, including Mrs. Jameson, Mrs. Howitt, and many other lady authors." The chairman said he was " greatly indebted to the ladies present, whom he was glad to see in such numbers, for the support they rendered to the movement ; it was most important that they should have the opinion, and consult the feelings of the fair sex in any legislation on this subject." The fair sex expressed their opinions only by their presence ; it was unusual for ladies to attend public meetings, and none of them thought of making a speech. The men made the speeches, and passed resolutions affirming the desirability of adopting the principle of equity as the basis of a general law of property with regard to married women.

In 1856 a ladies' committee was formed, including Miss Parkes, Miss Leigh Smith, Mrs. Bridell Fox, and Mrs. Howitt, who acted as Secretary, a task which was later undertaken by Miss Maria Rye. Miss Leigh Smith drafted a Petition,[1] stating the hardships occasioned by the law, especially among the poorer classes. The petition was circulated with requests for signatures, evidence as to the working of the law was collected, public meetings were held, and other petitions were got up all over the country. Over seventy petitions with 24,000 signatures attached were presented to Parliament.[2] The movement was supported in the press by

---

[1] *Law Amendment Society's Journal*, Vol. I, p. 72.
[2] *Law Amendment Society's Journal*, Vol. I, 1855-6 ; Vol. II, 1856-7 ; *Westminster Review*, April and October, 1856 ; *Edinburgh Review*, January, 1857 ; *Englishwoman's Journal*, Vol. I and Vol. II, 1858, pp. 76, 415 ; Mary Howitt, *Autobiography*, II, 114-16.

Harriet Martineau and W. J. Fox. Finally, over 3,000 women, including Mrs. Browning and others of acknowledged intellectual distinction, signed Miss Leigh Smith's petition, which was presented in March, 1856, to the House of Lords by Lord Brougham, and to the House of Commons by Sir Erskine Perry. On May 14, 1857, Sir Erskine Perry introduced a Bill into the House of Commons embodying the proposals of the Law Amendment Society, but it got no further than a second reading. The Divorce Bill, which came on about this time, occupied much time and attention, and its passage was attended with great difficulty. Lord Lyndhurst succeeded in introducing into this Bill a clause [1] affording protection to the property of married women separated from their husbands, and relief was thus provided for some of the hardest cases. It was impossible at the time to accomplish more, and the question was not adequately dealt with till 1882, when the first Married Women's Property Act was passed. [2]

Clause XXI of the Divorce Act was welcomed by opponents as depriving the supporters of the Married Women's Property Bill of their most telling point. " In the presence of the Divorce Bill," declared the *Saturday Review*, " which embodies the only parts of Sir Erskine Perry's scheme which are at all valuable— those which deal with the property of women legally separated —it would be absurd to consider his absurd and abortive proposal." " So long as the petticoat rebellion was confined to a mistaken petition of a few literary ladies whose peculiar talents had placed them in a rather anomalous position . . . we really had not the heart to say anything serious about it ; " but the

---

[1] Section XXI in the Act.

[2] *Law Amendment Society's Journal*, Vol. I, 1855–6, and Vol. II, 1856–7. See also *Report of Married Women's Property Committee presented at the Final Meeting of their Friends and Subscribers at Willis' Rooms*, November 18, 1882. This Report, which gives the history of the question, was the work of a new Committee, of which Mrs. Jacob Bright and Mrs. Wolstenholme Elmy were Secretaries. This Committee began by calling the attention of the Social Science Association (in which the Law Amendment Society had been merged) to the question. Success was attained, as the Report states, " after fifteen years of arduous and anxious effort." Cf. *Law and Opinion in England*, Chap. XI, by A. V. Dicey.

Law Amendment Society's proposals " set at defiance the experience of every country in Christendom and the common sense
of mankind " ; they were " enough to remove the whole discussion from the region of reality to that of burlesque." The
exceptional cases, thought the *Saturday Review*, in which a
woman's private means were squandered by a wicked husband,
were neither numerous nor brutal enough " to justify us in
revolutionizing society." [1] The existing state of things was " the
natural system " ; Sir Erskine Perry proposed an " artificial
system." " There is, besides, a smack of selfish independence
about it which rather jars with poetical notions of wedlock."

Such comments seem heartless, but the fact was that the public
had no general knowledge about the lives of women. While
there was no Divorce Court, there were no reports published of
divorce proceedings ; and the many cases of hardship of which
information was obtained and published by Miss Leigh Smith
and her friends revealed an amount of suffering of which most
people had previously heard nothing. Mrs. Norton's case had
had a quite exceptional notoriety. Now it was found that such
things were of every-day occurrence in all ranks of life. " In the
effort to obtain signatures," wrote Miss Parkes, " people interested
in the question were brought into communication in all parts of
the kingdom, and the germs of an effective movement were
scattered far and wide." Public opinion began to be stirred,
and Miss Leigh Smith and Miss Parkes were encouraged to feel
that though they had not succeeded in carrying their point, a
foundation had been laid for further efforts.

Meanwhile, a great change had taken place in Miss Leigh
Smith's life. About 1856 her sister Bella (Mrs. Ludlow) having
fallen into delicate health, it was decided to take her to Algiers.
The three sisters went, with their eldest brother Ben, and were
fascinated by the new world which was opened to them. " I
have seen Swiss mountains and Lombard plains," wrote Barbara, describing the view from her window, " Scotch lochs and
Welsh mountains, but never anything so unearthly, so delicate,
so aerial, as the long stretches of blue mountains and shining
sea ; the dark cypresses, relieved against a background of a
thousand dainty tints and the massive white Moorish houses

[1] Cf. *Caius and Caia, Saturday Review*, July 18, 1857.

gleaming out from the grey mysterious green of olive trees."
She delighted in sitting out of doors in November, sketching
amidst blue lilies, narcissus, cyclamens, and crocuses—" African
flowers such as Dido might have culled to deck the banquet for
pious Æneas." [1] All was new and fascinating. Excursions on
horseback were a great pleasure to the party, and they visited all
sorts of wild and lovely places. Stories of attacks by hostile Arabs
and man-eating lions gave an agreeable thrill. A pleasant society
was provided by " a constant influx of visitors from all nations."
A French colonist with whom they soon made friends was Dr.
Eugène Bodichon. Dr. Bodichon, who was born in 1810, belonged on the father's side to an old bourgeois family of Brittany,
who were Bonapartists. His mother, Antoinette Le Grand de la
Pommeraye, was descended from a noble family, Royalists and
Catholics of the old Breton type. Dr. Bodichon, when a medical
student in Paris, had become a Republican, and a friend of Louis
Blanc, Ledru Rollin, and other revolutionists. The conquest
of Algeria led many adventurous spirits to visit the new colony,
and in 1836 Dr. Bodichon decided to settle there. He took a
scientific interest in the varied native population of Arabs, Kabyles
and other races, practised among them, and rendered service
during an attack of cholera. In 1848 he was named Corresponding
Member of the Chamber of Deputies for Algeria, and he was
instrumental in procuring the abolition of slavery in the colony.
" Mes espérances pour l'avenir—" he wrote in his election
address—" le genre humain ne formera plus qu'une seule famille."
Tall, dark, and dignified, he was an attractive and romantic
figure, and in spite of seventeen years' difference in their ages, he
and Miss Leigh Smith became attached to each other. In 1857
he came to England, and they were married on July 2, at the
Unitarian Chapel in Little Portland Street.

Soon after their marriage, Dr. and Madame Bodichon visited
George Eliot and Mr. Lewes at Richmond, and later they set
out on a long tour in the United States. Madame Bodichon
painted much during this journey, and her pictures (including
some of Niagara) were exhibited at Washington, Philadelphia,

---

[1] *Algeria Considered as a Winter Residence for the English*, by Dr. and
Madame Bodichon, published at the *Englishwoman's Journal* Office,
1858.

and elsewhere. Events in the United States were at this time moving rapidly towards the Civil War, and feeling ran high on the question of slavery. Madame Bodichon sent some articles to the *Englishwoman's Journal* [1] in which we get glimpses of her views and experiences. The effect of slavery, she felt, was more hurtful to the white men than to the black, undermining their self-control in both temper and morals. The white ladies were ruined in health by their horror of all work and exertion ; even walking was not *comme il faut* for a lady who could send twelve slaves for anything she wanted. Madame Bodichon visited schools, churches, sugar plantations ; she mixed with whites, free coloured people, and slaves, although to call on a coloured lady was " an unpardonable offence against the social code." At New Orleans she saw a slave auction, where about 30 women and 20 men were for sale, as well as 12 or 14 babies. She attended negro services in Baptist and Methodist chapels, where she was often the only European present. " Sometimes," she writes, " when I hear them sing, the thought of slavery, and what it really is, makes me utterly miserable ; one can do nothing—nothing, and I see little hope ; it makes me wring my hands with anguish, sometimes, being so helpless to help ! " At the end of the service, there was generally a universal shaking of hands all round ; " my two arms ached," she wrote on one occasion, " with the shakes I received." Her proceedings were not only unconventional to the last degree, but were attended with some risk, as people even suspected of being abolitionists were liable to serious persecution. She was not, however, an abolitionist ; she wished for " gradual freedom for the blacks ; but freedom in all the States to buy themselves, and freedom to educate themselves." At Ohio she saw an institution which reminded her of her own Portman Hall School—a large mixed school for boys and girls, and an evening school for young men and women. " It rejoiced my heart," she writes, " to see this school, and to know that there are hundreds like it ; to see children of rich men and the very poor sitting side by side." [2]

[1] *Englishwoman's Journal*, October and November, 1858 ; March, 1860 ; October, November and December, 1861 ; and February, 1863.
[2] *An American School*, by B. L. S. B., in the *Englishwoman's Journal*, November, 1858.

45

The United States were extraordinarily interesting to Madame Bodichon, partly through her inherited interest in the slavery question, but still more because of her modern cast of mind. The North was in the full tide of its marvellous course of expansion, and she felt that many of her aspirations would be realized in America long before they could be hoped for in England. After her return home, another journey provided one of those contrasts of which her life was full. In 1861 Dr. Bodichon took his wife to visit his relations in Brittany, where she became acquainted with a society which in many ways seemed hardly to have changed since the Middle Ages. Many of Dr. Bodichon's relations had been killed in the French Revolutionary wars, but there were still a number of cousins, the chief of whom were a pious and benevolent great lady, Madame de Villebois-Mareuil, and her daughters. Madame de Villebois was, as Madame Bodichon said, a model revival of the *ancien régime*. Her days were spent in managing her invalid husband's farms, and in giving advice and medicines to the poor ; her evenings in spinning. Though some of the ladies knew a little Latin, they seemed to be unacquainted with " the commonest modern scientific truths." Few members of the family had ever travelled in a train ; they thought England, not being a Catholic country, a terrible place. Madame Bodichon was, however, received with warmth and kindness, and quickly made friends with her new relations, though, as she wrote home to one of her aunts, she felt she would have exploded if she had stayed much longer. The Royalist atmosphere would have been too much for her. " Think," she wrote, " of Garibaldi being called monster, and Cavour right hand of Satan."

In the early days of her marriage, Madame Bodichon hoped that she and her husband would settle in London. This, however, proved impossible. It was too late to transplant him from his free and unconventional life in Algeria, and they bought a house there, where she used to spend the winter months. She seconded Dr. Bodichon in his efforts to make the country healthy, and they both did much for afforestation, especially for the planting of the Australian eucalyptus. In Algeria as in England she busied herself with philanthropic work as well as with her painting. The difficulty was to avoid interruptions. She would declaim against casual visitors : " Devastators of the day, away, away ! " Yet she was very hospitable, and never seemed to be in a hurry. Free and friendly intercourse of French colonists and English visitors was promoted by her influence ; it was natural to her to ignore all differences in nationality as well as in social standing. Her hospitality had a character of its own, and the simplicity of her arrangements was considered rather Bohemian. This simplicity was also characteristic of her dress ; at a time when other women were wearing tight dresses, bustles, and caps, she wore what suited her—loose flowing dresses, made on simple lines, with no fussy draperies, and a plain velvet band round her braided hair. The freedom of her life in Algeria gave her great delight. " I confess," she wrote to William Allingham in 1862, " the enthusiasm with which I used to leave my easel and go to teach at the school or help Bessie in her affairs is wearing off, and if it were not that at thirty-five one has acquired habits which happily cannot be broken, I should not go on as I do ; I could not *begin* as I used ten years ago at any of these dusty, dirty attempts to help one's poor fellow-creatures, and it is quite natural that my life abroad and out of doors should make me more enterprising for boar-hunts or painting excursions, than for long sojourns in stifling rooms with miserable people. I think of the ' Palace of Art ' and know it is my temptation." [1]

Such were her feelings in Algeria. But every summer she returned to England, and spent some months there, dividing her time chiefly between Blandford Square and Scalands ; and when she was at home she threw herself into her old interests with a will, and was always ready to welcome new ideas and new developments in the causes for which she cared. She exercised much hospitality, welcoming old friends and new to her house. At Scalands a visit from Miss Davies was almost an annual institution, and in later years Girton students used often to stay there, and were especially welcome. One of the first students to enter the College, Miss Gibson, has described a visit paid by her in 1871.

" It was, I think, during the next summer vacation that Madame

---

[1] *Letters to William Allingham*, p. 79. Fifteen letters from Madame Bodichon are printed in this book.

Bodichon invited me to stay for a few days at her delightful cottage at Robertsbridge. That visit was a revelation to me. It showed me a new way of life, the charm of simple surroundings. The living-room with open hearth, wood fire and round table spread for a meal beside the open cottage door was entirely different from anything I had seen, although I am now a familiar guest at many such cottages. Dear Madame Bodichon was a forerunner in the revolt against the Victorian worship of smug, stuffy, pretentious comfort. Her little sitting-room, a frieze of the Bayeux tapestry for its only decoration, was delightful by lamplight when William Allingham, the only other guest, read aloud to us Shakespeare's sonnets and now and then a poem of his own.

" The whole picture was French rather than English, and the illusion was completed by the wonderful apparition of the master who appeared only at meals clad in his blue peasant's blouse, and by the French talk which one had to take part in when he came in. As I look back to these early days I find that though I never knew Madame Bodichon intimately, she had a considerable influence on my life. At her pleasant informal parties in Blandford Square I met some of my best friends—friends still to-day—and enjoyed many delightful evenings. She had too a wonderful gift of speaking the right word at the right moment—a gift that came I think from a combination of kindness and candour—so that some of her quite unimportant remarks have remained with me to this day."

Much has been recorded about Madame Bodichon in connection with another Girton student, Miss Marks, afterwards Mrs. Ayrton, in whose biography (by Miss Evelyn Sharp) may be found many delightful instances of the " kindness and candour " which were her great qualities.

CHAPTER IV

Miss Davies and Miss Garrett : Their Initiation into the Women's Movement. 1857–1862

THE agitation on behalf of the Married Women's Property Bill of 1857 proved to be the first step in a great movement. As George Eliot remarked, " The proposed law would help to raise the position and character of women. It is one round of a long ladder stretching far beyond our lives." The public interest which had been awakened in the question was quickly turned to account by Madame Bodichon and her friends. Mrs. Jameson (well known as the author of *Sacred and Legendary Art*) had recently delivered a lecture on *Sisters of Charity*, followed by another on *The Communion of Labour*, in which she pointed out the good that might be done by providing women with training and employment.[1] In 1857 Madame Bodichon pursued the matter further in a pamphlet entitled *Women and Work*. " There is no way," she wrote, " of aiding governesses or needlewomen but by opening more ways of gaining livelihoods for women." They ought to be trained as teachers, accountants, watchmakers, nurses, clerks, in fact, for any occupation for which they may be fit. She went, however, much further than the material point of view. " Women want work both for the health of their minds and bodies." Moreover, women are wanted as workers : they ought to be doctors and nurses, they should be employed in lunatic asylums, prisons, and workhouses ;

---

[1] The lectures, delivered in 1855 and 1856, were published as a book in 1859, with a letter to Lord John Russell " on the present conditions and requirements of the women of England," as Miss Davies notes in her *Family Chronicle*, p. 161.

" all the work of philanthropy is imperfect unless women co-
operate with men." These suggestions were practically all innovations ; even the possibilities of nursing as a profession for
women had only just been perceived, since Miss Nightingale's
work in the Crimea, two years previously.

The pamphlet on *Women and Work* is somewhat diffuse and
ill-arranged. Madame Bodichon never wrote easily ; her language has always a kind of abrupt simplicity and sincerity, but
her work was usually done with a care which seems lacking here.
Naturally the *Saturday Review* fell upon it with glee : " Miss
Barbara—we cannot bear to speak of so poetical a philosopher
as Miss Smith [1] . . . is a lady of large figures." She " has
much to propose, and no hesitation in proposing it." " If this
is at all a typical pamphlet—a fair sample of what a lady, who
boasts to have made the subject her own, is likely to publish—
we are afraid that the sex is really not so far developed as we had
hoped. As a piece of ' pretty Fanny's ' talk it would be charming ; but we should be sorry to trust ' pretty Fanny ' with any
business more important and intricate than the payment of a
milk bill."

Madame Bodichon and her friends, however, were not only
in earnest—they were more practical than the reviewer supposed.
Steps were now taken which led to an effective organization.
After consultation with Mrs. Jameson, they decided to start a
magazine devoted to women's questions. Money was collected
in the form of shares, subscribed by Madame Bodichon and others,
in a limited liability company ; Miss Parkes and Miss Hays [2]
were appointed editors ; and in March, 1858, the first number
of the *Englishwoman's Journal* appeared. The prospectus set
forth that " the present industrial employments of women, both
manual and intellectual, the best mode of judiciously extending
the sphere of such employments, and the laws affecting the
property and conditions of the sex, form the prominent subjects
for discussion in its pages." It was carried on, as Miss Parkes
wrote, " at a cost of responsibility and anxiety far beyond what

[1] The pamphlet was published not long before Madame Bodichon's
marriage.

[2] *Family Chronicle*, p. 263a. The prospectus is quoted in the *Englishwoman's Journal*, October, 1858, Vol. II, p. 75.

any merely literary journal could entail, inasmuch as the subject-matter touched at all points upon the dearest interests and safeguards of civilized society, was partially connected with the religious views of various bodies of Christians, and presented in other directions a perfect pitfall of ridicule, ever ready to open beneath the feet of the conductors." [1] Miss Parkes, in addition to her work as editor, wrote a great many of the articles, and Madame Bodichon often sent contributions. Among other contributors may be mentioned Miss Maria Rye, Miss Isa Craig, Miss Boucherett, and Miss Adelaide Procter.

Before a year had passed, the *Englishwoman's Journal* gave rise to a new development. Miss Boucherett, the daughter of a Lincolnshire squire, in her country home had felt the need for improvement in the condition of women. She was stirred by an article by Harriet Martineau on *Female Industry*, in the *Edinburgh Review* for April, 1859; and meeting about the same time with a chance number of the *Journal*, she was delighted to find in its contents exactly what met her wishes and hopes. She came to London and called at the office, where to her surprise she found, instead of some dowdy old lady, Miss Parkes, " a handsome young woman dressed in admirable taste," and Miss Leigh Smith, " also beautifully dressed, of radiant beauty, with masses of golden hair." She immediately set to work, with their sympathy and assistance, to organize a Society for Promoting the Employment of Women, in concert with Miss Adelaide Procter, and Miss Sarah Lewin, who had also been drawn in by a chance encounter with the *Englishwoman's Journal*. Much had to be done to induce people to employ women even as assistants in drapers' shops. Their ignorance of arithmetic was a serious difficulty, and among the undertakings of the society's first few years was a book-keeping class, which soon grew into a day school. Other enterprises included a Law Copying class and office; a printing business; and plans for the emigration of women, which developed (under the management of Miss Rye and Miss Lewin) into the Middle Class Emigration Society. A Registry Office was also established, and was soon besieged by applicants for work.

The Society for the Employment of Women and the *English-*

[1] Cf. the *Saturday Review*, April 10, 1858.

woman's Journal established themselves in the same house, No. 19, Langham Place, and worked in close co-operation with each other. Rooms were set apart for a ladies' club on a modest scale, comprising a luncheon room, and a reading room supplied with newspapers and magazines. It was a new thing for women to have a social centre of this sort. The whole affair was known as the Ladies' Institute, and served as a rallying point which gathered many recruits to the movement.[1] The members formed a group constantly on the look-out for new openings of all sorts for women—industrial, educational, professional, and philanthropic. By working together for a common cause, they gained for themselves a kind of experience new to women, and not at that time to be had anywhere else. When in London, Madame Bodichon went to Langham Place almost every day, " carrying into the work," as Madame Belloc says, " the sunshine of her vigorous intellect and her warm heart." [2] Among others of the " Langham Place circle," as Miss Davies called it, were Miss Boucherett ; Miss Isa Craig, the daughter of a hosier and glover in Edinburgh, who began her career as a contributor of verse to the *Scotsman* ; Miss Emily Faithfull, the head of the printing business ; and Miss Adelaide Procter, the author of *Legends and Lyrics*.

The offices in Langham Place had not long been established, when Miss Davies went in the spring of 1859 to pay a visit to her brother in London. She and Miss Garrett went together to tea at the Leigh Smiths' at their home in Blandford Square,[3] where they made the acquaintance of Miss Parkes and Miss Adelaide Procter. A year later, as Miss Davies records, " Jane Crow, proposed by Adelaide Procter, was appointed to the Secretaryship of the Society for Promoting the Employment of Women, founded by Miss Boucherett, and went to live at the office in Langham Place. This made another link with the Langham Place circle." [4]

[1] See *Women's Suffrage*, by H. Blackburn, Chap. IV and Appendix C ; the *Englishwoman's Journal*, March, 1859 ; August, October and November, 1860.

[2] The *Englishwoman's Review*, July 15, 1891.

[3] Now almost entirely destroyed to make room for Marylebone Railway Station.

[4] *Family Chronicle*, p. 165.

Inspired by the example of Langham Place, Miss Davies now began to try to introduce something of the spirit of the women's movement into her parish work at Gateshead. She did what she could for the young women of the parish, and among other things, started a weekly reading meeting and classes at Mrs. Austin's house. " Annie's [Mrs. Austin's] class for servants and young women sounds very promising," wrote Miss Garrett. " I fancy it will do the pupils no end of good to have friendly intercourse with anyone so refined and cordial as Annie." A little later, Miss Davies wrote three letters to a Newcastle paper, setting forth the new ideas about women, and urging that they should be not only allowed but encouraged to work, and given suitable training and education. Soon after, she started a Northumberland and Durham Branch of the Society for Promoting the Employment of Women; with herself as Treasurer and the Bishop of Durham as President. " I am glad," wrote Miss Garrett, " your meeting went off so well, and that you are fairly started now as a recognized worker for the cause. Miss [Leigh] Smith and I agreed the other day that it was just the work for your special powers." Miss Davies succeeded in forming a Committee, which was joined by some prominent local people. A book-keeping class was started with the view of preparing girls for the Examinations of the Society of Arts ; a Register for Governesses was opened ; and some enquiries were made into the conditions of women in neighbouring factories. These various efforts brought, as Miss Davies said, some significant facts into notice. Women could find employment only of the humblest kind, at a miserably low rate of wages, because they were unskilled. " It is indeed no wonder," she wrote in her report, " that people who have not learned to do anything cannot find anything to do." [1]

Among the members of this local Committee was Miss Anna Richardson, the eldest daughter of Mr. Edward Richardson of Newcastle, an unusually well-read and cultivated woman ;

[1] *Report of the Northumberland and Durham Branch of the Society for Promoting the Employment of Women,* 1861. Reprinted in *Thoughts on Some Questions relating to Women.* Miss Davies was later (1865–72) a member of the Managing Committee of the parent Society for Promoting the Employment of Women (see *Reports* of the Society).

practical too, and much occupied at home, according to the usual lot of elder sisters in large families. Miss Davies, happening to hear that Miss Richardson was a subscriber to the *Englishwoman's Journal*, felt sure they would have sympathies in common, and sought her acquaintance, which soon became a warm friendship. Miss Richardson stimulated and encouraged Miss Davies' taste for reading. In an early letter to her, Miss Davies writes : " My mind wants looking after dreadfully, and I consider you responsible for it." They discussed books together, particularly George Eliot's novels, which they admired immensely ; and Miss Richardson taught Miss Davies some Greek. Together they attended a course of lectures on Physiology given by Dr. Embleton of Newcastle to a class of ladies. " Though I did not care for the subject," writes Miss Davies in her *Family Chronicle*, " I very much enjoyed being associated with others in learning *anything*."

Although Miss Davies did not care for this subject, she was keenly interested in the question of opening the medical profession to women. In the second of her letters to a Newcastle paper, she had proposed it as being a suitable occupation for them. " There are at present," she wrote, " great and almost insuperable difficulties in the way of obtaining the necessary education in England. It is a fact, I believe, that the only female physician legally registered in this country—Dr. Elizabeth Blackwell, M.D.—was obliged to obtain the greater part of her instruction elsewhere, and though herself an Englishwoman, she is indebted to an American College for her degree." [1] Miss Blackwell took her degree in 1849, and in the following year came to London and succeeded in obtaining leave from Mr. (afterwards Sir James) Paget to pursue her studies at St. Bartholomew's Hospital, of which he was then Dean. Miss Leigh Smith and Miss Parkes, hearing of this, sought her out and made her work known with a view to encouraging other women to take up medicine. In 1859 she again visited London, and arrangements were made for her to give some lectures on her work. " The most important listener," wrote Miss Blackwell afterwards, " was the bright intelligent young lady whose interest in the

[1] Miss Davies had no doubt read about Miss Blackwell's career in the second number of the *Englishwoman's Journal* (April, 1858).

study of medicine was then aroused—Miss Elizabeth Garrett." [1] The lectures were followed by a *Letter to Young Ladies desirous of Studying Medicine*, in the *Englishwoman's Journal*, January, 1860. [2] The ladies of Langham Place were desirous of encouraging women to study medicine, but it was not easy to find any who could be induced to do so, still less to procure any training for them.

Later in the year Miss Davies paid another visit to her brother. " My time during this visit to London," she writes in her *Family Chronicle*, " seems to have been chiefly spent at Langham Place, helping in work either for the *Englishwoman's Journal* or the Employment of Women Society, and in helping E. Garrett in the first steps of her enterprise." This enterprise—the study of medicine—had been first proposed to Miss Garrett by Miss Davies, who felt that her friend's health and strength and energy would make her an admirable pioneer. Miss Garrett's own inclinations were urging her to take up work of some kind. A trifling circumstance led to an interview with Dr. Elizabeth Blackwell. [3] During a conversation in the Garrett family circle, Dr. Blackwell was spoken of very disparagingly, and Miss Garrett, in great indignation, told her father that if he wanted to know whether Miss Blackwell was a respectable woman, he could ask Mr. Valentine Smith—a cousin of Madame Bodichon's and a business partner of Mr. Garrett's. Mr. Smith, thinking that Miss Garrett wanted an introduction to Miss Blackwell, arranged for them to meet at Madame Bodichon's house, when Miss Garrett, who was still undecided, was somewhat taken aback (as she wrote to Miss Davies) to find herself already looked upon as a recruit. " She assumed that I had made up my mind to follow her, I remember feeling very much confounded, and as if I had been suddenly thrust into work that was too big for me, while talking and listening to her that evening at Blandford Square." Soon afterwards, Dr. Blackwell had to return to her practice in New York. " When Miss Blackwell went back to America," writes Miss Davies in her *Family Chronicle*, " she left

[1] *Pioneer Work in opening the Medical Profession to Women*, by Dr. Elizabeth Blackwell.
[2] *Family Chronicle*, p. 166.
[3] *Family Chronicle*, pp. 168-9 and 205.

as her representatives three ladies, one of whom was Mrs. Russell Gurney. In consequence of this, Llewelyn introduced me to Mrs. Gurney." Mrs. Gurney, whose acquaintance Miss Davies had sought in the hope of furthering her plans for Miss Garrett, proved a helpful friend in this, and in other enterprises which were to follow.

Gradually, as Miss Davies records in the *Family Chronicle*, " it came to be understood that E. G. would, if possible, enter upon the career. . . . She began to prepare for the course by reading, and having lessons in Latin. She was also trying to improve herself in English composition and sent me papers for criticism." Like other girls, she was not in the least prepared for a profession. She was one of the elders of a large family whose home was at Aldeburgh in Suffolk. Her father, Mr. Newson Garrett, had business interests of a varied kind both at Aldeburgh and in London. He got the best governess he could for his daughters ; she bore the distinguished name of Miss Edgeworth, and was niece to Maria Edgeworth, but she was of the old-fashioned type described by Miss Yonge in *The Daisy Chain*, and taught chiefly by means of lists of questions and answers, a system which broke down when her irrepressible pupils began asking questions which were not in the book. The Miss Garretts were then sent to the Miss Brownings' school at Blackheath. These ladies, who were aunts to the poet, had some taste in literature and music, and the school was above the average in efficiency, but there was no question of the girls learning Latin or Mathematics. Lessons from a brother's tutor in the holidays helped to fill up the gaps a little. Such as the school was, at fifteen Miss Garrett left it, and a tour abroad was considered to have completed her education, after which she of course returned to live at home with no special tasks to occupy her beyond those which naturally arise for an elder sister in a large and affectionate family. But she was deeply interested in the questions of the day—the slavery question in America, the struggle for Italian freedom, and above all the woman's question, and she soon began to feel that she could not live at home " in happy idleness " all her life—she wanted " something definite and worthy " to do. Miss Davies suggested the medical profession, and the possibility began to be talked of. Miss Garrett's mother was at first greatly shocked, and her father very anxious about the " almost insurmountable difficulties and dangers " which would beset her. As Miss Garrett wrote to Miss Davies : [" My father] would prefer my settling down into a douce young lady, with no awkward energies, but when this is admitted to be impossible, he will soon be reconciled to the other line, *if I succeed.* This is an all-important point, of course, and it will nerve one up to almost any exertion to remember how far the cause is identified in the minds of one's family with personal success." In the end, both parents heartily approved, and her father's exertions on her behalf contributed much to her success.

There was much to be done by way of preparation in elementary subjects, and Miss Garrett began by taking lessons in Latin, while continuing to work at English composition. Through all the time of her medical studies she used to send her medical papers to Miss Davies, asking her " to cut up the style." The question of how she could get any medical education was very difficult, and there was much consultation as to the possibility of getting apprenticed for three years to a doctor, and what doctor could be induced to take her. Miss Garrett's letters (carefully kept by Miss Davies and copied into the *Family Chronicle*) show how Miss Davies entered into every detail and every step in her friend's career.[1] The two friends set to work in a very diplomatic way, losing no opportunity, leaving no stone unturned, and seizing boldly on the slightest advantage. The first step was to approach Mrs. Russell Gurney, with whom Miss Davies had already made acquaintance. Early in July, 1860, Miss Davies and Miss Garrett visited her together and received a kind and encouraging welcome ; but it was not easy for Mrs. Gurney or anyone else to cope with the formidable difficulty of securing teaching. After many visits to doctors which led to nothing but disappointment, Mrs. Gurney suggested that Miss Garrett should see Mr. William Hawes, who had been connected with the Middlesex Hospital and was disposed to be helpful. The Gurneys invited her, therefore, to meet him.

[1] Miss Davies' letters to Miss Garrett are unfortunately not available, as they were destroyed.

(Miss Garrett to Miss Davies.)

July 8, 1860.

" Mr. Hawes was cordial enough yesterday morning, but he evidently feels that the individual fitness of those who make the first attempt in England is of the very highest importance, and he feels that the difficulties to be overcome will need a *very* strong determination. He asked me if I had any idea of the nature of these difficulties, and when I said that it was because I felt so ignorant about them that I dared not speak or think confidently of the strength of my determination, he suggested that some test should be found to prove my power of endurance, etc., *before* any time was spent upon direct medical studies. I thought this very reasonable, if there really are such great unknown difficulties, and as Mr. and Mrs. Gurney seemed to agree with Mr. Hawes on this point, I suggested that I should spend six months as hospital nurse at once, as a test. This suited Mr. Hawes very well, but he said I must go into a surgical ward, as the physicians' wards were not a sufficient test."

Mr. Hawes succeeded in getting her admitted to the Middlesex Hospital, and in August, 1860, she established herself in London, at first with a married sister in Bayswater, and later in nurses' quarters at the hospital. She had to be in the hospital every day from eight o'clock till about four, and after a short interval for relaxation she generally spent the evening in reading Latin and Mathematics. Work was allotted to her in two surgical wards, where she learned from the nurses how to dress wounds, and took every opportunity of being present when the physicians and surgeons went their rounds. All went smoothly at first, and her zest in the work carried her through the awkwardnesses of the position. She reported to Miss Davies that the doctors were " uncommonly civil," and the surgeons very kind and courteous in giving her information.

(Miss Garrett to Miss Davies.)

August 17, 1860.

" The house doctor is very cordial and gives me a great deal of instruction . . . and seems to think it quite natural for me to see and hear anything professionally, which I feel is a great comfort. The pupils too seem inclined to treat me as a student, several of them have volunteered scraps of information, and as long as they merely speak to me of the matter in hand, I think it is wiser not to appear too frigid and stiff with them. If they *will* forget my sex and treat me as a fellow-student, it is just the right kind of feeling. It does seem to be wrong in theory to treat them all as one's natural enemies, though I know that in practice an absence of stiffness might be misconstrued."

Though nominally a nurse, she did not wear nurse's uniform, and the question of how to dress suitably had to be considered. Both she and Miss Davies were vexed by some of their friends' deficiencies in this respect. " I do wish, as you said, the D's dressed better," she wrote to Miss Davies. " She looks awfully strong-minded in walking dress . . . she has short petticoats and a close round hat, and several other dreadfully ugly arrangements. . . . It is abominable, and most damaging to the cause. I will not have her visit me at the Hospital in it." As to her own dress, she wrote :

September 5, 1860.

" Experience is modifying my notions about the most suitable style of dress for me to wear at the hospital. I feel confident now that one is helped rather than hindered by being as much like a lady as lies in one's power. When my student life begins, I shall try to get very serviceable, rich, whole coloured dresses that will do without trimmings and not require renewing often."

Early in September she wrote to Mr. Hawes to tell him how she was getting on, and received a friendly answer. " Your note," he wrote, " gave me great pleasure—pleasure to hear you were comfortable, and still greater pleasure to hear you were so valiantly meeting difficulties which I am sure would appal many stout hearts."

The idea, generally entertained, that the difficulties were appalling, arose partly from the belief that women were incapable of serious application to work, or of enduring anything unpleasant. The care of sick people was regarded as a disgusting occupation which no person of refinement could be expected to undertake. " Perhaps they do drink a little," wrote Lady Palmerston of the nurses at the time of the Crimean war, " but so do the ladies' monthly nurses, and nothing can be better than them ; poor people, it must be so tiresome sitting up all night." [1] Nursing was a disagreeable task fit only for coarse people ; when it came

[1] *The Life of Florence Nightingale,* by Sir Edward Cook, Vol. I, p. 272.

to medical work, it was shocking to think of refined ladies making a study of the revolting details of illness, acquiring a knowledge of anatomy, and practising dissection. A passage in Tennyson's *Princess* gives expression to this feeling. Princess Ida is explaining to the Prince that in her college " there are schools for all."

> " ' And yet,' I said,
> ' Methinks I have not found among them all,
> One anatomic.' ' Nay, we thought of that,'
> She answered, ' but it pleased us not : in truth
> We shudder but to dream our maids should ape
> Those monstrous males that carve the living hound
> And cram him with the fragments of the grave,
> Or in the dark dissolving human heart,
> And holy secrets of this microcosm,
> Dabbling a shameless hand with shameful jest,
> Encarnalize their spirits ; yet we know
> Knowledge is knowledge, and this matter hangs.' "

It must be remembered that surgical practice at that time was very different from what it is now. It was only in this year, 1860, that Lister first published his observations on antiseptic methods. Such were the horrors of septic infection, that it was seriously questioned whether the system of gathering patients together in hospitals could be continued. Popular opinion had some cause for shuddering at the hospitals. With less reason but equal force it was felt that a knowledge of physiology was improper and should remain a decently secluded mystery in the hands of professionals. Evidence of this abounds, but a specimen may be quoted from a letter to the *Englishwoman's Journal* of April, 1862, expressing the view that it is practically impossible to teach such subjects to girls, on account of " the extreme repugnance, amounting to disgust, felt by many girls to this class of knowledge . . . an obstacle which could not be surmounted without the sacrifice of much that is very valuable in a young girl's mind." A variety of prejudices, therefore, combined to produce a formidable opposition to any instruction for women about physiology, and the care of health ; although, should " pain and anguish wring the brow," they were at once to become ministering angels, and of course they ought at all times to be able to look after their children.

Miss Garrett, however, was getting to be so deeply interested that she was hardly conscious of the difficulties for which Mr. Hawes offered his sympathy. She found the hospital work "delightful." "It is rather provoking," she wrote to Miss Davies, "that people will think so much of the difficulties, in spite of my assurances that so far from their being appalling, I am enjoying the work more than I have ever done any other study or pursuit." Her position at the Middlesex Hospital was, however, too irregular, and the work too desultory to be satisfactory.

(Miss Garrett to Miss Davies.)

October 5, 1860.

" I have come to the conclusion that it will not do to go on long in the false position I now occupy at the hospital. I am nominally a nurse, but without any duties, no regular scene of action even. . . . Dr. Willis treats me as a pupil, and the house surgeons do the same, and I am in the surgery every morning getting the teaching and practice gratis for which the pupils pay a fee. It appears to me that I should not go on receiving instruction as a pupil under the guise of a nurse, and that it will be right to ask the College authorities to allow me to pay the usual fees in these special departments and to have the run of the hospital as at present for medical observation."

She accordingly spoke to Mr. De Morgan, the Treasurer of the hospital. He would not allow her to pay fees, as that would be recognizing her to some extent as a student, but she might make a donation to the hospital, and stay through the winter, learning all she could as an amateur. She was allowed to go to the apothecary, Mr. Plaskett, as a pupil, and learn dispensing, but Mr. De Morgan was very discouraging about the ultimate chance of getting into the College. "He said it was impossible, but would not assign any grounds for such an opinion, except that a lady's presence would distract the students' attention. All that he said against it was as frivolous as this is, and on the whole I did not feel hopeful about ever bringing him round, he was too much inclined to treat the subject with amused contempt."

Individual doctors, as she reported to Miss Blackwell, were willing to help her privately and singly, though they were afraid to countenance her work in their collective capacity. The

Dean, Mr. Nunn, was encouraging, and Dr. Willis offered to take her as a private pupil, coming to teach her practical chemistry and anatomy three times a week at her sister's house. She wanted very much to get this teaching, but the plan suggested was so novel and unusual that she hesitated on the score of propriety. After consultation with her parents, as well as with Miss Davies and Miss Anne Leigh Smith, she decided to accept it. Miss Davies advised caution, but Miss Leigh Smith, though she saw the difficulties, was in favour of risking these for the sake of the teaching. " The vulgarity of people is *the* difficulty," wrote Miss Garrett to Miss Davies. " It is so impossible to forget that to many, simple and honest actions will seem wonderful and wrong. I consider my engagement with Mr. Plaskett [the apothecary] is some safeguard in this respect, it looks well to be taught by several doctors at once, and the sisters and nurses will know of this."

Miss Garrett was anxious to be admitted to the chemical laboratory and lectures, and to the dissecting room.

(*Miss Garrett to Miss Davies.*)

March 19, 1861.

" Mr. Nunn had been talking to the Chemists about me. . . . He says a great deal has already been done towards removing prejudices ; many of the doctors who were most confident that I should meet with unheard-of insults from the students are now admitting that perhaps in some cases the experiment may be safely tried : I do myself see some justification for their objecting to open the school as freely to women as to men, for one flirting woman would make a woful deal of mischief and annoyance. . . . Mr. Plaskett brought me an invitation for the remaining chemical lectures of this Session, last Monday . . . Wednesday. The lecture has gone off very pleasantly. I went early to get a seat before the students came in, and they only showed their astonishment by an occasional grin."

She continued to go round the hospital wards, both alone and with Dr. Willis, and was soon admitted to the Dissecting Room, which was controlled by the friendly Mr. Nunn.

(*Miss Garrett to Miss Davies.*)

March 23, 1861.

" I wish you were at hand to hear all the details I could give you of my *widening* hospital work. There is constantly some small advance being made, either in friendliness towards some one, or new openings for study. . . . You will be glad to hear the arcana of all has been entertained—the dissecting-room. Mr. Nunn took me in on Tuesday, and it was not nearly so shocking as I had been led to expect. The reports have been gross exaggerations. There were no bodies hanging over chairs or by their feet from the ceiling, nor any of the other horrors that had been painted to me. . . . I don't think it will be at all overpowering to work there. . . . I tell you that you may know what the worst difficulties really are, in case you should find anyone anxious to join in the work. I don't feel very anxious for a companion, nor am I at all sure that the authorities would be as civil to two as they are to one. Still a very nice companion would be a great enjoyment and help. The loneliness (as far as free intercourse goes) is considerable and rather trying."

April 12, 1861.

" I feel so mean in trying to come over the doctors by all kinds of little feminine dodges, but Mrs. Gurney seemed to think they did not matter. She said it was often a matter of perplexity to her, to know if feminine arts were lawful in a good cause. She thinks they have immense weight from any woman, and she attributes Miss Marsh's success among the navvies mainly to them. I can believe her own to be very powerful."

Miss Garrett and Miss Davies had the good sense to see that in unessential matters it was well to disarm prejudice wherever this was possible. For instance, when during her holidays Miss Garrett was with some relations who disapproved of her doings she was " always most carefully feminine, even to doing fancy work and playing croquet." She took pains, during visits to her home, to do what was expected of her in the way of helping to entertain visitors and so forth, and it is easy to see that any other line of conduct would have destroyed her chances of success. People had to be persuaded that a woman doctor could be a civilized member of society.

Difficulties arose before long in relation to the Dissecting-Room.

(Miss Garrett to Miss Davies.)

April 25, 1861.

" [Mr. Nunn] said, on consideration he could not allow me to work in the Dissecting-Room, except when he or some of the other Demonstrators were present : the reasons he gave were the general larkiness of the students, especially of those who did nothing else ; the work itself was not the objection, he was sure that men and women could do that together as well as anything else, but he would not risk putting me with the idle students. However, he made ample amends by saying that he would like to see a separate room given up to women for this branch of the work, and all examinations shared by them. . . . If he were to propose these things to the medical committee, they would probably meet with more attention if there were several women candidates, so I thought this was a good time to make a more vigorous attempt than I have hitherto done, to get some companions. As long as I am in an unrecognized position, it is almost better to be alone, but if there is any chance of the committee's admitting women as students (the separate Dissecting-Room being the sole line of distinction), they should know that there are several women ready at once to accept the offered privilege."

Accordingly, both Miss Garrett and Miss Davies were on the look-out for medical candidates, and Miss Garrett wrote a letter to the *Englishwoman's Journal*,[1] giving a short account of her work. " I would have sent the letter to you for revision," she wrote to Miss Davies, " but there was only just time to polish it up as well as we could, and send a fair copy to Miss Parkes." She was very sanguine about her prospects, and quite hoped that some suitable woman would be tempted to join her.

(*Miss Garrett to Miss Davies.*)

May 6, 1861.

" I feel quite sure that the chance of being admitted fully increases constantly. . . . On Wednesday I determined to ask Dr. Thompson to admit me to his lectures (on materia medica). It being the opening day of the session he had an unusual train of pupils, and for some time I thought it must be put off till another day. However, this seemed cowardly, and moreover as the course had begun any delay seemed injurious, so I screwed up my courage and asked him as he was leaving the ward. I think the students did me good service, for of course a flat refusal would have sounded very ungracious before so many men, and their presence made it impossible to tell me any of the commonplaces about the unpleasantness of studying with them. Dr. Thompson looked confounded with my boldness, and before he answered I told him that the chemical Professors had admitted me to

---

[1] June, 1861. The letter appears over the signature A. M. S., presumably " A Medical Student."

their classes ; this settled his doubts and he said very cordially that he had no personal objections and should be glad to see me. I felt tremendously triumphant, tho' it was not so much after all. The next day I avoided him carefully fearing he might have repented, and to-day I have been to his lectures and the Practical Chemistry."

Disappointment was, however, in store.

(*Miss Garrett to Miss Davies.*)

June 4, 1861.

" I am not satisfied with my progress with the physicians, especially with Dr. ——, whose outpatients I see. He is certainly less civil to me than he was at first, and I can't account for it at all, unless it is that he does not like to see me pushing into the lectures and other student privileges."

The truth was, her success had been too marked. Among both the officials and the students there were a number who, though not really favourable, were willing to tolerate her presence as an amusing novelty, taking for granted that she would soon find the work too difficult and give it up. It was startling to find that, on the contrary, she was a very able and successful student, and must be taken seriously. Matters came to a head when, at a *viva voce* examination, she gave better answers than any other member of the class. She soon heard that the students were getting up a memorial against her. Feeling that she must do something, she wrote a letter to the leader of that movement.

(*Miss Garrett to Miss Davies.*)

June 7, 1861.

" The answer came to-night, and is extremely amusing, though not quite as satisfactory as I wish it had been. They will not give up the memorial, but I don't mind that so much, now that I know there is as strong a division for me as against me—as strong in numbers, and more respectable, for as you may imagine, the idlest and least known of the students would be sure to give their names very willingly to anything that would bring them before the dons in a creditable (?) light. Mr. Plaskett called on me to-day, and told us many of the good ones were standing up against the memorial like bricks ; he found one of the medical assistants, whom I had never known as a friend, defending me and pitching into the memorial with a flushed face and an air of great annoyance. So, on the whole, it perhaps may do as much good as harm, though I fear some of the lecturers who are still against me will make the memorial a handle for their own prejudices."

The memorialists succeeded in their object, and it was decided that she was not to be admitted to any more lectures after those she was attending were over. The reasons given were, that the lecturers disliked the presence of women, and the school would suffer. " It is very disagreeable," she wrote to Miss Davies, " but I suppose one will overlive it somehow."

Applications for admission to the London Hospital and other medical schools were now made, but in vain; the College of Surgeons, in refusing to allow her to compete for their special diploma in midwifery, stated that they would not in any way countenance the introduction of ladies into the medical profession, and the *Lancet* took the same line. She had some thoughts of making a public appeal by means of a letter to *The Times*, but was advised that if the letter were printed, there would probably be a leading article in the opposite sense. One of the usual grounds of objection was, that as the examining bodies would not admit women to their examinations, the schools could not educate women who could only become illegal practitioners. She therefore came to the conclusion that she must secure examination somewhere, before making any more attempts to enter a medical school. " If any University " (she wrote to Miss Davies) " will promise to examine me either upon the general or a special curriculum, we should at least know how to shape our plans of study, and if no examining body will do so, on any terms, it will be no good troubling the schools." Applications were made, but in vain, to Oxford, Cambridge, Glasgow, Edinburgh, and Dundee. At one time it seemed likely that admission might be granted at St. Andrews, but the authorities drew back, and no formal application was made. At last some encouragement came from the Society of Apothecaries. One of the examiners of the Society, to whom Mr. Nunn had introduced Miss Garrett, told her that as there was no law against the admission of women to their examinations, he thought there would be no difficulty. Miss Garrett made up her mind that if necessary she would take legal proceedings to assert her right to examination, but happily this proved unnecessary. The

Society took counsel's opinion on the question of their power to admit her, and were advised that they were bound to do so. The news reached her on August 20 at Aldeburgh, and she wrote at once to tell Miss Davies.

" You will be almost as surprised and pleased as I am to hear that the Apothecaries are willing to examine me if I will go through the five years' apprenticeship and the usual routine of lectures, etc. Their decision reached me yesterday and was welcomed with a ' hurray ' and congratulations all round the table."

An examination having been secured, Mr. Garrett was anxious that she should at once proceed to try again to gain admission to some medical school. Miss Garrett, however, felt that though the Apothecaries' licence would enable her to practise, she would not be satisfied without winning the higher qualification of M.D. With a view to this, she decided that it would be better to put her medical work aside for the moment, and matriculate, if possible, at London University. If she could obtain leave to matriculate, the M.D. degree would follow later. But here she was faced with the obstacle, that London University was closed to women.

Earlier in the summer of 1861 she had been able to see something of Miss Davies, who spent some time in London with Mr. Llewelyn Davies (now married and settled at 18, Blandford Square), and later with Miss Garrett's sister, Mrs. J. W. Smith, in Manchester Square. During these visits Miss Davies enjoyed opportunities of meeting Madame Bodichon and others of the Langham Place circle, as well as of going to some parties and other diversions, including a visit to the theatre, when she saw Fechter in *Hamlet*. In April her father and mother came to London, for medical advice for Dr. Davies. Soon after, his health began to fail seriously, and after some months of anxiety he died rather suddenly, on October 20. This, of course, brought about a great change ; it meant that the life at Gateshead Rectory must come to an end. It had been Miss Davies' home since she was nine years old, and there were some friends, especially Miss Richardson, whom she would regret leaving. But it was soon decided to move to London, where the call of the new interests was strong, and in January, 1862, she and her mother established themselves in a small house, No. 17, Cunningham Place, not far from Mr. Llewelyn Davies and his family in Blandford Square. " It will be very nice to have you so near," wrote Miss Garrett. " I keep imagining all manner of ways of getting help out of your presence. I believe it is a great thing for me to have you near enough to speak to pretty constantly." To the solitary student, struggling against prejudice, a friend at hand was invaluable ; and Miss Davies was able before long to take an active part in helping Miss Garrett.

ELIZABETH GARRETT
(MRS. GARRETT ANDERSON)
ABOUT 1866
From a painting by Laura Herford

CHAPTER V

Miss Davies and Miss Garrett : Their Work and Life in London.   1862–1865

MISS DAVIES found great enjoyment in her new life in London, with its variety of interests, and in the friends, old and new, with whom she was brought into touch. An acquaintance with whom she now became intimate was Miss Adelaide Manning, whom she had first met in 1861 during a visit to Mr. and Mrs. Llewelyn Davies. Miss Manning's father, Mr. Serjeant Manning, had taken part, as a member of the Law Amendment Society, in promoting the Married Women's Property Bill of 1857. His second wife, Miss Manning's stepmother [1] (to whom she was much attached), was a cultivated woman, endowed with the social tact that has its root in real kindness of heart. Mrs. Manning had lived for some years in Calcutta, with her first husband, Dr. William Speir, with whom she had studied Indian literature, antiquities, and history ; she was the author of two scholarly and attractive books on India which she wrote with the object of making that country better known in England, and helping to draw the two together. The subject of India became equally interesting to her stepdaughter, who was afterwards well known as Secretary to the National Indian Association. This Association provided the main occupation of Miss Adelaide Manning's later life, but she had educational interests too ; besides being an early supporter of Girton College, she was the first secretary of the Froebel Society, founded in 1874. Endless kindness and patience, and a sustained cheerfulness of temper, formed the foundation of a

[1] See Biographical Index.

character which, contrasting with the strong feelings and nervous energy of Miss Davies, made Miss Manning perhaps especially helpful as a friend. The two had many interests in common, particularly as regards education.

Miss Davies naturally saw a good deal of her brother and his wife, whose children were a source of great interest and pleasure. On one occasion she went with Mr. and Mrs. Llewelyn Davies and a party of friends to hear Jenny Lind in the *Messiah*. She wrote afterwards to Jane Crow that it was " first-rate in every way. . . . My enjoyment of such things always depends very much on the people I go with, and our party was a very pleasant one. Robert Browning was there, looking very nice and genial but not in the least suggesting to my dull mind anything that he has ever written. He is not so astoundingly ugly as literary men generally. I had the pleasure of watching Mr. Russell Gurney. . . . His face is the most beautiful I have ever seen, I think, except Mr. Maurice's." As to the music, she makes no remark. A keen curiosity about life in general made her like to meet well-known people, but the artistic interests which came within her ken failed to attract her. Some letters to Miss Crow show that she was quite clear as to this :

January 12, 1864.

" Of course I know Art is not a little thing to you. It is almost everything. But to me it is just about as much of a meeting-point figuratively as a pin's head might be literally. I dislike ugliness as I dislike pain, but it no more interests me to be descanting upon the laws of beauty than upon the laws of health. Of course it is all right that there should be some people to study Art, as it is necessary that some one should study Medicine. Probably one may be as useful as the other, but by Jove, I have quarrelled with them all."

Miss Crow, who was travelling abroad, had written some descriptions of what she was seeing, on which Miss Davies commented characteristically :

January 23, 1864.

" I like your discursive letters, on general subjects, that you call flippant, much better than the descriptive ones. . . . I always skip descriptions in books. . . . Descriptions provoke no comment or reply. There is nothing to say but oh ! Of course, the oh may be said with various intonations, but that is all. Disquisitions on other subjects are something like Hutton's articles,[1] which always excite me. I am either vehemently agreeing, or contradicting, or questioning, and wishing I could get hold of him to ask exactly what he means."

She was a great reader of novels and current literature (" I do so love a novel," she told Miss Crow), and was intensely interested in her fellow creatures. What her eager, combative, inquisitive spirit most enjoyed was the clash of argument and the stir of social life and politics. " How London spoils one ! " she wrote to Miss Crow. " I feel quite injured now, if I don't see everything that's going, the moment it comes out. . . . As regards parties, business is dull just now. Lizzie [Miss Garrett] and I remarked with a sigh that we had no engagements in view. The love of dissipation grows upon me, as I get more at home in society. But it is always a risk and a really dull party is a dreadful sell." A diversion was afforded by Garibaldi's visit to London. Miss Davies, like every one else, was eager to see him.

(Miss Davies to Miss Richardson.)

April 19, 1864.

" I have been engaged in fine sports to-day, helping to present an address to Garry Baldy, as the Londoners call him. It was as being on the Committee of the Ladies' Emancipation Society that I had the honour and happiness of going. I felt rather unworthy of it. The face is very fine in its calm composure, not at all foreign in the common sense of the word. We were a disreputable set of people (except myself and one other lady) and our address was a most inflammatory production. I felt as if I had got among conspirators, and was relieved when I discerned two clergymen in the company. Mr. Forster was there and George Macdonald. Isa Craig was tearing her hair with disappointment at not being asked. She spent Sunday in writing a poem, and thought it hard that she might not present it."

Public interests had combined with family ties to make it natural for Miss Davies and her mother to settle in London. This much was easily settled ; but during the first few months

---

[1] R. H. Hutton, of the *Spectator*.

after her father's death, it was not easy to see clearly what her future way of life was to be. " During this time," she writes, " I was considering what to do for the future in the changed circumstances and came to the conclusion that to follow E. Garrett was the only course to which I could see my way. The practice of Medicine had no attraction for me, and I had no aptitude for the necessary study, for which I was very far from being prepared, but there seemed to be no other opening to any sort of career, and I did not care to take up parish work as the business of my life. The first necessary step seemed to be to qualify myself for passing some Examination in Arts, and with this view I made arrangements for taking lessons in Latin and Greek."

This idea was not entertained for long, as Miss Davies felt that it would involve leaving her mother too much alone ; and she quickly found that participation in Miss Garrett's plans gave her a great deal to do. It came to their knowledge that the University of London was about to apply for a new Charter, and this seemed a good opportunity for trying to obtain the admission of women to its degrees. They set to work, at first informally, without any committee, Miss Davies acting as Honorary Secretary, and Miss Garrett paying all expenses. The first step was an application from Miss Garrett for leave to enter for the matriculation examination. With a view to obtaining support, a list of members of the Senate was drawn up by Miss Davies, and printed, with an extract, as heading, from the original Charter, stating that the University was to provide a liberal education for " all classes and denominations, without any distinction whatsoever." After looking over the list of names, Mr. Llewelyn Davies said, " Oh, you'll get it. These men are all advanced Liberals." Miss Davies comments dryly : " As to a good many of them, it turned out that their liberality did not include women in its scope." A similar application had been made before, in 1856, by Miss Jessie Meriton White (afterwards Madame Mario) and was rejected on the ground that the Senate was not empowered under the Charter " to admit females as candidates for degrees."[1] Miss Garrett's application was likewise rejected,

[1] See Biographical Index.

by one vote, at a meeting of the Senate held on April 9, 1862.

The smallness of the majority was encouraging, and it was decided to try again. A Memorial was sent in, signed by Mr. Garrett on behalf of himself and his daughter, asking that the new Charter might contain a clause providing for the extension to women of the privileges of the University.[1] The Memorial submits that " as the University requires no residence, and the Examinations involve nothing which could in the slightest degree infringe upon feminine reserve, we believe that by acceding to our wishes you would be conferring an unmixed benefit." Miss Davies' characteristic forethought and attention to detail are shown in her account of her next proceedings as secretary :

" An organized effort was made to obtain support for Mr. Garrett's request. Copies of a letter asking for an expression of opinion, with a statement of the question, a form of adhesion for signatures, and a stamped envelope addressed to The Secretary, etc., for reply, were sent to persons of distinction and members of the University of London. It was thought best not to give my Christian name in full, M. Ll. D. [her sister-in-law] remarking that ' they'd think it was some horrid woman in spectacles,' and in consequence I received many letters addressed ' S. E. Davies, Esq.' . . . All possible friends were enlisted in the service." Miss Davies induced Miss Adelaide Procter to secure the support of Mr. Monckton Milnes. She asked the Committee of the Society for the Employment of Women to help ; she sent out over 1,500 copies of the circular, and she had a number of favourable opinions printed and circulated, including letters from Mr. Gladstone, Richard Cobden, and other members of Parliament, as well as Mr. Russell Gurney (Recorder of London), Mrs. Somerville, Mrs. Grote, Rev. F. D. Maurice, and other well-known people.

" A list of supporters " (writes Miss Davies) " was sent to the Senate of the University and made a great impression—so much so that its authenticity was questioned. Mr. Grote asked to see the signatures and went over them carefully with me, that he might be able to vouch for them all. He told me that of all

[1] See the *Englishwoman's Journal*, October, 1862, p. 123 ; December, 1862, p. 286 ; January, 1863, p. 325.

the names Mrs. Somerville's was the one that made the greatest impression, and thereupon urged that women should do things, showing their capacity. I remarked on their special difficulties, and he quite agreed, while still taking the view that evidence of capacity was of the greatest value."

Miss Garrett, at any rate, was doing all she could to prove her capacity, in spite of her disabilities as a woman. It was provoking that again success was only just missed. On May 7, 1862, the Vice-Chancellor moved that the Senate should endeavour to obtain a modification of the Charter providing for the admission of women to degrees but not to Convocation. The motion was lost by the casting vote of the Chancellor, after a long and earnest discussion. In a leaflet circulated by Miss Davies to announce the result she stated that such an amount of interest and sympathy had been called forth as to encourage the hope that the University would soon grant the privileges desired. In the following year (1863), the Annual Committee of Convocation passed a resolution in favour of provision being made for the examination of women. A fresh disappointment was, however, to come ; the resolution was thrown out in Convocation by a large majority,[1] and Miss Garrett gave up the idea of matriculating.

Meanwhile Miss Davies had been preparing a paper on *Medicine as a Profession for Women* for the National Association for the Promotion of Social Science, which in 1862 held its annual meeting in London. This Association, founded in 1857 under the presidency of Lord Brougham, was organized on the model of the British Association, but with aims that were so novel as to excite some ridicule. Its promoters included Lord Shaftesbury, Lord John Russell, Mr. F. D. Maurice, Charles Kingsley, Lord Lyttelton, and J. S. Mill. Mr. George Hastings, who as Secretary to the Law Amendment Society had helped to promote the Married Women's Property Bill of 1857, was Secretary to the Association, in which the Law Amendment Society was merged. He had the strength of mind to appoint a woman—Miss Isa Craig—as his assistant. The workers at Langham Place were naturally delighted at his choice, and still

---

[1] See *The Influence of University Degrees on the Education of Women*, *Victoria Magazine*, July, 1863, reprinted in *Thoughts on Some Questions relating to Women*, by Miss Davies.

more because, as the *Englishwoman's Journal* announced, " the Association has assumed the right of woman to sit in an assembly deliberating on social affairs—nay, to express her opinion in that assembly if she chooses." As Miss Davies notes in her *Family Chronicle* : " The Association was of immense use to the women's movement in giving us a platform from which we could bring our views before the sort of people who were likely to be disposed to help in carrying them out." [1]

In bringing the subject of *Medicine as a Profession for Women* before the Association, she would be addressing a far wider circle, and one more likely to listen seriously, than any she could reach by other means. The meeting of 1862, which was the first to be held in London, was of special importance and interest. Lord Brougham presided, and the proceedings opened with a special service in Westminster Abbey. Miss Davies records in her *Family Chronicle* that she " was asked to take part in the office work as a sort of Assistant Secretary *pro tem.*, with Isa Craig, under Mr. Hastings. This introduced me to people who afterwards became friends and allies, e.g. Mr. Westlake, for whom I did some writing, from his dictation, and Mr. Ernest Noel and Mr. Fitch,[2] who as Secretaries of the Education Section were friendly and helpful."

It was unusual for women to appear in public as speakers, and Miss Davies' paper on *Medicine as a Profession for Women* was read for her by Mr. Russell Gurney.[3] Besides the direct propaganda of Miss Davies and her friends, other influences

---

[1] Women were ready and eager to seize the advantage. At the first meeting, in 1857, papers were contributed by Miss Mary Carpenter (*Reformatories for Girls*) and Miss Louisa Twining (*Workhouses*) ; in 1858 there was one by Miss Florence Nightingale, in 1859 one by Miss Parkes ; and papers by women continued to be a feature of the meetings. The Society for Promoting the Employment of Women was re-organized in connection with the Association, with Lord Shaftesbury as President. See *Transactions* of the National Association for the Promotion of Social Science ; the *Englishwoman's Journal*, October, 1858, December, 1859, October, 1860 ; and an article (anonymous but by Miss Davies) in the *Victoria Magazine*, November, 1863.

[2] See Biographical Index.

[3] The paper was published by Miss Faithfull as a pamphlet, and re-printed in *Thoughts on Some Questions relating to Women*.

were at work on the same side. The Social Science Association, which had a Section devoted to the subject of public health, promoted the formation of a Ladies' Sanitary Association, for " the diffusion of sanitary knowledge and the promotion of physical education, especially among the working classes " ; and this no doubt helped to dispel the prejudice against women learning about physiology and health. It was, however, contended by many that nursing, and not medicine, was woman's proper sphere, and in the *Englishwoman's Journal* for April, 1862, we find a letter from " A Physician of Twenty-one Years' Standing " advancing this view, which roused Miss Davies to a reply in the May number.[1]

While she was busy with her work for the Social Science Association and for Miss Garrett, and an occasional day spent at Langham Place, Miss Davies found time for other things, as the following entry in the *Family Chronicle* shows :

" Miss Emily Faithfull was at this time carrying on the Victoria Press, for the employment of women as printers, and was prominent in the women's movement. I have notes of parties at her house in Taviton Street at which I met Anthony Trollope, Louis Blanc, and (at a breakfast party) . . . Mr. Maurice, Mr. Russell Gurney, R. H. Hutton [editor of the *Spectator*], Mr. Hastings . . . Madame Bodichon, Miss Craig, B. R. Parkes, etc. There were also evening parties at Madame Bodichon's . . . and Mrs. Peter Taylor's.[2] At Mrs. Taylor's I met Holman Hunt and G. Monro, and at Madame Bodichon's, William Allingham. Conferences were going on of Madame Bodichon, Miss Craig, E. Faithfull and Miss Parkes, at Waterloo Place (Social Science office)—again, with Isa [Craig] on the *Englishwoman's Journal*."

At these conferences it was arranged that Miss Davies should act as editor of the *Englishwoman's Journal*, which she did for about six months from September, 1862. The summer holidays of that year were occupied with visits to her old friends in the north ; and in September she paid a visit, the first of many, to Madame Bodichon at Scalands, her home in Sussex.

Early in 1863, in conjunction with Miss Emily Faithfull, Miss

---

[1] Reprinted in *Thoughts on Some Questions relating to Women*, where the date is erroneously given as 1861. The paper was originally signed " A. C. R.," perhaps " A Constant Reader."

[2] See Biographical Index.

Davies embarked on another literary enterprise. Miss Faithfull, who had literary and political friends, now started a monthly magazine, of which Miss Davies was editor. The *Victoria Magazine*, as it was called, made its appearance in May, 1864. The first number contained articles by Edward Dicey,[1] Tom Taylor,[1] and R. H. Hutton and Meredith Townsend (joint owners and editors of the *Spectator*); a poem by Christina Rossetti; and first instalments of a novel, *Lindisfarne Chase*, by T. A. Trollope, and of Nassau Senior's *Journal in Egypt*, written on the occasion of the Suez Canal Commission in 1855–6. Under the heading of *Literature of the Month*, there were short notices of books, written partly by Miss Davies herself, partly by special reviewers, one of whom was her friend Anna Richardson. Among occasional contributors were Matthew Arnold, F. D. Maurice, and Tom Hughes, as well as George Macdonald, Mrs. Oliphant, Miss Frances Power Cobbe, Professor Villari, Tom Hood, and Edwin Arnold. Though the magazine was of general and literary interest, Miss Davies took care to uphold the women's cause. The Annual Report of the Society for Promoting the Employment of Women is to be found in Volume I; and in 1863 Miss Davies contributed articles on *Needleworkers* v. *Society* (in which she urged that needlewomen should strike); on *The Influence of University Degrees on the Education of Women*; and on the Social Science Association (November, 1863). In 1864 an article on *Lady Doctors* drew attention to Miss Garrett's success in the Apothecaries' examination. The Garretts expressed their warm approval of the *Victoria Magazine*, and Mr. Garrett, at his daughter's instigation, asked Mr. W. H. Smith to give a general order to push it at the railway bookstalls. Unfortunately, however, the magazine was not a financial success, owing to unsatisfactory business arrangements. After about a year, Miss Davies gave up her editorship, and other interests soon became too strong to admit of literary work.

During the summer of 1862 a fund was started " for incidental expenses connected with the effort to obtain for women admission to University Examinations in Arts and Medicine." Miss Davies was Honorary Secretary, and the Treasurer was Lady Goldsmid, who was to become a valuable and lifelong ally.

[1] See Biographical Index.

The first step taken was to send the following advertisement to a number of newspapers :

THE MEDICAL PROFESSION.—Ladies who may be desirous of qualifying themselves for the Medical Profession are respectfully informed
that particulars concerning the prescribed course of study, and the
opportunities at present available, may be obtained on application to
Miss Davies, 17, Cunningham Place, N.W.

As an answer to the enquiries which this might produce Miss
Davies prepared a circular in which it was announced that the
Apothecaries were bound to admit women to be examined and
to receive their licence. Unfortunately, as to the " opportunities
available " for education, there was nothing to offer. All she
could say was, " Offers of help have . . . been received from
eminent medical men ; and there is reason to believe that if
two or three ladies should simultaneously offer themselves as
students, a separate class would be formed for them in connection
with some one of the existing medical schools." Miss Davies
received a fair number of enquiries, mostly from obviously
unsuitable people. As she notes in her *Family Chronicle*, " Not
one of them led to anything."

Miss Garrett therefore continued on her course alone, and
found a good deal of difficulty in getting the teaching she required.
The Apothecaries were willing to allow her to get private instruction from teachers in recognized medical schools, when she could
not gain admission to the public lectures. This meant the payment of heavy fees, but as Mr. Garrett supported his daughter
generously through every step, she had no anxiety on that score.
She was allowed to attend lectures at the Pharmaceutical Institute,
as well as some lectures by Huxley, but there was a great deal
of difficulty in making arrangements for the practical work of
dissection. Hospital practice was equally hard to come by ;
after trying in vain to enter the London Hospital as a student,
she could find no better way than to enter there as a nurse, and
pick up what medical knowledge she could. It was the same
kind of unsatisfactory anomalous position that she had occupied
at the Middlesex Hospital. In the autumn of 1863 she established herself in rooms at 8, Philpot Street, Whitechapel Road, in
order to be near her work. It was hard to have to begin the same

kind of struggle over again. As she wrote to Miss Davies :
" It is distressingly nervous work, standing about with nothing
definite to do, and the consciousness of being under a fire of
criticizing eyes, nurses', patients', students'. But this stage does
not last long, and when the novelty goes off, they look less, and you
feel less, thank goodness."

Difficulties arose, just as they had at the Middlesex Hospital,
and soon came to a crisis. Miss Garrett confided them as usual
to Miss Davies, and apparently received some rather bracing
advice in reply.

(Miss Garrett to Miss Davies.)

February 18, 1864.

" I agree with you in thinking snubbing won't be a serious evil in
the long run, still it is unpleasant and for a time hindering. You
cannot at once believe that personal effort can altogether make up for
all the help that teaching and guidance give other students. To-day
after I had been round a few beds with Dr. Powell he took me into
the nurses' room and told me he had been ' officially ordered not to
allow me to go round the wards with him, and that as he was only
a subaltern he was reluctantly obliged to obey.' So I must peg away
alone and do as well as I can. It is harder work and far less interesting—besides the painful sense of conflict which I must have whenever an enemy comes into the ward—but still the self-reliant frame
it puts me into will be good, it will force me to look closer than I
should be likely to do if I had anyone to appeal to in every difficulty.
Mr. Heckford reports that some of the older students are warmly on
my side. . . . He says the storm is going down, but that he never
saw the school in such an uproar about anything before. They seem
to have dwelt particularly on the shabbiness of my pretending to be
a nurse, but as I said, that was not my fault, I had given them two
chances of having me as a regular student."

April 16, 1864.

" I have had a skirmish with the arch enemy here, Dr. ——, which
has ended in a kind of drawn result. I yield the point about going
round the wards with him, and he yields part of his personal animosity.
He will not again order the resident medical officer to cut me. . . .
He became wonderfully civil and pleasant before we finished."

About this time Miss Garrett applied to the College of Physicians
for leave to take their examination. Both she and Miss Davies
did all they could to prepare the way with anyone they knew who

was likely to have influence. Miss Garrett reported that Dr. Watson, the President of the College, was " promising in manner," and her letter making the application was " a model of craft." But, as she had expected, the decision was against her ; the College were advised by Counsel that their charter did not empower them to admit females for examination.[1] At last, in 1865, she passed the final examination of the Society of Apothecaries, with great success.

(Miss Garrett to Miss Davies.)

April 18, 1865.

" I heard a charming account of the Hall Examination yesterday. Two of the Examiners had told Mr. C. that it was a mercy they did not put the names in order of merit, as in this case they *must* have put me first. . . . I am very glad, tho' the examination was too easy to feel elated about, it is a good thing that such as it was the people who manage it should go about saying this."

Being now qualified to practise, Miss Garrett was able, in 1866, to have her name placed on the British Medical Register, which contained the name of one other woman, Elizabeth Blackwell. Meanwhile the prospects of getting a medical degree from London University seemed still so remote that she gave up the idea, and decided to try Paris, where she took her M.D. degree in 1870. " Miss Garrett is quite determined never to be called Dr.," wrote Miss Davies to Madame Bodichon. " She feels as I do about it, and so does Mrs. Gurney. I should not consider it an act of friendship to present anyone to strangers under a title which excites repugnance." Her front door bore the inscription " Elizabeth Garrett Anderson, M.D.," but she was always known as Mrs., not Dr., Garrett Anderson. Her marriage to Mr. J. G. S. Anderson in 1871 proved no hindrance to her medical practice, which had been quickly established. In 1866 she opened a Dispensary for Women and Children, which afterwards grew into the New Hospital for Women, of which she was for many years Senior Physician ; and in 1883 she became Dean of the London School of Medicine for Women.

Other women soon followed her in attempting to get medical training, but in London they met with no success, for the Society

<hr>

[1] *Victoria Magazine*, June, 1864.

of Apothecaries in 1868 made a rule that in future they would not recognize certificates of private studies ; all candidates must have studied in the regular medical schools, which were closed to women. This closed the only avenue to a qualification that had been open to women ; and ten years were yet to pass before they could gain admission to the examinations and degrees of the University of London.

CHAPTER VI

First Steps towards the Higher Education of Women. 1862–1866

THE admission of women to University Examinations was one of the many questions relating to women which were discussed by the London meeting of the Social Science Association in 1862. A special meeting of the Association was held in the Guildhall, at which Miss Frances Power Cobbe read a paper on *University Degrees for Women*.[1] " Next morning," says Miss Cobbe in her *Autobiography*, " every daily paper in London laughed at my demand, and for a week or two I was the butt of universal ridicule." The Association however took the matter seriously, and held a special evening meeting at Burlington House, at which it was discussed.[2] Mr. Shaen opened the debate, with a proposal that representations should be made to the Senate of London University as to the desirableness of their undertaking the duty of examining women. The meeting was not prepared to go so far, but an amended resolution was finally adopted unanimously : " That this meeting is of opinion that measures ought to be provided for testing and attesting the education of women of the middle and higher classes, and requests the Council of the Association to take such measures as they may deem expedient for the attainment of this object."

A suggestion made by Mr. Shaen had important results. He

[1] Published by Miss Faithfull under the title *Female Education and how it would be affected by University Examinations*.

[2] *Transactions* of the National Association for the Promotion of Social Science, 1862, p. 339 ; *Family Chronicle*, pp. 259–61.

told Miss Davies that the University of London did not like being treated as a *corpus vile*, on which all experiments were to be tried, and advised her to try to get something from the old Universities. Thereupon she cast about as to what could reasonably be asked for, and the Local Examinations, as involving nothing in the way of residence, seemed to meet the case. These were a recent invention, and were known at this time as the Middle-Class Examinations, because they were instituted in order to supply middle-class schools with a test and standard of efficiency. While public schools looked to the Universities, and elementary schools to the examinations of H.M. Inspectors, schools of an intermediate character fell between two stools. They had no external standard or stimulus, and in order to meet this need, a scheme of local examinations, promoted by Dr. Temple (later Archbishop of Canterbury) and Mr. (afterwards Sir) Thomas Dyke Acland, was established by the University of Oxford in 1857. Cambridge quickly followed suit; and in 1858 a Syndicate, of which Dr. Liveing (afterwards a supporter of Girton College) was Secretary, was appointed to carry out the scheme adopted.

Miss Davies had already discussed with Miss Garrett the possibility of girls entering for these examinations, but no steps had been taken. Now, however, she began to think of getting up a memorial to the Universities.

(Miss Davies to Miss Richardson.)

July 12, 1862.

" The examinations would be worth having, tho' I do not care so *very* much for them in themselves, because I think the encouragement to learning is most wanted *after* the age of eighteen. It seems likely, however, that if we could get these Examinations, it would be a great lift towards getting the University of London. We are told that the real feeling of the Opposition in the Senate was the fear of lowering the dignity of the University, and that they would be very much influenced by any forward step on the part of the older Universities. This agitation is hateful work, but it becomes clearer every day that incessant and unremitting talking and pushing is the *only* way of gaining our ends. I stop sometimes and ask whether the ends are worth such horridly disagreeable means, and if one had only a personal interest in the matter, I am sure it would be impossible to persevere. But we are fighting for people who cannot fight for themselves, and as I believe, directly working towards preserving women from becoming masculine in a bad sense."

The last sentence may be explained by a reference to her paper in the *Victoria Magazine* [1] on *Women and University Degrees*, in which she says :

" Amazons have never been persons of high intellectual attainments, nor have the most learned women shown any tendency to rush into Bloomerism and other ugly eccentricities. It is true, indeed, and a fact of the utmost significance, that women with great natural force of character do, when denied a healthy outlet for their energy, often indulge in unhealthy extravagancies, simply because it is a necessity of their nature to be active in some way or other. But the fast women and the masculine women are not those who sit down to their books and devote themselves to an orderly course of study."

The next step was to write to the Local Examinations Secretaries at Oxford and Cambridge, to ask if there were any possibility of admitting girls to the examinations. Mr. Griffiths, of Oxford, replied that the University Statute gave authority only for the admission of boys, and expressed his opinion that " the University would think the examination of young ladies a matter altogether beyond its sphere of duty." Dr. Liveing of Cambridge was more encouraging. He thought the regulations would hardly bear such an interpretation as to admit girls, but he offered to gather the views of members of the Local Examinations Syndicate on the subject, with a view to the presentation of a memorial to them. Miss Davies now set about the formation of a Committee, which was constituted in October, 1862, for obtaining the admission of women to University Examinations. The Committee consisted of Madame Bodichon, Miss Bostock,[2] Miss Isa Craig, Mr. Russell Gurney, Mr. Hastings, Mr. Heywood, Lady Goldsmid (Treasurer), and Miss Davies (Secretary). The names suggest a close connection with the Social Science Association. It seems curious that no schoolmistress was included. There were of course very few of any standing or importance, except Miss Beale and Miss Buss. Miss Beale was not at first inclined to approve of the admission of girls to examinations ; and Miss Buss, though she strongly approved, may have been disinclined

---

[1] June, 1863.   [2] One of the founders of Bedford College.

to identify herself publicly with anything so controversial. The Committee decided to invite the Local Committees for both the Oxford and Cambridge Examinations (twenty-one in all) to co-operate in getting up a memorial to the Universities. The answers were fairly encouraging. Among the Oxford centres, the most useful results came from Exeter, where Mr. Dyke Acland was a member of the Local Committee. Although he did not at first quite like the idea of including girls, he took the question seriously, and was helpful in making enquiries and giving advice. One of his letters may be quoted as expressing the objections commonly felt:

" If publicity and freedom be by the general consent of educated men necessary to the full development of boys' nature, a certain degree of privacy and clinging for protection is equally indispensable for the full ripening of the precious qualities of womanhood. I confess therefore that I feel a shrinking indisposition to throw the girls of England into public competition with the boys. . . . I rather doubt whether University Examiners, who are as a general rule unmarried men, possess that experience of the ways of young people which many a country clergyman in frequent contact with his village school possesses. It requires considerable experience of family life and of the actual working of a schoolroom to judge of a girl's knowledge and mental training."

Mr. Acland thought, however, that the experiment might be made of " a parallel examination specially adapted to female schools," and he exerted himself to make enquiries at Oxford, as a result of which he reported that the Delegacy would probably be unfavourable ; he found " in conversation with friends, ladies and gentlemen, great repugnance to your plans, especially to the competition of the two sexes." But he gave some useful advice which Miss Davies took to heart, namely, to begin with a scheme of small dimensions at first, as he himself had done in establishing the Oxford local examinations : " This was the secret of my success, such as it was. We showed at Exeter that our ideas could march." Miss Davies notes that this advice was of the utmost importance to her. " The same policy," she writes, " was carried out in the struggle for Degrees at Cambridge, and it may almost be said that it was the secret of our success, such as it was."

A little later, in May, Mr. Acland reported that a considerable impression had been produced at Oxford by her letters to him, which he had shown to various friends there. He suggested that she should apply to the Delegates for leave to hold an experimental examination of girls, by private arrangements with the Examiners, writing at the same time a " fly-sheet " explaining her objects, to be sent round to the Common Rooms. " I am strongly .of opinion " (he wrote) " that the way to get an old institution to take up a matter is to prove its feasibility without committing the Institution. . . . I have had some conversation with Dr. Temple. I think the opinion he expressed most strongly was that with such ability and perseverance you would be sure to succeed." In May Miss Davies and Miss Bostock together visited Oxford to pursue the matter, but they found that there was no chance for anything but a scheme of examinations specially designed for girls. This they were firmly resolved not to accept, and the matter dropped for the time. An application in 1865 was unsuccessful, and the Oxford Local Examinations were not opened to girls till 1870.

The enquiries addressed to the Cambridge Local Centre led more speedily to success. Mr. Potts, the Secretary of the Local Centre at Cambridge, wrote that he had brought the subject before several men there. " As might be expected, some laughed, and others looked grave, and some considered that the subject was not unworthy of serious consideration." In the Secretary to the London Centre, Mr. H. R. Tomkinson, Miss Davies found, not only a valuable supporter on this occasion, but a friend for life. The Committee for the London Centre, as he informed her, never met, but he took the trouble to write to them all individually (there were twenty-eight of them), and reported favourable answers from the majority. He himself at once entered sympathetically into the question, and offered advice as to the wording of the circulars which Miss Davies was preparing to send out. Miss Davies, who always listened to advice (though she by no means always followed it), received Mr. Tomkinson's criticisms gratefully, and this incident was the first of many of the same sort. " There is nothing so provoking as being told vaguely that things will *do*," she wrote to him on a subsequent occasion. " I would much rather be told that they *won't* do." Mr. Tomkinson was that most useful kind of ally, a sympathetic but keen and candid critic, and moreover, one whose words carried weight. He had had a distinguished career at Rugby and Trinity ; he rowed in the Cambridge eight in 1852, played in the University eleven, and was a Wrangler in 1853. He was called to the Bar, but left it in 1855 to become an assistant master and Bursar at Marlborough, where his cousin Dr. Cotton (afterwards Bishop of Calcutta) had been appointed Head Master in 1852. Marlborough was in the throes of a very serious crisis, owing to defective organization, as regards both internal discipline and finance. It was therefore a task of no little difficulty in which Mr. Tomkinson was called on to help Dr. Cotton, but the finances of the school were gradually restored under his strict and skilful management ; and so great was his success that on leaving Marlborough in 1860 he was appointed Managing Director of the Sun Fire Insurance Office, and later Chairman of the Associated Insurance Offices of London. With great ability and practical experience of business, he was one of the kindest and most generous of men. Moreover, he was familiar with the working of the Local Examinations. When Miss Davies' Committee met again in April, 1863, therefore, they hastened to secure this valuable ally. Mr. Tomkinson was co-opted on to the Committee, and was asked to invite his Committee for the London Local Centre to support the demand for the admission of girls. Miss Davies' friend Mrs. Manning joined the Committee at the same time, and a little later another useful supporter was enlisted—Dr. W. E. Hodgson, the well-known economist and educational reformer, who had always taken an active interest in the education of girls.

The Committee now decided to ask the Cambridge Local Examinations Syndicate to allow arrangements to be made for a private experimental examination of girls, as previously suggested by Mr. Acland. A little later, the Dean of Canterbury, Dr. Alford, was asked to join as Chairman. He had some scruples, thinking that the Committee were aiming at obtaining degrees for ladies, and that " personal eminence would be dearly bought at the sacrifice of that unobtrusiveness which is at the same time the *charm* and the *strength* of our Englishwomen." Though herself of course in favour of degrees for women, Miss Davies managed to explain the Committee's views to the Dean's satisfaction, and he consented to become chairman.

Towards the end of October, a favourable answer came from the Cambridge Syndicate as to the experimental examination. Copies of the boys' examination papers were to be at the disposal of the Committee, who were to organize a centre at which girl candidates could be examined, making their own arrangements with the Examiners for the answers to be looked over. The examination was due to begin on December 14, to Miss Davies' dismay, as she wrote to Miss Richardson :

" Our breath was quite taken away on Saturday by receiving quite unexpectedly a favourable answer from the Cambridge Syndicate to our application. I fully expected they would politely get rid of us by saying it was ' beyond their powers.' It has thrown us into dreadful agitation. We have only six weeks to work up our candidates, and who can expect them to come up on so short a notice ? Do come to the rescue. We shall look unspeakably foolish if we have no candidates, after all, and people won't understand the reason. . . . I will send you a packet of circulars when they are ready, and please send them about. If any country girls like to come up, we will arrange to receive them and take good care of them during the Examination week. You might send us some *junior* candidates. . . . Why should not your youngest sister come ? . . . I am afraid no girls will come who are not certain to get a pass, whereas *hundreds* of boys failed the first year."

After the first terror lest there should be no candidates, the difficulty proved to be quite the contrary, and some anxiety was felt about hospitality for girls who were to come up from the country. However, the Russell Gurneys and other friends came to the rescue. Ninety-one girls entered, of whom eight afterwards withdrew. Miss Buss sent twenty-five candidates from the North London Collegiate School, and a number also came from Queen's College, and from Miss Octavia Hill's school. It was decided that the Committee should award certificates of proficiency to candidates who passed. There was a good deal of discussion as to the propriety of giving prizes and publishing names in class lists ; finally, the prizes were allowed, but it was decided that the names should not be published. Miss Davies wrote to Mr. Tomkinson on November 10 :

" Some of the schoolmistresses' letters are almost illegible and very funny. One is afraid the Examinations will foster the spirit of confidence and independence which is too common amongst girls of the present day. I fancy girls must be excessively insubordinate by nature, or they never would have a grain of spirit left, after going thro' school training. . . . Miss Bostock is very strong on the cupidity of girls. I hope the Committee will not support you and Miss Craig in restricting us to laurel wreaths as prizes."

November 11, 1863.

" You are very wrong about the prizes. We are not going to have a public distribution at all, and if we had, we should not want the Bishop of Oxford.[1] No one supposes that the girls would choose ear-rings or anything foolish, but the privilege of free choice is very dear to them, perhaps because they so seldom have the chance of exercising it."

There was some alarm lest the examiners should refuse to undertake so much extra work, and Miss Davies wrote to each one individually, asking it as a favour, and " offering unlimited time and fees at their discretion." They all consented, for the most part very cordially. The candidates were not asked to pay fees, so subscriptions had to be raised to cover the expenses, but with liberal support from Lady Goldsmid and Mr. Heywood, this was done without difficulty.

Miss Davies had some anxieties about the supervision of the examination, the duties of which were as new to her as to the candidates ; but with the help of Mr. Gray and Mr. Tomkinson, and the friendly co-operation of Mr. Chalker, who conducted the boys' examination, all went well, and she was able to write triumphantly to Miss Richardson : " Our examination came to an end last Saturday, having been all thro' as completely successful as could possibly be desired. Every one connected with the University was most kind and friendly, and there seems little doubt now that it will be permanent." All was not yet plain sailing, however, and there were some anxious moments in store.

The Report on the results of the examination was most illuminating.[2] The girls did creditably on the whole, but a very weak spot was found in their Arithmetic. Out of forty-five junior girls, eight failed, and none got three-fourths of the marks. Of thirty-eight seniors, only six got more than one-fourth of the

---

[1] Dr. Samuel Wilberforce.
[2] Reprinted in the *Victoria Magazine*, May, 1864, p. 82.

marks. " The senior girls," wrote the examiner, " showed very little knowledge of arithmetic, and it was clear to my mind that this was due to want of proper instruction." Out of Miss Buss' twenty-five candidates no less than ten failed—an experience which led her immediately to reform the teaching in her school. Similar failures among the candidates from Queen's College caused Mr. Maurice to reform the teaching there also. As Miss Davies wrote in her Report on the examination : " the want of an external standard could scarcely have been more conclusively shown than by this experiment."

The question was now taken up by the Social Science Association, and a special meeting was held on April 29, 1864, to discuss it. Miss Davies took immense pains with the arrangements for this meeting.

(*Miss Davies to Mr. Tomkinson.*)

April 14 [1864].

" We very much want you to come and testify (if you can, conscientiously ?) that everybody behaved properly, and nothing alarming or scandalous happened at the experimental examination. . . . Lord Lyttelton has promised to preside, and there is some hope that Mr. J. S. Mill will come. . . . They are going to invite Cambridge men, especially enemies, to give them a chance of being converted."

April 18.

" If you will state facts, that is just what is wanted. I only hope the speakers on our side won't go off, as our enemies always do, into theories. It is dreadfully unsafe."

Miss Craig was triumphant at securing " three lovely girls for the front row "—the three Miss Hares.[1] Miss Davies was anxious to know whether any of the ladies struck Mr. Tomkinson as " strong-minded looking." " We were afraid," she wrote, " that Miss Craig would have ruined us by her recklessness in inviting anybody that liked to come. She insisted that they had a right to have ' Mission ' stamped on their brows if they liked, but I don't think she did any serious mischief. Miss Garrett was sitting very near you, looking exactly like one of the girls whose instinct it is to do what you tell them."

[1] Daughters of Thomas Hare, author of the system of proportional representation.

Mr. Tomkinson, as requested, testified that the examination had been conducted in strict privacy, and that " as far as good sterling work and the readiness of the girls in following all the rules and regulations were concerned, the result was very remarkable. . . . There is no ground whatever for the notion that girls are unfit to take part in these examinations." Mr. Plumptre, of Queen's College, observed that no master or mistress of a private school would have the courage to admit what the Report had stated of the candidates for this examination—that a large proportion of his or her pupils had no knowledge of Arithmetic. Mr. Roby, though in favour of the admission of girls, thought there should be some modification of the subjects to suit their needs—laying stress on modern languages, omitting Greek, and " lightening " the higher mathematics. Miss Davies' wrath was roused by this suggestion, and still more by Miss Manning expressing her approval of it. " Your note," she wrote afterwards to Miss Manning, " confirms a remark I had already made two or three times, that Mr. Roby's was the most mischievous speech of the evening ! I did not think he would have converted *you* ! My views on this subject are exceedingly strong, and I do not despair of bringing you round to them when I see you and can explain them fully. . . . On the whole I think the discussion went well . . . were not you delighted with the ladies ? I gazed at them with serene satisfaction, feeling that their presence was doing as much good as other people's speeches."

A few speakers upheld the conventional view, that if music and needlework were neglected, the ladies would become strong-minded women instead of good sisters, good wives, mothers, and nurses. One (Mr. Elliott) asserted that the mental organization of the male differs totally from that of the female. The function of men, he thought, was to accumulate wealth ; that of women to distribute it. But in Mr. Elliott's view the distribution of wealth should not involve them in arithmetic or political economy. " Let them understand all domestic questions, and so much of the accomplishments of life as will tend to make the evening delightful, and then we shall secure all that is necessary." [1]

[1] The *Saturday Review's* comment was as follows : " Among the busybodies who compose the Social Science Association . . . the crochet [examinations] is as vigorous as ever. The most curious develop-

Dr. Hodgson, though he made only a brief speech at the meeting, felt that Mr. Elliott's reflections on the female intellect and political economy demanded a reply. On June 11 he delivered a lecture *On the Education of Girls considered in connection with the University Local Examinations*,[1] which dealt fully and forcibly with the matter. Education, he felt, was the key of the position in regard to the women's question. The lecture was commented on in the *Spectator* by Mr. R. H. Hutton,[2] who took up an intermediate position ; girls and boys might very well be educated alike up to the point of the Local Examinations, perhaps allowing a higher age limit for girls, but the later curriculum should be different.

Miss Davies, who attended Dr. Hodgson's lectures, was herself preparing a discourse on the subject for the meeting of the Social Science Association, to be held at York in September, 1864. The famous Schools Enquiry Commission of 1864–1866 had been appointed earlier in the summer, and this kindled a special interest in the question of education. The Archbishop of York,[3] who presided over the Educational Department at this meeting, expressed himself in his Address as unfavourable to the admission of girls to the Local Examinations. He thought that

ment of it is a proposal . . . for submitting young ladies to Local University Examinations. The idea almost takes one's breath away." Steps must be taken to secure fair play by having " learned men advanced in years " as examiners, with " their wives in a commanding position in the gallery." Even so, " it will be next to impossible to persuade the world that a pretty first-class woman came by her honours fairly." (This might impress people who did not know that examinations were conducted in writing, and not in the presence of the examiner.) " The object for which girls are supposed to be brought up is that they may be married." But " there is a strong and ineradicable male instinct, that a learned, or even an over-accomplished young woman is one of the most intolerable monsters in creation " (*Feminine Wranglers*, in the *Saturday Review*, July 23, 1864).

[1] Published in 1869 with another lecture, under the title *The Education of Girls ; and the Employment of Women of the Upper Classes Educationally Considered*. A copy of an early Report of Girton College is bound up at the end of the second edition. The volume contains a number of appendices and quotations which add to its value as throwing light on the women's movement.

[2] *Spectator*, October 1, 1864. *The Education of Girls.*

[3] Dr. William Thomson.

the education of girls ought to be organized separately, by a Council of ladies and clergymen—not by the Universities, who could know nothing about it. Canon Norris contributed a paper on *The Education of Girls*, in which he elaborated similar views, which he had already expressed to Miss Davies. " University men," he wrote to her, " are the last men likely to judge wisely as to such modifications of the girls' examinations as experience might suggest. The Examiners ought to be married men, of older standing and more knowledge of society."

The idea that unmarried men would not know how to examine girls, irrelevant as it now seems, is worth noticing because it indicates the curious ignorance about girls which prevailed. It is difficult to realize how little was known about their education, carried on as it generally was by individuals working privately and in isolation, with nothing to guide them beyond the fancies of their pupils' parents, most of whom paid little attention to the matter. " The average man of the middle classes is more than indifferent to it," declared the Rector of Lincoln College (Rev. Mark Pattison) in his evidence before the Schools Enquiry Commission,[1] " he rather dislikes an educated woman." Asked how he had gained his knowledge of the subject, he answered : " I have had no other means of knowing the classes of whom I speak than any other English clergyman has had who is fifty years old, and is married, and has had many sisters, and has been resident in a great variety of English counties, and has seen the farming class, and the clerical class, and something also of the daughters of shopkeepers." Married men had at any rate the chance of knowing about their own families : celibate Fellows of Colleges, living in the semi-monastic atmosphere of the University, knew only that girls were brought up in some private mysterious way to be as unlike boys as possible. Canon Norris ascribed the backward state of their education to its privacy and retirement. Public discussion was desirable, he thought, though the matter being so delicate must be treated " simply, modestly, and practically. Any declamation or mere theory will only damage the cause." He thought it most undesirable that girls should be admitted to the University Local Examinations, for it would certainly result in the course of girls' study being assimilated

[1] Report of the Commission, Vol. V, May 10, 1866.

altogether to that of boys. And then, forgetting his own warning against " declamation or mere theory," he asks : " Is this what the nation wishes ? . . . Are not the two sexes, in mental constitution as in all else, marvellously, beautifully, and distinctly supplemental one to the other ? . . . Surely the differences between men and women are differences of kind, not of degree. . . . Let men and women, by all means, if they wish it, study the same branches of knowledge with a most absolute liberty ; but let them do it each in their own way, following each their own nature freely ; and then, under nature's free unconscious guidance, each will develop their own congenital excellence, and the self-adjusting balance of humanity will not be disturbed."

Such vague phrases as " nature's guidance " and " the rules of common sense " seem generally to cover a want of exact knowledge, and an aversion to change. It certainly appears from the remarks of the Archbishop of York and Canon Norris that they had no exact knowledge as to how girls were educated. How should they ? There was no information available, except (as Mr. Mark Pattison said) what each man might glean from his own personal experiences. A vague idea prevailed that there was some mystery about it, with which ladies, clergymen, and married men were specially qualified to deal.

If girls could be admitted to the Local Examinations, the results would at any rate provide a little information as to their work, and this would do something to dispel the darkness which prevailed. But Miss Davies had perceived that much more was to be hoped from the newly-appointed Schools Enquiry Commission, if only girls could be included in its scope. The great point was to arouse public interest in the matter, and to this accordingly her efforts were directed. In her paper *On Secondary Instruction relating to Girls* she described the condition of depression and neglect which prevailed as regards middle-class girls.[1]

---

[1] Mr. Fitch read Miss Davies' paper to the meeting, while she sat with Mrs. Fitch among the audience. On hearing her own words read aloud, she whispered to Mrs. Fitch, " This is too strong ; Mr. Fitch will feel obliged to say afterwards that he does not agree ; it is much too strong." " Not at all too strong," Mrs. Fitch answered. Mr. Fitch was then Inspector of Schools for Yorkshire, and Miss Davies stayed with him and his wife for the meeting.

Those in the elementary schools had been dealt with by the Newcastle Commission of 1861 on elementary education. The Public Schools Commission (also of 1861) on the nine great schools (Eton, Winchester, etc.) was concerned with boys only. Why, asks Miss Davies, should middle-class girls alone be treated as of less importance than their brothers ? The reason, she thinks, is " partly a sort of inadvertence " ; men are unwilling to speak of what they imperfectly know. " It is one of the results of the prevailing indifference, that nobody knows enough of the interior of girls' schools to speak with authority about them. But there is a method by which we may test the quality of the schools : we can look at the quality of the thing produced. . . . I ask then, what are girls worth when their education is finished ? What are they good for ? "

Very little, is the answer, and she elaborates it with a careful reasonableness that does not hide very strong feeling.

" On all sides there is evidence that as regards intelligence and good sense, English women of the middle classes are held in small esteem. ' A woman's reason ' means, in popular phrase, no reason at all. A man who lets it be known that he consults his wife endangers his own reputation for sense. A habit of exaggeration, closely verging upon untruthfulness, is a recognized feminine characteristic. Newspaper writers, expressing the prevailing sentiment, assume towards women an indulgent air which is far from flattering, giving them credit for good intentions, but very little capacity. . . .

" Women are not healthy. It is a rare thing to meet with a lady, of any age, who does not suffer from headaches, languor, hysteria, or some ailment showing a want of stamina. . . . Dulness is not healthy, and the lives of ladies are, it must be confessed, exceedingly dull. . . . Busy people, and especially men, have a very faint and feeble conception of what dulness is. . . . They think dulness is calm. If they had ever tried what it is to be a young lady, they would know better. . . .

" Of literature, women of the middle classes know next to nothing. . . . Newspapers are scarcely supposed to be read by women at all. When *The Times* is offered to a lady, the sheet containing the advertisements, and the Births, Deaths and Marriages, is considerately selected. This almost complete mental blankness being the ordinary condition of women, it is not to be wondered at that their opinions, when they happen to have any, are not much respected. . . .

" It will be maintained that the defects pointed out are traceable, not to want of education, but to the natural inferiority of the female intellect. . . . Any objector is welcome to assert anything he likes about the inferiority of the female intellect, if only he does not rate it so low as to be incapable of improvement by cultivation. We are not encumbered by theories about equality or inequality of mental power in the sexes. All we claim is that the intelligence of women, be it great or small, shall have full and free development. And we claim it not specially in the interest of women, but as essential to the growth of the human race. . . . In one of the recent debates it was pointed out by Mr. Gladstone that the idleness and ignorance of Public School boys are largely attributable to the over-indulgent atmosphere of the homes in which they are brought up, and the Commissioners' Report contains repeated testimonies to the same effect. . . . What is the ideal presented to a young girl ? Is it anything higher than to be amiable, inoffensive, always ready to give pleasure and to be pleased ? Could anything be more stupefying than such a conception of the purposes of existence ? And is it likely that, constituted as society now is, young men will escape the snare which has been spread for their sisters ? Once again I would venture to urge, with the utmost insistence, that it is not a ' woman's question.' Let me entreat thinking men to dismiss from their minds the belief, that this is a thing with which they have no concern. They cannot help exerting a most serious influence upon it. Silence sometimes teaches more eloquently than words, and while they refrain from giving encouragement, their apparent indifference damps and chills. . . . So long as they thrust it aside, it will not come before the nation as worthy of serious thought. . . . If the proposition, often enough vaguely affirmed, that the true greatness of a nation depends as much on its women as on its men, be anything more than a rhetorical flourish, let it be acted upon. . . . In a word, let female education be *encouraged*—let it be understood that the public really *cares* whether the work is done well or ill—and the minor practical questions will ere long find for themselves a satisfactory solution."

Miss Davies' paper was followed by no debate at the Social Science meeting, but there were opportunities for informal discussion at the social functions which formed part of the programme of such gatherings. Meanwhile she was already busy getting up a Memorial to the University of Cambridge about the Local Examinations. She was advised by Mr. Potts to collect supporters from among " ladies of rank and influence " whose names would be likely to impress the Senate. Mrs. Russell Gurney, Lady Goldsmid, and Mrs. Manning threw themselves into the work. " I believe the names of *ladylike* ladies have great influence in a matter of this sort," wrote Miss Davies to Mrs. Manning. One hundred and two names were collected. As to the schoolmistresses, it was not easy to get at them, as there was no list of schools published anywhere, and all that could be done was to find out as many as possible privately, from friends. Nine hundred and ninety-nine signatures were obtained from Principals of schools, and men and women engaged in teaching all over the country.

It could not be expected that supporters would be found among the innumerable mistresses of small schools of inferior calibre, who were unwilling to face the ordeal of submitting their pupils to examination. A few of the more enlightened head mistresses shared this reluctance, for other reasons. Miss Beale, whose great work at Cheltenham was already well known, had declined to send in any candidates for the experimental examination. She thought that the subjects were unsuited for girls, and that an undesirable spirit of rivalry with boys would be encouraged.[1] Miss Hannah Pipe, a well-known teacher who had established a good school at Laleham, Clapham Park, also declined to send in her girls for public examinations. She feared lest cramming and overwork should " cultivate the intellect at the expense of health of body and peace of mind " ; she thought it a mistake to adopt a system which was admittedly imperfect —the system should be reformed first, and then perhaps its application to girls might be considered.[2]

Nevertheless the weight of support from people engaged in teaching girls was on the side of the Memorial, signed as it was by seventeen teachers and officials connected with Queen's College, and thirty-four from Bedford College, as well as by Miss Buss, Miss Clough, Miss Octavia Hill, and other well-known teachers.

---

[1] Later, when it became clear that the examinations had given a new impetus to education, she came to feel that it was necessary to fall in with the movement, and girls were sent up from Cheltenham to the London Matriculation, when that was thrown open to women.

[2] Miss Pipe's views were somewhat changed in later years. See *post*, Chap. XIII, p. 214.

Miss Hill had been " extremely pleased," as she wrote to Miss Davies, with the effect of the experimental examination on her pupils. She thought it was both invigorating and interesting to them, and the contact with other students was very good. She felt that it would be " almost invaluable " to have such a standard to test knowledge as this would offer. " Some such plan " (she wrote) " *must* be adopted before the education of our girls will improve. It is next to impossible for ladies to know what their governesses know. . . . I am sure the want is a very great one, and very generally felt."

Early in the October term of 1864, the Memorial was sent to the Vice-Chancellor of the University of Cambridge. " I am sure you will be gratified to learn," wrote Mr. Potts, " that the Memorial was respectfully received by the Council. . . . Not even Dr. Whewell uttered a voice against it." Both Mr. Potts and Miss Davies took great trouble to enlist supporters. At Miss Davies' request, Lord Lyttelton wrote both to Professor Thompson and to Dr. Whewell. The former replied that his impression was that the matter would be viewed without disfavour, " but naturally Fellows of Colleges know less about young ladies than a body of husbands and fathers would." Dr. Whewell said that the proposal would be fairly considered, " but the University must be allowed time and quiet, and not be disturbed by external agency. I say this because I saw in the *Spectator* a very urgent and ill-informed article." Mr. Gray, the Secretary to the Local Examinations Syndicate, reported that there was a good deal of division of opinion at Cambridge. The publicity of examinations for girls, he said, " rather grates upon one's feelings " ; and one objection seriously urged was that the admission of girls " would give rise to so many jokes." However, the first step towards success was gained by the appointment of a Syndicate to consider and report upon the Memorial.

Some anxiety was caused by the active opposition of the Committee of the Local Examinations Centre at Liverpool. This Committee sent up a counter-memorial to Cambridge, stating their opinion that the Local Examinations were too exciting for girls ; that the admission of girls would give rise to the impression that the University was in favour of educating boys and girls in the same manner ; and " might tend to expose to ridicule the existing examinations, and therefore cause them to be avoided by many of the most promising candidates." The Liverpool Committee had, of course, no experience of the examination of girls. "A stupider production [than the Liverpool Memorial] I never saw," wrote Mr. Markby to Miss Davies. "They talk of conclusions, but it really is a mere bundle of fears and impressions." Still it was felt desirable to issue a counterblast, and Mr. Tomkinson got together a meeting of the London Local Committee, to pass a resolution in support of the admission of girls, which was sent to the London and Cambridge papers. Miss Davies wrote a leaflet entitled *Reasons for the Extension of the University Local Examinations to Girls*, which was widely circulated, and sent to the *Guardian*, where she hoped it would be seen by the clergy, and University men. Circulars and pamphlets were sent to every member of the Syndicate, with offers of further information. The University was accustomed to go its own way as a body of experts for whom outside criticism had little meaning ; as Dr. Whewell had said, it did not like to be "disturbed by external agency." Yet the members of the Senate had somehow to be informed, as tactfully as possible, of the facts of the case.

In February, 1865, the Syndicate issued its report, recommending that girls should be admitted to the Local Examinations, on the same terms as boys. There were to be local committees of ladies, and care was to be taken "to prevent undue publicity or intrusion." No names of candidates or class lists were to be published. There was to be no difference in the regulations as regards the subjects of examination. The Syndicate considered it "quite inexpedient to introduce others which belong exclusively to female education."

This was a great step towards success. But the report had yet to be accepted by the Senate. It was discussed there on March 2, and among those who spoke in its support were Mr. Potts, Dr. Liveing, Mr. Markby and Professor Fawcett. Although the tone of the discussion was encouraging Mr. Potts wrote alarmingly to Miss Davies about opposition in the University, and there was much anxiety about the voting a week later. On March 8 Mr. Markby telegraphed to Miss Davies : "Send up all you can to-morrow, voting at 12, opposition organized." Miss Davies thought that all was lost. She was dining that evening at the Russell Gurneys', where she met Leslie Stephen, Edward Dicey, and Miss Smith, sister of Professor H. Smith, of Oxford. Miss Smith thought the situation looked very serious, as the telegram seemed to indicate that the country clergy were to be brought up. Mrs. Gurney asked Leslie Stephen to go up and vote, but he declined, as he had been writing on the opposite side in the *Saturday Review*. " On Thursday," Miss Davies writes, " the suspense was acute. Apparently it did not occur to Mr. Markby to telegraph, but as I was sitting in the little dining-room at Cunningham Place, longing for news, a note came from Miss Buss, announcing our victory. An undergraduate had telegraphed to her. I went to a party at the Westlakes' in the evening, and on my way called at 18, Blandford Square [her brother's house], with the good news." A letter from Mr. Markby confirmed it. " Fifty-five to fifty-one—so we are successful—it was a close contest. I got votes enough to turn the scale just before going into the Senate House." Miss Garrett's congratulations came promptly : " Your slip with the good news was most welcome. To win by ever so small a majority is delightful. This will be the stepping-stone to so much more." Miss Davies wrote at once to Mr. Tomkinson :

" Many thanks for your kind note. I know you would have gone up if you could. But after all, we are safe. The scheme has passed, by a majority of four. I had so thoroughly made up my mind to defeat, never having counted on success even when things looked most promising, that now it is come, I cannot half believe it. . . . I feel inclined to thank everybody very much who has helped us, and you especially, because I am quite sure it is to the experimental examination, which we could not have done without you, and to the general co-operation of the London Committee, that our success is mainly due."

Conditions are now so different, that some effort is needed in order to realize how much was gained by the admission of women to University Examinations. Instead of being in a kind of No-Man's Land, girls were now brought by contact with the University into the national system. A step had been gained towards the object so earnestly desired by Miss Davies—" let female education be *encouraged*—let it be understood that the public really *cares* whether the work is done well or ill." The examinations were most effective in throwing light upon the subject, and raising interest in it. The following years brought a rapid and steady increase in the number of candidates, together with a marked improvement in the quality of their work, and no harmful effects on health. This was most useful as evidence that girls were as capable as boys of profiting by good teaching. It was of real value to have a living demonstration of this, carried on quietly and continually. Only three years later, we find Mr. Markby, the Secretary to the Local Examinations Syndicate at Cambridge, writing to Miss Richardson : " My own opinion is quite clear that the success of girls in the Local Examinations has been such as to prove them worthy of means of carrying on their education to a high point similar to those open to boys of promise on leaving school. I hope to see Colleges built for them with a good staff of competent teachers and ample assistance and encouragement in the shape of Scholarships and Exhibitions."

To most parents and schoolmistresses, the examinations were a strange and alarming novelty. A passage in the Report of the Schools Enquiry Commission shows how unaccustomed people were to the idea. One of the Assistant Commissioners, Mr. C. H. Stanton, found, when examining girls' schools, that sometimes no paper was provided, or not enough ink, and that the girls copied from each other unblushingly. In one large middle-class school, he reports : " I found the girls all packed closely together on benches, as in the pit of a theatre, thrones on a stage being erected for myself and the teachers—the mistress' notion of an examination being that I was to ask questions of the crowd below, and all who could were to answer in chorus." [1] No wonder people wanted some assurance that the Local Examinations were conducted in a quiet and orderly manner ; especially as the candidates had to be consigned to an unfamiliar examination room, under the supervision of strangers. Here the prestige of the University combined with the careful chaperonage of Miss

[1] Report of the Schools Enquiry Commission of 1864, Vol. VII, p. 74. It should be added that Mr. Stanton found copying at examinations prevalent in private schools for boys also (p. 30).

Davies were invaluable. An article in the *Athenæum* [1] by Mr. Romer, the conducting examiner at the London centre in the winter of 1867, states that to most parents " the idea of sending their daughters to be examined is perfectly terrifying," but these examinations are conducted with so much care for the comfort and safety of the candidates, that there is nothing to be feared. A paper by Miss Davies, *On the Influence upon Girls' Schools of External Examinations*, contributed to a meeting of the London Schoolmistresses' Association, was designed to persuade schoolmistresses of the advantages of the examinations. [2] It may be noted that in spite of the Liverpool Committee's fears of ridicule, there was a steady increase in the number of boys entering for the examinations. [3] A Committee of ladies was appointed to undertake the conduct of the examinations for girls now regularly established at the London Centre, and Miss Davies acted as Secretary for some years, till she became too busy with other things. The work was a source of pride and pleasure to her. As she wrote to Miss Manning :

" I received my cheque for £10 from the Vice-Chancellor yesterday, for superintending the examination of girls. Miss Buss says I ought not to spend it, but to have it framed and glazed. I suppose it is the first payment ever made by the University to a woman for a service not menial."

The scheme as originally passed by the Senate was to remain in force for three years. During this time, the Committee for obtaining the admission of women to University Examinations did what it could to encourage girls to enter as candidates, offering prizes and scholarships on the results of the examinations. In 1867 the scheme was confirmed, and made permanent.

The Committee meanwhile was turning its attention to London

[1] *Athenæum*, January 4, 1868. Mr. Romer was afterwards Lord Justice Romer.

[2] Published in *The London Student*, May, 1868, and in *Thoughts on Some Questions relating to Women*, 1910.

[3] The total number who entered, counting Seniors with Juniors, was in 1865, 1,217 ; in 1866, 1,338 ; in 1867, 1,472. Under Mr. Forrest Browne (afterwards Bishop of Bristol), who succeeded Mr. Markby as Secretary, the work of the Local Examinations Syndicate was greatly developed.

University. A renewed effort to obtain admission to the London Matriculation met with no success, but the University began to consider the advisability of establishing special examinations for women. On April 25, 1866, Mr. Charles wrote to Miss Davies that he hoped to get a report in favour of the establishment of such examinations passed by Convocation. " The Senate," he wrote, " are certainly in advance of the popular body [Convocation] on the subject, and this month we hope to elect a new member of Senate, Mr. R. H. Hutton [of the *Spectator*], who is strongly in favour of some general educational standard in the University for women." Resolutions were carried in favour of establishing a special examination, of a less difficult standard than the Matriculation, for women over seventeen. Miss Davies' Committee at once declared its opinion that special examinations for women were not desirable. Miss Davies and Mr. Hutton engaged in a lively correspondence over this question. " I am afraid," she wrote to him, " the people who are interested in improving the education of women are a thankless crew. Instead of accepting as a great boon the admission of women to the London University Examinations ' *in the manner proposed*,' they have come to the conclusion that they do not consider a special examination any boon at all, and will have nothing to do with it. Please do not publish this, however, as we should not like to seem ungrateful. We are really obliged to Convocation for their kind intentions in offering us a serpent when we asked for a fish, tho' we cannot pretend to believe that serpents are better for us."

" I think you are thankless," answered Mr. Hutton. " As to the thing you wish for, I believe it to be (like some of the political wishes of some of you) altogether *premature* to say the least. When women in general are better educated it will be time enough to see whether the line of general education ought to be the same for them as for men. . . . But you are so eager to be reckoned equal, that you will not hear of *difference*, even tho' difference involve as much superiority as inferiority. . . . Why, too, if you repudiate what we offer should you be ashamed of its being known that you do ? You ought to blazon your view abroad, and it would give me great pleasure to comment on your view of the matter."

" The reason we do not wish to blazon abroad our discontent," answered Miss Davies, " is that we know that the people who carried this Report thro' thought they were doing us service, and that it was a great step to get even so much as this passed in Convocation. Of course we shall tell them privately that what they call a compromise we consider a capitulation."

" I am your best friend, if only you knew it," rejoined Mr. Hutton. " I think seriously you are making a great mistake . . . in not publishing your real views as to our resolution. . . . Is it not really that *you distrust the soundness of your own decision* ? Mind, I do not say that it *may* not turn out that the farther and later education of women *should* be on the same lines as that of men. I only say that for my own part I rather expect it will not be so, and that in any case you have not at present any means whatever of knowing that it will. Of course the elementary foundations of all common knowledge must be the same."

" All I maintain," replied Miss Davies, " is that neither the enlightened ladies nor the London University know what the intellectual differences between men and women may be, but what I argue from this is, that *therefore* existing examinations, having already a recognized standing, had better be thrown open without reservation and let us see what comes of it. The moment you begin to offer special things, you claim to know what the special aptitudes are. The London examinations do not strike me as eminently suitable either for men or women, but if girls like to go in for them, why should they not ? . . . So long as this arbitrary dictation of studies goes on, we have no chance of finding out what women would choose, if they had a free choice, say, between Ancient and Modern languages. As it is, all the encouragement goes to the last, which makes it the more surprising that, even now, so many women read and enjoy Homer and Virgil. I suppose it must be the same wilfulness which you discover in my holding on to my poor opinions. . . . The most amazing thing in your letter is where you ask, ' Is it not really that you distrust the soundness of your own decision ? ' If only one could see as clearly and feel as confident about a few other things ! I am sorry to say my stock of beliefs is but small, but on this point I have no doubt whatever—I mean as to the general principle. In practical measures, it may often be expedient to compromise."

Miss Davies' Committee did in fact compromise so far as to pass a resolution recommending " that women above the age of 18 be advised to avail themselves provisionally of this examination "—the special examination for women established by London University in 1868.[1] The results were such as to justify her contentions ; the chief distinctions attained by the candidates were not in the subjects set specially for the benefit of women, but in classics and science ; and the examinations were dropped in 1878, when women were admitted to all London examinations and degrees.

Miss Davies' Committee had now come to an end of what it could usefully do. It had secured the admission of girls to the Cambridge Senior and Junior Local Examinations, an example soon followed by the Universities of Edinburgh and Durham. Nothing further could be done at the moment with London, where special examinations had been established for women ; several applications to Oxford had failed. Even at Oxford success came in 1870, but by that time the Committee had ceased to exist. In August, 1869, a small meeting, attended only by Miss Davies, Madame Bodichon, and Mr. Tomkinson, dissolved the Committee, and handed over their balance in hand, amounting to £18 18s. 11d., to Miss Garrett, to be used in furtherance of medical education.

---

[1] See below, Chap. XII, p. 192. This examination was modelled on the matriculation, differing from it chiefly in giving a wider choice of subjects.

CHAPTER VII

Women's Suffrage and the London School Board. 1865–1873

THE few friends who set to work in 1862 to open the Local Examinations to women soon became the centre of quite a large group of allies and sympathizers, who found that they had interests in common beyond their immediate object. This object had been gained, and they felt the need of some new meeting-ground for the future. A ladies' discussion society (then something of a novelty) was accordingly started. It was called the Kensington Society, because Mrs. Manning, the President, lived in Kensington ; and it was managed by a Committee of three consisting of Mrs. Manning, President ; Miss Davies, Secretary ; and Miss Isa Craig. During the first year about fifty members were admitted, among whom were some of the older suffragists, such as Madame Bodichon, Miss Helen Taylor (Mill's step-daughter), Miss Boucherett, Miss Crow, and Miss Frances Power Cobbe ; some who had educational interests, such as Mrs. Joshua Fitch, Miss Bostock, Miss Buss, and Miss Beale ; besides Miss Garrett and her sister Mrs. J. W. Smith, and Miss Sophia Jex Blake ; Mrs. Westlake and Miss Wolstenholme (afterwards Mrs. Wolstenholme Elmy) ; Mrs. Russell Gurney, Miss Manning, and Mrs. Llewelyn Davies. Meetings were held four times a year, for the discussion of social and political questions. The first took place on May 23, 1865. " I am not very anxious about this evening," wrote Miss Davies to Miss Richardson. " The main responsibility lies with Mrs. Manning, and she always manages people beautifully." Miss Garrett sent in a paper entitled *What is the Basis, and what are the*

Limits, of Parental Authority? a question which had been prominent in her experience. Among subjects suggested by Miss Davies were the following :

What is the justification, if any, of a Church endowed and controlled by the State ?

What is the moral justification of the pursuit of the Fine Arts ?

Is it desirable for women to take part in public affairs, and if so, in what way ?

This last question led immediately to the discussion of women's suffrage. Electoral reform was the political question of the moment, and in 1865 John Stuart Mill, then at the height of his reputation, was elected Member for Westminster. In his election address he had the courage to announce his conviction that the franchise ought to be extended to women—an announcement which, had it come from anyone else, would have excited nothing but ridicule. The election was followed with lively interest by the public, and members of the Langham Place circle were active in Mr. Mill's support, as Miss Davies records :

" I remember that Madame Bodichon hired a carriage, occupied by herself, Isa Craig, Bessie Parkes, and myself, with placards upon it, to drive about Westminster. We called it giving Mr. Mill our moral support, but there was some suspicion that we might rather be doing him harm, as one of our friends told us he had heard him described as ' the man who wants to have girls in Parliament.' It may have been on this occasion that Madame Bodichon uttered her prophecy— ' You will go up and vote upon crutches, and I shall come out of my grave and vote in my winding sheet.' " [1]

(*Miss Davies to Miss Richardson.*)

May 10, 1865.

" Did I tell you that I had seen Mr. Mill ? He spoke a little while ago at a Social Science meeting. His outward shell does not to my mind express what he is, and in that respect he is very unlike Mr. Maurice, who sat near him at the same meeting. Miss Garrett says : ' Mr. Mill's characteristic is clearness, and his face expresses it ; Mr. Maurice's is reverence, and his face expresses it.' . . . I hope in the future state Mr. Mill's outward form will be more expressive of the

---

[1] Miss Davies walked to the poll in 1919, at the age of eighty-eight, and recorded her vote.

many-sided soul within. It may be, that being very shy, he does not *choose* to express anything but what he cannot help, namely, refinement. *That* cannot be concealed. It was very beautiful to see the varying expression of Mr. Maurice's face while Mr. Mill was speaking."

In November, 1865, the following question was proposed for discussion by the Kensington Society, at its second meeting : *Is the extension of the Parliamentary suffrage to women desirable, and if so, under what conditions* ? Papers were sent in by several members, including Madame Bodichon.

(*Miss Davies to Madame Bodichon.*)

17, CUNNINGHAM PLACE,
November 14, 1865.

" I find your paper capital. It is much the best that has come in, to my mind, as furnishing a basis for discussion. Miss Taylor has sent one, but I am a little disappointed in it. There are three very strong against. In your paper there are two or three expressions I should like to have altered, e.g. I don't think it quite does to call the arguments on the other side ' foolish.' Of course they *are*, but it does not seem quite polite to say so. I should like to omit the paragraph about outlawry. You see, the enemy always maintains that the disabilities imposed upon women are not penal, but solely intended for their good, and I find nothing irritates men so much as to attribute tyranny to them. I believe many of them do really mean well, and at any rate as they say they do, it seems fair to admit it and to show them that their well-intended efforts are a *mistake*, not a crime. Men cannot stand indignation, and tho' of course I think it is just, it seems to me better to suppress the manifestation of it. I should not mind *saying* a few indignant things at the meeting, but these papers travel about the country and go into families, where they may be read by prejudiced men. So it is necessary to be careful."

When the discussion took place a resolution in favour of women's suffrage was carried by a large majority. Miss Davies wrote to announce this to Miss Taylor, who was at Avignon with Mr. Mill, and had not been able to attend the meeting. Miss Taylor replied that she rejoiced to hear " such encouraging news." Madame Bodichon thought the time had now come to organize a regular Women's Suffrage Committee, but Miss Davies, with her usual caution, was inclined to hold back, as she wrote to Mr. Tomkinson.

(Miss Davies to Mr. H. R. Tomkinson.)

[*November*, 1865.]

" Some people are inclined to begin a subdued kind of agitation for the Franchise. I have rather tried to stifle it, and they are willing to be stifled if there seems to be any risk of their damaging other things by it. . . . I don't see much use in talking about the Franchise till first principles have made more way. The scoffers don't see how much is involved in improved education, but they are wide awake about the Franchise. You see I lean to compromise, though I should like also to keep clear of hypocrisy, and the line between the two is rather faint."

November 14, 1865.

" Thanks for your opinion of Mrs. Bodichon's plans. What you suggest about putting Mr. Mill's views before girls is I think pretty much what she proposed, only that she meant to put them before ' qualified women,' i.e. women who have the householder or property qualification. She thinks (and so do I) that more women care for the suffrage than is supposed, and that more still would care if they thought about it. Mrs. Bodichon would certainly wish her Committee to go very quietly to work. My doubt is whether a safe Committee could be formed, and if wild people get upon it, who would insist on jumping like kangaroos (the simile is not flattering), they would do harm. I don't think I agree with you that rights ought to be seized by force. Take the extreme case of Slavery. It would surely be better that the right of freedom should be restored by the people who have stolen it, than that it should be extorted by an insurrection of the slaves. As to the suffrage, my view is that, the object of representation being, not to confer privileges but to get the best possible government, women should be politely invited to contribute their share of intelligence in the selection of the legislative body. As to their ' asserting their rights successfully and irresistibly,' the idea is, if I may say so, rather revolting to my mind. But I remember you and Miss Craig always go in for hard hitting."

To Madame Bodichon she wrote as follows :

17, Cunningham Place,
November 14, 1865.

" I don't see my way about the Committee. I have taken further advice, and it is all against. If we could have a perfect Committee, it might do good, but I doubt whether the sort of people who can really help us would join, yet, and wild people might do great harm. I am inclined to think the first thing to do is to stir up women, chiefly through private channels, to use the rights they already possess, of voting for Guardians, etc. So long as these rights remain unused, they are an almost incontrovertible argument against us. To get women to work on mixed Committees is also very useful. It accustoms men's imagination to the spectacle of women taking part in public affairs."

Though hesitating to embark on formal organization Miss Davies began to see something of the more active suffragists, including Lady Amberley, Mrs. Peter Taylor,[1] Miss Frances Power Cobbe, and Lady Stanley of Alderley.[2] Lady Stanley, a woman of much ability and force of character, had always been a keen politician, and was before long to become a fellow-worker with Miss Davies in the cause of women's education. " Do you think it worth while to cultivate high society ? " wrote Miss Davies to Miss Manning, in the summer of 1866. " Lady Amberley has asked me to one of her parties, and Lady Stanley was very kind the other day and asked me to go any Wednesday. They have tea at five, and people go in and out. Dean Stanley and Lady Augusta were there, and Mr. Jowett, and the Bakers of Africa. It is rather nice seeing the people, but I don't feel as if I had exactly a *raison d'être* among them. Miss Garrett's case is different, because successful physicians always consort with the aristocracy, and she of course wants to make her way in the world. I like Lady Amberley very much. She seems very simple and good and alive." Miss Manning encouraged her to accept these invitations. " Your advice," wrote Miss Davies, " on high society seems to me sound, and I am going to follow it by going to Lady Amberley's to-night. There are difficulties, I think. The talk is apt to run on people that one does not know, and things (like picnics at Brocket [3]) that are quite out of one's way. This does not apply to quiet talks with a person like Lady Amberley because it is understood that each party has something to communicate to the other, but it tells in general talk, and I have an impression that people who are outside a circle are apt to be on *the hands* of the entertainers. I felt directly that

[1] Not to be confused with Mrs. Taylor, afterwards Mrs. Mill, who had died in 1858.
[2] See Biographical Index.
[3] Lord Palmerston's country house.

if I went to Lady Stanley's again, I must get a new bonnet. And is it well to spend one's money in bonnets and flys instead of on instructive books ? But on the whole, I think the advantages preponderate."

On April 25, 1866, Miss Davies paid a visit to Mill, who was living at Blackheath with his step-daughter Miss Helen Taylor. This was a great event.

(*Miss Davies to Miss Manning.*)
April 22, 1866.
" Miss Garrett says she should be too frightened to enjoy it, but I don't see why one should be. The only thing I mind is taking up their unspeakably precious time."

April 28, 1866.
" The thing that impressed me most in Mr. Mill and Miss Taylor was their simple goodness. They seemed to set no value on anything else, comparatively. I fancy too that they are a good deal nearer to us as to religious belief than I had thought."

Meanwhile the Reform Bill introduced by Gladstone in March, 1866, was being debated in the House of Commons, and it was decided to get up a petition from women for admission to the suffrage.[1] This was a piece of work which Miss Davies thoroughly enjoyed, as may be seen from the account of it in her *Family Chronicle* :

" I have a distinct recollection of the party of friends who met at Miss Garrett's house from day to day and worked it. One of the early signatures that we hailed with special delight was that of Mrs. Alford, the name, and the address—The Deanery, Canterbury—being so highly respectable and therefore influential. The list was closed with 1,499 names. Miss Becker used to say how much she regretted that she did not know of the Petition in time for her name to be the fifteen-hundredth.

---

[1] In her *Record of Women's Suffrage* Miss Blackburn states (p. 53) that a statement by Disraeli in the House of Commons on April 28, 1866, was " the spark that fired the train," and impelled Madame Bodichon, Miss Boucherett and Miss Davies to meet and draft a petition. Miss Davies noted in her copy of Miss Blackburn's book that on investigation by Miss E. A. McArthur, " it was found that the statement was not made on April 28, but appeared in *The Times* for July 20, 1848. Of the firing of the spark, and consequent meeting, I have no recollection or memorandum."

"Madame Bodichon had undertaken to convey the Petition to Mr. Mill, but when the time came, some domestic hindrance came in the way and she sent it round to me. Not feeling very competent to deal with it, I took it on to E. Garrett. We then took a cab and went together to Westminster Hall, and were fortunate in soon coming upon Mr. Fawcett, who sent his Secretary to find Mr. Mill. In the meantime, we walked up and down the hall, E. Garrett carrying the Petition, amid a crowd of people. The large roll was somewhat conspicuous, and not easy to conceal, so we asked an old applewoman to put it behind her stall. Almost immediately after, Mr. Mill suddenly appeared, finding us empty-handed. It was an embarrassing moment. E. Garrett, almost choking with suppressed laughter, said in broken accents, 'We've put it down.' It was of course at once recovered, and Mr. Mill, taking it up and waving it in the air, said, 'I can brandish this with effect.'"

The Petition was presented on June 7, 1866, in the name of "Barbara L. S. Bodichon and others." "I should like to see the faces of the Members when the question is brought forward for the first time in the House of Commons," wrote Miss Davies to Miss Helen Taylor. "I think there must be truth in your theory as to the peculiar fitness of women for fighting. I cannot help enjoying it." Soon afterwards, she received another invitation from Miss Taylor to visit her and Mr. Mill at Blackheath.

(Miss Davies to Miss Manning.)

June 26, 1866.

"I had a most interesting visit to Blackheath—much more so than the former one, as the conversation turned on more interesting subjects. I did not care very much for Mr. Bain, but his being there encouraged talking on quasi-philosophical subjects, such as the probable results in the future of free enquiry, Ecce Homo, the beginnings of Authority, etc. It was 'society' in a very delightful form. There were six of us, three ladies and three gentlemen. Mr. Mill and Mr. Bain talked most, and were best worth hearing, but we all put in our word, especially in the way of asking questions. You would have enjoyed it much."

The defeat of Gladstone's Reform Bill led to the formation of a Conservative government, which was followed by Reform demonstrations and riots. On the new government taking up the question, plans were set on foot for fresh petitions for women's suffrage, one from women householders, and two from the general public, one of which was to be presented by Mill to the House of Commons. Some differences of opinion arose as to the terms of this last.

(*Miss Davies to Miss Manning.*)

Wednesday [*October*, 1866].

" I shall be glad to have your opinion and Mrs. Manning's on the question whether the words ' Unmarried women and widows ' should be inserted in the last clause of Miss Taylor's Petition. She decidedly refuses to put them in, and repeats her old statement that ' freeholders and householders ' practically excludes wives. If we insist on inserting these words definitely limiting the claim, Mr. Mill and Miss Taylor will give us no help in getting signatures, and it is possible that Mr. Mill may refuse to present the petition. On the other hand, Lady Goldsmid feels so strongly the impolicy of leaving it an open question that she says she cannot be on the Committee *unless* those words are put in. And it is not only Lady G.'s help that we should lose, but that of other people who take the same view. I feel myself that it would almost drive us into prevarication (Miss Taylor's phrase I mean), or to say the least, we should be involved in controversies over the legal question, leading off from the matter in hand, and attention would be directed towards the position of wives question, which we do not want to raise at present."

" In the last paragraph [of the Petition]," wrote Miss Davies to Miss Taylor, " the words ' on the same conditions as men ' seem to me a little too definite. Commonplace people, women as well as men, have a horror of what they call ' women wanting to be on an equality with men.' And I should be glad to avoid anything that might possibly suggest that unpleasant phrase."
" I understood the drift of your suggestions to be, to avoid defining exactly what qualifications we ask for women," replied Miss Taylor, " and this would be desirable were it possible to do so without resigning the principle of equality." She could not, she added, conscientiously sign any form which by implication petitioned Parliament to establish a different qualification for women and for men ; and if any such form were adopted, Mr. Mill would not be willing to present the Petition. This did not meet Miss Davies' views, who felt, as she wrote to Madame Bodichon, that " the signatures will be the argument, so I wanted

to secure chiefly that the Petition should be what anybody could sign."

(Miss Davies to Miss Manning.)
[Undated, probably July, 1866.]

"My reflections on the subject of 'hobbles' have led me to the conclusion that if one's vocation is to work at public affairs, not at a definite profession, offences must needs come, but woe unto them by whom they come. In other words I think one must try very hard not to give unnecessary offence, but if trouble comes, say thro' injudicious proposals, one must accept it as part of the day's work without undue fretting. Mrs. Manning's hint as to the desirableness of letting people see that you appreciate their good while resisting their evil, is valuable. But I feel that to myself those personal considerations are tiresome (or irrelevant). I don't want people to be impressing upon me that they think very well of me though they disapprove of my projects. It does not comfort me."

A letter to Miss Richardson gives expression to the admiration of Mill which made a disagreement with him the more disappointing.

"I met yesterday again in Mill a passage which made a great impression upon me some years ago. 'Human beings owe to each other help to distinguish the better from the worse and encouragement to choose the former and avoid the latter. They should be for ever stimulating each other to increased exercise of their higher faculties, and increased direction of their feelings and aims towards wise instead of foolish, elevating instead of degrading, objects and contemplations.' That principle is at the bottom of everything I do (that is not bad) and perhaps accounts for what looks to you like love of power. . . . I see no disgrace in not having read Mill, but either a present loss or a vast fund of delight to come, according as you like to look at it. . . . I think there must be great fire in his writings tho' the form is so restrained, or they would not be so kindling. I feel glowing with hope and courage after reading Mill, tho' it would be hard to find a passage in which the enthusiasm is more than latent."

The Social Science Congress, to be held in Manchester in October, 1866, offered an opportunity of bringing the question of women's suffrage before an audience which was accustomed to listen seriously to contributions from women, and with Miss Davies' advice, Madame Bodichon prepared a paper for the

114

meeting, entitled *Reasons for the Enfranchisement of Women.* She asks for the suffrage on the broadest grounds :

" Among all the reasons for giving women votes, the one which appears to me the strongest is that of the influence it might be expected to have in increasing public spirit. . . . Give some women votes, and it will tend to make all women think seriously of the concerns of the nation at large. . . . As it is, women of the middle classes occupy themselves but little with anything beyond their own family circle. . . . They do not consider it any concern of theirs, if poor men and women are ill-nursed in workhouse infirmaries, and poor children ill-taught in workhouse schools. If the roads are bad, the drains neglected, the water poisoned, they think it all very wrong, but it does not occur to them that it is their duty to get it put right. . . . They do not bring their good sense to bear upon public affairs, because they think it is men's business, not theirs, to look after such things. . . . There is no reason why . . . women should not take an active interest in all the social questions—education, public health, prison discipline, the poor laws, and the rest, which occupy Parliament. . . . The result of teaching women that they have nothing to do with politics is that their influence goes towards extinguishing the unselfish interest—never too strong—which men are disposed to take in public affairs."

But even the Social Science Association was not ready to entertain the question to any serious extent ; Madame Bodichon's was the only paper on women's suffrage, and was barely mentioned in the Association's Report of Proceedings. It was not, however, without effect. Among the audience at Manchester was Miss Lydia Becker, who listened with keenly aroused interest, and from this time forward set herself to work for women's suffrage. A Suffrage Committee, of which she was Secretary, was formed at Manchester early in 1867. In the previous autumn a similar Committee had been formed in London, with Mrs. Peter Taylor as Treasurer, and Mrs. J. W. Smith as Secretary. With some misgivings, Miss Davies agreed to take part in the work. " It was arranged," she writes, " that I should do the Secretarial work with Mrs. J. W. Smith (E. Garrett's older sister) as figure-head. . . . My name was to be kept out of sight, to avoid the risk of damaging my work in the education field by its being associated with the agitation for the franchise."

The Committee set energetically to work on the Petitions. The paper which Madame Bodichon had contributed to the Social Science meeting was reprinted and circulated ; and she worked up the paper she had previously written for the Kensington Society into another pamphlet, entitled *Objections to the Enfranchisement of Women Considered.* Some correspondence arising out of a letter from Miss Davies to the *Morning Post* was also reprinted for circulation.

Miss Davies' work was now branching out so much in all directions that it gave her more than enough to do, and in the autumn of 1866 she made some attempt to withdraw from the suffrage work. It was, however, very difficult to replace her. " Miss Garrett," she wrote to Miss Manning, " has a counter-proposal that Miss [Harriet] Cook should be engaged . . . as a sort of private secretary to help me generally in what I have to do. Mrs. Bodichon and Miss Boucherett also wish this, and if the others (Mrs. Taylor, Mrs. Knox,[1] and Miss Cobbe) take the same view, I suppose it will be done." This plan was agreed to ; but had been only a few weeks in operation, when, in February, 1867, Mrs. Smith's sudden death made some rearrangement necessary. This was not an easy matter, with the time for presenting the Petitions so near at hand, and a somewhat unsatisfactory plan was adopted by way of stop-gap. Madame Bodichon's name was entered in place of Mrs. Smith's as a figure-head secretary. She could not be consulted, as she was in Algiers, and though her friends at home did not know it, she was very ill with fever.

(*Miss Davies to Madame Bodichon.*)

March 21 [1867].

" It was a very great pleasure to receive your note to-day. I am so glad to think of your being pretty well again and on your way towards England. I am glad you do not mind our using your name. We won't do it again. And we *did not do* it, knowing that you were ill. It was not till it was all arranged, which had to be done very suddenly, that I heard of your fever and that I must not write to you. Very little has been done in your name, except sending out formal notices and writing to Mr. Bruce and Mr. Gurney, who have both consented to present the Petitions. . . . We have circulated about 10,000 of each of your pamphlets. They seemed to be just what

---

[1] Miss Isa Craig.

was wanted. Sir Thomas Erskine May thinks *Reasons* ' unanswerable.' There is a strong letter from Kingsley too, which I must show you when you come to England. . . . I am longing for you to be at hand."

General Petitions were presented by the Hon. H. A. Bruce on March 28, and by Mill on April 5. The Women Householders' Petition was presented by Mr. Russell Gurney on April 8. The *Saturday Review*,[1] commenting on the Petitions, admitted that " when Mr. Mill makes a legislative proposal, something may probably be said in its defence. But Mr. Mill himself " (the reviewer continued) " can hardly be surprised at finding that his proposal for giving votes to women is generally treated as a joke."

On May 20, 1867, Mill moved an amendment to the Representation of the People Bill, to the effect that the word *persons* should replace the word *men* in the Bill, an alteration which would introduce women's suffrage. The amendment was rejected by a majority of 123. " I am glad you thought the Division good," wrote Miss Davies to Madame Bodichon, who had now returned to England. " It was pretty much what I expected, and certainly on the whole, encouraging."

This defeat was followed by no relaxation of the women suffragists' efforts, but some changes of organization took place.

(Miss Davies to Madame Bodichon.)

June 3, 1867.

" We have been considering what will be best to do about the Franchise, and have come to the conclusion that the Committee must be dissolved. Mrs. Taylor proposes it, so there will be no opposition from her side, and Lady Goldsmid, Miss Manning, and E. Garrett, who may be taken as representing the quiet section, agree that it is the only thing we can do. . . . We *might* have two Committees, one moderate, and the other under Mrs.[2] and Miss Helen Taylor's leadership. But that would expose our divisions to the world, and it would be said that ' women never can work together,' etc., which would be very damaging. So on the whole, I think with Lady Goldsmid that ' We had better quietly withdraw and stick to our middle-class ' (i.e. to education). The best course will perhaps be for you to write to me resigning the Secretaryship. If you could at the same

---

[1] *Saturday Review*, March 30, 1867.　　　[2] Mrs. Peter Taylor.

time suggest that the Committee might be dissolved, we could call a meeting for the purpose of receiving your resignation, and discussing whether to dissolve or not. So that all the Committee will know that it is going to be proposed."

A letter from Miss Davies to Miss Manning indicates the result.

June 14 [1867].

" Our meeting yesterday was pleasant in some respects but leaves one with a melancholy feeling behind it. Miss Taylor was perfectly unpersuadable, and I believe we might all have talked for a week without making the least impression upon her. It seems that Mr. Mill also is very strong in favour of excluding men from the Managing Committee, and Mrs. Knox went over to the enemy. . . . Mrs. Bodichon and I were obliged to give in. . . . I don't so much mind the having only women on the Managing Committee, as the sense I have that under the proposed management, the matter will get identified with the extreme section of the Liberal Party, and will be worked, as the Emancipation Society seemed to me to be, almost exclusively among the people who are convinced already. Conservatives and moderate Liberals will be treated, I am afraid, as hopelessly blind and stupid, and our chance of success will be very much injured, to say the least. But perhaps it may turn out better than I expect."

Writing many years afterwards, Miss Davies summed up the episode as follows :

" [The Committee] had been working through great difficulties, owing to the incompatibility of its chief elements. Mrs. Peter Taylor, the Treasurer, belonged to the extreme left of the Liberal Party, and looked at matters from a different point of view from other members of the Committee. This difference was the more embarrassing, as she was by far the most zealous and active member. Other members had other interests, and without any sort of quarrel, it was finally agreed to be best to leave the Women's Suffrage part of the women's movement to be worked for the time under the direction of the Radical section of the party. . . . The new Committee formed by Mrs. [Peter] Taylor, which met at her house (Aubrey House, Notting Hill), was not joined by any member of the former Committee except Mrs. Taylor herself. From that time until many years after I took no active part in the agitation for Women's Suffrage."

In a letter to Miss Richardson written at the time Miss Davies expressed her feelings with less reserve : " It is a great relief to me," she wrote, " to get away from uncongenial companionship and to abandon the vain effort to work with Radicals. Heaven protect me from trying it again ! The more I see of them, the worse they appear, *quâ* Radicals. No doubt some of them have the domestic virtues."

Madame Bodichon, though she did not join the new Committee, kept in touch with Miss Becker, Miss Cobbe, Mrs. Taylor, and other leaders. In 1869 a third edition was issued of her *Brief Summary of the most important Laws of England concerning Women.* In this edition, while something is said as to the Married Women's Property Bill of 1868, the chief stress is laid on exclusion from the franchise as the greatest disability suffered by women. The franchise question, scarcely noticed in 1856 when the pamphlet was first published, had now become a matter of importance to practically all the women engaged, in one way or another, in working for the women's movement. The agitation, hitherto carried on by suffrage committees in Manchester and London, was before long organized on a larger scale. Local committees, springing up in other places, led to the establishment of the National Society for Women's Suffrage. This elicited much comment in *Punch*, of which the following may be quoted as average specimens :

April 2, 1870.

" SUFFRAGE FOR BOTH SEXES.—The law which allows every male fool, not absolutely idiotic or insane, to vote for members of Parliament, and forbids the very cleverest and best educated woman, is clearly no specimen of the perfection of human reason."

And a fortnight later (April 16) :

" To Mrs. Professor Fawcett. . . . Has it not occurred to you that in parcelling out our life into two great fields, the one inside, the other outside the house doors, and in creating two beings so distinct in body, mind, and affections, as men and women, the Framer of the Universe *must* have meant the two for different functions ? . . . Surely . . . there lies a tremendously strong presumption against the wisdom of the feminine entry on the masculine domain of business and politics ? "

Punch was not alone in speaking with two voices ; public opinion was to some extent beginning to be moved. A considerable step was gained by the admission of women to the Municipal Franchise in 1869 ; and in 1870, under the Education Act, they were given the right not only to vote for members of the new School Boards, but to be elected as members of the Boards. Four ladies were successful at the first School Board Elections—Miss Flora Stevenson in Edinburgh, Miss Becker in Manchester, and Miss Davies and Miss Garrett in London. Miss Garrett became a candidate in October, 1870, at the invitation of a Working Men's Association in the Marylebone Division.

(*Miss Garrett to Miss Davies.*)

[*October* 12, 1870].

" They go for reading the Bible without note or comment, but they would vote for me even if I were put up by the Unionists. They selected their candidates by ballot from a long list. I was considerably ahead of all the others proposed, even of Huxley. It's queer why they want me. . . . I wish you were here to advise. . . . If I am certainly to be elected, as the deputation seemed to think, my friends might as well make the majority as telling as possible."

Miss Garrett did not at first realize how much was necessary in the way of organization, and was dismayed at finding that there would have to be a great deal of committee work, and speech-making.

(*Miss Garrett to Miss Davies.*)

October 24 [1870].

" This morning Mr. Alsager Hill called on me and offered his services on a Committee if I thought of having one. I believe this is what we ought to have, if we wish to succeed. The scattered work of individuals will count for so little if the opposition is really vigorous and as strong as Mr. [Llewelyn] Davies evidently thought it was. . . . Failing conspicuously will do us so much harm that it *must* be avoided if possible. . . . After Mr. Hill's visit I had a deputation from working men. . . . They think there must be meetings to teach people to be interested. . . . I suppose it is part of the whole thing and ought not to be refused, tho' I am sorry it is so. I dare say when it has to be done I can do it, and it is no use asking for women to be taken into public work and yet to wish them to avoid publicity. We must be ready to go into the thing as men do if we go at all, and in time there will be no more awkwardness on our side than there is on theirs. Still I am very sorry it is necessary, especially as I can't think of anything to say for four speeches ! and after

Huxley too, who speaks in epigrams ! However, I shall hope to avoid bad taste, even if I am commonplace. The first of these trials is to be some night next week. I hope you will be up in time to go with me.[1] Couldn't you and Annie [Austin] think of something to say, not quite hackneyed ? Quotations either from the Bible or Milton, especially one to wind up with, would be very precious. Bless us ! it's a tough and toilsome business."

Meanwhile, Miss Davies had also received an invitation to stand, Mr. Tidman, a friend of Mill's, having invited her to contest the City division. At his suggestion, she prepared an election address, which she sent to Mr. Tomkinson for criticism and advice.

(Miss Davies to Mr. H. R. Tomkinson.)
November 7 [1870].

" Would you be kind enough to criticize the enclosed in case I should rise to the point of issuing an address to the City electors ? My inviter is Mr. P. F. Tidman of the Kershaw tribe—34, Great St. Helens—uncle of one of the Hitchin students. He thinks success will depend very much on personal exertion, and he and his friends offer to take all the trouble and expense. They do not want me to do anything but write an address. I am torn in two between rival advisers. My mother and Miss Garrett urge that if a woman is wanted to try it, I ought not to lose time by holding back. My brother insists that it would be *too* audacious to offer to stand for ' the greatest constituency in the world ' without *more* invitation. . . . What do you think ? If one could be tolerably sure of a respectable failure, it would be enough. An ignominious and ridiculous defeat would do harm. . . . Do please give me some advice directly about the City. It strikes me as preposterous to think of. But preposterous things sometimes get done."

The address, which she sent to Mr. Tomkinson, concluded with the following paragraph on the burning question of the moment :

" I should be very sorry to see religion excluded from the schools. I believe that such religious instruction as is suitable to children may begin without entering into doctrinal differences, and that for practical teachers the ' religious difficulty ' can scarcely be said to exist. At the same time I should wish to see loyally carried out the pro-

---

[1] Miss Davies was at Hitchin, busy with the new College, afterwards Girton.

visions of the Act which enable parents who desire it to obtain education for their children in all the secular subjects without sharing the religious instruction."

Mr. Tomkinson dealt faithfully with the question, and answered her with a very discouraging letter. He pounced upon the word *loyally* in the last sentence of her address. " I hate the use of this term which every one is using in this matter," he scribbled at the bottom of the draft address. " It sounds as if great credit was being sought, and would be claimed, for condescending to comply with the Act ! and is often meant to imply that the loyalty is not without cost, and entails some sacrifice. Or rather as *you* put it, you contemplate the Act *not* being carried out—for hinting at which you would in a well-constituted community be executed at once."

(*Miss Davies to Mr. Tomkinson.*)

[*November* 8.]

" I do not feel guilty of having ' sought a conspicuous place ' in connection with elementary education. I should not have thought of standing for *any* constituency, least of all the City, except on the conditions proposed to me, that the people who *asked* me to stand would take all the trouble and expense. I am not sure that it would not have been better to refuse at once, without saying anything about it, but it is possible that some small good may be done by accustoming people to think of it. . . . The object of getting questions put to Miss Garrett is to avoid her having to make a set speech. The Chairman is to invite the meeting generally to ask questions. If the invitation is met with dead silence, he will then ask Miss Garrett to state her views, which will be more difficult and disagreeable for her than having them drawn out. We had not any of the crafty designs you attribute to us. . . .

" I am afraid you will find this a very cross letter, but I am really grateful to you for saying what you thought. I have been trying to remember the texts about the reproofs of the wise. Does it not say that they break one's head, or something of that sort ? It is quite true."

Miss Davies was not adopted as a candidate by the City committee, but Mr. Tidman proposed that she should stand for his own district, Greenwich, where he thought there would be a better chance. Miss Davies at first declined, as she would be

" brought forward by Radicals in opposition to what they call a clerical and sectarian list, and it would be a false position," but as Miss Shirreff (whose sister Mrs. Grey was a candidate for Chelsea) and others begged her to come forward, she consented to stand, and the energetic Mr. Tidman began to organize meetings.

(*Miss Davies to Mr. Tomkinson.*)

November 14 [1870].

" I am going to do it after all. Mr. Tidman came up on Saturday evening and again yesterday, and made out such a moving case of the anxiety of the electors of Greenwich to return a Woman (*what* woman being a secondary consideration) that I thought I ought not to refuse. I am not to pretend to represent the secularists. It is a coalition of very respectable ladies, ' Low Church parsons ' (perhaps High Church too), and Mr. Mill. . . .

" I am very sorry you and Mrs. Tomkinson [1] do not approve, but I think perhaps you would if I could explain exactly with what intentions I am going into it."

November 25 [1870].

" You ignore the philanthropic period of my history. The twenty years at Gateshead were *all* schools and District visiting, and I feel that the experience counts for a good deal as a qualification for the School Board."

Meetings were soon in full swing, and among the speakers on her behalf were Tom Hughes, Miss Garrett, and Mr. Roby. " I am a little disappointed," Miss Davies wrote to Miss Manning, " at finding that speaking does not get easier as one goes on. . . . The chief feeling I have thro' it all is a kind of sense of being half asleep, and having nothing to do with it. But I cannot help wishing you had been at Greenwich instead of Blackheath. You would have liked Miss Garrett's speech—it was only too generous —and the meeting was enthusiastic. The Hall was fuller than it would hold (it holds 1,000) and the women came crowding into the Committee Room at the end to shake hands and promise their votes. Shaking hands seems to be a chief part of a candidate's business."

The elections took place on November 30, 1870. Both Miss Davies and Miss Garrett were elected, the latter coming out at

[1] Mr. Tomkinson's mother, with whom he lived in Lower Seymour Street.

the head of the poll in Marylebone, with 47,858 votes, Huxley coming next with 13,494. " I am very glad and happy," Miss Garrett wrote to Mr. Anderson, " both for the victory itself and also for its having been given to me to have a share in it. I am sure it will do the women's cause great good." There was some idea that Miss Garrett as the member with the largest majority might be called to the chair, to open the proceedings at the first meeting of the School Board.

(Miss Davies to Miss Garrett.)

EXAMINATION ROOM,
December 7.

" The temporary Chair question does not seem to me very impor-tant. I was a little sorry that you should tell people, whether in jest or earnest, that you would very much like a position which, to my mind, would be incongruous even to the point of absurdity. I should feel it so in my own case, tho' as the Scotsman observed, I am ' of comparatively mature age,' and have had more experience of that sort. It is not being a woman (tho' that probably enhances it) but your youth [1] and inexperience that makes it strike me as almost in-decorous to think of presiding over men like Lord Lawrence, etc. It may not strike others in the same way, and if there were a rule, it might be worth while to submit to it, but there can scarcely be pre-cedents enough to constitute a custom, and unless necessary, I should be sorry for you to do anything which might give colour to the charge of being ' cheeky,' which has been brought against you lately. It is too true that your jokes are many and reckless. They do more harm than you know. . . .

" I have had a nice note from Mr. Anderson. I like him the best of all your friends."

(Miss Garrett to Mr. J. G. S. Anderson.)

December 8 [1870].

" Most people like compliments, particularly when they have the charm of perfect sincerity, so I send you one from Miss Davies. The contrast between my share and yours is rather trying, but I do not mind a little north-east wind, and I know it is good to have it as a check upon any tendency to uppishness which 47,000 might induce.

" Miss Davies is a good deal my senior, and if I live to be 100 she will still be so and will feel it as much as she did when I sat at her feet in girlhood. I enjoy thinking how I can crush her with the

---

[1] Miss Garrett was thirty-four, and Miss Davies forty.

Recorder's and Mrs. Russell Gurney's decided opinion on the other side.

" I ought to have been luminous in the dark last night, I had been dining with such a constellation. Robert Browning, Jenny Lind, Dean Stanley, and Lady Augusta, and Prof. Mohl. It was very delightful to be thought fit for such companions. Lady Augusta sees all the advantages our victory brings to the general cause and rejoices over them very cordially."

Another letter to Mr. Anderson described how the question about the Chairmanship was settled.

(*Miss Garrett to Mr. J. G. S. Anderson.*)

December 15 [1870].

" I had no choice about the Chair, after all ! It had evidently been arranged beforehand that I should have none. When we assembled Miss Davies and I were asked to take two seats apart, this we resisted, and with the Recorder's sanction sat on a level with the other members on the seat round the table facing the House. Without a moment's pause some one moved that the oldest member should take the Chair : then some one amended it that Aldn. Cotton should. It was seconded and carried without discussion. After a few common-places from him, Huxley opened the battle by moving that *no* salary be given to the Chairman. . . . To my surprise most people agreed to the no-salary principle. Lord Sandon, Dr. Barry, Mr. Thorold, and Mr. Smith were all on our side. They said nearly all I had thought of, but as I thought it would look less like being sore about the Chairmanship to say a word or two in a good-humoured way, I just added that I heartily supported Mr. Huxley's motion—without giving reasons. Then we voted, and it passed by 32 to 14. . . ."

[Lord Lawrence was then elected as Chairman.]

" The new Chairman recognized us, which no one else had done, by beginning ' Ladies and Gentlemen,' and what he said was sensible and manly, though he is evidently no orator. . . . It was very pleasant to Miss Davies and me to have the Recorder's friendly presence all the time. I felt the atmosphere to be decidedly hostile, but of course that is not surprising, and it is not a bad discipline to find it so after the intoxication of one's 47,000. The anteroom was full of my supporters who gave me a very hearty welcome as I came in. I hope they will get to know that I did not shirk the Chair. The Recorder [Mr. Russell Gurney] took us out by a back door, so I had no opportunity of explaining."

Perhaps none of the members realized how heavy the work of the new School Board would be. Elementary education had to be systematized, and there were immense gaps to be filled. The work was done principally through Standing Committees, of which there were six. Miss Davies was put on two of these—the Statistical Committee and the Bye-Laws Committee. The Statistical Committee, which had to advise as to the amount of accommodation required in the different localities, had a tremendous task before it, and its investigations during Miss Davies' two years of service on the Board resulted in plans being passed for over one hundred new schools. The Bye-Laws Committee was concerned chiefly with the enforcement of attendance, a thorny question in those days. This was the part of the work in which Miss Davies took the most active share, both as a member of the Committee, and locally, in enforcing the Bye-Laws in the Greenwich division. She prepared a plan which was submitted to the School Board early in 1871, in accordance with which Visitors were appointed in each district, to make house-to-house visitations, working under the guidance of a Superintendent. In each Division there was a Committee consisting of the members for the Division, sometimes with local residents co-opted, and the Clerk to this Committee was also Superintendent of the Visitors. During the twelve months ending in June, 1873, the attendances in the Greenwich division had been increased by about 5,500.[1] What with the weekly Board meetings, and the local work at Greenwich, involving long and toilsome journeys, she soon began to find that she had undertaken more than she could do. She was during these years absorbed in the foundation of Girton ; the College was going through a critical period, and from March, 1872, till 1875, Miss Davies was residing there as Mistress. In October, 1873, therefore, she said farewell to the School Board.[2]

Miss Garrett, who in 1870 had become Mrs. Anderson, was a member of the Statistical Committee and of the Officers and Clerks Committee ; she interested herself in the sanitary arrangements of the schools, and succeeded in introducing Domestic Economy among the subjects taught.[1] Her professional work

[1] Minutes of the London School Board, June 28, July 19, and November 15, 1871.

[2] A picture of the first London School Board, painted by J. W. Walton in 1873, now hangs in the County Hall.

was meanwhile fast increasing, and in October, 1873, she, like Miss Davies, decided not to stand for re-election. Mrs. Anderson's sister, Mrs. Cowell, succeeded her as representative of the Marylebone division, together with Miss J. A. Chessar, a well-known teacher. It was a satisfaction to the retiring members that two women had been elected to carry on their work. In her farewell address [1] to her constituents at Greenwich, Miss Davies urged women to come forward and offer themselves as candidates. " We have felt continually," she said, " the want of more women on the Board. . . . Repeatedly it has been felt that on this or that Committee there ought to be a lady, and we have been obliged to decline to serve because we could not spare the time. We were willing to do our best, but when it is remembered that the Board has consisted of forty-seven gentlemen and two ladies, it will not be a matter of surprise that the two ladies have proved incapable of doing their half of the work."

[1] Published in the *Kentish Mercury*, October 11, 1873.

CHAPTER VIII

The Schools Enquiry Commission (1864–1866) and its Effects

MISS DAVIES' withdrawal from the Women's Suffrage agitation in 1867 left her free to devote herself to the question of women's education. Her interest had, as we have seen, been first attracted to this side of the women's question through Miss Garrett's efforts to enter the medical profession, which led immediately to the desire to open degrees to women. The admission of girls to the Cambridge Local Examinations in 1865 was the first move in the direction of degrees, and it was also the first step towards the general improvement of girls' education.

It had long been admitted that improvement was needed. At the first meeting of the Social Science Association, in 1857, a speaker remarked that it was even more difficult to obtain a good education for girls than for boys, observing that " the great defect in ladies' schools is the utter absence of all solid and valuable teaching, and this is fatally influencing our social condition." [1] This was a mere passing allusion to the subject, the speaker being mainly concerned with boys. At the meeting of the Association in 1860, there were no fewer than three papers by ladies, dealing with girls.[2] All three agree in condemning

[1] *The Education of the Middle Classes*, by Rev. Evan Davies, D.D., *Transactions of the National Association for the Promotion of Social Science*, 1857.

[2] *Girls' Schools*, by Miss Louisa O. Hope ; *Middle Class Schools for Girls*, by Madame Bodichon ; *On the Education of Girls with Reference to their Future Position*, by Miss Jessie Boucherett. Madame Bodichon's paper, which was printed in full in the *Englishwoman's Journal* for

the education given in girls' schools. We hear from one that it is
" frothy and superficial," from another of its " miserable ineffi-
ciency," and from a third of the " pretentious ignorance " of the
teachers. Yet, as Madame Bodichon pointed out, it was a matter
on which exact information was hard to get. " It is exceedingly
difficult," she writes, " to visit such establishments ; they are
private, and I have found the mistresses exceedingly jealous of
inspection, most unwilling to show a stranger (and quite naturally)
anything of the school books, or to answer any questions."
Madame Bodichon enquired into as many girls' schools as she
could, and saw enough to convince her that they were very inferior.
But investigation by one private person could not be carried far,
and any attempt at an organized enquiry would have to overcome
the timidity of the schoolmistresses and the prejudices of the
parents. The opportunity for such an enquiry came through the
awakening of the public to the fact that boys' schools were in
need of reform, and the consequent appointment of the Schools
Enquiry Commission. In Lord Brougham's opening Address
to the Social Science Congress of 1864, we find the following
account of this matter :

" The state of education for the middle classes has long been com-
plained of, and petitions to both Houses had more than once been
presented on the subject, a great number, more than 120, by myself
to the Lords, and with those to the Commons signed by above 40,000
persons. . . . The general complaint was that while due care is bestowed upon the schools for the highest and the humblest classes,
none whatever is given to the schools for the middle class. . . . No
provision whatever is made to superintend the teachers of the schools
frequented by their children . . . the person least qualified by learning or talents, and even of the most exceptionable character and habits,
may set up schools for either sex, so that it has become a saying,
when anyone has failed in all other ways to procure a livelihood, let
him keep a school, or let her be a schoolmistress. . . . The Council
of the Social Science Association, taking this important subject into

---

November, 1860, is remarkable for its anticipation of the principal
measures afterwards taken to improve girls' education, such as the investigation by the Schools Enquiry Commission, the admission of girls
to the Local Examinations, and the establishment of the Girls' Public
Day School Company.

their consideration, appointed a deputation on it to wait on the Minister.[1] . . . It has since been announced in Parliament that a Commission will be issued on the whole subject of middle-class education in compliance with the recommendations of the Council."

It soon appeared that in " the whole subject of middle-class education " the education of girls was not included. The Social Science Association had heard Miss Davies's appeal for their interest to be extended to girls : " Let me entreat thinking men to dismiss from their minds the belief that this is a thing with which they have no concern. . . . So long as they thrust it aside, it will not come before the nation as worthy of serious thought." [2] But girls, though not formally excluded from the enquiry, were overlooked ; it had not occurred to anyone to think of them. The general appeal having fallen flat, some immediate action must be taken if the precious opportunity were not to be lost. Miss Davies wrote to enquire of Lord Lyttelton, who replied, " I have no doubt girls are to be included in our Commission, which is to enquire into the education of the middle-class generally, but I will mention it to Lord Granville." [3] No definite announcement was however made, and towards the end of December Miss Davies wrote to Matthew Arnold :

" I am sorry to see that your name is not included, as we hoped it would have been, in the new Royal Commission. . . . Do you happen to know with whom it rests, whether girls' schools are included in the enquiry ? Lord Lyttelton told us he thought they would be, as a matter of course. Mr. Norris has since stated, on I do not know what authority, that ' the Commission will not extend their enquiry to girls unless a strong effort is made to persuade them.' If this is the case, I suppose we ought to do something, but we do not wish to torment people with appeals unless it is necessary. One does not see what objection there can be to enquiry, except the work, which some of the Commissioners would perhaps be glad to lessen."

" I can hardly think," wrote Matthew Arnold in reply, " that the new Commission, with all it will have on its hands, will be

[1] I.e. the Prime Minister, Lord Palmerston, who received the deputation on June 18, 1864.
[2] See *ante*, Chap. VI, pp. 92, 94–6.
[3] Lord Granville was Lord President of the Council.

willing to undertake the enquiry into girls' schools as well as that into boys ! " This was very discouraging. Mr. Acland, with whom Miss Davies was at this time corresponding about the Local Examinations, had been appointed a Commissioner, but could tell her nothing. " We shall think it very hard," she wrote to him, " if the Commissioners narrow their field by shirking half their duty."

Feeling that the attack must be pushed further, she made another attempt to get at Lord Granville, and wrote to Mr. Grote :

December 30 1864.

" I hope you will not think it unpardonably troublesome when I again venture to ask your help in connexion with female education. We are very anxious that ladies' schools should be included in the enquiry by the new Royal Commission. Hitherto we have not been able to discover what is intended, reports and opinions being contradictory, but it appears that the decision rests with Lord Granville, and it occurred to me that you would perhaps be kind enough to speak to him on the subject. In the Commission for enquiry into the education of the poor, there was no thought of leaving out girls' schools, and it will be a great disappointment to those who are interested in middle-class female education, if a different course should be adopted in the present case."

Mr. Grote answered that as he was not living in London, he would have no opportunity of speaking to Lord Granville. " All I can do is, to forward your letter and request his attention to it. I have no information as to the details of the contemplated enquiry. If it includes Female Schools, the amount of the work, and of course the time employed by the Commissioners, must of course be greatly increased. I should be glad to see Female Schools investigated and improved, but I have some doubt whether this Commission is likely to undertake the task."

The matter was too important to be left there, and it was decided to get up a memorial to the Commissioners. This was quickly organized by Miss Davies and Miss Bostock, one of her colleagues on the Committee for securing admission to University Examinations. It was signed by representatives of Queen's College and Bedford College, and by a number of teachers

and people interested in education.[1]   A favourable answer was
soon received.   Mr. Roby (Secretary to the Commission) wrote
that the limits of the investigation would necessarily be narrower
in the case of girls than in that of boys, firstly because girls were
more often educated at home, or in schools too small to be entitled
to the name, and the Commissioners were not to deal with either
domestic education or private tuition ; secondly, because the
endowments appropriated to girls were not at all comparable in
number or value to those provided for boys.   But the Assistant
Commissioners, who were to be sent to inquire in selected districts,
were to report on the state and prospects of girls' education as well
as on boys' ; and the Commissioners sitting in London would be
prepared to examine witnesses.

Mr. Roby sent a message to Miss Davies through her brother
to say that he would be glad to aid the enquiry in any way he
could—an offer which he made good with the most cordial
co-operation.   Much correspondence and many interviews with
him and with the Assistant Commissioners followed.   Mr. Roby
sent to Miss Davies copies of the circulars to be addressed to
schools, instructions to Assistant Commissioners, and questions
for witnesses, for her to criticize ; and at her suggestion Mark
Pattison, Huxley and Mill were included among the witnesses.
" I should like," she wrote to Mr. Roby, " to have Huxley examined about the brain, because that physiological argument is
constantly used, and people believe it.   It seems to me the most
rational plan to examine schoolmistresses, who know the subject,
but considering the Commissioners' native propensities, and also
that the evidence of distinguished people has some chance of
being read, it might answer our purposes best to get some men
like Mark Pattison and Lord Wrottesley to testify.   I don't think
they know anything, but they might be primed."   She wished
some enquiry to be made as to what was done for girls over
sixteen, and " whether in the case of public schools for girls
it is desirable that ladies should take part in the management."

The value of the step gained by the inclusion of girls' schools

[1] *Report of the Schools Enquiry Commission*, Vol. II, p. 272.   The
signatories include Dean Stanley and his wife Lady Augusta Stanley,
Dean Alford, Lady Stanley of Alderley, Mr. Russell Gurney, Miss
Boucherett, Miss Clough, Miss Beale, Miss Buss, Miss Wolstenholme.

in the enquiry was perhaps hardly realized to the full at the moment. The Commission proved to be of the utmost national importance. It was the first attempt to survey the field of secondary schools in general. The personnel was a strong one, and the Report, which broke entirely new ground, was very full and searching. Its publication in 1868 led immediately to the Endowed Schools Act and other reforms, and was immensely powerful in stimulating interest in education. That the needs of girls should be included in this epoch-making enquiry was a great step in the progress of women. The Report showed that the boys' as well as the girls' schools were far from satisfactory— a fact that must be remembered in relation to the much-discussed question as to whether girls' education should be assimilated to boys' or should strike out on new lines.

The enquiry into endowments attracted a great deal of attention, and here it was desirable to bring the needs of girls before the public. Miss Davies set to work to prepare a paper on *The Application of Funds to the Education of Girls* for the next congress of the Social Science Association. Referring to the evidence of the four Commissions which had reported on charities between 1819 and 1837, she notices that the terms of many foundation deeds suggest that the educational charities were intended for children of both sexes, but in many cases it had become customary to allow only boys to benefit.[1]

" The modern theory," she writes, " which when pushed to its extreme length, almost implies that whatever learning is good for boys must be bad for girls, and *vice versa*, was in earlier times scarcely known. The framers of school programmes offered to boys and girls alike a common curriculum, the best they were able to devise ; sometimes specifying the particular subjects, sometimes summing them up in some such general formula as ' grammar and other virtuous and

---

[1] The most striking case was that of Christ's Hospital. This charity expended about £49,000 per annum on education. Their boys' school contained over 1,000 pupils, with twenty-seven masters, of whom more than half were University men. The girls' school at this date contained eighteen girls under one mistress. " They are neither intellectually nor industrially trained. They have no physical education," wrote Mr. Fearon in his Report (*Report of Schools Enquiry Commission*, Vol. VII, Appendix V).

godly learning,' but never prescribing, on the one hand, classics and mathematics for boys, and on the other, modern languages and the Fine Arts for girls. We are not told that it was with any special view to girls that, at Stow-on-the-Wold, the schoolmaster was required to teach, in addition to the Latin tongue, ' other more polite literature and science '; that in the City of Coventry Free Grammar School, ' grammar and music ' were the subjects prescribed ; and that ' music and good manners ' formed part of the ancient curriculum at Dulwich College."

On the other hand she quotes the statutes of several charities where it is expressly stated that boys and girls alike are to learn reading, writing, arithmetic, and Latin grammar.

" The general impression produced by a perusal of these reports is that the founders were not as a rule thinking about sex at all. . . . This was natural at a time when it was the prevailing custom in the highest classes for the boys and girls of a family to be taught together by the same tutor. It seems probable that the founder of a school for ' the children of the parish,' in the time of Queen Elizabeth, would almost as soon have thought of specifying that it was for both boys and girls, as the builders of a parish church would now of announcing that it was intended for both men and women. No doubt many people in those days considered learning more the business of men than of women, just as some people now consider religion more the business of women than of men ; but it appears that, in either case, the thought of exclusion would be almost equally remote."

She goes on to say that, mixed education being now not looked on with favour, some separate provision ought to be made for girls. Endowments are wanted for new girls' schools, for teachers' salaries, and for scholarships. " The foundation of scholarships and exhibitions, though as yet very unusual in girls' schools, is not without precedent." The great thing wanted, she thinks, is to strengthen the existing Ladies' Colleges (Queen's College and Bedford College) and extend the range of their influence. " It is certain that those who know much about the lives of girls just entering upon womanhood are strongly convinced of the injurious effect of suddenly throwing them upon their own resources, removing the restraints of school discipline without any intermediate process, and leaving them exposed to all the temptations of idleness and vanity."

The paper was read at the Social Science Congress held in May, 1865, at Sheffield. Miss Davies and Miss Garrett attended the Congress together, and went on from there to visit Miss Richardson at Grasmere. The Assistant Commissioners had begun their investigations, and she had some correspondence with them about their work. Mr. Bryce, whose district was Lancashire, visited the Lake district in October, and went to see Miss Richardson, through Miss Davies's introduction. "Please be kind to him," wrote Miss Davies to Miss Richardson, " he gets plenty of cold water thrown upon him by other people."

In the middle of November, 1865, Mr. Roby wrote to Miss Davies warning her that she would be wanted as a witness before the Commission at the end of the month. " Whom shall I ask to follow you ? " he wrote. " I thought of the Principal of Bedford College, but shall be quite ready to adopt any suggestions you will kindly give me as to that."

(Miss Davies to Mr. Roby.)

November 18, 1865.

" I have seen some of the Bedford College ladies and we think Miss Buss will be the best person to summon for the 30th. . . . What I have to say might I think be arranged under four heads :

Local Examinations,
Education of girls after leaving school,
Uses of Endowments, and
Government of Endowed Schools.

' Education ' of course means the absence of it. I suppose that head will be understood as including the want of examinations for women. If you think these four points would make a very long story, the Uses of Endowments might be left out. I should be very sorry to take up too much time, so as to run Miss Buss short, as she can speak from long experience in school work and knows the subject thoroughly. . . . I suppose it is not worth while to exert oneself to invent schemes for Colleges or schools, as the Commissioners are not likely to make specific recommendations. I have an extreme repugnance to thinking about details any more than is necessary."

This last sentence means only that she had a repugnance to wasting thoughts on castles in the air. When it came to practicable schemes, Miss Davies worked at details, down to the smallest, with untiring interest and enthusiasm, and her care in mastering

135

them and preparing them beforehand counted for much in her success. But she did not get lost in detail. A criticism which she once made on a Girtonian with whom she had worked may be recalled : " X does not know which things are important and which are not ; that's a bad fault." It was a mistake which she herself seldom made ; she did not let details smother the end in view. On this occasion, having thought out the heads of her evidence beforehand, and being already personally acquainted with some of the Commissioners, including Lord Lyttelton and Mr. Acland, she was able to answer their questions with self-possession. Her evidence brought out the advantages of the Local Examinations ; the need for endowments, for inspection, for the better training of schoolmistresses, and for some provision for the education of girls after school age. Asked what she would recommend for this last need, she answered that some examination for women over eighteen was what was chiefly wanted, and the opening of the London University Examinations would be the most useful direct means that she knew of. More Colleges were needed. " There are two in London," she said (meaning Queen's and Bedford), " but they are kept down very much by the ignorance of the girls who come to them." [1]

Miss Buss was examined exhaustively on the teaching in her school, and as to her views on the condition of girls' education generally. She too felt the want of some provision for girls on leaving school. " I think," she said, " the want of inducement is such as to make it almost impossible for girls to go on cultivating themselves when they leave school. They are not old enough and strong enough to work by themselves without any help or encouragement."

Miss Davies reported to Miss Richardson that the examination was not so terrible as she had expected. " Seven people asking questions are not so bad as one alone, and they were good-natured and encouraging to the last degree." She gives the following account of it in her *Family Chronicle* :

---

[1] The age of the students at Queen's and Bedford Colleges was at this time from fourteen to eighteen (Schools Enquiry Commission, Mr. Fearon's *Report*, Vol. VII). At both colleges, junior schools had been established because it was found that the senior girls who entered were generally too ill prepared to profit by advanced teaching.

" We were both nervous, but I had some success in concealing it, and was encouraged by finding that the Commissioners instead of being banded together against the witness, so to speak, showed a disposition individually to back up the witness against his colleagues. After I had given my evidence, and was being regaled with claret and biscuits in Mr. Roby's room, Mr. Acland came hurrying in, with ' This witness is not so self-possessed as the other,' and asking me to go back, to support Miss Buss. She was almost speechless with nervousness, but she managed to give good answers to questions."

This was probably the first time that women had given evidence in person before a Royal Commission ; [1] and it was so unusual for them to appear in public except as figure-heads or spectators, that it was not surprising that the witnesses felt afraid of the unsympathetic curiosity that might be caused by their appearance. People were apt to credit " advanced " women with motives of vanity and self-seeking, and it was not understood by an indifferent public that women like Miss Buss and Miss Davies were moved by real feeling for the neglected girls whom they wished to help to a fuller and more reasonable kind of life. Miss Buss however wrote to Miss Davies that the Commissioners were " indeed kind, and more than kind . . . I cannot get over my astonishment at their civility." She need not have felt anxious as to the impression she made. Many years afterwards, Mr. Fearon, one of the Assistant Commissioners, in recalling the occasion, said, " We were all so much struck by their perfect womanliness. Why, there were tears in Miss Buss's eyes ! " [2]

(*Mr. Roby to Miss Davies.*)

December 5, 1865.

" I thought your and Miss Buss's examination went off capitally. The proofs I have not yet got. I must congratulate you on the greater

---

[1] Mrs. Chisholm gave evidence in 1847 before the House of Lords Committee on the Execution of the Criminal Laws, and Miss Carpenter in 1852 before the Parliamentary Committee of inquiry on juvenile delinquency. Miss Nightingale's evidence for the Royal Commission of 1857 on the health of the army was given in writing. Three ladies gave evidence before a Select Committee on Poor Relief in 1861. The *Englishwoman's Journal* (Aug., 1861) remarked that this " marks an epoch in social history."

[2] *Frances Mary Buss*, by A. E. Ridley, pp. 3, 4.

self-possession. . . . The Commissioners are going to have a variety next week, a Wesleyan, a Quaker, an Independent or perhaps two, and a Jesuit. No more ladies before Christmas."

After Christmas, evidence was given by six more ladies, including Miss Beale, Miss Wolstenholme, and Miss King, the Secretary to the Society for the Employment of Women.[1] Their evidence, like the Reports of the Assistant Commissioners, brings out very clearly the need for a reform in public opinion. We find it said again and again that parents neither demand nor will pay for good teaching for their daughters ; nothing is thoroughly well taught to girls ; their want of education shows itself in after life, as one witness [2] said, " most miserably," making them restless and unreasonable, and wasters of time. It was a satisfaction to know that this wretched state of things had been brought to light.

(Miss Davies to Madame Bodichon.)

(Date missing.)

" I am sending you the evidence Miss Buss and I gave before the Commission. We got thro' very well. The Commissioners were excessively kind and encouraging, and they struck me as being favourably disposed towards women generally. I think you will be pleased with Miss Buss's evidence. . . . I feel very hopeful about things in general. The schoolmistresses seem very ready to join in any efforts at improvement, and of course that is an immense point. It is quite striking and almost pathetic to see the eagerness with which they respond to any encouragement or anything like a helping hand held out to them. We had a gathering last week to meet some of the Commission people. We put Dr. Hodgson in the Chair and he conducted very nicely. To my surprise, several of the schoolmistresses spoke, and did it very well. The best speech was from Mr. Roby, the Secretary to the Commission. He said he thought there was a great ferment going on about the education of women, and he hoped it would go further and be helped by the investigations of the Commission. This is exactly what I think is the fact. The Assistant Commissioners, with scarcely an exception, go in for the girls, and it is most useful to have them going about, stirring up and encouraging the schoolmistresses. I send you some questions propounded by

---

[1] *Report of Schools Enquiry Commission*, Vol. V.
[2] Miss E. E. Smith of Bedford College.

Mr. Fearon.[1] Will you kindly answer those that you have an opinion upon, and return them to me as soon as you can. . . . It is very amusing to hear the Assistant Commissioners' theories about the female mind. I am looking forward to their Reports with great curiosity. They are all drawing them up now. . . . I write about nothing but business, because I really have not time for anything else, and I hear of Nannie and your other concerns from Jane Crow."

The Assistant Commissioners found, like Madame Bodichon, that schoolmistresses were apt to be frightened or offended by their enquiries. They succeeded however in visiting a large number of schools, and their reports concur in giving a depressing picture of the education of girls. Mr. Fitch found it generally assumed that " ladylike manners and deportment " were more important for a girl than intellectual training, and that the two were incompatible. " Everywhere the fact that the pupil is to become a woman and not a man operates upon her course of study negatively, not positively," he writes. " It deprives her of the kind of teaching which boys have, but it gives her little or nothing in exchange." Mr. Bryce writes of the " frivolity and languor " of girls' schools ; the teaching, he found, was scrappy, lifeless, and superficial, and the girls suffered from the want of any real interest as much as from the want of games and physical exercise. " The thing most needed," he writes, " is to get rid of that singular theory of girls' education by which parents are at present governed—to make them believe that a girl has an intellect just as much as a boy, that it was meant to be used and improved, and that it is not to refinement and modesty that a cultivated intelligence is opposed, but to vapidity and languor and vulgarity of mind, to the love of gossip and the love of dress." The Commissioners endorsed Mr. Bryce's views, though in more guarded language. We read in their Report that " there is weighty evidence to the effect that the essential capacity for learning is the same, or nearly the same, in both sexes "; although " there is a long-established and inveterate

[1] Mr. D. R. Fearon, Assistant Commissioner for London. Madame Bodichon's experience with the Portman Hall School made useful material for evidence. Unluckily Mr. Fearon could not inspect the school as it had been closed in 1864, owing to difficulties consequent on Madame Bodichon's frequent absences abroad.

prejudice . . . that girls are less capable of mental cultivation, and less in need of it, than boys." [1]

Mr. Bryce's Report concluded with the proposal of some practical remedies, namely, that girls' schools should be established under public authority and supervision ; that the subjects and methods of instruction should be thoroughly revised ; and that higher education should be provided for women. All these proposals were approved by the Commissioners, and were gradually carried into effect by various agencies, which the Report of the Commission did much to stimulate.

One of the chief initial difficulties was, of course, the provision of competent women teachers. Among the difficulties under which schoolmistresses laboured, Mr. Bryce mentioned their isolation. This was a matter which Miss Davies had already set herself to remedy.

(Miss Davies to Madame Bodichon.)

February 19, 1866.

" We are about to organize a Schoolmistresses' meeting, a thing analogous to a clerical meeting, which I expect will be useful, partly as a propagandist institution, the more intelligent gradually enlightening the dark and ignorant, and partly as a body (if it ever grows strong enough) which can speak and act with some authority."

This was the London Schoolmistresses' Association, which was formed at a meeting held at Miss Davies's house on March 9, 1866, when twenty-five ladies were present. Meetings were held at the houses of members in rotation, at intervals of two or three months, when papers were read on subjects interesting to teachers. Among the early members were Miss Buss, Miss Chessar, Miss Manning, Miss Octavia Hill, Mrs. Malleson, Miss Metcalfe, and Miss Bostock. Miss Davies was Secretary during the whole twenty-two years of the Association's existence. It was the first organized attempt in London to break down the isolation which had been the lot of teachers. There was a Schoolmistresses' Association in Manchester, with which the London Association was in touch from the first, and others soon sprang up in Bristol, Leeds and elsewhere. It is curious to read in one of the early Reports that some teachers have " scarcely so

---

[1] Report of Schools Enquiry Commission, Vol. I, Chap. VI.

much as a speaking acquaintance with any professional associate."
The Cambridge Local Examinations had done something to
bring teachers into communication with each other, and further
organization became necessary in connection with some proposals
made by Miss Clough for co-operation in teaching. These proposals, which were discussed by the London Association in
January, 1867, led to fruitful results through the formation
in the following winter of the North of England Council for
Promoting the Higher Education of Women.

That a Council of men and women should be established for
such an object was a sign, among others, of the new interest that
was being awakened in the education of women. The stimulus
given by the Schools Enquiry Commission will be appreciated if
its Report is compared with the Report of the Royal Commission
of 1894 on Secondary Education. This Commission, with Mr.
Bryce as its chairman, was not likely to overlook the interests of
girls ; and there are many signs in its Report of the revolution that had taken place in public opinion during the past thirty
years. We find three women [1] among the seventeen Commissioners, and five among the fourteen Assistant Commissioners ;
women are not only called as witnesses, but their evidence is
treated in the Report as contributing to the general subject, and
not kept in a separate compartment for girls. It is assumed
throughout that the education of women is a matter of national
importance, and that girls are capable of profiting by good teaching. Mixed schools for boys and girls are spoken of with approval
in several passages,[2] and in one of these, relating to the provision
to be made for rural districts, it is expressly stated that " the
duty and the interest of the community require equal provision
to be made for both sexes." As regards endowments, the
advance made since the Commission of 1864 is compared with
the great movement for the endowment of boys' schools after the
Reformation. Whereas twelve endowed girls' schools were
reported in 1864, there were in 1894 about eighty. Private
schools had greatly improved, and schools under public manage-

[1] Lady Frederick Cavendish, Mrs. Bryant, D.Sc., and Mrs. Henry
Sidgwick.
[2] *Report of the Royal Commission on Secondary Education*, 1895,
Vol. I, pp. 159, 285, 297.

ment (such as those of the Girls' Public Day Schools Company) had sprung into existence. In the words of the Report of 1894, " There has probably been more change in the condition of the Secondary Education of girls than in any other department of education." [1]

As regards higher education for women, the advance recorded is at least equally striking. The thing did not exist in 1864. In 1894, no fewer than eleven University colleges were open to women as well as to men ; five new colleges had been established expressly for women (Girton, Newnham, Somerville, Lady Margaret Hall, and Holloway) ; while, as the Report says, " another women's college (Bedford College, London) has attained a rank equal to that of these five." The ancient universities had not been injured by this new movement ; on the contrary the number of undergraduates at Oxford and Cambridge had doubled. [2] The correlation of girls' schools with the Universities is discussed in a passage of the Report [3] which alone would suffice to show that women's education had come to be viewed in an entirely new light by the experts, if not by the general public.

It was the Commission of 1864 that first enabled this new light to penetrate the darkness in which the subject had been enveloped. In Miss Davies's contribution to the Social Science Congress of that year, *On Secondary Instruction as relating to Girls*, she described the then existing state of things—the ignorance, idleness and dullness which were accepted as the normal lot of girls. In 1866, while the Commissioners were still at work preparing their report, she published a book on *The Higher Education of Women*, in which the matter is carried a step further. What, she asks, ought the education of girls to be trying to make of them ? " Many persons will reply, without hesitation, that the one object is to make good wives and mothers." This, she argues, is too limited ; education ought to aim at producing " women of the best and highest type," without limitation as to their subsequent functions. But what is the best and highest type ? " The only intelligible principle on which modern critics show anything like unanimity is that women are intended to supply, and ought to be made, something which men want. What that

[1] P. 75 *et seq.*   [2] Introduction to Report of 1894, p. 11.
[3] Report of 1894, pp. 232–4.

may be, it is not easy to discover." She quotes the current contradictory opinions ; some men want women to be accomplished, others (including the *Saturday Review*) are bored with accomplishments ; Anthony Trollope likes them to be timid, Arthur Helps complains of their want of courage ; some would like them to be gently tyrannical and charmingly capricious, while Mr. Coventry Patmore demands patient and soothing treatment for a husband's ill-temper.

" Conceive a governess or schoolmistress, duly impressed with the obligation of training her pupils to be accomplished pleasers of men, and trying to fashion for them a model out of such materials ! Must not the result be simply blank despair ? . . . Might it not be as well to abandon this distracting theory—to discard the shifting standard of opinion, and to fall back upon the old doctrine which teaches educators to seek in every human soul for that divine image which it is their work to call out and to develop ? "[1]

In a chapter entitled *Things as they are*, Miss Davies put the case of the untrained and unemployed girl with much feeling :

" There is no point on which schoolmistresses are more unanimous and emphatic than on the difficulty of knowing what to do with girls after leaving school. People who have not been brought into intimate converse with young women have little idea of the extent to which they suffer from perplexities of conscience. ' The discontent of the modern girl ' is not mere idle self-torture. Busy men and women— and people with disciplined minds—can only by a certain strain of the imagination conceive the situation. For the case of the modern girl is peculiarly hard in this, that she has fallen upon an age in which idleness is accounted disgraceful. The social atmosphere rings with exhortations to act, act in the living present.[2] . . . The advice given,

---

[1] A similar thought was expressed by Mr. Fitch, in connection with the fact that most of the endowments for girls were not for grammar schools but for charity schools where they were trained as servants. The boys were trained " to serve God and the State "—the girls to contribute to the comfort of their betters, as apprentices or servants. A. E. Ridley, *Frances Mary Buss*, p. 9 ; *Women and the Universities*, by J. G. Fitch, *Contemporary Review*, August, 1890.

[2] Cf. " Be good, sweet maid, and let who will be clever.
Do noble things, not dream them all day long."

so easy to offer, so hard to follow, presupposes exactly what is wanting, a formed and disciplined character, able to stand alone, and to follow steadily a predetermined course, without fear of punishment or hope of reward. . . . What society says to girls seems to be something to this effect. Either you have force enough to win a place in the world, in the face of heavy discouragement, or you have not. If you have, the discipline of the struggle is good for you ; if you have not, you are not worth troubling about. Is not this a hard thing to say to commonplace girls, not professing to be better or stronger than their neighbours ? Why should their task be made, by social and domestic arrangements, peculiarly and needlessly difficult ? And why should it be taken for granted that, if they fail, they must be extraordinarily silly or self-indulgent ? "

The remedy she proposes is to provide an education corresponding with that given by the Universities to young men— " in other words, ' the education of a lady,' considered irrespectively of any specific uses to which it may afterwards be turned." How far it may be desirable for women to take part in politics, she says, is a vexed question, but there is no doubt that an intellectual training is needed for all the purposes of life—for all kinds of work, social, philanthropic and professional, educational and literary, and as " the best corrective of the tendency to take petty views of things, and on this account is specially to be desired for women on whom it devolves to give the tone to ' society.' " She meets frankly the objections that women may be tempted to neglect their home duties :

" It does not follow that because a temptation exists, it must be irresistible. To construct a plan of life absolutely free from temptation is a simple impossibility, even supposing it to be desirable. Every career has its snares, and a life of narrow interests and responsibilities is no exception to the rule. The true safeguard seems to consist, not in restraints and limitations, but in a vivid sense of all that is involved in the closest relationships, and in a steadfast habit of submission to duty. In the present case it may be noted that, however fascinating the temptation may be, it is at any rate open and well understood. . . . The paramount importance of home duties is enforced by all the sanctions of an overwhelming public opinion. . . . Any neglect is liable to be punished . . . by universal disapproval."

These general considerations form the main substance of the book, but in a chapter entitled *Specific Suggestions* she mentions and enlarges on some of the points contained in her evidence before the Schools Enquiry Commission—the admission of women to examinations of a high standard, an increase in the number of colleges, and a reduction of the cost of girls' education by the organization of larger schools and the application of endowments.

A copy of the book was sent to Matthew Arnold, who wrote that he thought it " very pleasantly written, as well as full of things that are true." It was received with warm approval by women who shared Miss Davies's views, and were delighted to see their own feelings expressed. Miss Helen Taylor wrote : " I have just finished your book, which I like better and better. . . . It will be well that the matter of this should sink into many half-prepared minds, and when it has had time to do its work, you can carry out the same ideas still further." Miss Cobbe wrote :

" I must thank you for sending me your *capital* book. I have not read anything which delighted me so much this many a day—the sense, and the fun ! Your quiet bits of sarcasm are *impayable*. I think the book can't fail to do good, for you have met the enemy at every point. . . . The tone of calm good sense is precisely the one to be assumed in the question. Half our mischief comes from *screaming* American advocates. Of course I shall be delighted to review the book."

Mrs. Grote thought that Miss Davies had described admirably " the moral and mental disease which now disfigures female existence," but that the remedies proposed were inadequate. Miss Davies's " specific suggestions " were indeed set forth very modestly and occupied a small space in the book. But all were practicable and she was working hard to bring them into practice. Feeling her way towards some plan for establishing a College of University standing, she applied in April, 1866, for the post of Assistant Secretary at Queen's College, Harley Street. Mr. Plumptre (the Dean) had informed her of the vacancy in a letter which seemed almost to amount to an invitation to apply. " My idea," she writes in her *Chronicle*, " was that if I were inside the place, I might be able to help forward some plan for the affiliation of the College to the University of Cambridge, which at that time was our modest aspiration."

Though not appointed to the post, she did not give up the

object in view, and after an interval she wrote to Mr. Plumptre to sound him as to the possibilities of her plan.

(*Miss Davies to Mr. Plumptre.*)

[*September*, 1866.]

" I have been asked to attend a meeting of schoolmistresses at Manchester on the 6th [of October], chiefly for the purpose of talking to them about the London Colleges. . . . I find among the higher class of schoolmistresses in all parts of the country a strong disposition to put themselves into friendly relations with the London Colleges. They would like their schools to be to the Colleges what the Public Schools are to the Universities, but with that view they want the Colleges to be *really* places of higher education than schools can be. Hitherto they have been more like rival schools. In fact I have heard of a case in which a girl was sent first to College, and then to school to finish. I do not see how this can be got over excepting by raising the age of the College students and giving them some higher kind of examination than any that is open to schools. I believe there would be no difficulty in getting these from Cambridge, if the Colleges are willing to accept what the University has to give, that is, the examinations for Ordinary Degrees. . . . It seems to me that this kind of affiliation to Cambridge would in the case of Queen's College be much more satisfactory than anything we are likely to get from the London University, and I am sure it would make the College much more popular with the schools and more looked up to in the country generally than it now is. I am afraid Bedford College will be shut out by its constitution, as the Cambridge Little-Go examination includes some little Theology and at Bedford College they get over the religious difficulty by excluding it. I suppose Greek is more likely to be the stumbling-block at Queen's. . . .

" The schoolmistresses insist very much that they want something to work up to. They would gladly prepare for the Colleges if they knew in what direction to work. I do not know how far it may be possible to meet them in this and other respects. There are now means of mutual communication which might be made use of, if necessary. There are Associations of Schoolmistresses already in London and at Manchester, and one is in course of formation for the West Riding. I think there will probably be some similar organization before long for Newcastle and the neighbourhood. We have come to these thro' the Local Examinations, but we are finding more and more that the Local Examinations are not enough. They are very useful so far as they go, but the higher class of schools are not satisfied to ' finish ' their pupils at seventeen. In fact they distinctly prefer not finishing at all, but transferring them to a different kind of teaching."

Mr. Plumptre did not think that anything could be done at Queen's College. " I doubt," he wrote, " whether it would be wise to raise the age limit of admission until public opinion has ripened on the matter of employment for women. As it is, our girls stay often till 18 or 19, and, without professional objects, not many fathers would keep them later. I am glad to hear of the Cambridge idea, but I anticipate the same kind of difficulty."

" I had reason to know," writes Miss Davies in her *Chronicle*, " from informal communications, that at Bedford College they were equally unwilling to move. They were afraid that raising the age of admission and setting up an Entrance Examination would reduce their numbers to a ruinous extent. The failure of this effort was a great disappointment to me at the time, but it was no doubt a blessing in disguise, as if the existing Colleges had responded to our overtures, it would probably have stood in the way of the better things which were in store."

Events were in fact leading her to the point at which she perceived that what was wanted could only be supplied by the foundation of a new College. This was soon to become the absorbing interest of her life, and her chief occupation for nearly forty years.

Before entering on the story of the new foundation, a word may be said as to some of the various works which had hitherto occupied Miss Davies's time. The Kensington Society was dissolved in the spring of 1868. It had been in operation for only three years, but it had served a useful purpose, and Mrs. Manning was anxious that it should come to an end " before it had become a bore." Its objects were met partly by the Suffrage societies, partly by educational associations such as the London School-mistresses' Association. In course of time, this last was in its turn supplanted by newer organizations, such as the Associations of Head Mistresses and Assistant Mistresses. When the London Association came to an end, in 1888, an address, together with a gold watch and chain, was presented to Miss Davies by the members, in recognition of her work as Secretary during the whole period of its existence.

CHAPTER IX

The College : A Vision. 1866–1867

SO long ago as 1847, Tennyson had portrayed in *The Princess* a college where women could enjoy the highest kind of education. The vision, though fantastic, was not forgotten ; and it remained, in the clouds indeed, but occasionally seen and remembered. A college for women became a definite object of aspiration to Madame Bodichon when, a couple of years later, she visited her brother Benjamin, then an undergraduate at Jesus College, Cambridge. But it was too soon ; she was only twenty-two ; and public opinion was as yet comfortably unconscious of any deficiency in the education of women. Ten years later, the deficiencies were beginning to make themselves felt. " When shall we see anything like ' a University for maidens ' ? " asked a writer on *Colleges for Girls* in the *Englishwoman's Journal* of February, 1859, quoting *The Princess*. The idea was becoming familiar, but Tennyson had given to it associations which were sublime, sentimental, absurd—anything rather than practical. Miss Davies set herself to bring the castle in the air down to earth, a task for whose practical difficulties her previous experience had been the best of preparations.

The meeting of schoolmistresses at Manchester on October 6, 1866, at which the subject of colleges was discussed, put the final touch to the train of events which, as Miss Davies notes in her *Family Chronicle*, " led—or drove—me to the conclusion that our case could only be met by starting a new College for Women." As she drove back from the meeting to the house at which she was staying (Mr. and Mrs. Herbert Phillip's) it was borne in upon her that there was nothing else for it. Fired with the idea, she confided it to her friends, and was soon glowing with enthusiasm and full of plans for its accomplishment. Madame Bodichon was, of course, quickly secured as an ally.

(Miss Davies to Miss Richardson.)
October 25 [1866].

" I am very glad you like the idea of the College—people take to it so kindly that I have great hopes of seeing it done some day. Mrs. Bodichon is quite fired by the vision of it. . . . It is to be as beautiful as the Assize Courts at Manchester and with gardens and grounds and everything that is good for body, soul, and spirit. I don't think I told you how intensely we enjoyed the beauty of the Assize Courts. I have seen no modern building to be compared with it, and the delight we felt in it made one realize how much one's happiness may be influenced by external objects. If Mr. Waterhouse will build us a college as noble and beautiful, Mrs. —— shall have a high place in it as a reward."

December 29, 1866.

" I am very much encouraged about the College. All the Cambridge men I have spoken to about it seem to take to it. Have you seen the Students' Guide to the University of Cambridge ? We shall not be able to follow exactly, as there are no ladies (I fear) competent to be exactly what College Tutors are, but it may be made right by giving more prominence to the Professorial teaching. Professor Liveing suggests, as you did, that ladies should learn some subject with a view to teaching it. I think we may get the actual teaching done by men. What I feel most anxious about is to have connected with the College some ladies of a very high stamp, on whom the girls might fitly bestow the reverence ' dearer to true young hearts than their own praise.' "

Before the year ended, Miss Davies had drafted a " programme," as she called it,—a short leaflet stating the need for a college which should provide for young women something analogous to what the Universities provided for young men. After submitting this to the criticism of Miss Wolstenholme and Mr. Roby, who both approved it, she had a number of proof copies printed and sent to about twenty friends and possible supporters. Madame Bodichon had gone back to Algiers for the winter, and Miss Davies wrote to her there.

THE COLLEGE:

January 29, 1867.

" I wonder whether you are still full of the earthquake. I hope not *quite*, as I am full of the College and must discourse about it. Since I wrote to you last, I have been staying with the Brodies and learnt a good deal from them and in other ways, at Oxford. I saw Mr. Mark Pattison, and he entered warmly into the idea. It grieves him that we look to Cambridge instead of Oxford, but Lady Brodie says they are not ready for it yet, and if we can do it with Cambridge first, they will get up another by and by, perhaps at Reading. In the meantime, both Lady Brodie and Sir Benjamin take to ours in the friendliest way, and will I believe give us very valuable help. It raised my spirits still higher than they were before to find them so interested in the idea, because they can look at it from both sides, knowing both the College system, and the sort of young women whom we hope to get. Their approval seems like the sanction of practical people. I believe it is partly owing to their having found it answer so well to send their eldest girl from home. They did it with great hesitation, and it has worked most satisfactorily.

" Now that the scheme is about to be brought down from the clouds, it seems necessary to make some sort of a statement about it. I have drawn up the Programme of which I enclose a proof. Several people have seen it and approve, but it is only a kind of preliminary statement, subject to modification. I believe the next step must be to get up a Committee. I propose bringing it before our Examination Committee at our next meeting, but not asking them to take it up *as* a Committee, as I think we want a larger and more influential body, to give weight. The best plan seems to be to have a rather large general Committee of distinguished people, to guarantee our *sanity*, and a small Executive, to do the work. Mr. Roby, the Secretary of the Schools Enquiry Commission, who has befriended us very much all thro', thinks Lord Lyttelton will very likely accept the office of Chairman, and that we could not have a better. If we can get Lord Lyttelton, who has the reputation of being rather High Church, to be Chairman, and Lady Goldsmid to be Treasurer, I think the comprehensiveness of the scheme will be pretty well guaranteed.

" The next question will be how to set about raising the money. We are told that we ought to ask for £30,000 at least, as besides the expense of building we ought to have something in hand, in case we do not at first get students enough to make the College pay. It is not a large sum, considering that there is to be but one College of this sort for Great Britain, Ireland and the Colonies, and considering how easy it is to raise immense sums for boys' schools. But considering how few people really wish women to be educated, it is a good deal. Everything will depend, I believe, on how we start. If we begin with small subscriptions a low scale will be fixed, and everybody will give in proportion. I do not know yet what anybody is going to do, except myself. I mean to give £100, and I believe Lizzie Garrett will do something the same, but she cannot put down her name at present, as she is still partly dependent on supplies from home. Will you consider what you can do, and will you also talk to Nannie [Madame Bodichon's sister] about it. The money need not of course be paid at present. What we want is a few promises of large sums, to lead other people on. I think that, for one thing, it will make a good deal of difference as to getting support in other ways. I don't think Lord Lyttelton would like to be Chairman of a beggarly concern that would be struggling with pecuniary difficulties all its days. And I am anxious to get him, as besides being a thoroughly *good* man personally, and very much respected, he has access to the Prince of Wales and Miss Burdett-Coutts and all sorts of people. As soon as I hear from you, I shall go to Lady Goldsmid, Mr. Russell Gurney, Mr. James Heywood, the Westlakes, and two or three other people who are likely to be interested, and we may then I hope make a beginning at looking out for a site, etc. I hope we shall be able to get Waterhouse, the architect of the Manchester Assize Courts. He is going to restore Balliol College, which, as Lady Brodie says, is the very best training he could have for our purpose. I am anxious that the building should be as beautiful as we can make it. As we cannot have traditions and associations we shall want to get dignity in every other way that is open to us."

At the moment, Madame Bodichon could make no answer to this letter, for she was very ill with fever. Miss Davies soon heard that she had been ill, and was on her way home to England. " I am longing for you to be at hand," wrote Miss Davies to her. " I have so much to say to you about the College. . . . The remarks upon the Programme are very encouraging, and I think we must certainly make a beginning this year."

(*Miss Davies to Miss Anna Richardson.*)
February 4 [1867].
" I send you also a kind of Programme of the College, by which you will see that the vision is beginning to come down from the clouds. . . .
" Are you coming up for the Yearly Meeting ?[1] Do come at any

---

[1] The Friends' Meeting.

rate for something. I will take you to see Mrs. Russell Gurney, who grows more and more heavenly. . . . I want you very much to talk about the College. There is so much to say about it—to talk over, I mean—and it must be done with a kindred spirit. Miss Cook and I talk about it continually . . . We are composing a hymn in its praise, partly adapted from an ancient composition. It begins :

> For thee, O dear, dear College,
> Mine eyes their vigils keep ;
> For very love, beholding
> Thy happy name, they weep.
>
> O sweet and blessed College,
> The home of the elect,
> O sweet and blessed College,
> Which eager hearts expect.
> Etc., etc.

" Will you finish it ? (Remember, I *have* a reverent soul at the bottom, tho' it is a little way down.)"

A second and somewhat expanded version of the programme defined the main features of the plan a little more fully. " During the last few years," it ran, " an increasing desire has been manifested by young women of the upper and middle classes to carry on their education beyond the period usually assigned to it."

" In the hope of supplying the want which has been indicated, it is proposed to establish a College, in which the instruction and discipline will be expressly adapted to advanced students, and the results tested by sufficiently stringent examinations. It is intended to place the College in a healthy locality, about equidistant between London and Cambridge, thus putting it within reach of the best teaching in all the subjects of the College course. The religious instruction will be in accordance with the principles of the Church of England ; but in cases where conscientious objections are entertained, such instruction will not be obligatory. There will be University Examinations of an advanced character, open to, but not enforced upon, all students. There will also be annual examinations in all the subjects taught in the College. Briefly, the projected institution is to be, in relation to the higher class of girls' schools and home teaching, what the Universities are to the public schools for boys."

" Polly, B.A.," was Mr. Tomkinson's frivolous comment, scribbled in pencil on his copy of the programme. Other critics were not quite so light-hearted, though there was a good deal of approval. Mr. Plumptre, though friendly, was " a little startled at the magnitude of your enterprise." The schoolmistresses, who felt in their daily lives the urgent need of the College, were very cordial, and more encouraging than anybody else. " What they say," wrote Miss Davies to Lady Brodie, " is that they think the girls will want to come to the College and that if girls set their hearts upon a thing they can generally persuade their parents."

The point of religious instruction in accordance with the principles of the Church of England gave rise to some difficulties. Miss Davies took a firm line about this from the first. Miss Helen Taylor (Mill's step-daughter) declined to help the scheme, as she doubted whether it was right for people who were not members of the Church of England to subscribe money " for the direct teaching of what they believe to be untrue." Mr. Roby wrote as follows :

[*February* 27, 1867.]

" I have had a letter from Dr. Temple this morning, and in it he says that your scheme deserves encouragement, but it will fail, the public not being yet in a right frame of mind to accept such schemes. . . . I am disappointed at Dr. Temple's not being more sanguine, but at the same time am not at all inclined to be deterred by it."

Mr. Westlake fell upon the rash assertion in the programme that there would be University Examinations of an advanced character. " What University," he wrote, " has promised these ? " The statement was altered in a revised version to run as follows :

" Application will be made to the University of Cambridge to hold Examinations at the College in the subjects prescribed for the Ordinary (or Poll) Degree . . . in the final Examinations for which a choice is now offered between Theology, Moral Science . . . Natural Science, . . . and other subjects. In case this arrangement should be found impracticable, it is proposed to hold equivalent Examinations under the direction of the Syndicate appointed by the University to provide for the Examination of Schools. . . . There will also be periodical Examinations in all the subjects taught in the College, including, in addition to those above referred to, Modern Languages, Music, Drawing, and other subjects which usually form part of the education of an English lady. . . . Students will be admitted at the age of sixteen and upwards."

The College here sketched is not really analogous to an institution of University rank. It falls below that standard as regards both the age of the students and the curriculum. Honours examinations form no part of the scheme. The College is to be connected with the University by means of the Poll Degree examinations. The inclusion of "modern languages, music, drawing, and the other subjects which usually form part of the education of an English lady," is a departure from the University curriculum, in which at that time none of these were included. Mathematics and Classics still held the first place at Cambridge. The range had in recent years been somewhat widened owing to the action of the Master of Trinity, Dr. Whewell, in promoting the study of Natural Sciences and Moral Sciences. But these subjects were not popular, and for modern languages and history there was no provision whatever. It was of course precisely in Mathematics and Classics that girls were specially ill prepared and supposed to be incapable of excelling. It therefore seemed natural to ask for the Poll Degree examinations, but unluckily these were thought unsatisfactory by many good judges. Professor Seeley, Mr. Bryce, and Professor Sidgwick considered that they were of little value as an educational test, and that it would be a mistake to tie the new College down to a system that was bad for men, who were at least supposed to be prepared for it, and still more so for women, who were not. It must be remembered that at this time the air was full of plans for University reform. "At both Oxford and Cambridge a powerful body of men, representing much of the highest intellect of the country, and becoming increasingly influential between 1850 and 1882, was constantly promoting the cause of Reform."[1] The agitation for the abolition of religious tests at the Universities had been renewed with fresh vigour since 1864, and was soon to be carried to a successful issue, in 1871.[2] Naturally the reformers felt that

[1] *Report of the Royal Commission* of 1919 *on the Universities of Oxford and Cambridge*, p. 20.
[2] *History of University Reform*, by A. I. Tillyard, Chap. IX.

women, being untrammelled by educational systems of any kind, had a precious opportunity open to them of striking out on new lines.

(Professor Seeley to Miss Davies.)

VIENNA,

August 15 [1867].

" I shall be most happy to give my name to your scheme if it can be of any use to you . . . for tho' I do not feel able to judge whether a University education would be good for women generally, there are evidently some for whom it would be good, and the experiment is worth trying for the others. I only hope you will not copy Oxford and Cambridge too closely, at any rate Cambridge, which I think is in a very bad state. The German Universities seem to me to be the right model, not the English ones."

Mr. Bryce sounded a similar note.

(Mr. James Bryce to Miss Davies.)

June 4 [1867].

" The circular seems to me so clear and well drawn that I don't find any suggestions to make. As to the religious difficulty, I can't say that I like the solution proposed, but I suppose no other is admissible. I doubt rather as to the propriety of holding examinations exactly similar to the Cambridge examinations for a degree. These examin-ations—so far as they are pass or poll examinations—are really very bad and quite unworthy of a University. Those of Oxford are just as bad—in fact they are little better than a farce. It would be much better for a new institution not only to set up a higher standard than the contemptibly low one of Oxford and Cambridge, but to let the examinations be in subjects and on text-books better chosen and of more educational value. . . ."

June 12 [1867].

" Last Sunday I was at Cambridge and showed your prospectus to Mr. Henry Sidgwick, the fame of whom you have perhaps heard. He is an earnest sympathizer. He regretted greatly that you should choose a place between London and Cambridge only, urging that you were likely in the end to get at least as much help from Oxford as from Cambridge, and hoping therefore that Bletchley would be pitched upon as accessible from all three places. At Hertford or Hitchin you would be quite cut off from Oxford.

" He also agreed in the view that it would be a mistake to start with an examination exactly similar to that at Cambridge. . . . The poll examination at Cambridge has quite too low a standard to be really useful, the honour examinations, i.e. the mathematical and classical triposes, have too high a one, not too high for the natural abilities of girls, but too high for any training schools now give them, or can for a good many years be made to give them. . . ."

November 26 [1867].

" Mr. Roby tells me some things which make me desire to send you a word or two to remove misapprehension.

" It is not in the least because you propose to imitate Cambridge rather than Oxford that I or any of the other objectors have objected to your plan—we, at Oxford, are not quite so pettily jealous of our rival as all that. Nor is it because we desire to have one system of training for girls and another for boys. On the contrary it seems to me that the more the two are assimilated the better for both. It is simply because we think the present examination system a bad one, and the present standard too low a one, both at Oxford and at Cambridge—because we think it a pity to load a new institution at starting with those very vices whose existence we deplore in an old one. In our view the course at your new College ought to be a model for men's Colleges to follow, instead of a slavish copy of their faults. . . .

" I don't say this by way of asking you to resume a discussion of the matter, for I don't expect to convince you, and very likely you are practically right and we wrong. I desire only to explain what we mean."

Miss Davies felt it to be of supreme importance that women should be admitted to a place in the educational system already in existence. She was convinced that they could secure the means of progress in no other way than by taking their place in the system already devised by men—a system the reform of which, as we have seen, was engaging some of the best minds of the Universities. If any new scheme specially devised for women were to succeed, it would have to win the general approval of those who cared for education, and had the knowledge and experience necessary for putting such a scheme into execution. The practical difficulties would thus be enormously increased, and the dangers of introducing a double standard made any compensating advantages very doubtful. Neither Mr. Bryce nor any one else, therefore, ever succeeded in turning her aside from her determination that women students should be submitted to the same tests, and have the same opportunities as men. Mr. Bryce and Mr. Roby, however, continued to help with her plans, in spite of these differences of opinion.

Meanwhile, it was necessary to get together a working committee to carry out the College scheme. In March, 1867, Miss Davies wrote to Lady Brodie : " We shall not begin to do much till the Local Examinations Scheme is confirmed, which will probably be this month or next. It seems to be pretty safe. . . . As soon as we get the Report of the Syndicate, we shall have a meeting of our Examinations Committee, and I mean then to talk to them about the College and see if they will help."

The Committee met early in April, and considered a proposal " to found a College for women, with a view to preparing candidates for the examinations of the University of Cambridge." After a good deal of discussion they resolved not to undertake the project. This was just what Miss Davies wanted, as she had written to Madame Bodichon. In a letter to the same correspondent she described their discussion :

(Miss Davies to Madame Bodichon.)
April 6, 1867.

" We had an exciting debate over the College project. Lady Goldsmid, who could not come, wrote to say that she could not make up her mind to take any part at present. She thought we had better wait till the ferment about the Franchise is over. Mr. Gurney sent word that he could not give his adhesion till he knew more about the domestic arrangements and how the young ladies were to be looked after. Mr. Hastings said he would do anything he could for us and then went away. (He had an engagement.) Miss Bostock made a protest against mixing it up with the Examinations Committee. So we agreed to consider that the Chairman had left the Chair, and then went on. Miss Bostock opposed, Mrs. Wedgwood hesitated, Mr. Tomkinson and Mr. Clay were very strongly in favour. Mrs. Wedgwood asked whether we thought young women would like to go from home to College, and then our side had to admit that the weak point of our scheme was that the girls would want to come and would hate to go home. . . . Mr. Clay and Mr. Tomkinson are almost too strong on our side and too determined to make the College a paradise. They insisted that the girls should have breakfast in their own rooms (instead of all together like a school) as if the whole thing depended upon it. Mr. Clay said if we could only open it, he was sure we should be overflowing with students. . . . It was amusing to hear them talk about the examinations. They evidently thought the ordinary Degree examinations, which we are going for, rather beneath their notice. Mr. Tomkinson, who was a Wrangler himself, said he was sure girls could take Mathematical Honours with very little teaching. I see that we shall have to change our order of procedure, and instead of beginning with a large general Committee and then appointing a small one to carry out the project, we must first get together a small Committee and work out the scheme in detail, and then get as many great people as we can to sanction it. I do not think we shall be ready to come to the public before the autumn or next spring, but the delay is perhaps rather an advantage."

May 26, 1867.

" I must just send you a word of welcome on your coming back to England. It is hard to have you escaping away to Oxford and passing us coldly by, but perhaps it is best till you are stronger. . . . We are getting out a fuller Programme of the College, which I will send to you as soon as it is ready. I am longing to talk to you about it. We cannot do anything of a public sort before the autumn, but in the meantime there are endless things to talk about. It frightens me a little to see our castle coming down from the clouds and *substantiating* itself on the solid earth. For I really think it will be done.

" You will tell me when you are within reach. I feel already elated by the sense of having you in England."

On a suggestion from Mr. Bryce, it was decided to apply to the Schools Enquiry Commission, asking that a grant should be recommended for the proposed College. Mr. Roby encouraged the idea, and helped Miss Davies to draft a Memorial. The Schoolmistresses' Associations in London and Manchester gave their support, as did also Miss Clough, Miss Buss, Miss Beale, and many others. " The chief object," Miss Davies wrote to Mr. Tomkinson, " is to give the Schoolmistresses an opportunity of stating their views, as people are generally very much surprised to hear that *they* want anything beyond their own schools. If you know any nice orthodox people whose names are known, would you kindly ask them to ' support ' the Memorial ? We could get plenty of people with peculiar views of the most various sorts, but unfortunately two contradictory heretics do not make one reasonable person, which is what we want."

Plenty of contradictory heretics and reasonable persons joined in supporting the " Memorial respecting Need of Place of Higher

A VISION

Education for Girls "[1] which was sent in by Miss Davies on July
9, signed by 521 teachers of girls, and 175 others.

(*Miss Davies to Miss Anna Richardson.*)

July 18, 1867.
" It has been I think a successful stroke. The Memorial was
signed by about five hundred schoolmistresses, and ' supported ' by a
row of other people of the most singularly varied character—Tennyson,
Browning, Ruskin, Tyndall, Huxley, Sir Charles Lyell, Mr. Martineau,
Mr. Grote, Professor Bain, the proprietor of *The Record*, Dr. Angus,
champions of orthodoxy of various sects, the Bishop of St. Davids,
five Deans, a good sprinkling of Archdeacons, Canons, Fellows and
Tutors, and Professors, M.P.'s, eminent lawyers and physicians, with
Mr. Frederic Harrison and a few others to complete the medley.   I
have had some curious letters about it.   Most of them are from people
who cannot yet see their way, but there are a few for or against. . . .
Ladies generally are very shy about it.   I suppose they know that if
they give their names, they must be prepared to fight, and unless they
are very clear about it, the prospect is not pleasant."

It may be added that among the memorialists were Cambridge
en of influence, such as Dr. Henry Jackson, Professor Lightfoot,
Mr. Aldis Wright, Mr. (afterwards Professor Sir Richard) Jebb,
Dr. Kennedy and Professor Seeley.   The Memorial did not lead
to any substantial results.   The Commissioners' Report, which
appeared in twenty volumes early in 1868, contains one short
chapter on girls' schools,[2] at the end of which the question of
higher education is touched on briefly but sympathetically.
Mention is made of classes and lectures for advanced women
students, which had been set on foot at Oxford by Dr. Mark
Pattison, and in the north of England, under the inspiration of
Miss Clough.   It is then stated that a proposal has been set forth
for the establishment of a new College for women, to provide
something analogous to University education.   The Commissioners express their " cordial approval," and go on to state that " the
fact alone that ladies of so much ability and observation as those
with whom we have communicated, have applied themselves to
providing in these ways enlarged sources for occupation of time

[1] *Schools Enquiry Commission Report*, Vol. II, pp. 194–7.
[2] See above, pp. 139, 140.

159

by their own sex, and that whether as heads of families or remaining unmarried, is a strong argument for encouragement to be given to Colleges in any suitable manner by the Crown and by Parliament." Nothing came of this. Encouragement from the Crown or from Parliament could hardly have been expected at this stage. Still, it was something to have received the blessing of the Commissioners.

CHAPTER X

The College : Propaganda. 1867–1868

EARLY in 1867 Miss Davies began to look out for a working Committee for the College. " As there will be very various kinds of business to do," she wrote to Mrs. Russell Gurney, " I should like to have one or two members in each peculiar walk, who would not be expected to come when there was nothing going on in their line. On this principle, if you would be one, I could always let you know beforehand whether you would be specially wanted or not." She made out a list of people whom she had in view, with a note, against some of the names, of the " peculiar walk " attributed to the person :

Lady Stanley of Alderley.
Lady Goldsmid—Economy.
Lady Hobart—Sweetness.
The Dean of Canterbury—Greek, Divinity.
James Bryce, Esq.
Mrs. Russell Gurney—Drawing.
James Heywood, Esq.—Business.
G. W. Hastings, Esq.—The world.
Mrs. Manning.—Domestic Morals.
H. J. Roby, Esq.—Latin.
H. R. Tomkinson—Conciliation.
Rev. Sedley Taylor—Music and Mathematics.
E. D.—Principles.

Lady Brodie, Lord Lyttelton, and Dr. Temple were also invited to join, but declined, as did Lady Stanley of Alderley. Lady Stanley was in full sympathy with the scheme, but was obliged to decline because, as she wrote to Miss Davies, " it is not liked to see my name before the public." [1]

" It may be observed," writes Miss Davies in her *Chronicle*, " that the list includes no one specially known as advocating the Rights of women. It was felt to be important to put forward only such names as would be likely to win the confidence of ordinary people." For this reason, Madame Bodichon was not at first included.[2] The point was doubtless discussed and settled in August, when Miss Davies spent nearly a month at Scalands, resting after the summer's labours, which ended with a tiring week of Local Examinations.

(*Miss Davies to Miss Anna Richardson.*)

SCALANDS,

August 24, 1867.

" Many thanks for your kind enquiries and projects for my mother. She is better again, but far from strong. . . . Annie Austin is with her and Elizabeth Garrett has been looking after her very sedulously, or I could not have stayed away . . .

" This place reminds me much of Heugh Folds,[3] only that it is not a place for all the year round, but in the heat of summer it is delicious. I don't think I have ever been in such a perfectly reposeful retreat. . . . There are noises, but they are all rural, the murmuring of the wind in the trees, the buzzing of insects, barking dogs, lowing bullocks, birds twittering—nothing to remind one of mental labour and strain. I have been entering into the spirit of the place, and *almost* forgetting even the College. I send you however a list of signatures to the Memorial to the Schools Enquiry Commissioners. I have had some letters since it was sent in, from people who were abroad, etc.—a very cordial note from Lady Hobart, and one from Professor Seeley. . . .

" Mrs. Bodichon is, I am sorry to say, sadly broken down by her fever. It was a very bad attack and she has never had a fair chance of recovery, for people *won't* let her alone. It is quite a caution against forming the habit of benevolence, it is so difficult to break it off.

" I have been reading down here a novel or two (*Tancred, Ruth,* and *Quentin Durward*), Shakespeare, and I am now in the middle of the Duke of Argyll's book [*The Reign of Law*], which I find extremely

---

[1] She joined the Committee in 1872, after her husband's death.

[2] She joined in February, 1869 (Letter from Miss Davies to Madame Bodichon, February 16, 1869).

[3] Miss Richardson's house at Grasmere.

interesting. Are you reading ' Stone Edge ' in the *Cornhill* ? It is by Lady Verney, Miss Nightingale's sister. Llewelyn and family are at Aberystwyth, all flourishing."

The visit to Scalands was a time of rest from active work and correspondence, but good use was made of the opportunity to talk over plans and a number of circulars about the College project were sent out. Madame Bodichon now declared her intention of giving £1000 to the College. It was a great thing to have so large a sum with which to begin the process of " bringing the College down from the clouds." It gave substance and reality to the scheme, and showed the scale on which subscriptions were wanted. As Miss Davies said, " Everything will depend on how we start." Certain conditions were discussed. Miss Davies thought the money should be promised subject to their being able to raise a total sum of £30,000. Madame Bodichon, who held strong views as to the harm caused by mismanagement and neglect of health among women, wanted precautions to be taken to safeguard the future students. They would no doubt be as ignorant about health as the average young woman of the day, and they would be in a new position of independence and responsibility, which would have its dangers. An agreement was soon reached. " I like your Committee very much," wrote Madame Bodichon to Miss Davies, a little later. " We must do this well if we do it at all. My whole heart is in the idea."

(Madame Bodichon to Miss Davies.)
November 22 [1867].
" About giving the £1000 conditionally, I will follow your advice, so you can say it is to meet £29,000.
" I do still think something special must be done about hygiene, but I have decided to leave it to your influence and mine over you ! So now you can say you have my £1000 promised."

A set of four " resolutions," summarizing the essential points of the scheme, was now drafted by Miss Davies, and sent to each person whom she asked to join the Committee :

(1) That the following ladies and gentlemen, with power to add to their number, form a Committee for the purpose of founding a College for the higher education of women [here followed the list of names].

(2) That the College shall be, if possible, connected with the University of Cambridge, and that efforts shall be made to obtain the admission of the students, under suitable regulations, to the Examinations for Degrees of that University.

(3) That the religious services and instruction shall be in accordance with the principles of the Church of England, but that where conscientious objections are entertained, attendance at such services and instruction shall not be obligatory.

(4) That the resident authorities shall be women.

(Miss Davies to Mr. H. R. Tomkinson.)
November 9 [1867].

" You will see by the enclosed draft that we are preparing to carry out the College scheme and to claim your promised help. . . .

" People who join the Committee are supposed to agree to the four Resolutions. There has been a question whether to mention Cambridge definitely from the beginning, but it seems not unreasonable, as the whole thing has grown up out of the Cambridge Local Examinations, and it saves trouble to have the matter settled."

Mr. Tomkinson accepted his place on the Committee, and suggested that some Cambridge men, in residence at the University, should be asked to join.

(Miss Davies to Mr. H. R. Tomkinson.)
November 15 [1867].

" I quite agree with you that it will be much better for the College to be carried thro' by a large number of people than by a few fanatics, and there seems a fair prospect of very general support. We shall get Local Committees soon in several of the large provincial towns, and they will enlighten their respective neighbourhoods. . . .

" Your note was forwarded to me at Birmingham,[1] and I acted at once upon your suggestion about Cambridge, in so far as to ask Mr. Sedley Taylor, who happened to be staying in the same house, to be on the Committee, to which he very readily consented. We had thought that Cambridge residents could not conveniently attend meetings in London, and that as we hope to get a Local Committee there [at Cambridge], it might be better for them to be on that. There is another slight difficulty, that I suppose they are all young men, and our Committee is I am afraid rather deficient in the due proportion of age and

---

[1] Miss Davies was visiting Mr. and Mrs. C. E. Matthews at Birmingham, for some educational congress.

PROPAGANDA

experience. If we could get a few more old ladies like Lady Stanley of Alderley, who has six grown-up daughters and a multitude of grand-children, they might counterbalance the levity of young Cambridge."

(*Mr. Bryce to Miss Davies.*)

November 20 [1867].

" If by accepting the draft resolutions you mean that we are to waive our objections to them for the sake of giving such help as we can towards a project whose success we desire more than we dislike what we think blemishes in it, I am willing for my own part to accept the resolution about Cambridge and the examinations. You do not mean, I presume, to shut our mouths altogether upon the matter, but merely that when the majority is against us we are not to be factious.

" As to the ' religious difficulty ' . . . I need not tell you that I would far rather there was no mention of one denomination any more than another, but of course you have to look to the practical aspect of the plan, and the feelings of the English upper class. All that we care about is that the thing should not seem to be on the face of it—a denominational institution, which is just what Oxford and Cambridge are ceasing to be. In a few more years we shall have no more tests there, and no more conscience-clauses in schools : why bring them in here ? "

The College Committee met for the first time on December 5, 1867, at the Architectural Gallery, 9, Conduit Street, where rooms were usually hired for the Local Examinations. " Only Mrs. Manning, Mr. Sedley Taylor, Mr. Tomkinson, and myself were present at the meeting," writes Miss Davies in her *Chronicle*. " Mr. Roby was pressed with work on the Report of the Schools Enquiry Commission, and others were kept away by various hindrances." No exact record of the business exists, as the Minute Book was lost by Miss Davies in 1872, to her lasting regret. Letters were, however, preserved by means of which the gap may be partly filled. The four Resolutions were formally adopted, and the formation of a General Committee was discussed, as well as the " Programme," and finance. The upshot of the meeting may be gathered from Miss Davies' correspondence.

(*Mrs. Manning to Miss Davies.*)

December 6 [1867].

" In January I shall wish to be presenting £100 to the College Fund. You can announce the same at whatever time most suitable. . . . I praised our Committee very much to Adelaide. Each willing to hear and consider and suggest, and I thought your two advisers able as well as in earnest."

(*Miss Davies to Mr. H. R. Tomkinson.*)
December 7 [1867].
"Thank you very much for negotiating with the Bank. . . . I should think the best plan will be to pay in at once all the money I have received, amounting to £14 6s. There is no need to draw the £20 authorized by the Committee till we have a respectable sum to draw upon, which will probably be pretty soon. . . . I am so much obliged to you for instructing me about business. I feel very ignorant about it, and it would be disastrous to be making mistakes."

(*Miss Davies to Miss Anna Richardson.*)
December 13 [1867].
"To lose no time, I send you a Proof of the Programme finally agreed upon at the first meeting of the College Committee. We have come to no decision as yet upon details. With regard to beginning on a small scale, the counsels of experience seem to be these, that to adapt an old house is apt to cost more in the long run than to build a new one, but that it would be unwise to put off opening till we have accommodation for the full number of students. We shall *probably* (but nothing is fixed) provide for only about twenty-five at first.[1] We should like to be obliged to refuse some at first. That would be much better than having empty rooms. But there will be a great deal to consider about the staff of teachers, etc., etc., and I do not see my way even to an opinion as yet."

A General Committee was gradually got together, including three Bishops, two Deans, and other prominent people, to give the air of solidity and dignity to the proceedings which Miss Davies desired. Naturally there were a good many refusals. Sir Charles Lyell, for instance, declined on the ground that he would prefer the establishment of non-residential colleges, where young women might attend lectures and be examined, "without entirely quitting the parental roof," and without being obliged to attend Chapel.

(*Miss Davies to Miss Anna Richardson.*)
December 17, 1867.
"Your suggestion that we should get High Church names on our

---

[1] The number of students at the College did not rise to twenty-five till 1876.

Committee is admirable. I made the same myself to Mrs. Gurney the
other day. Please get us some at once. I should like Dr. Pusey."

(Miss Anna Richardson to Miss Davies.)
December 23, 1867.

" I am sorry Dr. Pusey should ' violently oppose ' a useful measure.
At the same time, one cannot expect elderly people—especially elderly
people whose own close work prevents them from seeing near needs—
to enter into what may well look rather like a volcanic upheaval in the
old paths. . . . Do you so entirely abjure Miss Yonge, as to refuse to
ask her ? Her name is so well known, and so well liked by vast numbers of young ladies, and her own claims to solid culture so real. Also,
do you think Mrs. Gatty [1] a likely lady ? She is a very nice, wise,
thoughtful woman."

(Miss Davies to Miss Anna Richardson.)
December 28 [1867].

" There are few names I should like better to have than that of Miss
Yonge, but I despair of getting it. I wrote to Miss Sewell [1] about the
Memorial and she declined on the ground that the project reminded
her of the *Princess*. Miss Rossetti declined joining anything that did
not belong to the Catholic Church (Anglo-Catholic I suppose) . . .
Miss Longley (the Archbishop's daughter) says the idea of the College
is quite contrary to her notions of women's sphere. You see I have
some reason to be discouraged . . . but I certainly should not wish to
lose either Miss Yonge or Mrs. Gatty, for want of asking. . . ."

The applications to Mrs. Gatty and Miss Yonge, as Miss Davies
had foreseen, met with refusals. " I have the greatest fears,"
wrote Mrs. Gatty to Miss Richardson, " as to the *general result
upon the tone and manner of women*, from such publicity as is proposed. *Frivolity* is sooner cured than *conceit*, and I think your
experiment dangerous. Can you blind yourself to the effects of
' publicity ' on the ladies, however excellent, who are prominent
in Social Science ? " Miss Yonge wrote that she felt that girls if
brought together in large numbers " always hurt one another in
manner and tone if in nothing else." Home education, she
thought, was " far more valuable both intellectually and morally
than any external education. . . . Superior women will teach
themselves, and inferior women will never learn more than enough

[1] See Biographical Index.

for home life." [1]   Miss Yonge's words almost seem to suggest that " inferior women " will do well enough for home life.   This she would, of course, have denied with horror, but it is not far from what Miss Davies wrote in her Birmingham paper : " It is often taken for granted that though for women who have only themselves to think of, it may be a good thing to have some intellectual resources, for *mothers* there is nothing like good sound ignorance."

(*Miss Davies to Miss Anna Richardson.*)

[*Friday*] *March* 6 [1868].

" I hope you will not get very tired of the arduous business of talking. . . . Let me tell you my Programme for Monday. 1. Lunch with Lady Goldsmid, on purpose to talk about the College. 2. Afternoon tea at Mrs. Gurney's, to meet Lady Colville and Lady Rich [2] ditto. 3. Professor Seeley and Mrs. Bodichon coming to dinner, to talk over the College curriculum, a most important and difficult business. I ought to begin the day with Bedford College, [3] but Annie [Austin] is going to take it for me. This will not sound much to you country people, who pass your lives in the extraordinarily fatiguing process of ' spending the day ' with each other and talking from morning till night —but to a quiet, not to say stagnant, Londoner so much working of the jaws is a considerable effort."

" I will do my best," wrote Professor Seeley to Miss Davies, in accepting her invitation to dinner, " with the resolution you put into my hands, though there is a good deal of difficulty in planning the course of studies."

(*Madame Bodichon to Miss Davies.*)

(*No date.*)

" I know you thought I was damped but that is not true, but I should have shut my eyes and closed my reason to all evidence if I had not seen up and down the world this last two months that there is a frightful coolness about the College. I felt at your house Mr. Seeley was

---

[1] In later life Miss Yonge changed her views somewhat. One of the principal characters in *Modern Broods* (published in 1900) goes to an Oxford women's college, and comes home much improved in character and manners.

[2] See Biographical Index.

[3] Where she was a Lady Visitor.

bored by it, and if I had followed my instinct I should not have mentioned it to him that night at all—perhaps another time he might not have been slightly oppressed and oppositive (if there is such a word). I don't know him, but I felt he was not inclined to discuss : did not you ? What really staggers me is the work before you ! I can't lose faith in the cause that was in me before you were born, and every experience of my life makes that faith more certain and more ardent. . . . I am astounded at the wonderful interest in the ' higher education,' it is going on everywhere, rolling about, this great wave of interest, and your book partly set it going.

" I am very anxious, my dear, that you should not neglect any sources of sweet waters, and I want you to call on the Lewes [' George Eliot ' and Mr. Lewes] at 2 or 2.30 before people come to-day, because they (Lewes) go away for a month on Monday. I shall be there exactly at 2.30, so you will have a seconder."

(*Miss Davies to Madame Bodichon.*)

Sunday [*March* 15 ?] 1868.

" Thank you much for your kind words. I did not think you were losing faith in the cause, but I thought you were more discouraged than need be by other people's coldness, because you expected more from them than I did. You go about bravely talking to people and expecting sympathy from them, when I should not open my mouth, and so you get the cold water showered upon you. I did not think Professor Seeley was nearly so tired of the subject as I was. . . . I am well used to the cool Cambridge manner. It is not half as pleasant as the kind, gushing way Oxford men have, but it comes to more.

" I could not go to Mrs. Lewes to-day. It would have interfered with family things. It is rather curious that she should be the only person who favours it to you. I should not have wondered much if she had been against. In fact the only thing that ever surprises me is to find anybody for it. As Lady Augusta said, ' Of *course* it is received with shouts.' I expected no less, but that is because I got so used to them and to working really almost single-handed thro' the Local Examinations and winning at last. It was carried by the help of people who were dragged in, almost against their will. So now, we glory in tribulations also ; knowing that tribulation worketh patience ; and patience, experience ; and *experience, hope*. All the good things are done (and they *do* get done) by faith and patience. The shield of faith quenches the fiery darts of the wicked. Let us run with patience the race that is set before us, looking unto Jesus the author and finisher of our faith ; who for the *joy that was set before him*, endured the cross, despising the shame. Consider him that endured such contradiction of sinners (the Fawcetts,[1] etc.) against himself, lest ye be wearied and faint in your minds. It is astonishing how much there is of parallel experience in old times. I often think of St. Paul, with his sensitive, highly strung, nervous temperament, and the amount of worry he went thro', with the care of all the churches upon him, all quarrelling and fretting and disgracing themselves, and he, *feeling* it all to the heart's core, held on, appealing and persuading and remonstrating, and every now and then coming out with songs of triumph. It makes one's own little vexations look very small.

" You will forgive my quoting so many texts as it is Sunday. Sundays and churches and prayers and sermons are my sources of sweet waters (not the only ones) and I think they will last my time whatever science may do for the next generation."

Miss Davies had made the acquaintance of George Eliot in the previous winter. " Mrs. Bodichon assures me," wrote George Eliot to her, " that you would like to call on me for the sake of some conversation on the desirable project of founding a College for women. I shall be very happy to see you on Tuesday at 4 o'clock if that time will be convenient to you."[2] The project was received with enthusiasm by George Eliot and Mr. Lewes. " We strongly object," wrote George Eliot a few days later, " to the proposal that there should be a beginning made ' on a small scale.' To spend forces and funds in this way would be a hindrance rather than a furtherance of the great scheme which is pre-eminently worth trying for. Every one concerned should be roused to understand that a great campaign has to be victualled for."

Many people would have hesitated to visit George Eliot. " I have been to see Mrs. Lewes," Miss Davies wrote to Miss Richardson, " as Mrs. Bodichon wished me to hear what she had to say about the College. She is warmly in favour of it, on good grounds. I am not sure what your feeling is about her, and till I know that you have as great a reverence for her as I have, I cannot talk to you or tell you all she said."

[1] Professor and Mrs. Fawcett were supporters of the Lectures for Women and the special examinations for women. Cf. *What I Remember*, by Dame Millicent Garrett Fawcett, pp. 72–3.

[2] Letter dated November 16, 1867.

PROPAGANDA

(Miss Davies to Mrs. Manning.)

November 25 [1867].

" Mrs. Gurney was extremely interested in hearing about Mrs. Lewes. She says it would be like a gin palace to her to have the temptation so close at hand, and prophesies that now I have once crossed the threshold I shall be constantly going. She takes the same view that you do, that it is justifiable to go and see Mrs. Lewes herself, but not to meet people at her house. She also thinks that having once taken the false step, the only thing they can do now is to stick together to the end."

Mrs. Gurney's prophecy came true. " I went afterwards," Miss Davies records, " from time to time, always at the same hour, when she had had her afternoon walk, and was to be seen alone, except that Mr. Lewes sometimes appeared."

Meanwhile, the " great campaign," as George Eliot called it, was being carried on unceasingly. Miss Davies and Madame Bodichon talked to people about the College, wrote letters, sent out circulars, and organized meetings, generally small and private, sometimes on a larger scale.

(Miss Davies to Miss Anna Richardson.)

February 21 [1868].

" I am to go down to Bristol towards the end of March, and see what can be done, and I expect to get a tolerably strong propagandist body there, to do exactly what you propose, that is, to use the local press and in other ways to diffuse information. . . . I think you are on the right track in looking for county names. They are useful by way of sanction. But the really important people are the Secretaries. We had a full and satisfactory meeting of the College Committee yesterday. It was agreed to hold a little conference or semi-public meeting some time in March. . . . Lady Augusta Stanley (who was present) and Professor Seeley were added to the Executive Committee. Their names will not give confidence either to the extreme right or the extreme left, but we are not likely to get much help from either of those quarters, and the enlightened moderates are strong enough to carry thro' a little bit of a thing like this if they get heartily interested in it. . . . Mr. Bryce thinks we might as well throw our Programmes into the fire at once, as propose a College *in* Cambridge. . . . *I* should not have asked Mr. Trevelyan to join the Committee, but it is thought that he may be useful as representing the flippant interest. . . .

171

The " little conference " was held at the Architectural Gallery on March 28, 1868. About two hundred people attended, and the audience was thought most satisfactory as to quality. The Dean of Canterbury (Dr. Alford) presided, and speeches were made by Mr. Roby, Professor Seeley, Mr. Llewelyn Davies, Mr. Hastings, Professor Lightfoot and Mr. Tomkinson, followed by some discussion. Ladies were present, but none ventured on speaking. Mrs. Austin sent an account of it all to Miss Richardson :

" Professor Seeley took up what Mr. Roby said about the desirability of residence, in answer to the objection that ' it will take girls from home,' and said that while boys generally have too little of home, girls perhaps have too much of it (buzz of approbation and assent in the audience) ; that the college will only take them away for six months ; that as popular feeling is so strong in favour of seclusion for girls, this College being in the country will give greater privacy and freedom than will be possible in a town ; that the course of study proposed at first is to aim at the ordinary Poll examination ; but, he added, of *course* we don't mean that the ladies of our College are to stop at *that* (with extreme scorn). (Great laughter and applause from audience.) . . . He ended by drawing attention to the report of one of the Commissioners (they were frequently alluded to throughout the meeting) as to the busied, engrossed lives of many fathers of families, they have no time to look after their children's education, children look most to the mothers, and for them there must be higher culture if motherhood is not to end in infancy, but in guidance and sympathy and companionship is to continue to the end. . . . All spoke as if their minds were made up, and of ' our college,' as if it certainly is to be done, which was very good to hear. . . . Mr. Tomkinson ended, with suggesting a system of nominations, saying also a good deal against nominations in general, and put it to the audience quite pathetically, ' Are they to be a necessary evil in the College ? ' . . . Mr. Roby admitted that £30,000 is sometimes a large sum, but £50,000 had been raised in a fortnight for the City of London Schools. . . . All whom we spoke to afterwards seemed much pleased, and another £100 has come in this morning from some one who professes to be only half-hearted."

(*Miss Davies to Mr. H. R. Tomkinson.*)

April [1868].

" I hope you were satisfied with the meeting. I thought the mastery of the subject shown by the Executive Committee was quite remarkable. I expected every minute that somebody would be offering to sacrifice some vital principle, but nobody did. My brother thought your part was ' perfectly done.' The Dean thought it a capital meeting and wishes our religious meetings could be cast in the same mould.

" Mr. Courtney has put his name down for £100."

George Eliot sent £50 " from the author of *Romola*," and bestirred herself to ask others to subscribe. A subscription list had already been inserted at the end of the Programme, showing (besides Madame Bodichon's £1,000) contributions of £100 each from Miss Davies, Lady Goldsmid, Mr. Heywood, Mrs. Manning, and Mr. Tomkinson. " I enclose another cheque," wrote Miss Davies to Mr. Tomkinson, " the first instalment of Miss Garrett's £100. She says it is a signal instance of faith that she promises to pay £20 yearly. She is always expecting that patients will suddenly come to an end—all get well at once—or something as calamitous as this."

The subscription list grew but slowly, and by the middle of July, 1868, only about £2,000 had been promised. An advertisement setting forth the main features of the scheme, and its needs, was sent to the papers and called forth some comment. Some of the favourable opinions were collected by Miss Davies and reprinted as a leaflet for distribution.[1] As a specimen of the unfavourable opinions, the following will show the kind of thing which had to be faced :

" Our age has been so prolific of absurdities, that we cannot well be expected to feel any very great surprise at the incubation of one foolish project more ; we therefore receive with a feeling of quiet, if somewhat contemptuous resignation, an enthusiastic appeal to us to subscribe for the foundation of ' A True College for Women.' . . . It is difficult to treat with gravity this preposterous proposal of a University career for the potential wives of Englishmen, without being betrayed into an indignation such as, nowadays, is never effective, and is not unfrequently ludicrous. Still it must on no account be supposed, because we have approached the subject in a tone of levity, that we do not consider it to be of the most serious importance. Manhood suffrage, triumph of Trades Unionism, and Secularism rampant, would be

---

[1] *Proposed New College for Women*, giving extracts from articles in *The Literary Churchman*, *The Economist* (by Mr. Hutton), *The Jewish Chronicle*, *The Queen* (by Miss Chessar), and *The Express*.

almost minor evils, compared with a system, if extensively adopted, calculated to unfit women for the performance of the very duties to which . . . women only are intended and adapted." [1]

Such were the " shouts " with which, as Lady Augusta Stanley said, the College was received. But the situation was on the whole encouraging. " It is a remarkable fact," wrote Miss Davies to Miss Richardson, " that all the people who take up the College are the very best and nicest one knows. The pleasure of working with them makes up for a great deal of cold water from the inferior sort."

Miss Davies was now preparing a paper entitled *Some Account of a Proposed College for Women*,[2] for the next Congress of the Social Science Association, to be held at Birmingham in the autumn of 1868.

(Miss Davies to Miss Anna Richardson.)

August 1, 1868.

" The Committee have arrived at the discovery that we have not been definite enough in our statements about the College life. People do not *see* it, and they hesitate about giving money to a thing about which they feel so much in the dark. Mr. Roby suggested that in the papers to be read at Birmingham, I should give a sketch of the daily life of a student. The idea seems to me a good one, but rather difficult to carry out, as we do not know yet exactly what the life will be, and one has to steer clear between the temptation to make it look very pleasant, so as to attract students, and the risk of exciting the jealousy of parents."

(Miss Davies to Mr. Tomkinson.)

August 5, 1868.

" I will try to be respectful to parents, but how is it possible to describe College life without showing how infinitely pleasanter it will be than home ? It is the weak point which I am utterly at a loss to defend. I do not believe that our utmost efforts to poison the students' lives at College will make them half so miserable as they are at home. (The bad homes, I mean, of course. Please remember that the weather is still very hot.)"

---

[1] *Essays in Defence of Women*, 1868, republished from *The Imperial Review*.

[2] Reprinted, with some omissions, in *Thoughts on Some Questions relating to Women*.

PROPAGANDA

In her paper, after noticing the deficiencies of girls' education, Miss Davies points out that something is needed to meet the wants of the two thousand sisters of the two thousand undergraduates of Cambridge.

" These sisters will be found for the most part scattered about in country houses and parsonages, and in the families of professional men and retired merchants and manufacturers. . . . Their abundant leisure and many opportunities of influence have hitherto been turned to small account. Yet how much might be made of them ! The Hall and the Rectory are the centres of light for a whole parish. If their light be darkness, how great is that darkness ! . . .

" This will be the aim of the College work. It will not be specifically directed towards changing the occupations of women, but rather towards securing that whatever they do shall be done well."

All this was only general. The details were more difficult to fill in.

" It is intended to apply, in due time, to the University of Cambridge for admission to the examinations for degrees. But . . . in the plan of study . . . a certain amount of option will be allowed. It is needless to say that no subject which competent authorities regard as fit and desirable for the higher education of an English lady will be excluded from among the studies . . . the College will be, as far as possible, officially connected with the University of Cambridge. It is not proposed to set up a new female University. . . . The College is intended to be a dependency, a living branch of Cambridge. It will aim at no higher position than, say, that of Trinity College." [1]

Stress is laid on the fact that " the discipline and internal arrangements will be under the direction of ladies " ; the Mistress and resident teachers " will exercise just so much of supervision and control as would be practised under the same circumstances by a wise mother." There will be " out of door recreation. . . . Active games, not too violent and straining, but amusing enough to be a real distraction, will alternate with country rambles as a relief from too great assiduity in the pursuit of learning." Miss Davies dwells on the advantages to the students of quiet and privacy.

---

[1] " Such a degree of humility will not be considered excessive," was *The Times'* comment (Oct. 10, 1868).

175

" Each student will have a small sitting-room to herself, where she will be free to study undisturbed, and to enjoy at her discretion the companionship of friends of her own choice. Of all the attractions offered by the college life, probably the opportunity for a certain amount of solitude, so necessary an agent in the formation of character, will be the one most welcomed by the real student. . . . It has been decided, after much consideration, to locate the College in the country. One of the strongest reasons for preferring the country is, that it would be almost impossible for young ladies of eighteen and upwards to be in London without being in London society. . . . And as most of the members of the College will come there very much for the sake of temporary seclusion, it would be cruel to bring about them in their supposed retirement the distractions from which they are trying to escape."

One cannot but feel that the College has not become quite such a calm and quiet retreat as is sketched here by Miss Davies. But her longing for privacy was in reality a longing for freedom. That the students should be unsociable was not her wish. In a letter to Miss Manning she writes : " With submission, I don't like your idea of studying in a partition. I could not *rest* (which is half the battle) in a partition, and besides, I want the students to be able to ask their chosen friends to tea in their own rooms, and one could not have a five o'clock in a partition."

The paper ends on a practical note. In order to carry out the project, two things are necessary—students and money. The former will certainly be forthcoming ; for the latter, she appeals to " the wealthy class, who in the persons of their daughters, sisters, nieces, cousins, god-daughters, and young friends will derive benefit from the College."

No discussion of Miss Davies' paper is recorded, but it was referred to by Lord Lyttelton, when addressing the Education Section as Chairman, in a friendly but cautious tone :

" Lastly, a few words on Female Education. This question is one to which I had to pay particular attention on the Schools Enquiry. . . . Its importance cannot be exaggerated, but its formal investigation in this country is of recent date, and I am strongly impressed, not only with the difficulty and uncertainty of the question in many respects, but with the consequent tentative and experimental nature of it regarded practically.

" On one point I desire that the public mind should be carefully fixed : the opinion which was stated to us on much weighty authority, that, simply looked on in the intellectual view, the capacity of girls to learn is similar and equal to that of boys. . . . I cannot say that I look upon it as a settled opinion. . . . At present I only desire that the opinion should be fully tried : that the freest scope should be given to the exertions of the excellent and energetic persons, such as Miss Emily Davies, who are attempting to give large extension to the educational appliances in this country for women, and through them to their social functions and employments."

A few days later, *The Times* published a leading article on the proposed College, mentioning with approval that " the Education Department [of the Social Science Association], under Lord Lyttelton's guidance, withheld its formal recommendation from a scheme brought before it for the establishment of a Ladies' College on a somewhat novel and ambitious scale."

" The scheme will, we believe, be at least attempted. . . . This social enterprise is scarcely less bold on the part of the fair sex than the political schemes of which we have recently heard so much. It would be easy to indulge in raillery or poetry on such a theme. . . . But the names which have been subscribed for the proposal demand for it at least serious consideration." And *The Times* does give it serious consideration, but without any idea that a women's college could ever dream of approaching the University standard of learning. Girls are superficial, *The Times* thinks, because they " do not generally possess the physical strength which minute and thorough study requires. . . . An instinctive sense of this peculiarity leads teachers to be less exacting with girls than with boys."

Such views are easily explicable. Girls were allowed very little in the way of fresh air and exercise, and they were judged to be nervous and fragile creatures ; they were not taught thoroughly and intelligently, and they were judged to be by nature superficial. But *The Times*, while accepting weakness and superficiality as a matter of course and in the order of Nature, thought that great improvements might be effected if a college were established for women who intended to be teachers.

" But the projectors of this College appear to go further. They think it would be desirable for young ladies in general . . . to devote a year or two to advanced studies and to collegiate life. It is, we believe, the best method of dealing with such innovations to let them be tried, but we confess we shall regard the experiment with some anxiety, and we think it is founded on a false conception. Until physical facts are altered, the life of women will always be essentially different from that of men, and the presumption is against any scheme which proposes to educate the two sexes in the same way. . . . The virtues of home must be learnt at home, and a girl's proper University, at the age when her brothers go to College, is to be found in her own family. For exceptional cases . . . this proposed College may be serviceable. . . . But anything would be mischievous which tended to place the standard of female education in intellectual excellence, in mutual competition, and in a kind of public life."

The average opinion of the day had in fact been moved so far as to think it might be well to improve the education of women ; but " intellectual excellence " was still regarded as incompatible with the domestic virtues—" for mothers there is nothing like good, sound ignorance." [1] It was, however, satisfactory that *The Times* should bestow even qualified approval, and should encourage its readers to treat the topic seriously.

Miss Davies, as usual, enjoyed herself at the Social Science Congress, with which she combined a holiday. Miss Garrett and her sister Mrs. Cowell joined her, and they visited Leeds, Bolton Abbey, and the Yorkshire Moors, on the way to Birmingham. " We did a great deal of conversion at Birmingham," she wrote to Miss Richardson. " The doctors were delighted with Elizabeth Garrett."

(*Miss Davies to Madame Bodichon.*)

September, 1868.

" We had an encouraging week of Social Science and enjoyed it. The College was a very new idea, but it was well received. Judging by the size of the audience, there was more interest about it than about anything else, except strikes. The discussion was poor, but it seems to have done no harm, and that is something. . . . To get a room full of people to listen attentively to a paper for more than an hour, is something ; and the foolish parts of the speeches afterwards fell dead. Mr. Samuel Morley was present, and seemed much interested. I wrote a

---

[1] *Thoughts on Some Questions relating to Women*, by Emily Davies, p. 104. Cf. *The Cry of the Women*, by J. B. Mayor, in the *Contemporary Review*, Vol. XI, May–August, 1869.

PROPAGANDA

letter to him yesterday. . . . He has £50,000 a year and does not spend £10,000, and gives largely to things that he approves. Mrs. E. Noel seems likely to be a capital ally. She has a large acquaintance, and will diffuse information, as you are doing, among the clergy and gentry. I am sure this is most useful work. We want to make as many friends as possible, not only for the present, but with a view to getting public money by and bye. *The Times* article will do some good, I hope. There is a great deal to be done. I find people are much more interested in the College when they have *seen* somebody who is concerned in it. And prejudice melts away beautifully."

CHAPTER XI

George Eliot : A Digression

IN George Eliot's letters, published in her *Life* by Mr. Cross, many expressions may be found of her sympathy with the women's movement. " I do sympathize with you most emphatically," she wrote to Mrs. Peter Taylor, " in the desire to see women socially elevated—educated equally with men, and secured as far as possible along with every other breathing creature from suffering the exercise of any unrighteous power."[1] Like many another woman of ability, however, she shrank from taking any active part in the movement. " The part of the Epicurean gods," she wrote to her friends the Brays, " is always an easy one ; but because I prefer it so strongly myself, I the more highly venerate those who are struggling in the thick of the contest." On seeing a picture by Rosa Bonheur, " What power I " she wrote. " That is the way women should assert their rights." Some passages in a letter to Madame Bodichon show how strongly she felt that as a general rule whatever women did was poorly done, and that a new standard was needed.

(George Eliot to Madame Bodichon.)

[April 6 1868.]

" What I should like to be sure of as a result of higher education for women—a result that will come to pass over my grave—is, their recognition of the great amount of social unproductive labour which needs to be done by women, and which is now either not done at all or done wretchedly. . . . I believe—and I want it to be well shown—that a more thorough education will tend to do away with the odious vulgarity of our notions about functions and employment, and to propagate the

---

[1] *Life of George Eliot*, by J. W. Cross.

180

true gospel that the deepest disgrace is to insist on doing work for which we are unfit—to do work of any sort badly. There are many points of this kind that want being urged, but they do not come well from me, and I never like to be quoted in any way on this subject. But I will talk to you some day, and ask you to prevail on Miss Davies to write a little book which is much wanted." [1]

George Eliot's own intellectual powers, and her pre-eminent position in the literary world of her day, were striking evidence as to the possible achievements of women ; and it is no wonder that Miss Davies felt an intense interest in her, mingled with gratitude and admiration. It was delightful to receive encouragement from such a woman for the new venture of a college for women. George Eliot had, however, some misgivings as to Miss Davies' views about family life. As Mr. Cross writes : " The danger she [George Eliot] was alive to in the system of collegiate education, was the possible weakening of the bonds of family affection and family duties." What Miss Davies rebelled against was really a false conception of family duties, a narrow and selfish family life, founded on the separation of women from men in education, interests, and ideals.

(George Eliot to Miss Davies.)

August 8 1868.

" You must have numbered me yesterday among the women of the ' glittering eye ' and excited demeanour. Not liking that sort of identification I want to tell you that I had all the morning been mentally agitated and in bodily pain, and that I was additionally restless in the prospect of Mr. Lewes' return. The pleasure of a visit from you made me thrust away all that pre-occupation, but I was not very successful, and I fear I talked on serious subjects in a sadly flurried imperfect way, which makes me feel guilty. Ineffectual rash talk is an offence, only not so bad as ineffectual rash writing. Pray consider the pen drawn through all the words and only retain certain points for your deeper consideration, as a background to all you may judge it expedient to say to your special public. 1. The physical and physiological differences between women and men. On the one hand, these may be said to lie on the surface and be palpable to every impartial person with common sense who looks at a large assembly made up of both sexes. But on the other hand the differences are deep roots

---

[1] Part of this letter appears in the *Life of George Eliot*, by J. W. Cross.

of psychological development, and their influences can be fully traced by careful well-instructed thought. Apart from the question of sex, and only for the sake of illuminating it, take the mode in which some comparatively external physical characteristics such as quality of skin, or relative muscular power among boys, will enter into the determination of the ultimate nature, the *proportion* of feeling and all mental action, in the given individual. This is the deepest and subtlest sort of education that life gives. 2. The spiritual wealth acquired for mankind by the difference of function founded on the other, primary difference ; and the preparation that lies in woman's peculiar constitution for a precious moral influence. In the face of all wrongs, mistakes, and failures, history has demonstrated that gain. And there lies just that kernel of truth in the vulgar alarm of men lest women should be ' unsexed.' We can no more afford to part with that exquisite type of gentleness, tenderness, possible maternity suffusing a woman's being with affectionateness, which makes what we mean by the feminine character, than we can afford to part with the human love, the mutual subjection of soul between a man and a woman—which is also a growth and revelation beginning before all history.

" The answer to those alarms of men about education is, to admit fully that the mutual delight of the sexes in each other must enter into the perfection of life, but to point out that complete union and sympathy can only come by women having opened to them the same store of acquired truth or beliefs as men have, so that their grounds of judgment may be as far as possible the same. The domestic misery, the evil education of the children that come from the presupposition that women must be kept ignorant and superstitious, are patent enough.

" But on that matter you know quite as much as I do.

" I have it on my conscience that I did not make a little protest against something that fell from you about ' the family ' and also about the hurrying industrial view of life that infects us all in these days—but I should never have done, and I am not well. Come again, when you can, if I did not weary you."

Both George Eliot and Miss Davies were intensely in earnest, intensely interested in questions of morality and conduct ; and they soon found that they had a great deal to say to each other.

(*Miss Davies to Miss Jane Crow.*)

August 21 [1869].

" I went to see Mrs. Lewes this afternoon, and tho' I did not stay very long, she said a great deal. We spoke of her health, which is such that she has scarcely ever had the feeling of being really well or can work without a sense of drag, but it does not come to an illness, and she is afraid she inherits from her father longevity. The anxiety about Mr. Lewes' son [1] upsets her a good deal, ' but one hates oneself for being perturbed.' Then she remarked how easily we fall back into any little vice that belongs to us, after being disturbed in it, and spoke of the state of perturbation as entirely caused by not being sufficiently occupied with large interests. I referred to something in *Felix Holt* about Mr. Lyon's preoccupation which set him above small cares, and said what an enviable state it must be. She said Yes, one only knew it by contrast, by the sense of the want of it. Somehow we got to talk of the *Mill on the Floss*. She said her sole purpose in writing it was to show the conflict which is going on everywhere when the younger generation with its higher culture comes into collision with the older, and in which, she said, so many young hearts make shipwreck far worse than Maggie. I asked if she had known actual people like the Dodsons, and she said, ' Oh, so much worse.' She thought those Dodsons were nice people and that we owe much to them for keeping up the sense of respectability, which was the only religion possible to the mass of the English people. Their want of education made a theoretic or dogmatic religion impossible, and since the Reformation, an imaginative religion had not been possible. It had all been drained away. She considers that in the *Mill on the Floss*, everything is softened, as compared with real life. Her own experience she said was worse. It was impossible for her to write an autobiography, but she wished that somebody else would do it, it might be useful—or, that she could do it herself. She could do it better than anyone else, because she could do it impartially, judging herself, and showing how wrong *she* was. She spoke of having come into collision with her father and being on the brink of being turned out of his house. And she dwelt a little on how much fault there is on the side of the young in such cases, of their ignorance of life, and the narrowness of their intellectual superiority.

" Then we got to talk of fiction, and she was eager to explain the difference between prosaic and poetical fiction—that what is prosaic in ordinary novels is not the presence of the realistic element, without which the tragedy cannot be given (shown)—she herself is obliged to see and feel every minutest detail—but in the absence of anything suggesting the ideal, the higher life. She seems quite oppressed with the quantity of second-rate art everywhere about. It gives her such a sense of nausea that it makes it almost impossible for her to write— ' such a quantity of dialogue about everything, every hole and corner being ransacked, every possible incident seized upon '—not *well* done,

---

[1] Thornton Lewes, very seriously ill.

but done in such abundance that good art is discouraged and the higher standard works are thrust aside. She was anxious to impress upon me what she felt about the difference between prosaic and poetical work, because she thought I might disseminate it. She said in an appealing tone : ' Then when you talk to young people and teachers, you *will* advise against indiscriminate reading ? ' She thinks she has done very little, in quantity. She cannot write what she does not care about. She has not that kind of ability. Whatever she has done, she has studied for. Before she began to write the *Mill on the Floss*, she had it all in her mind, and read about the Trent to make sure that the physical conditions of some English river were such as to make the inundation possible, and assured herself that the population in its neighbourhood was such as to justify her picture. It is still amazing to me, tho' she only seemed to feel how little she had done, how she has managed to get thro' so much work, actual hard labour, in the time. A great deal of it must have been very rapidly done.

" Mrs. Lewes said a good deal besides what I have put down. She thinks people who write regularly for the Press are almost sure to be spoiled by it. There is so much dishonesty, people's work being praised because they belong to the confederacy. She spoke very strongly about the wickedness of not paying one's debts. She thinks it worse than drunkenness, not in its consequences, but in the character itself."

Some years after this, the question of moral training in schools was considered by the London Schoolmistresses' Association ; and a prolonged and exhaustive discussion, lasting through a number of meetings, was summarized by Miss Davies and published by the Association in 1875, with a short scheme for a course of lessons on the " relations of life and consequent duties." The idea was carried into practice by Miss Adelaide Manning, who gave a course of lessons on moral training in the following autumn. It was a subject that could not fail to interest George Eliot.

(*Miss Davies to Miss Crow.*)
September 24, 1876.
" I mentioned that I was going to see [Mrs. Lewes] yesterday. I went late in the afternoon and found them at home. They have been abroad, in Switzerland and the Black Forest, and have not been long back. They were going on to Italy, but Mrs. Lewes was so ill that they thought it better to stay in the cooler parts. She was ailing all the time she was writing her book and very much knocked up at the

end. This Mr. L. told me before she came in. She said herself that she had had rather a bad two years, having had much pain in the hip, which was new. I asked if it was sciatica and she said it was not, and did not seem to know what it was. She is much better now. The talk was chiefly on Morals. It came in this way. Something being said about M. Thiers, Mr. Lewes repeated a bon mot of Royer Collard's— ' M. Guizot *sait* la morale ; M. Thiers ne la connait pas.' I threw out that really to know morals would be about the highest possible attainment. Mrs. L. did not agree. She thought people generally knew that there was a better and a worse thing to do. Then I told her of a controversy as to whether Morals should be taught as a lesson in schools, and that a friend of mine (Adelaide) was going to do it. She said at first that she thought it would be a most dangerous thing to do, but explained afterwards that she meant that, if it was as a set of dry maxims. Such lessons as Adelaide proposes she thinks may be very useful and interesting, and went into what they should be with zest. She spoke of truthfulness as *the* most important thing to teach —that it should be explained how important it is as the basis of mutual confidence. She said she thought she had succeeded ' with these servants, by talking to them,' in making them understand this, but it was the first time she had ever succeeded with any servants. Usually they only see the harm of falsity in the form of injury by backbiting. She would not admit the difficulty of deciding when truth ought to be spoken and when not. I instanced keeping secret the authorship of a book. She thought that might be done, by refusing to answer questions, but Mr. L. agreed with me that often that is as good as telling, and maintained that denial in such a case was not lying. He said he had himself said No, flatly, when he had been asked about the authorship of her books. She said she did not know that he had, and did not support his view. She thought pains should be taken to avoid situations in which truth cannot be told, so as to keep up the habit of truthfulness. She thinks you are not bound to say all that you think, but would use as a test, whether your silence would lead to action being taken under a false impression. In teaching, she would ask the children to say for themselves *why* it is right to speak the truth, etc. She was anxious that my friend should impress upon them the wide, far-reaching consequences of every action, as a corrective of the common feeling that it does not signify what we do—and on the other hand how society reacts upon us, and how much we owe to it. People are always asking, *Why* should I do what is good for society ? What is society to me ? The answer is that if it were not for the accumulated result of social effort, we should be in the state of wild beasts. Something was said about ' Assuming life to be a blessing.' I asked if we were entitled to assume that, and she said, Certainly not, in talking to people who deny it, and she knew several people who think it a curse. But she says that so long as you don't commit suicide, you must admit that there is a better life, and a worse life, and may try for the better. Some deny even this, but when you come to such stupid scepticism as that it's no use talking to them. She hoped my friend would teach the girls not to think too much of political measures for improving society—as leading away from individual efforts to be good, I understood her to mean. I said I thought there was not much danger of that with girls. It is so much more inculcated upon them to be good and amiable than anything else. She said, was there not a great deal among girls of wanting to do some great thing and thinking it not worth while to do anything because they cannot do that ? I said there might be, but I had not come across it. What I had met with more was not caring to do anything. She said, Yes, no doubt stupidity prevails more than anything. Then she hoped my friend would explain to the girls that the state of insensibility in which we are not alive to high and generous emotions is stupidity, and spoke of the mistake of supposing that stupidity is only intellectual, not a thing of the character—and of the consequent error of its being commonly assumed that goodness and cleverness don't go together, cleverness being taken to mean only the power of *knowing*. Mr. L. put in, ' and of expressing.' Mr. L. was taking an active part in the conversation all the time, but what I have repeated is hers, except when he said something that seemed to express her views, and in which she was concurring. At this stupidity stage I thought I had staid long enough and came away promising to try to remember to tell my friend what she had said. . . . It will be of great interest to her to have so much advice from such an authority. She is going to give a series of lessons on such subjects as Truth, Courage, Temperance, etc., at Miss Leighton's school . . . a small boarding school, the girls mostly from 15 to 18 or 19, largely drawn from the millocracy, rich, and when they come, profoundly ignorant. Adelaide's lessons will be an experiment. I think *she* will succeed, but whether many teachers would be found competent for such work, I doubt."

" The error of its being commonly assumed that goodness and cleverness don't go together " was one which George Eliot would care especially to refute. While feeling, as she wrote to a friend, " the intense enjoyment which accompanies a spontaneous, confident, intellectual activity," she wanted, as Mr. Cross writes, " to impress on ordinary natures the immense possibilities of making a small home circle brighter and better." She was anxious that the students of the new college for women " should be favourable subjects for experiment—girls or young women whose natures are large and rich enough not to be used up in their efforts after knowledge." This wish was fulfilled, and her acquaintance with several of the early students of the College, in particular Mrs. C. P. Scott and Mrs. Ayrton, was afterwards a source of great pleasure to George Eliot.

CHAPTER XII

A Rival Principle.   1867–1869

WHILE Miss Davies was aiming at the foundation of a women's college which should aim at preparing its students for the Cambridge degree examinations, other forces were tending to organize higher education for women on lines considered to be especially suitable for their needs and powers. Miss Clough's suggestions for the co-operation of girls' schools in organizing lectures and classes in advanced subjects led to the formation, in the autumn of 1867, of the North of England Council for the Higher Education of Women.[1] Lectures were organized in a number of large towns, and their success soon led the Council to consider the question of establishing an examination for women over eighteen, mainly with a view to providing a test for teachers. The examination, however, was to be open not only to intending teachers, but to all women, with no restriction but that of age.

(Miss Davies to Miss Anna Richardson.)

December 30 [1867].

" I cannot help wishing that the introduction of the Lecture scheme into new places might be postponed for the present. It is working against the College at Liverpool and Manchester. At the meeting of the Northern Council the College was opposed on the ground that the Lectures would develop into what was wanted. . . . At Sheffield, the Lectures have prospered, and the [Senior and Junior] Local Examinations, which had been successful for two years before, have gone to the wall. They have had no candidates at all this year. At Liverpool,

---

[1] See *Memoir of Anne Jemima Clough*, by B. A. Clough, Chap. V.

188

A RIVAL PRINCIPLE

Miss Clough and Mrs. Butler have begged us not to do anything for either the Local Examinations or the College, lest the Lectures should suffer. And we shall of course not think of interfering with their field. I do not mean by this that the different agencies are in the least really antagonistic. It is simply that we have not strength to work so much machinery. . . . As to the comparative importance of the two things, opinions will of course differ. . . . The notion that the Lectures would prepare the way for *the* College is showing itself to be a mistake. Wherever there is a Local Examination, the demand for the College naturally arises, because there are always young women too old for admission, who take to clamouring for a test, and wear out the lives of the Local Secretaries, and of Mr. Markby,[1] with their letters. These tiresome creatures have been most useful to us, both at Cambridge and elsewhere. But it is not lectures that they want. The *knowledge* they think they could get, by hook or by crook. What they want is the test."

February 4, 1868.

" I think we ought not only to accept, but to *desire* the introduction of the Lectures into every large town, with a view to their growing into local Colleges. . . . We have not found hitherto that the Lectures are paving the way for the *Cambridge* College, but the contrary. You see one must take into account that when you give the choice of the difficult best, or the easy second best, the latter is most likely to be taken. It is what Mat. Arnold might call an appeal to our relaxed self, and such appeals are very likely to be successful. . . . It seems to me that in the nature of things [local Colleges] can never reach a high pitch of excellence. There are not enough first-rate people to supply all the towns in England with first-rate teaching. . . . To my mind it comes to this. It is better frankly to acknowledge that at present the Lectures stand in the way of the College. Then one has to consider *how much*, in each case, one will have to sacrifice of the College interest. . . . I incline to think that where there is a strong local feeling in favour of the Lectures, it is better to take advantage of it, but without entirely abandoning the College. Let the thorough people form an auxiliary Committee and help as much as they can, and let them also join the unthorough in working for the less perfect measure. . . .

" Mr. Bryce definitely gives in his adhesion to the College. He said with a suppressed sigh that he supposed one must sacrifice something. So I asked what he was sacrificing, and it seemed to be the religious

---

[1] Secretary to the Cambridge Local Examinations Syndicate.

point. As to the connection with Cambridge he said he had pretty nearly come round to our opinion, and he admitted that the religious difficulty was a merely sentimental one. He is a very strong voluntary and cannot bear the faintest recognition of a National Church. It is rather important to have Mr. Bryce secured, as he is the governing mind of the Liverpool faction."

To meet the need for a test in connection with the Lectures for Women, a proposal was made to establish a Voluntary Board of examiners from Oxford and Cambridge. This project seemed to Miss Davies, as she wrote to Miss Richardson, " very unthorough and likely to waste the energy we want so much for the machinery already at work." She feared that the institution of special examinations for women, carried on by such a Board, would make it impossible to secure identical or equal tests for men and women. An opportunity for discussing the matter with friends and opponents occurred, during a visit which Miss Davies paid to Professor and Mrs. Liveing at Cambridge.

(*Miss Davies to Miss Richardson.*)
[THE PIGHTLE], CAMBRIDGE.
February 28 [1868].

" I am going home to-day, and I have not time to tell you any particulars of the delightful visit I have had here, but I want to let you know without delay, that there is a prospect of getting all our differences arranged. I have been seeing, by their own wish, the promoters of the Voluntary Board, and have succeeded in making them understand the objections to it. . . . And as they now *take in* the objections to a female examination, they will at any rate be fairly considered. It convinced them (indirectly) that the opposition to the Voluntary Scheme has nothing to do with jealousy on behalf of the College. . . . The sweetness and light here are very refreshing. I am amazed, bewildered, almost stupefied by the reception of the College idea. It is far beyond anything I had hoped for."

Mr. Sidgwick was in favour of the Voluntary Board scheme, as a means of showing that there was a demand for examinations for women. He thought it unlikely that the University would take up the matter in its corporate capacity, but the Board would at any rate attract the interest of University men. Dr. Henry Jackson was more sanguine as to the University, and he proved to be right. Memorials sent up to the Senate by the North of England

Council, and by a large number of teachers, obtained so much support that the Voluntary Board scheme was dropped, and a scheme for Women's Examinations was brought before the Cambridge Senate.

(*Miss Davies to Miss Anna Richardson.*)

March 17 [1868].

" The negotiations with the Voluntary Board have come to a sad end. I am glad the matter has come to this point so quickly. I felt sure that the Voluntary was *tending* to a special scheme under University authority, tho' they kept asserting that it was merely a stop-gap. . . . We shall be having a meeting of our old original Examinations Committee next week, and I shall bring the matter forward and get instructions from them."

March 23 [1868].

" I think you do not know quite how much depends on the movement now going on. The new scheme [the Cambridge Examinations for Women] has nothing about it of a stop-gap character. It is urged forward on the ground of female examinations for females, and if Cambridge is beguiled into granting it, it will be urged with equal pertinacity upon all the towns which have accepted the Lecture scheme. I have been talking to Mr. Hales about it this morning, and explaining to him that we did not want anything which would lead away from Degrees. He said : ' But Miss Clough and her section don't want Degrees.' And I have heard otherwise that she is pressing the scheme expressly on the ground that it will be specially adapted to women's needs. I have known this all through, but it has not hitherto been necessary to dispute about it. *Now*, however, the question is being put : Do practical, thoughtful and working women want Degrees and a common standard or is it only the clamour of a few fanatics and women's rights people ? The Memorial for an independent examination will be a complete answer, one way or the other. That is why I am afraid of it. . . . The idea of the new scheme is not that it is easy and a stop-gap, but that it is to be womanly. . . . What it is best to do, is difficult to say. . . . I don't mean to make up my own mind finally till after the meeting of our Examinations Committee on Thursday. The reason I write now is that in a letter from Miss Wolstenholme received this morning, she says—' Mrs. Butler heard from Miss Richardson about a week ago, and certainly from her letter understood her to be favourable to our examination plans.' You see it won't do to blow the trumpet with an uncertain sound. It only leads to misunderstandings, and the misunderstandings reappear at Cambridge in the form of a unanimous cry from ' the North '—(they *dare* not include London) for female examinations."

March 27 [1868].

" I think there is a great deal in what you say about getting the true thing for the *highest* education, which will naturally govern the lower. But we have not got it yet, and to have our best friends employed in working a false scheme would be a great injury. People so easily get to love the thing they are working at, and think it the best thing possible. . . . It is a dangerous thing to create an organization. It has no idea of getting out of the way when its work is over.

" On looking into the London Programme [of examinations for women], I find that it is almost identical with their own Matriculation. The differences are that Greek is not compulsory, and women are to have only the *First* instead of the *First four* Books of Euclid. It seems to me a great point that the subjects are substantially the same, as it will make it possible for young women to avail themselves of the teaching which must be in existence all over the country for preparing their brothers. . . . My idea at present is to advise young women of twenty and thereabouts to occupy the next two years in working for this London Examination, which will be a temporary help to them, and will prepare them for entering the College when it is ready."

The Committee for the admission of women to University examinations met on March 26, and considered the proposed Memorial to Cambridge asking for advanced examinations for women, as well as the London scheme. Miss Davies, as she said to Miss Richardson, felt that the trumpet must be blown with no uncertain sound. The Committee accordingly resolved that it could take no part in the proposed Memorial to the University of Cambridge for examinations for women over the age of eighteen, on the ground that such special schemes of examination tended " to keep down the level of female education." While regretting the special character of the proposed London examinations, they adopted Miss Davies' idea, that young women should be advised to make use of them provisionally.

" Only three members of the Committee," writes Miss Davies,[1] " Mrs. Bodichon, Miss Bostock and myself, were present at this meeting, but those who were absent made no objection to

[1] *Family Chronicle*, 597.

the step decided upon. It was the only action taken of anything like a public nature, in opposition to the Women's
Examination scheme. We suffered silently, rather than provoke the familiar charge that women were quarrelling among
themselves."

(Miss Davies to Miss Anna Richardson.)
May 23 [1868].
" The Myers-Butler project [the examinations for women] has
brought much troublesome and painful and perplexing correspondence.
Mr. Roby thinks that if it passes, which seems very likely, it will be
almost fatal to our getting Degree examinations from Cambridge.
They will offer us a Myers examination instead. . . . My impression is that it will be used as an excuse, but that we shall
carry all our points in the long run. In the meantime, it is no
doubt doing harm both in absorbing interest and energy and stirring
up strife."

The scheme for a Women's Examination was discussed in the
Cambridge Senate on October 23, 1868. Mr. Markby stated
that since he became Secretary to the Local Examinations Syndicate, hardly a day passed but petitions arrived from women
praying for the institution of such an examination. Some doubt
was expressed as to the powers of women in Mathematics and
Classics, but the scheme was carried without opposition, and the
first examination took place in 1869. This was a blow to Miss
Davies, but she did not lose heart. " I don't feel (*altogether*)
discouraged by opposition," she wrote to Madame Bodichon.
" It rouses me, and when it gets *very* bad, it begins to assume
a grotesque aspect and I feel inclined to laugh. I learnt
that from Friends in Council a long time ago. There
is always something humorous in a very desperate state of
affairs."

Mr. Bryce expressed the view that the women's examinations
would pave the way for Miss Davies' projects, by stimulating
education and awakening public interest. They did in fact provide a curriculum and a test, by means of which the supply of
qualified teachers was increased much more quickly than would
otherwise have been possible : and this soon reacted upon the
schools, helping to improve their standard of teaching, and thus
enabling them, before very long, to supply Girton and Newnham

with increasing numbers of reasonably well prepared students. To Miss Davies, however, this counted for nothing in comparison with the fact that the University, as it seemed to her, had " put its stamp on the principle that women's education is to be lower and narrower than that of men." This view of the matter did not appeal to Mr. Sidgwick and other University men, who took an educational, and not a feminist, view of the matter. " The Cambridge residents," as Dr. Jackson wrote, " not seeing how soon women would be ready for Tripos examinations, and fearing the low standard of Pass examinations, very decidedly preferred the establishment of a special examination for women." [1]

" It makes me very unhappy," wrote Miss Davies to Miss Richardson, " to see the Ladies' Lectures, Ladies' Educational Associations, etc., spreading. It is an evil principle becoming organized, and gaining the strength which comes from organization." She was determined to make a stand against the evil principle, and an opportunity soon came, in connection with her most cherished plans. In August, 1868, a Sub-Committee, consisting of Mr. Roby, Mr. Tomkinson, and Mr. Sedley Taylor, was appointed to draft a Constitution for the College; and early in the following January, Mr. Tomkinson reported to Miss Davies on what they were thinking of proposing. There was to be a governing body of fifteen, which should include representatives of the Universities of Oxford, Cambridge, and London. The objects of the College were to be set forth in general terms. Mr. Tomkinson thought it would be better to make no mention of

---

[1] *Life of Henry Sidgwick*, p. 181. The examinations did not long remain restricted to women candidates. In connection with the University Extension Lectures for men and women instituted in 1873 in provincial towns, a demand arose for some kind of examination, and the Women's Examinations were thrown open to men, under the name of Higher Local Examinations (*Cambridge University Reporter*, Nov. 1, 1873, and 1877–8). These continued to be made use of for the upper forms in schools, for many years; they were done away with in 1922, having been superseded by the School and Higher Certificate Examinations, instituted by Oxford and Cambridge. Long before that date, the standard of women's work had so much improved that at Cambridge the Higher Local was no longer to be feared as a rival to the degree examinations in honours.

granting Certificates. " By the time we really attest with any
force," he wrote, " we shall be ripe for a Charter and the Queen's
leave to grant Degrees."

In a long letter, docketed by Mr. Tomkinson as " a fundamental
letter," Miss Davies explained that this would not do at all.

(*Miss Davies to Mr. Tomkinson.*)

January 6, 1869.

" . . . As to the composition of the Council, it seems to me that the
proposal to represent *three* Universities departs altogether from the
fundamental idea of the College, which is, to be at the earliest possible
moment, a constituent part of the University of Cambridge, and adopts
the totally different (not to say antagonistic) idea, of a new, independent,
female University. . . .

" The ground of expediency and prestige . . . many people can
understand. But *you* understand the real ground on which all separate
schemes for women are objectionable, I mean the extreme undesirable-
ness of drawing lines of demarcation and setting up artificial distinctions.
And it seems to me that tho' there is an increasing disposition to give
women fair play, there is also some tendency to increasing separation.
We have not yet come to it in religion, but with Ladies' Committees,
Ladies' Associations, Lectures to Ladies, and the rest, one does not
quite see why we should not soon have also Ladies' Churches and
Chapels, in which the duties of women as such should be specially
inculcated. We have the principle already, in the double moral code,
which most people believe in.

" I daresay this will seem to you an extravagant tirade on a very
small provocation. Perhaps I exaggerate, but I think it is discouraging
to see so many of the new things for women started on the basis of
separation. It seems like getting into more of a *system* of separateness,
and it makes one suspicious of anything like a step in that direction.
You know of course that my feeling against raising barriers between
men and women has nothing to do with the assertion of equality or
identity, in neither of which I believe. . . .

" I am sorry to send you such a cross letter (and such a long one), but
when you go so terribly astray, what can I do ? It was very good of you
to let me know what you were about."

" The Constitution Committee is to meet to-morrow," wrote
Miss Davies to Miss Manning on February 1. " I feel ' strung
to persistency,' to borrow a phrase from yesterday's sermon."
After considering the whole matter again, in the light of her

explanations, the Committee drafted a fresh Report, which was adopted, with the following declaration of policy :

" That the Council shall use such efforts, as from time to time they may think most expedient and effectual, to obtain for the students of the College admission to the Examinations for degrees of the University of Cambridge and, generally, to place the College in connection with that University."

This made it clear that their ultimate aim was to secure the inclusion of the College in the University. Miss Davies had no illusions as to the difficulties of this course. " Of *course*, we should not get anything at all from Cambridge, if we asked now," she wrote to Miss Manning. " The only chance is to prepare students before asking for anything for them, and then to do it by small steps, carefully timed." But she felt, as she wrote to Mr. Tomkinson, that " there is a kind of force gained by working at a positive programme, however warily, which you cannot have when the ultimate aim is obscure." George Eliot, she told him, agreed with her : " Mrs. Lewes said she thought the great thing to be hoped for from the College was that it would modify the opinions of men about the education of women, and assert in an emphatic way that whatever it is, it ought to be on a par with that of men." Madame Bodichon shared this view, but the Committee were by no means unanimous, and it needed all Miss Davies' force and persistence to carry the day.

The same principle was at issue in connection with the work to be done by the future students of the College. A Sub-Committee of Studies had been appointed in August, 1868,[1] to prepare plans for the College curriculum, as well as a scheme of discipline. The Sub-Committee consisted, in addition to Miss Davies, of Professor Seeley, Mr. Roby, and Mr. Bryce, as educational specialists ; Miss Metcalfe, who as a Headmistress was a specialist in both education and discipline ; with Mrs. Manning and Mrs. Gurney, who from their social position would have views as to the kind of discipline desirable for the students.

" Mr. Seeley is working at our curriculum," wrote Miss Davies to Madame Bodichon. " There is nothing to stop us from making it the very best that the most enlightened people can devise."

[1] Letter from Miss Davies to Miss Anna Richardson, August 1, 1868.

In reality, however, there was but little room for new devices, for the curriculum was already tied to the announcement in the Programme drafted by Miss Davies, that it was proposed to hold examinations in the subjects prescribed for the Poll Degree. Professor Seeley, however, in a long report on the subject, submitted that they ought not to be content with the Poll examinations ; the Cambridge system was defective in that it omitted English, French, and History, and included Natural Science only as an optional subject. He proposed that the two Cambridge General Examinations for the Ordinary Degree should be supplemented by papers in English, French, Chemistry, and " the political institutions of the principal existing states of the world, and the elements of political economy." As for classics, he could not see why any special prominence should be given them in the education of women.

To meet these views, it was decided that while the Poll examinations (if they could be had) were to be adhered to, a " College Certificate " should also be offered, on similar but somewhat modified conditions, as well as Certificates for proficiency in single subjects. Here the variations desired by Professor Seeley could be introduced. French, German and English were to be available as substitutes for Latin and Greek ; and the examination in English was to include questions on Language and Political Institutions.

(Professor Seeley to Miss Davies.)

January 13 [1869].

" I am well content with our compromise. It puts the stationary and progressive principles side by side. I am not afraid for the result if justice is done to both. . . . I agree with all you say about the Classics, but it does not touch me, it does not affect me at all. Let the education of the sexes be the same, if you will. I only want to anticipate by a short time the change which I see coming over the education of men. We have made the mistake of erecting what ought to have been a special study into a universal study. We are fast finding out our mistake. We are discovering that instead of using the Classics to train the reasoning power, to form literary taste, to convey political information, and to form habits of observation, all which things they can be made to do in a fashion, the proper way is to teach Logic, English, Political Philosophy, and Physical Science, and to do all these things directly and not indirectly. My belief is that if you take this course the result will be no separation of the sexes, but that women will know the same things as men, and will threaten so soon to know them *better* that men will be shamed into reforming their own system."

Miss Davies was not in the least shaken. She was convinced that the adoption of Professor Seeley's ideas would mean that women would continue to put up with the second best and the superficial. In vain she quoted Matthew Arnold on the value of classics.

(*Professor Seeley to Miss Davies.*)

January 20 [1869].

" I shall stand up to you as long as you continue the controversy, though I believe you think that sleeping and waking my mind is always occupied with the demerits of a classical education."

March 4 [1869].

" I hope you will not be restrained by the small requirements of the first pupils from securing a good list of teachers in a good number of subjects. We must show the world what we are prepared to do, and not merely what it will be enough to do so long as the lists are thin. For instance, Venn writes to say that he will take Logic or Political Economy. The world, I think, ought to know that we have secured him even though next year there may be no class for him.

" Your view of the small amount of teaching required rather startles me, though I am not prepared to say it is wrong. At Cambridge men certainly attend on an average only about two lectures a day, but then they coach besides."

The list of teachers announced included, as Professor Seeley wished, Mr. Venn and others for whom there would probably be no students to begin with. Mr. Bryce pressed for the appointment of a teacher in History. The Committee asked him to undertake it himself, but though he was ready to give an occasional course of lectures, he would not take a regular appointment lest it should injure his position at the Bar.

(*Miss Davies to Miss Manning.*)

June 2 [1869].

" Mr. Stuart is to be recommended as undoubtedly the best man for Mathematics. Mr. E. C. Clark, Senior Classic, etc., married, and in other ways commendable, is to be recommended for Latin *and* Greek. . . . It was agreed that we ought to appoint the teacher of Vocal

Music, as it is part of the regular course, and I am to find out whether Madame Sainton Dolby would undertake it."

February 1, 1869.

" I quite feel with you the importance of putting forward the Cambridge Examination as the distinctive feature and of not letting an alternative College Certificate appear as equal and parallel. But I think this has been avoided. . . . I do not see the same reason for keeping the *additional* subjects out of sight. Our position is this. Our students take the Cambridge Degree, as evidence that they reach *that* standard, at any rate. But the Ordinary Degree is obviously and notoriously adapted to ordinary men (or as some say, the refuse), and our students will not be ordinary women. Therefore there is no objection to their *adding* anything that it is desirable to learn. It is quite common for men to do this at Cambridge. I know one man who is going to take a Poll Degree and is learning Hebrew besides. . . . There is all the difference to my mind, between supplementing and substituting. I think perhaps you scarcely know what a strong feeling there is among the younger University men against the present University education. . . . Their idea is that women, who don't know what it is, are bent upon getting it because men have it, and it strikes them as ignorant and childish. Of course they are wrong, but I don't think we can afford to disregard their feeling, as we shall be in a great degree dependent on their support for getting what we want from Cambridge, and I think it can be met by the supplementary plan. . . .

" It seems to me that we do want to charm people by an animating view of the studies and by the names of teachers. We want to attract the students, and for myself I feel decidedly more heartbroken at not being able to go, after realizing what the teaching will be. And also we want to enlist support by making people feel that what we are going to offer will be of a higher quality than women will have the least chance of getting anywhere else."

The compromise effected between Professor Seeley and Miss Davies was adopted by the Committee on March 23, 1869,[1] but in fact Miss Davies had her way. All her influence was exerted in favour of classics and the University course, and during the early years of the College, most of the students entered for the Tripos

---

[1] Present, Mr. Heywood (in the Chair), Mrs. Bodichon, Miss Metcalfe, Mr. Tomkinson, Mr. Roby, Mr. Sedley Taylor, Mrs. Gurney, Miss Davies. (Letter from Miss Davies to Miss Manning, March 24, 1869.)

or Poll Degree examinations. The College Certificate was awarded on only two occasions, and a certificate for proficiency in a single subject only once. The Poll examinations ceased to be available after 1881, when the University authorized the admission of women to the Tripos examinations, and expressly excluded them from the others—an exclusion which Miss Davies regretted. Naturally she was glad that the students should take honours, but she wished to extend the benefits of the College to as many women as possible, and thought that the course for the Ordinary Degree should be open to them as much as to men.

Madame Bodichon, though supporting Miss Davies' policy, did not wholly agree with her, as may be seen from a letter to Miss Helen Taylor, written under a misapprehension, but interesting as a characteristic expression of her views. It owed its origin to a letter in the *Spectator* on *Women's Suffrage*, signed " Helen T.," in which the statement was made that to Madame Bodichon " not only the college at Hitchin owes its origin,—not less to her energy than to the gift of a thousand pounds,—but the women's suffrage cause two of its best and most widely circulated pamphlets."[1] Madame Bodichon naturally thought the writer was Miss Helen Taylor, Mill's step-daughter. She was not ; but the following letter has been preserved among Miss Taylor's papers :

(*Madame Bodichon to Miss Helen Taylor.*)

August [1869].

" I must write and thank you for your capital letter in the *Spectator*. There is nothing which has given me so much pleasure for a long time, it is such a delight to have the approbation of people one religiously respects. I am the more pleased because I felt a little that you were not altogether in favour of Miss Davies' scheme, neither am I, but I am so happy to see anyone work with perseverance and good sense that I feel we cannot do better than help her. I do not think I deserve to be called the originator of the College, for tho' ever since my brother went to Cambridge I have always intended to aim at the establishment of a college where women could have the same education as men if they wished it, I certainly could not have carried out the plan as Miss Davies has done. I am not strong enough, or orthodox enough.

" Of course you understand that I do not approve of the Cambridge education as much as Miss Davies does, but I think we are likely to get

---

[1] See the *Spectator*, July 24, July 31, and August 7, 1869.

something really good in time if we attach ourselves to Cambridge and Cambridge to us, and such good workers as Miss Davies ought to be helped and not too much hindered by criticism."

Madame Bodichon, like Miss Davies, saw that it was the old Universities which offered the greatest promise for the future ; and while she did not think Cambridge above criticism, she was convinced that women would gain most by being attached to the highest educational forces in the country, and sharing in their growth and expansion.

CHAPTER XIII

Preparations for Opening the College.
1868–1869

THE College had now been announced publicly and talked about privately to such an extent that it was becoming urgent to begin on the practical work of getting together some students and arranging how to house them. An auxiliary Committee was formed of Cambridge men, with Mr. Sedley Taylor as Secretary, and they took the question of locality into consideration. Though Miss Davies was anxious for the closest possible connection with the University, she was no less anxious that the College should not be situated in Cambridge. While the students were to take the University curriculum and examinations, they were to be taught separately at the College ; she thought it impossible for them to attend lectures and demonstrations with the undergraduates.

(*Miss Davies to Miss Anna Richardson.*)

January 31 [1868].

" I sympathize entirely with Mr. Watson's [1] view about the desirableness of mixed education, and I admit that the foundation of a separate college seems to stereotype the idea of separation. I feel this so much that if there had seemed any reasonable chance of getting the whole, by waiting, I would not have grasped at the half. But all good things have to be worked up to, and the only way open to us of working towards common education seems to be to stand out for common subjects, common examination, and common standards. It is not a case in which you can begin at the top end. You cannot artificially separate

---

[1] Mr. Robert Spence Watson, of Gateshead, who was married to Miss Richardson's sister Elizabeth.

202

boys and girls, and then suddenly throw young men and women together at eighteen. . . . I do not think it would be true policy at present to throw our strength into fighting for common instruction."

February 4 [1868].

" Since I wrote last, we have added the names of Mr. Maurice and Dr. Gull to the General Committee. Mr. Maurice came to Blandford Square on Sunday and there was a long talk about the College and also about mixed education. As to the latter, we all seemed to agree that it was a thing to be desired, but not to be tried for in the present case. Llewelyn mentioned one objection, which I think is a real one and very strong, namely, that if the College were at Cambridge, the discipline must be much more strict. It would be impossible to give as much liberty as we may hope to do in the country. The experience of the Local Examinations at Cambridge is evidence of this. Whether all the precautions they take are *necessary*, I very much doubt, but at any rate they think they are, and the result is to make the girls very uncomfortable. . . . I suspect that this timidity would tell especially in hindering the thing I sigh for more, that is, the society of cultivated men for the mistresses. There would be such an amount of gossip and scandal ready to cluster round the College, that its managers and their male friends would be obliged in self-defence to shun each other, and we should perhaps be in the position of shutting ourselves out from Cambridge society even more than if we were fifty miles off. This may be a fancy, but I have been told that at Oxford, unmarried ladies are obliged to be excessively cautious in their demeanour."

It must be remembered that at this date the Universities retained a good deal of their monastic character. Fellows of Colleges were not allowed to marry, and the society of Cambridge was almost entirely masculine. The separation of the sexes during education was so complete that boys were ashamed to be seen with their mothers and sisters. Young women were not in the habit of going about the world unchaperoned, and any breach of this rule would appear even more conspicuous in a University town than anywhere else. Miss Davies had spent her life in fighting for a cause, and in the course of the fight had been obliged always to bend herself to the necessity of conciliating public opinion. She wanted not only to conciliate public opinion, but to convert it. She did not want merely to produce a handful of brilliant women ; she wanted to raise the general level, to convert the average parent to the necessity of educating the girls as thoroughly as the boys—a much harder task. Conciliation had counted for much in her previous successes ; it was something that that influential champion of the proprieties, Miss Yonge, should advise girls to go in for the Cambridge Local Examinations, as these did not seem to her " to involve anything unfeminine or undesirable." [1] We have seen what Miss Yonge replied when asked to support the College : a passage in her book *Womankind* expresses similar views :

" As to paths in life and education, womanhood is no obstacle to our being as highly educated as our brains will allow. That this should be done in close *juxtaposition* with a number of male pupils does not, however, seem desirable, because there is a tendency in large masses to rub off the tender home-bloom of maidenliness, which is a more precious thing than any proficiency in knowledge." [2]

Miss Davies felt sure that the average parent would never be got to send his daughters to the College if it seemed likely " to rub off the tender home-bloom of maidenliness." As to " proficiency in knowledge," she thought that efficient teaching could quite well be got at some place within reach of Cambridge and London, and that this would be enough. Mrs. Manning and Mrs. Russell Gurney (like Miss Davies) knew very well what kind of criticism of the new experiment might be expected from society in general. Madame Bodichon wished for Cambridge, but she was well known to be unconventional in her views. Moreover, Miss Davies felt strongly that girls needed freedom and protection from interruption. Cambridge therefore was barred. Baldock, Stevenage, Mill Hill, and Hitchin were all thought of, and finally Miss Davies set her heart upon Hitchin. So early as March 27, 1868, she wrote to Miss Richardson : " No site has been decided upon, but I think we are shut up to Hitchin as the only place which combines the essential conditions of rurality, healthiness and accessibility."

(Miss Davies to Miss Anna Richardson.)

April 23 [1868].

" I am going down to Hitchin to-morrow on a visit of exploration. Mr. Seebohm has kindly promised to take me about, if Mr. Tuke should be prevented. We have made a valuable discovery about the locality.

---

[1] *Womankind*, by C. M. Yonge, p. 84.   [2] *Womankind*, p. 236.

The Vicarage of Hitchin and the adjoining parish of St. Ippolyt's are Trinity College livings and therefore always likely to be held by scholars, who may be available as teachers in the College. The present Vicar of Hitchin was a Senior Wrangler, and Mr. Hort, of St. Ippolyt's, was a first-class man in Classics, and has been an Examiner for both the Moral Sciences and Natural Sciences Triposes. He could himself teach nearly everything we want, and is a warm ally. It makes a difference as to the possibility of starting with a small number, one of the objections to which is the expense of the staff. If we give up, as I am much disposed to do, the idea of having a grand lady at the head, we might begin with one woman as resident Mistress, and have all the teaching which she could not do supplied by non-resident people. This would make it possible to begin with a very small piece of building."

Funds, however, did not at present admit of building at all, and Miss Davies proposed that a beginning should be made in a hired house, and that meanwhile a site should be bought at Hitchin, in readiness to begin building directly it could be afforded. Madame Bodichon was averse to this plan. She thought the temporary house a mistake, as involving too much waste of their small resources. It did not seem to her difficult for young women to avoid scandal while living and working in Cambridge, and she felt that the College could not prosper, if it were set down in isolation, out of reach of the life of the University.

(Miss Davies to Madame Bodichon.)
November 23, 1868.
" I seem not to have explained properly about the ' small beginning ' idea. I never thought of spending any of your money upon it, or mine either. If it is done at all, which is very doubtful, my notion was to manage it very cheaply and make the students' fees pay the expenses. We should have to ask them whether they were willing to endure misery of various sorts for a year or two, rather than wait on indefinitely for perfect happiness. I am not in the least giving up the building project—scarcely even postponing it. But I think it might help us to get the money to come into existence in *some* shape, as soon as possible. . . . If we had a certain number of students actually collected together and at work, we could proclaim the astonishing fact, and show that the thing is actually begun. That is why I should like to buy the site. We want by every possible means to make ourselves look substantial. As you see I only propose the hired-house plan for a

year or two while the College is building. You will see that it would
not do to have it at Cambridge. An insuperable difficulty would be
that there is no house in Cambridge big enough. Even for a dozen or
twenty students, an ordinary dwelling-house would not be large enough.
This is besides the other objection, of the strong feeling against us that
we should stir up in Cambridge, just at the beginning when it will be
pre-eminently necessary to conciliate. And the more I hear of Cambridge society, the less I regret the impossibility of going there. If
the College was *strong* it might reform the society, but at first it would
be weak, and I think the social influence of the place would be not
helpful, but very injurious. Lady Brodie and the Radicals will not
help us, whatever we do. . . . I am not altogether sorry for their
defection, though of course it makes our work harder and slower. If
they had been at all reasonable, we should have worked with them and
been influenced by them, and the more I see of Radical women, the
less I desire to increase their number. I went to a Radical dinner-
party last week, and the bold, unfeeling faces of some of the ladies, and
their reckless talk, quite shocked me."

The search, both for a house, and for a building site, was carried
on through the year without success. At last a house that seemed
possible was found at Hitchin. Objections however were raised
by the Cambridge Committee. Mr. Sedley Taylor wrote that
the difficulties in the way of obtaining first-rate teaching at Hitchin
would be extremely formidable. Cambridge railway station was
" half an hour's walk from the two large colleges," and the average
journey to Hitchin took an hour, so that each teacher would have
to throw away three hours spent in travelling ; for a lecturer going
there twice a week, the cost of this unproductive time would
amount to £34 7s. 6d. a year for each teacher ; and even at this
cost, it would be impossible to get first-rate men to undergo the
perpetual railway journeys. A few days later, the Cambridge
Committee reported formally their opinion that it would not be
found practicable to procure first-rate University teaching at
Hitchin. They could see no substantial difficulties in the way
of the temporary experiment being made in, or in the immediate
neighbourhood of Cambridge itself.[1] Both Professor Liveing
and Mr. Taylor pointed out that at Hitchin the students would

[1] The report was signed by J. C. Adams, G. D. Liveing, Robert
Burn, T. G. Bonney, H. Sidgwick, Sedley Taylor.

be quite out of reach of museums and libraries.   Professor Lightfoot was the only member of the Cambridge Committee who
wished for Hitchin.

Miss Davies remained unshaken in her views.   For the moment
it was possible to secure some lecturers of high standing—Professor Seeley, Mr. Hort, Mr. E. C. Clarke, Mr. James Stuart,
Mr. Venn, and Professor Liveing, of Cambridge, with Gustave
Masson of Harrow, and Dr. Althaus of London University.   " I
do not feel at all humble about our teachers," she wrote to Madame
Bodichon.   " Those we have in view at present are all of the first
rank, and I do not feel inclined to look lower."   With some
exultation, she felt a little envy of the students who were to enjoy
opportunities so far beyond any that had been available in her
girlhood.   " Are they not spoiled children of Fortune ? " she
wrote to Miss Richardson.   " What might not have been done, if
we had had such chances ! "

(*Miss Davies to Miss Manning.*)
February 26, 1869.
" I am glad you do not want us to start at Cambridge.   Mrs. Bodichon has gone off upon that tack, and has been talking to Lady Goldsmid
about it.   She (Mrs. B.) seems to have made up her mind that we shall
have no more students than we have promised now, and that we ought
not to provide for, or look forward to, any more. . . .   I fancy it is
partly that Mrs. Bodichon has taken a dislike to Hitchin, and that being
of a physical turn of mind, she cannot separate the essential idea of the
College from the accident of the place in which it is located . . . It is
curious that you and I and Mr. Tomkinson, who in our *ultimate* ideas
go the farthest, are the most decided against this Cambridge notion.
Mrs. Gurney and Mr. Seeley however were very clear against it too, and
their remarks were very practical.   I was obliged to tell Lady Goldsmid
that Mrs. Bodichon had had an attack of timidity, and she said she
thought I had got an attack of audacity, but she seemed rather to
admire it than otherwise."

As to audacity, it seems rather that the honours were divided.
Madame Bodichon was audacious about Cambridge ;   Miss
Davies about building at once.   She had, however, been over-
sanguine as to the number of students, thinking that it would
be easy to get twenty-five to begin with, and a more prudent
estimate had to be taken as a basis.

(*Miss Davies to Madame Bodichon.*)

March 2 [1869].

" From what Lady Goldsmid said to me last night, and Mrs. Austin also tells me, I think there must be some misunderstanding about what was proposed at the College Committee. The estimate of expenses, as to teaching and everything else, was based on the supposition that there would be ten students to provide for. If there should be fewer, of course the estimate would be lower. . . .[1] It is quite impossible to make a conjecture as to the probable number, for months to come. I should think people would think they were doing very well if they let their daughters put down their names three months beforehand. And here we are, at eight months' distance, and we have not so much as announced where the College is to be, or how much the students are to pay.

" It is clearly a case in which some party must venture something, and evidently it must be the promoters, who believe in the idea, not parents, who do not. It is no use putting off till we can be certain of a certain number of students."

Thursday, March, 1869.

" If there *is* a person who is *not* tired of the College, it is Mr. Tomkinson. You would have said so if you had seen him here the other night, talking over every detail for about two hours, and willing to take any trouble . . . Mr. Tomkinson said the other day that he found even people who had *dis*approved were glad we were going to begin. It actually produces faith. In practical working, one finds that the way to kindle faith is to *show* it, by running risks. . . . A parallel case occurs wherever a Local Examination is started. Some cautious person suggests making the schools promise a certain number of candidates, before starting. Of course they won't promise. A Committee has to be formed, and an announcement made that there will be an examination, and in due course the candidates appear."

(*Miss Davies to Mr. Tomkinson.*)

March 13 [1869].

" Since I wrote to you last, I have grown very patient, under the influence of despair. I see that if we succeed in getting the house taken, and the teachers appointed, it is as much as we shall accomplish this season, and perhaps it is enough. . . ."

March 16, 1869.

" Having been discomfited about the sites, my desire now is to get the house taken and the staff appointed, that we may be able to

---

[1] The College was actually opened with six students.

tell parents into whose hands their daughters are to be committed.
" From what you say, I think I must have omitted to mention that
Mr. Seeley offered his services as a teacher with the proviso—if we
were not afraid of him. The Committee don't seem at all afraid. We
are only cowards when it comes to spending money. . . . I don't want
to buy an acre at a time, but I think if we had two acres in possession
it would be something for people's imaginations to build upon, and
also for Mr. Waterhouse to make a plan upon."

The question of finding some one to act as a resident authority
was one of great difficulty. Miss Davies, as she wrote to Miss
Richardson, felt that she herself was " not old enough nor distinguished enough," apart from the fact that her mother, from
whom she could not separate, hated the idea of living at the
College in any capacity. Professor Sidgwick and Mr. Sedley
Taylor suggested that an attempt should be made to prepare
suitable women for the position. A house might be hired in
Cambridge where a few such persons could live " under the
superintendence of some competent lady." They would probably
be admitted to lectures by some of the Professors, and they could
get the best private teaching available. The house and the
superintendent Miss Davies thought " quite unnecessary and
objectionable, but the opportunity of getting class tuition of the
highest kind, and seeing methods of high teaching, I should
consider most valuable." Living quietly in lodgings would,
she thought, be better than the conspicuousness of taking a
house. Mr. Sedley Taylor, however, thought it would not do
for ladies, even the middle-aged, to live in lodgings at Cambridge.

(Miss Davies to Miss Anna Richardson.)

" If we could get a very nice lady of sixty to take a house on her own
account, and if we could find some very nice students who would be
her guests (paying, of course) it might work. . . . I am not quite
sure as to the good effect of living at Cambridge on *young* women.
What you have heard of Oxford society applies I believe equally to
Cambridge, and it is discouraging. The idea of student life at a University is, as you say, most captivating, but when one comes to the working
out, the risks begin to appear. Without much power of control, we
should be responsible, and the smallest indiscretion on the part of any
student would be disastrous."

E.D.

A suggestion that Miss Richardson should take charge of a house was declined, and the scheme came to nothing. Academic training and experience being impossible, the best that could be done was to try, as Miss Davies said, for " ladies of a very high stamp." Her old friend Mrs. Manning was the person on whom she set her heart to fill the post of Mistress. They had worked together on the Kensington Society, and the London Committee for Women's Suffrage, and Mrs. Manning knew something of Queen's College and the Cambridge Local Examinations. She was a cultivated woman, with a touch of the scholar in her character, and her dignity, social tact, and goodness of heart would be of great value in dealing with such a new and unknown quantity as the students. Since her husband's death in 1866, she had continued to live in London, with her stepdaughter. She was elderly, and not very strong, and it was a great deal to ask of her that she should give up all she was accustomed to, and undertake the practical direction of the new venture. But Miss Davies asked it, and begged Miss Adelaide Manning to urge it on her stepmother.

(Miss Davies to Miss Manning.)

October 29, 1868.

" I feel impelled to write and beg you both not to harden and stiffen into a fixed decision about the College. I have seen Mrs. Gurney, and she is not going to let Mrs. Manning go. She says, Cannot we all besiege her ? Mrs. Gurney pleads for *one* year. She thinks that of course one cannot judge for other people, but that the good done would be worth making a *great* sacrifice for, unless there is something which really *cannot* be sacrificed. I do not feel as if you had yet realized how much there is to be gained, and I want you to wait till you have, before influencing Mrs. Manning on the other side."

Mrs. Manning was half persuaded, and began to think of the terms of her appointment. " Her conditions seem to me most liberal," Miss Davies wrote to Madame Bodichon a fortnight later, " and on such terms it may be possible to begin in a hired house. The first thing seems to be to find out how many students are ready to come." After considerable hesitation Mrs. Manning offered to undertake the College for one term only, to Miss Davies's great satisfaction. The Committee accepted " with great pleasure Mrs. Manning's kind offer of taking the direction of the College during the first term." Miss Davies's relief at having got the question settled, even though only for the moment, shows itself in the following letter :

(*Miss Davies to Mrs. Manning.*)

April 16, 1869.

" I enclose the motion passed at the meeting this afternoon. It is soberly expressed, as seemed to befit a solemn Resolution, but the Committee said a great deal which Adelaide would have liked to hear. They think it a great sacrifice for you to make, and a grand thing to do. We were quite unanimous. . . . Our number was small to-day, only Mrs. Gurney, Mr. Roby, Miss Metcalfe, Mrs. Bodichon, and Mr. Tomkinson. We were sure however that the absentees would agree with us. . . . I saw my brother this morning. He was of course much pleased but he greedily demands *more* sacrifice—a year, at least, not one term only. Miss Metcalfe spoke very nicely. . . . Mrs. Bodichon was very cordial too. It really is a delightful thing. It grows upon one. I do hope you will not find it too great a burden."

A suitable title had to be found for Mrs. Manning. " Is there no euphonious feminine to be discovered," wrote Miss Richardson, " of one of all these names—Rector, Warden, Provost, etc., which prevail at Oxford ? . . . Dean *has* a feminine in Spanish, but alas, it is duenna." The title of Mistress was chosen, as being in conformity with Cambridge custom.

While the question of the Mistress was under consideration Miss Davies had been angling for students in various quarters, and had already heard of some who wished to enter. It was remarkable, as she said, that " the people who say we shall *not* get students, have no particular means of knowing, and the people who say we shall, such as the schoolmistresses, etc., *have.*" The schoolmistresses wanted to send their girls, and a good many girls wanted to come, but the College was considered " dangerous " by parents. " I am more and more impressed," wrote Miss Davies to Miss Manning, " with the difficulties of conscience in the way of young women, as I hear more about them. They think they ought not to urge their own wishes against those of their parents, who, as Miss E. says, ' don't see the use of learning such a lot ! ' " Even parents who approved in theory hesitated in practice, when it came to a question of their own girls. Mr. Seebohm, who was to be their neighbour at Hitchin, had four daughters whom Miss Davies coveted, but though he was most

friendly, she did not succeed in enlisting them as students.[1]
Hopes were raised when an enquiry came from Mrs. Bradley,
wife of the Rev. G. G. Bradley, who had succeeded Mr. Tomkinson's cousin Bishop Cotton as Headmaster of Marlborough. She
was the mother of a family of daughters whom Miss Davies would
have been delighted to welcome as students—they were exactly
the kind of girls she wanted to get. But Mrs. Bradley, after
studying the prospectus sent to her by Miss Davies, felt afraid lest
the College might draw them too much away from home duties.

(Miss Davies to Mrs. Bradley.)

January 22, 1869.

" I have been waiting for a quiet morning to reply to your kind
letter, as I wished to say something of the difficulty you refer to. It is
one which has constantly been on my mind, and is *the* difficulty which
cannot I think be treated as a mere prejudice. . . . You feel I think
that those in whom the sense of duty was strong would not let the
passion for study interfere wrongly with home claims. . . . The real
difficulty perhaps is rather to decide which *is* the duty, as in some
families the most trifling and useless faddles put on the air of home
duties and are considered of more importance than any possible claim
of any other sort. In these cases, a sound judgment is wanted, and it
seems to me that wisely trained young women of twenty-one will be
better fitted to decide, than girls of eighteen, suddenly thrown upon
themselves after the strict routine of the schoolroom, often with no
guidance worth speaking of, either from their mothers or anybody else.

" Then as to the dulness of domestic duties as compared with study.
Anyone who cares much for learning would no doubt feel this, but she
would probably be less discontented and troublesome than one who
was dull from the opposite cause of emptyheadedness. . . . With
regard to the College, I cannot deny that the stirring intellectual and
spiritual life will awaken a craving for *more* work than homes in the
country can supply, where there are several daughters.

" I am afraid parents must make up their minds to as much as this
—that when home life manifestly does not supply more than enough
work for one, while there are two able and willing to work, one must be
allowed to leave home and find work elsewhere. It seems to me that
where the home is what it ought to be, the home ties will be strong
enough to bear as much strain as this. It looks like a consciousness of

---

[1] Mr. Seebohm shared the office of Treasurer of the College with
Mr. Tomkinson, from 1870 to 1873.

weakness and unsoundness, when there is so much fear that the home ties will snap at the least pull."

A month later, Miss Davies wrote again to Mrs. Bradley, and sent a circular announcing that the College was to be opened " in a temporary manner, on a limited scale," in October, and inviting intending students to send in their names. " Shall you have a daughter for us ? " she asked. Mrs. Bradley was not to be persuaded. She felt that the College was too much of an experiment and that it could not succeed unless great improvements were first carried out in the schools.[1] A few students had, however, already been enlisted. Early in August of the previous year, Miss Davies had a visit from " a real girl, who is definitely preparing for the College." This was Miss Emily Gibson. " She is nearly eighteen, ladylike, and intelligent," wrote Miss Davies to Miss Richardson. " She came for advice about the subjects to take up for the Entrance Examination, and decided upon Latin and Greek. Seeing her gave me a vivid impression of how delightful to teach and how pleasant as companions, our students will be." Soon afterwards came a slightly older recruit, Miss Lloyd, a friend of Miss Richardson's. " I find her original and amusing " (wrote Miss Davies to Miss Richardson), " with the hint of seriousness without which amusingness is rather disagreeable. It gives me extreme pleasure to have a student of her age and character, and only to know of her will be an encouragement to others." Three more names had come in by January, 1869. " More are in prospect," wrote Miss Davies, " but I daresay we shall not get many till we can announce the place and time of opening. And *then* we shall have more than there is room for." In April a prospectus was issued, announcing that an Entrance Examination would be held in London early in July, the examiners to be Professor Liveing, Mr. Roby, Professor Seeley, and Mr. Sedley Taylor. Two scholarships, each of the value of one hundred guineas a year for three years, were to be awarded to the best candidates, and

[1] A few years later, Mrs. Bradley was an active supporter of the Oxford High School for girls. In 1870 Miss Davies visited the Bradleys at Marlborough, in order to study the Bursar's department and gain some knowledge of the business side of a College. See *Education and the Victorian Matron : A Recollection of Emily Davies*, by Rose M. Bradley, in the *Cornhill Magazine*, March, 1922.

would cover their fees for the whole of the College course.[1] Miss Fanny Metcalfe, one of the best known head mistresses of her time, sent copies of the Prospectus to schools, with an appeal for recruits ; and finally eighteen candidates were secured for the Entrance Examination, a very good total.

The first student who entered, Miss Gibson, was a former pupil of Miss Pipe, head mistress of Laleham School, Clapham Park. Miss Pipe, it will be remembered, had in 1865 been opposed to the admission of girls to the Cambridge Local Examinations, but her views were now somewhat changed, and she encouraged Miss Gibson. It was through an article by Mr. Llewelyn Davies in *Macmillan's Magazine* [2] that Miss Gibson discovered the College. She was at once inspired with the wish to enter it. What followed is best described in her own words :

" I was eighteen then, and was longing for an opportunity for study, so the information when it came in my way was deeply interesting. My school days had been cut short by money troubles at home before I was sixteen. . . . I had been for three years at a private school at Clapham, a Methodist school kept by a very remarkable woman. . . . Miss Pipe was the daughter of a Manchester shopkeeper and began teaching at seventeen. When I knew her at thirty-five she was a person of ripe wisdom and intelligence, a most ingenious and inspiring teacher. One of her plans was to keep us in touch with the growth of her own mind, and I remember that she read us passages from Emily Davies' *Higher Education of Women* when it was published, and when I wrote and told her of my wish to go to the new College, she was kindly and sympathetic.

" As a result of the *Macmillan* article I called on Miss Davies to ask for further information. I told her that my education was very defective and asked her advice as to whether I should attempt the first

---

[1] It was courageous of the Committee to fix the fees so high as £105 a year ; probably this was owing to Mr. Tomkinson's experience of Marlborough, where there were serious financial troubles owing to the fees having been at first fixed too low. The Girton fees remained at £105 a year till 1918, when they had to be raised owing to the increased cost of living consequent on the War.

The Scholarships were subscribed by Mrs. William Cowper (afterwards Lady Mount-Temple), Mrs. Russell Gurney, Mrs. Scaramanga, Countess de Grey, Lady Marian Alford, and Miss Dunb Masson.

[2] *A New College for Women*, in *Macmillan's Magazine*, June, 1868.

entrance examination and how soon it was likely to be held. She told me that the examination might probably take place in the following June, and urged me to put my name down for it, saying that it would do me no harm to fail, and that it was very important that there should be plenty of applicants. She advised me to spend the intervening months in studying Latin (of which I knew nothing) and mathematics. This advice was not easy to act on, for money was scarce . . . but I was determined to let nothing interfere with the examination, though I felt quite unprepared for it.

" When it came I thoroughly enjoyed it and was immensely interested in seeing the other students, about seventeen I think in number. Two specially impressed me—Miss Cook, who was very handsome and dignified, and Miss Townshend. . . .

" My place was fifth, I think, in the result. The first scholarship was awarded to Miss Townshend for her essay, and the second to Miss Woodhead for excellence in Mathematics.

" After the examination Miss Davies had a reception or afternoon party for the purpose of introducing the students to the Committee. It was then that I first saw Madame Bodichon, and the little talk I had with her made an outstanding event in my life. Her frank, direct manner went straight to my heart. I felt that the College meant a great deal to her, and that it was a great privilege to have a chance of helping to make it a success. I seem to remember that her face was framed in a cottage bonnet that made a halo for her blue eyes and golden hair. She told me that she had been talking to Miss Townshend and felt sure she would be a leading spirit among the students, a sound prophecy, for her interests were wide and her mind original."

The Entrance Examination was held at the University of London (Burlington Gardens) under Miss Davies's superintendence, and she took the opportunity of writing to Madame Bodichon while she was sitting in the room with the candidates doing their papers. She was able to tell her that it had at last been definitely decided to take Benslow House, Hitchin, for the College.

(*Miss Davies to Madame Bodichon.*)
UNIVERSITY OF LONDON.
July 13, 1869.
" We got thro' a great deal of work on Friday at the Committee. We appointed the rest of the teachers, and decided to take the house, which is eminently desirable (far more so than the one we could not get), and agreed upon a daily routine, which practically determines the discipline.

" Eighteen nice young women are under Examination. They vary widely in attainments. Some of the French and Latin papers are extremely bad, and some I *think* very good. This morning is devoted to the struggle with Arithmetic."

Thirteen candidates passed, and in October, three more were examined, at Madame Bodichon's house in Blandford Square. One of these was Miss L. I. Lumsden, now Dame Louisa Lumsden.

(Miss Davies to Madame Bodichon.)

June 4, 1869.

" I have had a delightful letter from Miss Lumsden, one of the most distinguished of the Edinburgh students. . . . She does not wish to hold a Scholarship, lest it should be depriving some one else who wants it more. She is 28, manifestly a lady, as well as an eager student, and I should think eminently desirable for us to have in our first group."

July 2, 1869.

" I have been seeing more of the students, and like them much. Those we are sure of are all past 20, and look like discreet young women. They seem, too, inclined to be good-natured about their accommodation, which is fortunate, as we shall certainly be cramped *inside* Benslow House, if we take it. It is offered now, and the House Committee go down to inspect next week. There are good grounds, and the right of walking over fifteen acres. The young people are beginning to plan games and bring their varied experience to bear."

August 2 [1869].

" I get delightful letters from the students. There is not one as to whom there need be the least fear that she would do anything foolish."

The arrangements which Miss Davies had to make as to lectures and studies were a matter of some difficulty. The lecturers were tempted to see in the College a field for interesting work on new lines, and the students wanted to take the subjects they preferred rather than those for which lectures could most conveniently be arranged. If Miss Davies had not been perfectly clear and determined as to the aim which had been laid down for the College, chaos would have set in as regards the curriculum.

(Miss Davies to Miss Anna Richardson.)

August 24, 1869.

" Yesterday . . . I had . . . a staggering letter from Mr. Clark, our Classical lecturer. He had alarmed me when he was here a few weeks ago by remarking that Greek was of no use to ladies, and showing in other ways a narrow tone, and yesterday I had a letter to say that in his teaching he did not intend to make any reference to the Cambridge curriculum, having devised one of his own which he considered superior. . . . It is curious to see how possessed he must be with the female idea. He suggests the Cambridge Examination for women as the right thing for our students, having been devised expressly for their class. About the best thing that can be said of this Examination is that it is *probably* just a step above the Senior Local, i.e. about on the level of our *Entrance*. It was devised to suit struggling governesses, with no teaching, and no time for study except their evenings. But they and our students are alike females, and beyond this, Mr. Clark fails to discriminate. . . .

" As to what you say about Modern Languages, if questions are asked, the answer is that there will be classes as soon as there are enough students. Hitherto only Miss Woodhead asks for them, and we cannot have Lectures for only one pupil. . . . Our students have to pass in Latin and Greek grammar in a year, or rather more, and most of them are at the very beginning in Greek, besides having Mathematics, which to some will be very difficult.[1] I look forward to helping them with Greek during the first term. It is quite a waste of a University man's time to be hearing people say their declensions and verbs, and it will be a pleasure to me as a meeting-point with the students. . . .

" I hope the College students will find it possible to be in the highest spirits without trampling upon reverence. We are very happy in having a well-mannered group to start with, to set up good traditions."

September 14, 1869.

" I am delighted to tell you that the difficulty with Mr. Clark is quite disposed of. My letter to him brought an answer by return of post which was almost a retraction, and a day or two later I had another, still more satisfactory. . . . I believe there is no doubt as to his being a first-rate teacher. . . . It is a little tiresome that they all dislike the Little-go subjects so much. . . . I think we are bound to do as *much* as the Poll requires, but if our students should prefer trying for Honours, it is open to us to prepare for the Triposes instead. Whichever they do, the Little-go must be passed, and the further question need not be decided for a year or more.

" I want you to . . . influence Miss Lloyd not to give up Classics. . . . For her own sake, it might *perhaps* (tho' I doubt it) be best to

---

[1] These were the Little-go subjects.

217

confine herself to Modern Languages.[1] But while the number of our students is so very small, it would be most inconvenient to have them divided into two Sections. Apart from any considerations of expense, it would be dispiriting to have such small classes as they must be, if divided. I will explain this to Miss Lloyd, but I want you to make her feel what a great loss it would be to herself to give up Classics, especially as she has done a little already at both Latin and Greek. It is not as if she had to begin the alphabet."

A House Committee, consisting of Mrs. Gurney, Miss Davies, Miss Garrett, and Mrs. Austin [2] was appointed, and Miss Davies wanted Madame Bodichon to join it, " to help in making the house pretty and picturesque." Though Madame Bodichon had joined the Executive Committee, she was not strong enough at this time to undertake so much work as the House Committee would involve. " I don't think we shall be able to make very much of the house at Hitchin," Miss Davies wrote to her, " but having a foundation of plainness and solidity, we may by touches of prettiness and originality here and there save it from being ugly or depressingly commonplace. So please let us have hints if any come to you." Mrs. Austin took possession of the house towards the end of September, and worked hard to get it ready. Miss Davies joined her on October 9.

(*Miss Davies to Mrs. Manning.*)

THE COLLEGE, HITCHIN.

October 9, 1869.

9.30 *p.m.*

" MY DEAR MRS. MANNING,—

" One line just before going to sleep for the first time at the College. I seem to have almost too much to say, for a hasty note. Mrs. Austin has made a good deal of progress in getting the house into order, and I am sure we shall be ready for you by Thursday. As soon as you and Adelaide come, we can all work together at preparing for the students, if our time does not all go in talking, which I rather fear. . . . Mr. Tomkinson has been down to-day, to take possession of his property. . . . Our little band of undergraduates seem to be coming in the best possible *tone*. If not numerous, they are certainly select."

---

[1] There was at this time no Honours Examination in Modern Languages.

[2] The two latter were not members of the Executive Committee.

I.H.Gamble   R.S.Cook   Professor E.C.Clark   Dame Louisa   By kind permission of Mrs. Webber
(Mrs.Otter) (Mrs.C.P.Scott)   Lumsden   A.A.Bulley
            S.Woodhead   E.C.Gibson   I.F.V.Townshend   (Mrs.Brooke)
            (Mrs.Corbett) (Mrs.Townshend)

THE EARLIEST STUDENTS OF GIRTON WITH PROFESSOR CLARK
AT BENSLOW HOUSE, HITCHIN, EASTER TERM, 1871

CHAPTER XIV

The College : The Vision Realized. 1869-1871

THE first five students were Miss Gibson, Miss Lloyd, Miss Lumsden, Miss Woodhead, and Miss Townshend; besides Miss Manning, who hardly counted as a regular student, as she was to be there for only one term, and did not intend to take any examination. Miss Gibson has described her reception by Miss Davies, on her first arrival at Hitchin. Before she had time to knock or ring, " the door was opened, and on the threshold there stood the keen little lady to whose courage and energy the whole scheme of a College for women was due, and who was now quivering with excitement, thinly veiled under a business-like manner, in this moment when her cherished hopes were actually beginning to materialize."[1]

(Miss Davies to Miss Anna Richardson.)
October 20, 1869 [*Wednesday*].

" MY DEAR ANNA,—

" We are here. The little band arrived in due succession on Saturday, and we have now had three lectures. It is difficult to know what to say, except that you must come and see us. Adelaide has just been ejaculating ' It *is* so pleasant to be at the College,' and the students are saying it in their bright faces and in their tones all day. I scarcely expected that they could all have worked together with such entire cordiality and that so small a number could be so ' jolly.' Miss Lloyd is most valuable. Being a little older than the others, she makes a' link between them and the authorities. . . . Miss Lloyd is a little behind the rest both in Latin and Mathematics, and incessantly proclaims her despair of doing anything. She sends you a message that she doubts whether she will live till Christmas, but whatever happens,

---

[1] Communicated by Miss Gibson.

she will stick to it till she dies. Mr. Clark's teaching of Latin is most interesting. . . . They say Mr. Stuart's explanations of Mathematics are exceedingly clear. . . . I find a great deal of time goes in talking with the students. They come here by ones and twos and we get into talks. Mrs. Manning is delighted with their faces, and wants to have photographs of them all. We are pretty civilized now and quite comfortable. We have good plain food, milk, bread, beef, and mutton, and it disappears very fast. The fresh pure air, and perhaps also being in good spirits, gives everybody an appetite. . . . Mrs. Austin undertook the worst of the furnishing and settling and did it admirably, but it is not quite finished yet."

Benslow House, as Miss Davies said, had a foundation of plainness and solidity, and it was beautifully placed on a chalk cliff above Hitchin, with wide views over Hertfordshire. The garden was large and pleasant, with flower borders and shrubberies, and it was shaded with well-grown trees. One room served both as bedroom and sitting-room for each student, except two, who had, as well as a bedroom apiece, a small study—in one case a converted china closet. Miss Davies was not expected to reside at the College, but she would have to pay at least one official visit at the beginning of each term, to arrange about lectures, and a room was therefore set apart for her. A room on the ground floor, known as "the Library," had to serve as a common room for the students, and a lecture room. In the basement was what Miss Davies called "the dining-hall." Everything was planned by her in detail, and with careful regard to the dignity and correctness befitting a college. "The plan proposed," she wrote to Mrs. Manning, "is a students' table, and a Mistress's table, the first long and narrow, to sit only on one side, with their faces towards the Mistress's table, the other a rather small oval, for the Mistress and the Supernumerary [Miss Manning], and (if invited) the Sec. [Miss Davies herself].' Miss Lumsden has described the students' view of these arrangements :

" The dining-room was in the basement, a bare ugly room with two tables, at one of which we students sat, while the Mistress and her friends sat at the ' High table ' alongside. It was at first expected that we should sit in a formal row down one side of our table, lest we should be guilty of the discourtesy of turning our backs upon the 'High.' But this was too much, and we rebelled. Conversation cannot but flag if people have to sit in a row, and we quietly ignored rule and insisted upon comfortably facing each other. So academically formal . . . was the order imposed from the first at Hitchin—we might have been fifty undergraduates instead of five harmless young women." [1]

Beneath this formality there lay a definite purpose. Miss Davies was determined that the College should be a real College, and not a new variety of girls' school ; she wanted everything to be done from the very beginning with due regard to dignity and decorum. Down to the smallest detail, she felt that all they did was of historic importance, and that the lines which future generations were to follow must be rightly laid down. This feeling was understood and shared by the students.

" It needed an effort of imagination to recognize Dons and high table and undergraduates all complete, though as it were in embryo : but it was an effort that Miss Davies was fully prepared to make and to insist upon. Just at first she did not need to insist, for there was not one of these five first-comers who was not weighted with a sense of responsibility for the new start. They were all much on their guard against being treated as school-girls, and in the case of three, at least, out of the five, age alone was not enough to differentiate them." [2]

The students, as Miss Gibson recalls, were very various in age, experience, and attainments. Miss Townshend, the youngest daughter of an English family resident in Ireland since the time of Cromwell, was a quick-witted, clever, and sensitive girl, a great admirer of William Morris and the Pre-Raphaelites, and her " æsthetic " enthusiasms brought a novel element into the little circle. Miss Lloyd, in particular, used in after-years to say that her fellow-students had opened her eyes about art, and that she had learned from them that it was one of the foundations of happiness.

" Miss Woodhead, the youngest, aged eighteen " (writes Miss Gibson), " had only recently left a good Quaker school, but had already begun teaching : Miss Lloyd was older than any of us, a woman of culture, and also a Friend. She did not come with the intention of reading for a degree examination, but for a quiet time of leisure and

---

[1] *The Ancient History of Girton College*, by Miss L. I. Lumsden, *The Girton Review*, Michaelmas Term, 1907.
[2] Communicated by Miss Gibson.

study. Her presence was valuable as a mellowing influence. This was even more true of the gracious and charming lady who was our Mistress during the first term. Mrs. Manning was frail and elderly, and one cannot wonder that she felt unable to occupy the post permanently, but we all regretted her leaving us, and felt that we had lost a friend. The College has never had a more suitable and dignified Head than during its first term. Her suavity and gentle courtesy complemented perfectly Miss Davies' eager abrupt decisiveness."

The furnishing of the house was made more complete during the Christmas vacation, and Madame Bodichon sent some of her sketches, which were hung in the library. " I have not expressed sufficiently *how* welcome the pictures are," Miss Davies wrote to her. " Hitchin keeps up its health and spirits delightfully." With the Lent term, there came a new student—Miss Rachel Cook, who had previously been kept away by illness. Miss Cook's character and personality were such as to make a great impression on her fellow-students. " Her presence made itself felt the moment she entered the room," writes Miss Gibson. " It is impossible to convey an impression of her charm by any inventory of her features, but no man or woman ever failed to feel it. George Eliot once described her as nymphlike. . . . One did not need to wait for the delicate staccato idiom of her speech to decide that her romantic type of beauty could belong only to Highland blood." Miss Maynard, who entered the College two years later, has also described some of the first generation of students. Miss Cook was " beautiful in face as in mind, and had the endowment of that scholarly instinct that industry alone can never attain. . . . Her father had been Professor of Moral Philosophy at St. Andrews, and she had been brought up in the atmosphere of a University, as none of the rest of us had been." Miss Woodhead was " a stalwart north-country girl with an erect figure and a fine pair of shoulders . . . more given to long walks and to gathering branches of trees than to any sort of literary interest." Miss Woodhead and Miss Gibson read Mathematics, Miss Cook and Miss Lumsden Classics. Of the last named Miss Maynard writes : " We all . . . looked upon her not only as the senior student, but as our true head and representative. In her we saw the life of the College at its intensest and most glowing point, for there we found the widest sympathies, the highest aspirations, the severest struggles. . . . She appreciated the new outlook in a wider and more sagacious manner than any one of the rest of us at the time. . . . It would be hard to tell the gain to any one of us, and a definite part of that gain was her gift."[1]

Some one said that the students were " the happiest women in England." Miss Lumsden, on being asked, during her first term at Hitchin, what was the uppermost feeling in her mind, answered " Gladness." She had had a free and happy life at home ; but country pursuits and travel both at home and abroad had not satisfied her. Hitchin brought the one thing that had been lacking in her life—aim. Miss Maynard had similar experiences. She first heard of the College from a sister of Miss Cook's, who was able to describe it exactly. " The whole was a new world to me," Miss Maynard writes, " yet even while she was speaking, a conviction came to me, ' *That's* what you have been waiting for ! ' . . . The extraordinary happiness of that first year at Hitchin is a thing that cannot come twice in a lifetime. . . . I was . . . adopted at once by R. Cook and L. I. Lumsden, and I need hardly say they opened a new world of thought to me." Miss Maynard has recorded elsewhere that she used to wake every morning in her first term or two " with a sort of sting of delight, and think, ' Here is a whole day more at College ! ' "

The life at Hitchin was on the whole a very quiet and studious one. Miss Dove, who entered in 1871, has described some of their recreations :

" The old students were very good to us newcomers, and many were the delightful walks we had in the country round about, to St. Ippolyt's, to Wain Wood, full of primroses and anemones, and on one great occasion to Lily Hoo, where we found anemone pulsatilla. On another very memorable occasion, I remember, we went by train to Stevenage, and then walked to the woods at Knebworth, where we found yellow nettle in flower and other treasures. On our return, when we had the road to ourselves, we marched along singing College songs. I am afraid Miss Davies would have been sadly horrified if she had happened to meet us. But we really had very few amusements. The grounds being on a hillside were not suitable for games, and there was nowhere

---

[1] *Between College Terms*, by C. L. Maynard. See also *Girton Review*, October Term, 1905, pp. 6–7, for some account of Miss Cook.

else to play, besides which we were too small a party for any organized games, and I remember this was felt as a great privation by some. . . . The first year of students were really very outstanding people, and the interest of making their acquaintance, which we juniors considered a high privilege, and studying the varying points of view which they represented, together with the novelty of the life, the interest of our studies, and the beautiful country walks, were quite sufficient to keep us in health and vigour. One favourite amusement at Hitchin was to rush out after dinner to the walk on the edge of the cliff and see the Edinburgh express slip its carriage. Then we found after a time an open-air swimming bath in the town, and that became in the summer a great resource . . . we used to go down in parties and enjoy it."

(Miss Davies to Miss Manning.)

June 23 [1870].

" Have I told you how much we have been enjoying the Swimming bath ?—to which I must now pay a visit. I have been done out of it twice this week by excess of letters, and I don't want to miss it to-day, tho' I am not quite in Miss Townshend's state of mind. She announced this morning that she *must* learn to swim this Term, whatever became of the Examination. We have taken to croquet too, and find Mr. Heywood's implements particularly handy."

Miss Davies took great pleasure in joining in the students' diversions so far as she felt it proper for her to do so. She had that power of intense enjoyment of little things which is often seen in people whose youth has been spent in quiet and austere surroundings. The students played cricket and fives in the garden, as Dame Louisa Lumsden tells us, " with great laughter and fun, but with small success from the point of view of the game." Mr. Tomkinson taught them to play fives.[1] " I am learning to play fives," Miss Davies told Miss Manning ; " Miss Gibson is at the bottom of the class, Miss Cook and I are bracketed next above her." Miss Maynard describes a little scene in the garden :

" It was a great point to get much exercise in a short time, and one day I dragged out the heavy iron roller and began rolling the lawn. Other students, E. Welsh among them I remember, saw me, and came out to have a share. When they pulled it, I said ' I could walk on the roller, I think ! ' so they gave me a hand up and I found that by a

---

[1] *The Ancient History of Girton College*, by L. I. Lumsden, in the *Girton Review*, Michaelmas Term, 1907.

little practice one could balance oneself and keep up with its steady progress. Miss Davies came out of her room and stood watching us, and when I jumped off she came forward saying, ' I believe I could do that. Will you hold my hand ? ' She seemed small and light of weight as I helped her to her foothold, and then without the least mistake she went carefully from one end of the lawn to the other. She kept a very light hold on my hand, and the team in front did their best to draw the chariot evenly. Her life seemed so much apart from us, and so solitary, that a ' human ' incident like this was refreshing."

When the students began, in a mild way, to play football on the lawn, Miss Davies felt this was going too far. It was necessary to avoid criticism as far as possible, and " football for ladies " would certainly shock the world, if it were known.[1] Most of the students had to encounter some disapproval of the College among their families and friends. Miss Lloyd, who was one of a family of nine, had to face quite an outcry. " Hearing that Hitchin College was prepared to begin," she writes, " I said, ' Farewell, farewell,' but my farewells were almost drowned in exclamations of ' How worldly ! how shocking ! ' One of my nieces has told me she was led to think her aunt quite unchristian."[2] People generally thought the College either shocking, or ridiculous, or both. Miss Lloyd had a story of a fellow-passenger, a clergyman, in a train passing Hitchin, who said as he looked out of the window towards the College, " There go the infidel ladies ! " at which she was moved to say, " Indeed we are not infidels—we have morning and evening prayer," and he replied dryly, " I'm glad to hear it." When Miss Dove went to Hitchin, " it was an unheard-of event in the lives of all our neighbours and friends, and I was at once set apart by them as an eccentric and somewhat awesome person, and in vacations found myself avoided by all

[1] Cf. *Punch*, May 10, 1873. " *Pretty Batswomen.*" " Irrepressible woman again in the field. ' Ladies' Cricket ' is advertised, to be followed, there is every reason to apprehend, by Ladies' Fives, Ladies' Football, Ladies' Golf, etc. It is all over with men. They had better make up their minds to rest contented with croquet, and afternoon tea, and sewing machines, and perhaps an occasional game of drawing-room billiards." The last sentence gives a pretty accurate description of the games then thought proper for girls.

[2] Communicated by Miss Lloyd. See also an article by her in the *Girton Review*, May Term, 1915, pp. 15–17.

young persons, and was obliged to take refuge in the society of those who had known me from childhood. My contemporaries, I think, suffered from sheer fright lest they should be humiliated by being addressed in either Greek or Latin—poor things, if they had only known ! "

The process of living down these prejudices was a trying one, but reasonable people soon began to see that the College had no very terrible effects upon the students. Miss Maynard, for instance, had some difficulty in persuading her parents to allow her to enter it ; leave was at first given for one year only, on condition that she would not try for a degree but would come home again " as if nothing had happened," and not take to teaching or do anything eccentric. Before long, however, these conditions were willingly withdrawn ; and she was able, with their approval, to stay for three years and take the Moral Sciences Tripos, after which she took up teaching as the business of her life, and became the first Principal of Westfield College.

Prejudices, however, generally die hard, and Miss Davies naturally felt it of the first importance that the inhabitants of Benslow House should be most careful to avoid exciting remark of any sort. The students were all people of some force of character, or they would not have been there. " We were rather an awkward team to drive during the first two or three years," writes Miss Gibson, " and it is useless to deny that there was occasional friction, though on the whole, we were all very happy and got on well together." Miss Davies had some anxious times, but strong feelings of loyalty and goodwill held the little community together. On one occasion, when a visit from Mr. Tomkinson had given Miss Davies an opportunity of pouring out some of her difficulties to a sympathetic confidant, she afterwards repented of her criticisms and wrote to him as follows :

November 16 [1870].
" I have been half sorry since for disclosing any part of the imperfect side of anyone here, but you will not think more of it than was meant. I have been feeling strongly this evening how much nearer perfection they are than almost anybody else one knows. They have been in one of their mirthful moods, going off at little jests as if they had fountains of laughter within them. That. kind of innocent spontaneous hilarity is not common, I think, and is very pleasant."

226

THE VISION REALIZED

(" *George Eliot* " to *Miss Davies*.)

November 19, 1869.

" I am cheered by hearing that the beginning at Hitchin looks so happy and promising. I care so much about individual happiness that I think it is a great thing to work for, only to make half-a-dozen lives rather better than they might otherwise be."

George Eliot and Mr. Lewes gave some of their books to the library, which was still very meagerly supplied. Books were also given by Miss Richardson and her sister, and other friends, including Mr. Roby, who gave copies of his Latin grammar to the Classical Students.

(Miss Davies to Miss Anna Richardson.)

" So far as we can judge at present, the studies are going on well. Mr. Stuart thinks that Miss Gibson and Miss Woodhead, who wish to go in for the Mathematical Tripos, would have a very good chance of doing well in it. They know already more than is wanted for the Little-go. Miss Lumsden and Miss Townshend would like to try for the Classical Tripos, but we have not consulted Mr. Clark yet about their chances of success. The want of early preparation seems to be a greater drawback in Classics than in Mathematics. . . . I hope we shall before long be able to announce the time of the next Entrance Examination. There will certainly be some Scholarships awarded in connection with it. Mrs. Manning is going to give one of 50 guineas a year, for three years. . . . I wish I had time to tell you more about our life. Miss Lloyd and I sympathize in longing for you to come. We take in the *Times*, the *Spectator*, and the *Guardian*, and we all go to church except the two Friends."

December 10 [1869].

" How exhausting it must be to belong to a large family [a brother of Miss Richardson's had been ill]. . . . It is worse than the College, which I find an exciting thing to belong to. On the whole, our course this Term has run very smooth. It has been an exhilarating and encouraging time. We end to-morrow. . . .

" Do you know anything of a Miss Emily Shirreff who wrote a book a long time ago on the *Intellectual Education of Women* ? She is to succeed Mrs. Manning, as a volunteer. In some respects, I like her better than anyone else that has been thought of. She has a Stoical way of talking which attracts me. Her view of coming here is simply that if she is wanted, and can do it, she ought. She takes a modest view of her duties, and undertakes them simply, without any grand air of self-sacrifice. It is a spirited thing to do, from mere interest in the idea, at her age. She is I believe about 55, ladylike and gentle in manner, and I fancy a good deal of a student."

December 30 [1869].

" The College reopens on February 5th and I shall go down a few days before. . . . I do not intend to be so much at Hitchin next Term as I was last, but I find it difficult to arrange my time. Besides wanting to be at *home*, I want to be in London, but then I also want to be at Hitchin for the sake of getting people to come down. We find that seeing is believing, and I am afraid saying to people, *Go* and see, will not be so effectual as saying *Come*. Evidently there is still a great deal to do in making the College known. . . . I am hoping that Miss Shirreff will bring in friends of a new set. She belongs to the Antrim family, and moves in such high circles that scarcely anybody I know has ever seen her. . . . We are to have Miss Wedgwood also next Term. The students think it would enable them to get on faster with Classics if they had some help from a resident Tutor, so Miss W. has kindly consented to come for a month, as an experiment. The difficulty in the way is her deafness. We can only find out by trying whether that is too great a drawback. . . . To have a person of her noble nature and keen interest in study is worth sacrificing a good deal for."

Miss Shirreff took up the duties of the Mistress in the Lent Term of 1870. Miss Gibson remembers her as " elderly, beautiful, and beautifully dressed, of the fine-lady type, a contrast to the plain-speaking and downright manners of Miss Davies and Lady Stanley of Alderley. She was full of reminiscences and talked in an interesting way about the distinguished people she had known—Buckle, for instance, to whom she had been engaged." The new Mistress, for her part, was delighted with the students. " Miss Shirreff is as much struck as Mrs. Manning was by the elevation of their talk," wrote Miss Davies to Miss Manning. Miss Richardson, who visited the College in the following year, thought " the whole life of the students looked only *too* intellectually luxurious ; but they are a remarkably interesting set of young women."[1]

The intellectual luxury was, however, not so great as it seemed to Miss Richardson. " Our teaching during the first year was

[1] *Memoir of Anna Deborah Richardson*, 1877, printed for private circulation.

scanty but excellent," writes Miss Gibson. " We should no doubt have been the better in those early days for a little more advice and teaching. Our lecturers came once or twice a week, and there was no one to appeal to in between. Miss Julia Wedgwood stood in the gap for a time. I do not know that her classical teaching was of great assistance, but she was an interesting and delightful personality, and enriched the life of our little community." " Four lecturers came to Hitchin in the first term, Messrs. Seeley, Hort, Clark and Stuart," writes Dame Louisa Lumsden,[1] " and we had one lecture every day which everybody attended, the length of this lecture being fixed neither by our capacities of taking in knowledge, nor by the convenience of the lecturer, but by the hours of railway trains. The only exception to this rule was Mr. Hort, as he came from the neighbouring rectory of St. Ippolyt's, therefore his lecture lasted only the reasonable time of one hour." Mr. Clark came twice a week from Cambridge for both Latin and Greek. Miss Gibson describes the work as " very elementary, for we were all beginners, but the class was small and eager, and Mr. Clark the most patient, painstaking and thorough of teachers, so that we got on pretty quickly and enjoyed the lectures immensely. . . . For a single term we had lectures on English from Mr. Seeley. This had been looked forward to as a signal honour and great opportunity, for *Ecce Homo* was to many of us the book of the day, but the lectures were disappointing. Seeley was not a born teacher ; dry, critical, and sarcastic, he demanded bricks without straw."

Professor Seeley, as we have seen, despised the Cambridge course, and instead of keeping to the subjects required for it, he lectured on *Lycidas*, and set the students to write original verse ; Dr. Hort likewise lectured on the Acts, though St. Luke's Gospel was the book set for the Little-go ; Mr. Clark alone took a practical view of the position and kept strictly to the Little-go subjects. " By this, as well as by his most interesting and stimulating teaching, he earned our warmest gratitude," writes Dame Louisa Lumsden.[2] She was becoming anxious about her work. " I have been thinking a great deal lately about Latin," she wrote to Miss Davies, on February 28, 1870. " I am so dissatisfied with the work I am doing in it this term. Every day is of importance,

[1] *Girton Review*, Michaelmas Term, 1907.   [2] *Ibid.*

for I certainly have no time to lose. . . . Could you possibly arrange some plan by which Miss Gibson and I might go on really satisfactorily with Latin ? Could we have one Latin lesson every week ? I fear this request is a very troublesome one. . . . I can only say that I would not make it if I did not feel the need of additional Latin teaching to be a very pressing one. . . . Everything is going on here very pleasantly, but I think we shall all be the better for having you among us again to cheer us on."

Miss Davies advised that the question should be laid before Mr. Clark, who proposed that he should spare half an hour for Latin out of his Greek lecture once or twice a week, an arrangement which hardly looks satisfactory, but no doubt he could not spare another day for Hitchin, and they had to make the best of it. Next term, however, an additional classical lecturer was appointed, Mr. C. E. Graves. " No words," writes Dame Louisa Lumsden, " are enough to do justice to the services of Mr. Clark and Mr. Graves." Mr. Stuart was prevented from continuing his mathematical lectures by measles, " a disease that seemed to suit his youthful appearance," as Miss Gibson remarks. It seems, however, that in any case he would have resigned his lectureship before long. " I observe that a new mathematical lecturer is to be appointed," wrote Mr. Sedley Taylor to Madame Bodichon. " This is a direct consequence of our distance from Cambridge—at least, I imagine from what Mr. Stuart said to me that he resigns on account of the amount of time taken up in going to and fro between Cambridge and the College. Here then we have at once the serious evil of a change of teacher within a few months of our start." Mr. Stuart was succeeded by Mr. J. F. Moulton,[1] fresh from his honours as Senior Wrangler and Smith's Prizeman. " He poured an amazing illumination on elementary mathematics " for Miss Gibson and Miss Woodhead. They found the work a severe struggle, but were urged on by Miss Davies.

(*Miss Woodhead to Miss Davies.*)

THE COLLEGE, HITCHIN.

March 4, 1870.

" I was very much interested in the message you sent me about the use of Mathematics. . . . I have hitherto generally looked upon it

---

[1] Afterwards Lord Justice Moulton.

as a delightful study, but one which very few people cared about. . . .
Now I begin to see that it is rather a source of true pleasure. . . . I
am rather discouraged however at the very small progress I have made
this term. . . . At present I feel that it is perfectly hopeless to dream
of the Tripos. . . . My own private feeling is that I should like to
have some other subject next term. . . . I should rather have Natural
Science than anything else."

Natural Science would not have done at all, as there were no
laboratories. Miss Woodhead, however, persevered with her
Mathematics, and eventually succeeded in passing the Tripos.
Miss Gibson was lured away by a growing interest in other matters.
" As soon as opportunity offered for a wider choice of subjects,"
she writes, " my allegiance wavered. I had already begun to take
an interest in Political Economy, and when Mr. Venn's lectures
began in my third year, I spent a good deal of time in reading for
them, and was much thrilled to find at the end of it that we were
to be examined by my saint and hero, the author of *The Subjection of Women*.[1] . . . Perhaps if one had gone up straight
from school, one would have been inured to the restraint of
reading with an examination ahead, but the definite goal grew
more and more unattractive to me as time went on. I always
wanted to spend my time on the wrong things, and when I found
that the last term must be spent in revising tiresome elementary
work, I made up my mind not to stay for it."

Want of preparation made the burden of the examinations very
heavy. The long pull of elementary work to pass the Little-go
and the Additional subjects (all Mathematics) was, as Miss Maynard recalls, a very great strain, and with some of the students
two years had to be spent upon this before they could enter (well
tired out) on the Tripos work, with barely four terms at their
disposal. " No allowance whatever was made for our colossal
ignorance of the special subjects required. . . . Three years
and one term was in those days the time allowed to men in which
to take the Tripos, and Miss Emily Davies scorned all com-
promises and her students must conform to the same rule."[2]
The students were there for the College, not the College for the

[1] The papers set for the students by J. S. Mill are to be found in his
Letters, Vol. II, p. 336.
[2] *Between College Terms*, by C. L. Maynard.

students. To Miss Davies, the individual, as Dame Louisa Lumsden has said, was " a mere cog in the wheel of her great scheme. There was a fine element in this, a total indifference to popularity, but . . . it was plain that we counted for little or nothing, except as we furthered her plans." We have seen how Miss Davies pressed Miss Woodhead and Miss Lloyd to take the subjects which she thought would bring most credit to the College, and for which the teaching could most conveniently be organized, rather than those in which they felt themselves most competent. It must be added, that she had a strong faith in Classics and Mathematics as the established subjects, and the best means by which women could get the exact training which she so much desired for them ; and she was apt to under-estimate the drawbacks arising from want of previous preparation. Any other Tripos than these two was, in her view, " a soft option."

Among other members of the Committee, Mr. Bryce was the one who took most interest in the students' work. He visited the College several times, gave a few lectures on Greek History, and invited the students to write essays during the vacation for him to criticize. On one occasion he paid an unexpected visit, and, as Dame Louisa Lumsden relates, " unfortunately only one student was in, Miss Townshend. On our return from a long walk, we were greatly amused by her description of her interview with the visitor. ' You see,' said she to him, ' nobody here knows anything ! ' It was a startling criticism of Hitchin arrangements." And it was true—no one at Benslow House could be guided by experience. The ladies on the Committee were not familiar with University work, and did not realize the task set before the students. The lecturers had never before had pupils quite like these, mature, intelligent, and eager to learn, but wonderfully ignorant ; and they found it difficult to enter seriously into the plan of preparing them for the Honours examinations. The students had to grope for what they needed. Though they felt the kindness of Mr. Seeley and Mr. Hort, they were forced into the ungracious position of having to rebel and demand to be taught the subjects essential for their purpose. In a conversation with Mr. Seeley they explained that they wished to give up his classes owing to the necessity of spending all their time on the examination subjects. This was more than he could bear, and he resigned his place on the Executive Committee.

(Mr. Seeley to Miss Davies.)

" It seems to me a great misfortune that the College should seem to the outer world, just at this critical time, to be nothing but a reproduction of Cambridge with all its faults. . . . Just at the moment when education is taking a new shape I cannot take any pleasure in attending to the details of a College where the old and to me obsolete routine goes on. . . . I cannot do more than passively wish you well. . . . I do not feel prepared to give my time to you."

Other lecturers were appointed on the staff ; and the students helped each other, Miss Lumsden, Miss Woodhead, and Miss Gibson adding to their own work by coaching others in the Little-go subjects.

Difficulties as to the work and the teaching naturally made themselves felt in the second term, as the students began to find out what the work really meant. There were other troubles as well. Complaints as to the food seem to show that the housekeeping was perhaps too economical, and some details of discipline proved irksome to the students. Certain points, such as having to ask leave of absence from morning service on Sundays, and the presence of chaperones at lectures, were waived by Miss Shirreff. The rule that the gates must be closed at a certain hour was disliked by some of the students, who did not know that this was usual in a College. There was no custom or tradition to guide them or the authorities in their relation to each other. Miss Shirreff was the constituted resident authority, but Miss Davies was felt to be the real though not the official head. " In spirit she was continually with us," writes Dame Louisa Lumsden, " and her will was felt to be the driving force throughout." Miss Shirreff found her position not altogether easy. Neither in her case nor in Mrs. Manning's had the duties been clearly defined. During Mrs. Manning's short tenure of office, this had given rise to no difficulty ; she had been content to act as mistress of the house, and leave the organization of studies to Miss Davies. Miss Shirreff was not satisfied, and wished to be (like Mrs. Manning) on the Executive Committee. This was the first appearance of a perpetually recurring difference of opinion between Miss Davies and successive Mistresses.

THE COLLEGE:

February 28, 1870.

" No doubt [Miss Shirreff] would prefer to have the whole internal management, including the direction of studies, in her hands. But . . . nothing was said to justify her expecting it. . . . We really want a person with sufficient resources in the way of pursuits of her own such *as can be carried on at Hitchin,* to make her independent. . . . This seems to me to make it useless to think of Lady Rich, as her pursuits can only be carried on in London. A student, or a writer, might live contentedly at Hitchin."

March 2 [1870].

" Miss Shirreff is certainly an amiable, affectionate person, and warmly interested in the College, and I feel inclined to persuade her to stay on, if she is willing, considering how difficult it is to find anyone exactly made for the post. . . . She evidently thinks that the power of active helping depends much more than it does on being on the Committee. . . . It is quite true, I think, that the position of the Mistress will alter as the College grows. It will tend more and more to be governed by the resident body, when there *is* a body, over which the Mistress will preside. But this cannot be till there *is* a body grown up in College traditions and qualified by previous training to direct the studies, as well as the other departments. There are *no* women as yet fit to direct the studies, and to put such an important matter into the hands of a single, untried, and necessarily ignorant person (ignorant I mean of University arrangements of all sorts, to say nothing of the actual studies) would be manifestly unwise. . . . As to influencing the characters of those about her, that surely depends on the Mistress herself. It seems to me a position in which a powerful character might command great indirect influence without *doing* anything very definite. But *we* cannot confer the power."

March 30 [1870].

" I think it would be a great advantage to have age and experience more strongly represented. I do not mean that the representation of authority is weak, but that *one* older person among so many strong young spirits is not enough. The difficulty is, as we have felt all along, how to supply the deficiency. The School Board makes it still more difficult than it was before for me to be constantly there, and as to visitors, one feels it of extreme importance that they should be the right people, and our choice is limited."

Among visitors who came often to the College were Madame Bodichon, Lady Stanley of Alderley, Lady Rich, and Miss Manning ; among occasional visitors were also Mrs. Garrett Anderson, Miss Richardson, Miss Frances Power Cobbe, and Mrs. Grey (Miss Shirreff's sister).

(Miss Davies to Miss Manning.)

April 4 [1870].

" I have had a little talk with Miss Lumsden about the life here. She says it is not amusement that they want, but *interests*, and I believe it is so. They want to *feel* the links between the large outer world and their own work, not to be distracted from it. They are cheerful enough now, and were unanimous in wishing for a short vacation and a long term, rather than vice versa."

The isolation at Hitchin and the extreme smallness of the community were beginning to be felt by the students. But their interest was still keen in the new life and in each other, and they used to sit up at night discussing everything in heaven and earth. Miss Lloyd, who was obliged to leave before long owing to ill-health, often said afterwards that the short time she had spent at the College was full of stimulus and inspiration, and that what she had absorbed there was a source of joy through the rest of her life.

(Miss Davies to Miss Anna Richardson.)

June 23 [1870].

" The old students—they begin to grow venerable—separated in a pleasant state of mind ; I had a talk with them the evening I left on the results of one year, putting it in the form of the question whether it would be worth while to come for a year only. The thing Miss Lloyd feels to have gained is some appreciation of the scholarly, as distinguished from the man-of-business way of looking at things. Miss Lumsden said that before she came, she used to feel fearfully solitary. She was always having said to her, ' Oh, but you're so exceptional.' Now, she feels herself belonging to a body, and has lost the sense of loneliness. Miss Townshend has learnt that she does not know how to study. Before she came, she thought she did. Also, she feels it a relief to have taken a step, from which she could not go back even if she wished. She has got rid of the harass of the daily self-questioning about what she had better do with herself. Miss Gibson replied briefly that one year was much better than nothing. Miss Cook said she would rather not come at all than that, and being asked why, explained that it was because she would be so sorry to go away. Miss Gibson said she should feel that just as much at the end of the three years, to which there was a chorus of assent. Miss Woodhead an-

swered my question with an emphatic ' Oh, I should think it *quite* worth
while.' I asked what was the good of it and she replied with a still
more emphatic *Oh !*—which remains unexplained, as my train would
not wait. You will understand that we were not talking about the
amount of *learning* to be gained. I do not wonder that they like being
at the College for the sake of each other's company. They are delightful to live with. I only hope the new set may turn out as nice."

Miss Shirreff's appointment had never been regarded as permanent, either by herself or by the Committee. She retired after
two terms, and the difficulty of finding a Mistress had again to be
faced.

(*Miss Davies to Mrs. Manning.*)

March 19 [1870].

" Mrs. Gurney thinks the *best* thing would be to have a transcen-
dently fit person (such as Lady Rich) who could be entirely trusted
on all points. But in the absence of this transcendent person—who
is not likely to be found by advertising or by ' looking out,' the next
best thing is to have some one like Mrs. Austin, whom we know well
and could trust thoroughly as to the most essential things."

In the printed Report of the College for 1871, the impersonal
announcement was made that " a permanent Mistress has now
been appointed." Mrs. Austin, however, held the office for
only two years. She was a gentle, amiable woman, with some
sense of humour, most conscientious and willing in all she undertook, and always ready to befriend the students in illness or
trouble. She had not, however, the wide intellectual outlook of
Mrs. Manning, and she was not strong in health, and inclined to
be over-anxious. Naturally she leaned much upon Miss Davies,
whom she consulted constantly, even as to small details of housekeeping and discipline. The task was growing. Three new
students [1] came in October, 1870, and as the house could not hold
them all, a long iron building was set up in the orchard, and
divided by curtains into small rooms.

(*Miss Davies to Miss Manning.*)

THE COLLEGE, HITCHIN.

October 14, 1870.

" I came here on Tuesday. The Term begins to-morrow. A hard
struggle has been going on for the last fortnight to get the new rooms

[1] Miss Gamble, Miss Slade, and Miss Tidman.

ready. It is fortunate that Mrs. Austin has been here to drive things on, or I don't know what would become of us. . . . The immediate prospect as regards [new] students is not very encouraging. . . . I am amused at your having had the shine a little taken out of London life by comparing it with Hitchin. Mrs. Austin finds it very exciting to be here, and I think it is a reviving atmosphere, physically and mentally. . . .

" I suppose it is true, as Mrs. Bradley thinks strongly, that the badness of school education is a great hindrance to the College *for the present*."

(Miss Davies to Miss Anna Richardson.)

October 24 [1870].

" Even the present small increase of number is working advantageously, as to the Lectures. It enables us to have more of them, and shorter hours at a time. The new Lecturers are much liked. The new rooms also (we call them the Tabernacle—in the wilderness, on the way to the Promised Land) have turned out pretty and comfortable. And the old and new students work in together pleasantly."

Miss Davies viewed the Tabernacle through rose-coloured spectacles. " Life in the tin house," writes Dame Louisa Lumsden, " was a misery. If it rained, the rattle on the roof was maddening ; if the sun shone we were baked as in an oven ; and the rooms were so small that Miss Woodhead, a tall athletic young woman, declared that in her doll's house sitting-room, without rising from her chair, by merely reaching out a long arm she could either poke the fire or open the door." Miss Kingsland (now Mrs. Higgs) relates that she could hear the scratch of her neighbour's pen as she sat at work. Mice gambolled between the tin walls and the paper with which they were lined, and the nightingales in the orchard added more pleasantly, but quite as noisily, to the disturbance.

As the number of students increased, things became more lively, and it was possible to have dancing in the evenings, as well as debates, Shakespeare readings, and so forth. Miss Davies attended these functions as an onlooker, and generally took a quiet and rather reserved part in all that was going on. " Self-suppression and pertinacity " were the qualities most remarked in her by one of the younger students. She was greatly overworked at this time, and must often have been very tired ; it was noticed that she did not go out much, and when not actually at

237

work, was obliged to take refuge in her knitting and the sofa. Nevertheless, beneath a surface of quiet decorum, she enjoyed life at Hitchin intensely. " A mere sight of the students," she wrote to Miss Richardson, " does not convey any adequate sense of the delightfulness of living among them." A good many varieties of religious opinion were represented in the College. Some of the students went to a Congregational chapel, some to the services at the parish church, or to Dr. Hort's services at St. Ippolyt's, where among the congregation were to be seen old labourers dressed in smocks, standing during the sermon. Miss Davies put no pressure on anyone to go to church. All were left free to do as they chose, and though differences of religious opinion made themselves felt, the strong College spirit which ruled from the first helped them, as a student of that time has said, " to shake down together."

In the October term of 1870 came a great event in the life of the College—the Little-go. Despised as it was, this examination was regarded by Miss Davies and the students as the first touchstone on which to prove their worth. Every step in the process was a crisis. Application had first to be made to the University authorities for leave for the students to take the papers, and a refusal would have demolished the whole object of their first year's work. When the answer came from the Council of the Senate, it was to the effect that it was not within their province to give the permission asked for, but that there would be no objection to a private arrangement being made with the examiners. Miss Davies accordingly wrote to the Senior Examiner, Mr. Cartmell, asking him to take the matter into his hands, and make what arrangements seemed right with the other examiners. The examiners consented to undertake the work, and the five second-year students prepared themselves to face the ordeal at the end of the October term. Dame Louisa Lumsden describes her experiences as follows :

" We went up to Cambridge for it, and Miss Davies did me a good turn, for she kindly introduced me to a countrywoman of my own, Mrs. Latham, a most kind and charming woman, whose guest I became. With her I saw Cambridge under delightful guidance. We lunched, for instance, at Queen's, and I recollect how kind old Dr. Phillips, the President, froze my blood by innocently remarking, in his slow and somewhat pompous fashion, that he believed there were ' some young women up in Cambridge to pass the Little-go ! '

" ' Yes,' said Mrs. Latham coolly, ' and there sits one.' I could have sunk under the table ! But both Dr. and Mrs. Phillips were so kind, and they took the terrible revelation so calmly, that I was soon reassured.

" Not so, however, did it fare with me at Jesus College. Before we ventured into these once conventual precincts, Mrs. Latham warned me on no account to divulge the secret of my quest at Cambridge ; the result might, she said, be that I might find myself summarily ejected from the house. Nothing was farther from my desires than to be either a martyr or a nine days' wonder, and I need hardly say that I kept a discreet silence."

(*Miss Davies to Miss Richardson.*)

EXAMINATION ROOM, CAMBRIDGE.

December 10 [1870].

" This is the last day of our Little-go, and a viva voce examination in the Greek Testament (Gospel of St. Luke) is now going on. Miss Woodhead is at this moment in an adjoining room, being questioned. The others are writing. . . . Everything has gone quite smoothly and the kindness shown on all sides has been exhilarating. . . . We have managed to see a good deal during our leisure intervals, and the three Classical students went with me to dine at our Greek Lecturer's, where we met a pleasant party, Mr. Jebb (Public Orator), Mr. H. Sidgwick, Mr. John Mayor, and Mr. Sedley Taylor. We go back to Hitchin this evening and shall all be scattered on Monday. I go up by an early train to be ready for the Local Examination in London. We have more than 200 girls this year."

The success of the Hitchin candidates was recorded by *Punch* [1] as follows :

" THE CHIGNON AT CAMBRIDGE.

" At the examination lately held at Cambridge, a number of students from the Ladies' College at Hitchin passed their ' Little-go,' the first time that such undergraduates ever underwent that ordeal. It is gratifying to be enabled to add, that out of all those flowers of loveliness, not one was plucked. Bachelors of Arts are likely to be made to look to their laurels by these Spinsters. . . ."

All five passed in Classics, and two (Miss Gibson and Miss Woodhead) entered also for the Additional Mathematical Subjects,

[1] January 14, 1871.

239

and were successful. Not till the Michaelmas term of 1871 were the other three (Miss Townshend, Miss Cook and Miss Lumsden) ready for the Additionals. On enquiries being made, the Senior Examiner was reported to be unfavourable to their admission. Happily Mr. Cartmell, who was one of the examiners for the year, consented to look over their papers. Miss Cook and Miss Lumsden passed but their companion failed. Miss Lumsden's account may again be quoted :

" There still remained for my torment the Additional Mathematical Subjects—to me an almost insuperable barrier. Was ever anybody, I thought, so hopelessly stupid at Mathematics as I ? The only resource was to devote all my energies to them, and I gave up Classics entirely.

" You can imagine perhaps what it cost me to take such a step as this in my third year. However, my plan answered, and I got through in the Additionals, whereas Miss Townshend, who had no difficulty in Mathematics, but had not cut down her other work for their sake, failed, and gave up the Tripos altogether. It was no doubt the only wise thing to do at that late stage, but it was a great disappointment to us all. To Miss Woodhead and Miss Gibson, who were endlessly patient with my Mathematical deficiencies, I owe my success. For a sort of mutual help society had existed among us from the first, and thus to some extent we supplied gaps in teaching by coaching one another."

It was a difficult and anxious business for inexperienced people to work for a Tripos, hampered up to the last moment by the Little-go, and by doubts not only as to whether they would pass, but even as to whether they would be allowed to try. Relief was needed from the strain, and the students felt the want of interests and recreations which could not easily be supplied in such a small community. This led to an episode which illustrates the difficulties encountered by those who had to work out a system of College life and discipline, on the smallest possible scale with the scantiest materials, and without previous experience of anything of the kind. As Miss Gibson relates, it nearly caused a catastrophe " owing to Miss Davies' somewhat exaggerated anxiety about the proprieties and our equally exaggerated jealousy with regard to the rights, privileges, and liberty of students." Her story continues :

" Our number by this time was almost doubled, and we had become perhaps a little less earnest about our work, the Little-go being behind us, and a little more enterprising about amusements. There was an institution which had been started during the first term, called ' The College Five.' It held weekly evening meetings for reading and discussion of a more or less formal kind. This little club now aspired to run a small dramatic entertainment. We were bold enough to undertake to act a number of selected scenes from Shakespeare. Of course we wanted to make the performance as realistic as possible, and various stage properties were invented or procured. . . . , When all was ready, we decided to invite the Dons, Miss Davies, Miss Wedgwood and Mrs. Austin, and also the servants, to witness a dress rehearsal in the common room . . .

" We, the actors, were painfully conscious during the performance that our efforts were not being well received, and after it was over, the storm broke. Our men's clothes were a scandal and the whole performance an outrage on the proprieties which might prove fatal to the future of the College.

" The hot-heads among us took umbrage and disputed, with distant politeness, the right of the College authorities to interfere in such matters. Relations with Miss Davies became strained, and the upshot was that the College Committee was to be summoned to discuss the whole affair, and we were requested in the meantime not to proceed with the performance.

" It was an absurd instance of making mountains out of molehills, and I am afraid I was one of the worst offenders, for I remember that I and one or two others seriously considered whether we ought not to play the part of the village Hampden, and leave the College as a protest against tyranny."

The catastrophe was averted, but the affair caused Miss Davies much anxiety, as may be seen from her letters.

(Miss Davies to Mr. Tomkinson.)

March 8 [1871].

" A new kind of difficulty has arisen at Hitchin. The students have taken to acting, and last night they asked Mrs. Austin and me to see a rehearsal in the Library. It turned out to be, first, a passage from Swinburne's *Atalanta in Calydon,* then some scenes between Benedick and Beatrice, then Olivia and Malvolio, and the Page. We did not like any of it much, but what seemed to us seriously objectionable was the taking male parts and dressing accordingly. . . . Mrs. Austin intended to speak to some of the older ones in the morning, but they had seen that there was something we did not like, and began asking her before break-fast what it was. (They thought it might be their taking possession of the Library, which they had done without leave in rather a lawless way.) So she asked Miss Cook and Miss Lumsden to come to the drawing-room and explained to them what it was. They would not admit that there was anything to object to (Miss Lumsden said she had done the same thing at home). . . . Mrs. Austin was decided in refusing to allow it in any public room, and the discussion then shifted to the point whether they might have it in their own rooms, and gen-erally to the question whether in their own rooms they might do exactly as they liked, without any cognisance on the part of the authorities. This, they felt, was a question of principle, which they were not pre-pared to yield. . . . I told them that Mrs. Austin and I had agreed that the question was one which we did not wish to decide alone, and that I should get two or three other opinions as to whether it should be referred to the Committee for decision. Mrs. Austin particularly begged me to consult you about it, partly because she was sure you would be inclined to give as much freedom as possible. . . . Mrs. Austin thinks . . . this trouble is partly due to much reading of *The Earthly Paradise*, which one sees constantly about, and other things of that sort. It is a kind of mixed notion of being artistic and wor-shipping Nature. Miss Wedgwood, who has been there lately, found them all (i.e. the elder ones) ' Pagan.' "

(Miss Davies to Mr. Tomkinson.)

March 17 [1871].

" I find Mrs. Bodichon is extremely unwilling to have the student difficulty brought before the Committee, and thinks that if we give them time, they must see their mistake. Mrs. Austin also urges delay. . . . They seem to have been irritated by my references to under-graduate discipline, and some of them have made out to Mrs. Austin that before they came I held out expectations that the first students would have more share in the moulding of the College life than we are now willing to give them. Of course this is not so, but the moment of dispute is not a good time for people to listen to reason. . . . Mrs. Austin thinks the students look upon her and me as Evangelical and nar-row and unartistic, and therefore unfit to judge in such a case as this."

Mr. Tomkinson, and other members of the Committee whom Miss Davies consulted, agreed that acting could not be allowed, even in the students' rooms. " Russell says," wrote Mrs. Gurney, " in his Cambridge days this very thing was put a stop to, tho' carried on only in a private way." [1] Madame Bodichon consulted her friends, George Eliot and Dr. Elizabeth Blackwell, and they shared her disapproval of the students' acting in male attire. Apart from the question whether acting in itself was objectionable, the students felt strongly that they ought to be free to choose their own amusements, and that the question involved the principle of independence and responsibility which they felt to be one of the most valuable and necessary elements in the training given by the College. All parties, however, wanted to avoid a discussion of the matter by the Committee.

(Miss Davies to Miss Manning.)
March 17 [1871].

" I have promised to postpone it for the present. Mrs. Bodichon has promised a visit to Hitchin next week, and Mrs. Austin thinks that will do more good than anything. Mrs. Bodichon thinks the students *must* see what a mistake they are making, if we give them time, and they are more likely to listen to her, as an artist and a theatre-going person."

(Miss Davies to Mr. Tomkinson.)
March 24 [1871].

" Mrs. Bodichon had her talk with the students last night, and reported that in all her experience she had never met such a spirit of revolt, and such self-confidence. She thought she had made no impression at all, but I hope her words (which were strong) may have told, more than she was aware of. She seems to have spoken wisely

---

[1] Mr. Gurney took his B.A. degree in 1826. Acting was not countenanced in the University till much later. In 1854 the A.D.C. was founded by F. C. Burnand and his friends, who for some years acted in secret and under feigned names, so as to evade the proctors. The club only succeeded in gaining the recognition of the University authorities, when in 1861 the Prince of Wales attended a performance, to which (by his wish) ladies were invited, and which the Vice-Chancellor and other Heads of Houses had to attend in deference to the Prince. In 1871 rules were accepted from tutors by the Club. These particulars are taken from *The A.D.C., being Personal Reminiscences of the University Amateur Dramatic Club, Cambridge*, by F. C. Burnand. In his preface, dated 1879, Burnand writes : " Ladies . . . no matter how gifted for the stage, are nervously shy of having anything to do with it, except as a *dernier ressort* of absolute necessity." It is clear from this that in 1871, amateur acting was by no means the matter of course that it is now.

243

as well as strongly. I am going down again on Monday, and before they leave, I shall tell them all individually that this thing is not to go on in the College."

The impression made by Madame Bodichon on one of the rebels is described by Miss Gibson :

" To me the most important outcome of the imbroglio was an interview with Madame Bodichon who was deputed . . . to pay me a domiciliary visit, and reason with me with reference not only to my rôle as ringleader in the theatrical revolt, but to the style of dress which I was beginning to affect. With regard to the latter I scored. It happened that I had recently gone into mourning and, as a protest against the hideous and fussy fashions of the time, I had contrived a simple little frock of fine paramatta not unlike the coat-frocks of to-day. . . . It was jeered at, at home, as my 'preacher's gown,' but when Madame Bodichon found me in it in my room at Hitchin she was charmed with it. It was a case of the prophet coming to curse and remaining to bless, for she asked me for the pattern and said she would have a gown made like it to paint in."

Out of the difficulty arose a friendship, a not uncommon experience in such matters. The question of acting was never formally discussed by the Committee ; the performance was dropped, and no more said. On the other hand, no difficulties were raised when at Girton a dramatic club was started, only a few years later. At the moment, Miss Davies was greatly relieved. In a memorandum written long afterwards, she notes : " It seemed at the moment as if the existence of the College was at stake, as while it was felt to be impossible to allow the practice, the withdrawal of some of the students might have been ruinous."

The incident made it clear to Miss Davies that the students really needed something in the way of outside interests. It was difficult to achieve anything of the sort while the College was small, poor, and isolated ; and the Hitchin students felt this the more because they were not the products of school routine. Their previous experience of life made them feel the College in some ways a restriction, and not an enlargement of interests. Nevertheless they had something which is perhaps lacking in the full-grown Girton of to-day. The infant college had something of the child's zest in life, when the most ordinary things are new discoveries, and every day brings adventures. The spontaneous gaiety and happiness, in which Miss Davies took such delight, were like an overflow when some barrier has been burst. The students revelled in newly found intellectual interests, and in a novel and delightful relation with each other ; the thrill of a new movement, as Miss Gibson has said, gave comradeship to their intercourse. And they knew that upon their success it would depend whether others would be able to follow after them. They had the stimulus (new to women) of feeling that much was expected of them, and they rose gallantly to the occasion. There were of course moments of discontent and disappointment, but the whole thing was an adventure, and a mixture, as all great adventures should be, of the highest spirits with the most intense determination. Experiences such as these cannot last, and cannot be repeated.

CHAPTER XV

Decision to Build at Girton. 1870–1872

THOUGH students were not yet crowding to the College " in overwhelming numbers," as Mrs. Austin expected, still their number had increased so much as to make the need of better quarters very pressing. The house was supposed to hold six ; by the end of 1871 there were five more students in the " tabernacle," and one in the gardener's cottage.[1] It was hard to manage with only one room to serve as lecture room and library, as well as for reading and recreation. The lease of Benslow House was due to expire at Michaelmas, 1872, and it was becoming urgent to decide where the permanent home of the College was to be. In relation to this question, a new element had now to be considered. In the autumn of 1869, Mr. Henry Sidgwick, Mrs. Fawcett, and others took steps to organize Lectures for Women in Cambridge, in connection with the newly established Women's Examinations. The Lectures began in the Lent Term of 1870, and had an immediate success, being attended by nearly eighty ladies, residents in Cambridge. Students from a distance were soon attracted by the Lectures, and by scholarships offered in connection with them,[2] and by the end of the year it was evident that a house of residence was wanted. In January, 1870, Mr. Sedley Taylor wrote to Madame Bodichon : " You will have seen by the circular I sent you a few weeks ago how very much more comprehensive and how much

[1] The new students were A. A. Bulley, R. Aitken, E. Welsh, J. F. Dove, M. G. C. Hoskins, M. Kingsland.

[2] One scholarship was given by Mr. J. S. Mill and Miss Helen Taylor, who had refused to support Girton owing to the provision of religious services there.

cheaper are the lectures proposed to be given in Cambridge than what we can by any possibility offer at Hitchin." The Lectures were soon organized on a more permanent basis through the formation of the Association for Promoting the Higher Education of Women in Cambridge, which included many influential members of the University.

The new scheme, therefore, seemed likely to prove a serious rival to the College, but Mr. Sidgwick, who as a member of the " Cambridge Committee " was a supporter of the College, thought the two might coalesce. He had always wanted the College to be in Cambridge, and hoped that some arrangement might now be made for it to be moved thither, and to supply what was wanted in connection with the Lectures for Women. To this Miss Davies was by no means willing to agree. To support a scheme devised especially for women would have been to sacrifice the principle on which all her work was based ; and she was, as we have seen, strongly averse to the idea of moving the College into Cambridge. Her plan was to build immediately at Hitchin, with a view to preparing the way for moving into Cambridge when public opinion should have become more favourable—perhaps after ten years, perhaps after fifty.

(*Miss Davies to Miss Anna Richardson.*)
Twelfth Day, 1870.

" As to what you say about the College. . . . Getting our building at Cambridge seems to me so impossible that I might almost answer briefly—It cannot be done. But I would rather show you, if I can, why I am not inclined even to try. You say that if the Females set up at Cambridge, we, for the sake of equal vantage ground, ought to be there too. But in saying this you assume that we should gain by being there, whereas it is because (chiefly) there is reason to believe that we should lose in numbers and influence, that we do not try going there. . . . I think you do not give quite weight enough to the fact that we are pledged to the present plan. We have been asked, with hands held up in horror, were we going to Cambridge ? and have answered emphatically that nothing of the sort was proposed. . . . The question was brought forward at the last meeting of our Committee by Mrs. Bodichon, in connection with a letter from Mr. Sedley Taylor, about the Female Lectures. Mrs. B. wrote to him afterwards, and told him that she wished to go to Cambridge, but she thought no one else on the Committee did. . . . Young women are kept away now by parental fears. Their mothers would let them come if it was considered a creditable thing to do. Ladies of influence have to make other people think it creditable. It takes a good deal of zeal and courage to speak of the College as it is. If the more extreme course were adopted, a whole system of propaganda would be stopped. People like Mrs. Gurney and Lady Augusta would feel their mouths closed. As Mrs. Gurney said, they would be almost ashamed to speak of it. . . .

" Experience has not certainly made me think less of the real difficulties which would attend the location of the College in a University town. We had two visits from brothers, and tho' everybody concerned behaved with the utmost propriety, we felt thankful that brothers did not live within thirty miles. Without actually seeing something of College and University life, you can scarcely understand how disturbing it would be to have 2,000 undergraduates, most of them idle and pleasure loving, close to your doors. . . . I do not say that this will always be so. I am only speaking of English human nature as it has been made by social habits and by the system of separating boys and girls from childhood. We contemplate a removal to Cambridge as possible even so soon as in ten or twelve years. But what we have to do now is to meet present facts. And one fact is that we cannot wait ten or twelve years for our building. We shall want it next October. . . .

" You mention among the advantages that we lose at Hitchin, the wider choice of teachers. I do not think we lose anything in this way. There is not the least difficulty in getting eminent men to teach. . . .

" As to the ' associations,' surely the true bond is a spiritual one, and does not depend on locality. . . . As a *College*, we must create our associations. There is nothing to prevent our becoming part of the University, and taking our humble share in its traditions, in the fact of our being a few miles away from its local habitation. It seems to me that the excessive clinging to the visible locality is part of the superstitious and carnal habit of this age. I wish you could have heard a sermon of my brother's a few weeks ago, on the worship of relics. . . .

" One reason why I am not anxious to join hands with the ultras is that I do not care to have a set of lawless young Radicals, thinking it clever to disbelieve, and setting aside Christian teachers as narrow old fogies, not to be listened to."

The question of locality came before the Committee on July 23, and Miss Davies was at some pains to find out beforehand what views people were likely to take.

DECISION TO BUILD AT GIRTON

(Mr. Tomkinson to Miss Davies.)

July 22, 1870.

" I almost dread plunging into the ' situation ' controversy on paper : you give me a lot of people's views ; I can only give you my own stale ones : I think I am clear to myself as wishing simply that Hitchin were within half an hour, from door to door, of Cambridge with ready communication by rail or road, I don't much care which. Until Cambridge becomes Cornell in many respects I shall wish us to be anywhere rather than actually at it. Half an hour off we should be safe from its evils and sure of its advantages. Can a place be found ? If not now I would rather wait."

Mr. Tomkinson's view as to position was the one adopted by the Committee. As to money, the high hopes entertained in 1867 had to be dropped. It seemed useless to try for £30,000, and the modest figure of £7,000 was now adopted as the sum to be aimed at.

(Miss Davies to Miss Richardson.)

August 1, 1870.

" Apart from the impulse to answer your letter, it is my duty to inform you of a decision come to at the last meeting of the College Committee—namely, ' That as soon as the sum of £7,000 be raised, the Committee resolve to purchase an adequate site and to build, on a plan capable of future additions, rooms for a Mistress and thirty students, with the necessary lecture-rooms, kitchens, etc. The site to be at Hitchin or near Cambridge, but not in or close to Cambridge.' There is a strong preponderance of opinion against Cambridge *itself*, but some of those who most object to that, think that the evils can be avoided and the advantages gained by being about three miles off. . . .

" I have asked Mrs. Austin to look out for a Local Secretary for Newcastle (keeping you for Grasmere), but I doubt her finding anyone zealous enough. We seem to want some one in the state of mind Lady Goldsmid said she found me in the other day—ready to go round a corner and garotte somebody. I am preparing to garotte Sir Francis [Goldsmid] at the first opportunity, and the Lord Chancellor, etc., but one gets on slowly with letters, this weather."

The Committee met again after the long Vacation on November 5, and a few days later Miss Davies wrote to Madame Bodichon : " The Cambridge Committee are formally asked to look out for a site, or by Mr. Heywood's suggestion for a house that could be adapted to our purposes, not less than three miles from Cambridge. The Lecturers say this will be quite near enough for them." The Cambridge Committee, however, were by no means satisfied with this, and unanimously expressed their opinion " that it would be far more advantageous for the College to be established in Cambridge or its suburbs, rather than at a distance exceeding three miles from it." [1] In a letter to Miss Davies rehearsing the grounds for this opinion, Mr. Taylor urged that the College would now be able to take advantage of the Lectures for Ladies, as well as of University Lectures by Professors, which would help to reduce expenses. " Some of the Professors' courses," he wrote, " are already attended by ladies who have a separate gallery for their use in more than one of the University lecture-rooms, and where this is not the case, chairs placed near the lecturer. . . . The moral objections seem to be imaginary. There has never been the slightest difficulty with the ladies' lectures, though many of those who attend are young girls. . . . With regard to our fitness for judging such a question I may ask you to remind the Executive Committee that four of those who have signed our Resolution are married men."

Mr. Sidgwick, too, wrote to Miss Davies, to try and persuade her. He felt that by remaining at a distance, the College would be missing a great opportunity. If in Cambridge, it should become the nucleus of an academic female education which might extend far beyond its limits, through non-collegiate students. Teaching in the routine subjects of the University curriculum could easily be provided at a distance of three miles from Cambridge, but for the exceptional subjects such as Moral and Natural Sciences, it would be difficult or impossible. " As these subjects," he wrote, " are novel and nascent, they will be, for some time, taught with considerable enthusiasm to comparatively small numbers of men ; in them, therefore, you would be able to obtain a great variety of careful instruction at small expense." This was a point which was not likely to appeal to Miss Davies, whose feelings were strongly engaged on behalf of the old-established subjects. " The arguments on the other side," Mr. Sidgwick

[1] Dated November 15, 1870, and signed by J. C. Adams, G. M. Humphrey, G. D. Liveing, W. G. Clark, Robert Burn, T. G. Bonney, J. Venn, H. Sidgwick, Sedley Taylor.

concluded, " I am perhaps not competent to estimate, and there-fore will not discuss. But whatever their force may be, it must I think diminish every year : while the force of those that I am urging will for the most part steadily increase."

Miss Davies felt this difficult to answer. She knew that, as Mr. Sidgwick said, the objections to Cambridge must diminish progressively with the success of the cause for which she was striving. What neither of them could foresee was the reduction of all distances by means of telephones, bicycles, and motors. These inventions, and the ever-continuing growth of the town westwards, have brought Girton and Cambridge much nearer together. But distance was indeed a formidable insulator when there were no means of communication faster than a horse. In a very carefully considered letter Miss Davies stated her case to Mr. Sidgwick, not without some consciousness of its weak points. It will be noticed that she takes her stand on grounds rather different from those urged to Madame Bodichon and Miss Richardson, of which, indeed, she here seems almost to make light. But there is no doubt that she felt strongly that freedom from interruption was one of the things most needed by women.[1] Before sending her letter to Mr. Sidgwick, she showed it to Miss Metcalfe. " I have read your letter to Mr. Sidgwick," wrote Miss Metcalfe, " and it commends itself to my judgment entirely."

(Miss Davies to Mr. H. Sidgwick.)
December 31, 1870.

" As you have been good enough to put the arguments in favour of having the College in writing, I should like to try to do the same on the other side, tho' it is a more difficult task. . . . The advan-tages are obvious and tangible ; the objections are more subtle, and difficult to put into words without making them look foolish.

" I must speak first of some objections to which I do *not* attach much weight. These are : 1. The undergraduate difficulty, i.e. the supposed danger of annoyance to the students when out walking. 2. The mothers' fears, i.e. the supposition that mothers would be

---

[1] " Miss Nightingale has said, in her forcible way, that she has never known persons who exposed themselves for years to constant interrup-tion who did not muddle away their intellects by it at last. . . . If it were universally true, there would be comparatively few middle-aged women with any intellect left." (From a paper read by Miss Davies before the Nottingham Literary and Philosophical Society, 1871.)

afraid to send their daughters to a University town. 3. The possible loss of supporters. No doubt there is some force in all these objections, but they do not seem to me to be formidable enough to keep us away from real advantages. I should choose to face them all, if I could see it to be for the real good of the College itself to be in Cambridge.

" My difficulty is, the impossibility for women to carry on a free, healthy, undisturbed student-life in a town at all, and especially in a University town. It has come out pretty clearly in the course of the discussion that the promoters of the in-Cambridge scheme are divided into two parties. One party admit the difficulties, but would meet them by restrictive rules—the other, which is not represented at all I think on the Executive Committee, would trust to the strength of mind of the students and I suppose to the moral influence of the authorities. The first plan might possibly succeed, but it also might destroy the College altogether. We must not forget that the very existence of the College depends on its being very much liked by the students. They come because they like it and feel that it gives them what they want. And it is very questionable whether they want—or rather they emphatically assert that they do *not* want—anything like a grown-up boarding school. But supposing that we succeeded in getting a different kind of students—say girls fresh from school, to whom restrictions would not be galling—we should still feel that we were sacrificing one of our chief aims, that of giving to women an opportunity of laying out their own lives, in circumstances which may help them to lay them out wisely. Women have plenty of practice in submitting to little rules. We want to give them the discipline of deciding for themselves and acting upon their own responsibility. Then, it may be said, why not choose the other plan, which would give them such abundant opportunities of practising self-control ? I think people who urge this so easily can scarcely have realized what young Englishwomen are from say 18 to 25. . . . I am quite sure that even our present students, who are as you would say the élite of mankind, are not all . . . superior to the attractions of society. I do not at all believe that they would feel the interest in their work that they do now, if they were constantly being diverted from it by interests of a different sort. . . . And then only consider the difference between the influences acting upon men and women in such a case. A man knows that his success in life depends to a great extent on the Degree that he takes, and everybody else knows it too, and the most worldly can see some sense in his sticking to his work and approve of him for it. But a woman would know that her success would not depend in at all the same way on her place in an examination, even supposing that we wished to encourage that kind of racing for places. On the contrary, the reasonable thing, from a worldly point of view, would be to take advantage of opportunities which she might not have at home, and make the most of them. This is what her friends and relations would urge upon her. . . . Then too, in the case of women, much visiting means much time and thought bestowed upon dress, especially by those who are not rich and have not maids to do things for them. And this would tell upon the tone of the College generally.

" But supposing many should resist—and I do not mean to say that *all* the students would be severely tempted . . . it would, I believe, be at the cost of so much worry as would be likely to injure health. There is perhaps nothing more trying to the nerves than to be constantly called upon to make choices, where there is much to be said on both sides. Hitherto, the singularly good health of our students has been one of our strongest points. No doubt we owe it partly to the bracing air of Hitchin, and we shall lose in this respect by being even near Cambridge. But I trace it in great part to the quiet, regular, unperplexed life. And I cannot believe that we should sacrifice this to at all the same extent at two or three miles off as we should in the town itself. There would not be the morning calls and the dropping in and the servants coming with notes to wait for an answer, and the general victimization by idle ladies. It seems to me to make just the difference between the moderate amount of society which would be refreshing and cultivating, and the excess which would be injurious to mind and body. Then we would of course make a point of having a large garden (we hope also a swimming bath and gymnasium) so that the students could still, as they do now, go in and out without bonnets at all hours, getting air and exercise without fatigue whenever they want it. If we were to attempt this *in* Cambridge, the cost of the land would I suppose be more than we should make up by some saving in the expense of Lectures. . . .

" I believe the sum of what I have to say is this—that, supposing the superior convenience of Cambridge as regards Lectures and Museums to be all that it is said to be—and I cannot help thinking that this is somewhat exaggerated—this advantage would be counterbalanced by a decrease in the eager receptiveness of the students and possibly also a lower standard of health ; and that the loss would be decidedly greater than the gain. I say nothing to the argument about University recognition, tho' I think it also can be met, because tho' it has more weight with some of us than any of the others that you adduce, it is not, I know, a thing that you care about much.

" I am quite prepared to hear that now the objections are stated, they seem to you to have less in them than you were willing to give them credit for, but I would rather risk this unfortunate result than say nothing. . . .

" I am sorry it is so long, but a *great deal more* might be said ! "

On the back of her draft of this letter, Miss Davies noted, many years later : " If I remember right, Mr. Sidgwick told me afterwards that I was wrong in supposing that he did not care much about University recognition." But she was so far right, that his main interest was the improvement of women's education, while hers was to give them equality of opportunity with men. Though they both wanted women to have higher education, this difference of outlook hindered co-operation in these early days. With the immense development in the range and variety of University studies which began after 1882, it became gradually clear that higher education was not to be divided into two types only, male and female ; and thus, as time went on, Miss Davies and Mr. Sidgwick found themselves travelling on the same road. The two colleges which have in consequence been established are now as much alike in their aims and methods as any two colleges may be, and they benefit mutually by being in close touch with each other. But the views of their founders originally seemed likely to lead to results of very different character, and it was at first doubtful whether the friends of women's education were numerous and rich enough to make it possible for two foundations to succeed.

(*Miss Davies to Mr. Tomkinson.*)

December 22, 1870.

" I think we may consider the Cambridge question settled, and that the Committee will only have to consider at the next meeting in what terms to express their decision to the Cambridge Committee. Lady Augusta Stanley says she is quite with Mrs. Gurney, and Mrs. Gurney agrees more entirely with our view than I had quite understood from her before. The case now stands thus—The real strength of the Committee is all on one side. If the proposers of a boarding-school at Cambridge mean to carry out their plan, they must do it themselves, and this they will certainly not undertake. I doubt whether there will be any voting on the question."

The Cambridge Committee felt that there was now no further

need for them, and their meetings were discontinued.[1] Their Secretary, Mr. Sedley Taylor, remained on the College Committee, and took an active part in the search which now began for a building site near Cambridge. Mr. Sidgwick's proposals for amalgamation having been rejected, he set about the establishment of a house of residence in Cambridge. His Committee, though they did not object to girls coming to Cambridge to attend lectures, did not wish to be responsible for them.[2] Mr. Sidgwick, however, decided to take the responsibility himself, and to open a house for students as a separate enterprise unconnected with the Committee. He asked Miss Clough to take charge, and by May, 1871, it was arranged that the house should be opened in the Michaelmas Term.

This was a great blow to Miss Davies, who considered the new venture a most serious rival to the College. While Mr. Sidgwick, in his whole-hearted attachment to the cause for which they were really both working, felt it painful and perplexing to be forced into antagonism,[3] she felt quite clearly that the principle on which she was working was the only right one, and therefore it seemed to her peculiarly hard that obstacles should arise from what ought to have been a friendly quarter.

(*Miss Davies to Mr. Henry Sidgwick.*)

May 19 [1871].

" I am sure it is generous inconsistency and not cruel mockery that makes you say you are willing to help us, when your scheme is the serpent which is gnawing at our vitals. It glides in everywhere. As soon as any interest is awakened, people are told there is something else, as good or better, and which does not ask for money. I daresay it does not end in their doing much for the Lectures, but it is enough to hold them back from doing anything for the College. We meet this hindrance at every step, and lately it has seemed to me that it bids fair to crush us. However, we are not going to give in yet."

The difficulties did indeed seem crushing. With infinite labour the College had been opened at Hitchin, and after eighteen

---

[1] The Committee came formally to an end in 1872, when the College was reconstituted (Minutes, June 24, 1872).

[2] *Henry Sidgwick : A Memoir*, p. 242. *Memoir of Anne Jemima Clough*, by B. A. Clough, Chap. VI.

[3] *Henry Sidgwick : A Memoir*, pp. 247, 255–6.

months of precarious existence—just enough to show that there was a real demand for it, and to open up a tantalizing vista of future developments—it seemed that the obstacles to a permanent foundation were as great as ever. In a letter written about this time to some one who was enquiring about the College, Miss Davies described the position as follows :

" Since we began . . . our position has been seriously altered by the well-meant but from our point of view mistaken action of the University of Cambridge in instituting a new Examination exclusively for women. It has made it impossible for us to urge that without Degrees there is no authoritative certificate of attainment, and it may damage our case with the University, as we seem now to be wilfully rejecting what University wisdom has contrived to suit the special needs of women, and to be grasping, without any real necessity, at the privileges of men. We have in fact been gravely advised by a good and sensible man of high University standing,[1] to prepare our students for the women's examination instead of for Degree examinations. If such advice comes from the University, what can we expect from an ignorant and bewildered public ? . . . Add to this the great amount of zeal and energy which might fairly have been calculated upon for the promotion of the College, and which is now expended on the Women's Examination and the Lectures which prepare for it, and you will see how the difficulties in our way have been increased and will not wonder that our progress has been slow. We do not change our policy, which is based on a principle we cannot give up, on account of the difficulties, but we are obliged to reconcile ourselves as well as we can to an immense deal of misunderstanding and to painfully slow progress. It seems slow, at least, to our impatient minds."

(Miss Davies to Mr. Tomkinson.)

May 4 [1871].

" I had a talk with Mr. Roby on Monday and begged him to propose shutting up, if he disapproved of our present plan, as we cannot go on in our present course (I mean, at Hitchin). He said he should not like to be the person to propose it. He admitted that we must do something, and will not object I think to what we. propose. The Committee were very disheartening on Saturday, but I felt afterwards that I had been impatient. Things naturally sound more hasty to people who only think of them now and then at a meeting."

---

[1] Professor Lightfoot.

Want of funds was the most formidable obstacle. It was a great come-down, after having aimed at £30,000, to find a difficulty in raising even £7,000. Now that this was admitted, Madame Bodichon sent £100 to the Treasurer as the first instalment of her gift of £1,000, waiving the conditions originally attached. A great effort was needed to raise fresh subscriptions, and it was decided to organize a campaign of public meetings all over the country. A circular was issued setting forth the position and prospects of the College, and asking the public to subscribe £10,000. As Miss Davies wrote in the circular :

" If the College were within a short distance from Cambridge and relieved from the burden of rent, the students' fees on the present scale would at once cover the current expenses. . . . The sum which it is proposed to raise by public subscription is simply the amount required for starting on the smallest scale consistent with economical arrangements. We are not asking for funds to pay salaries, or to found Chairs, or even for Scholarships. The provision of a building in a convenient situation is all that is claimed from the public. It may be asserted that no similar institution has ever been founded without some such aid from external sources, while, in most cases, the building has been but a small part of the assistance rendered."

And a reproachful glance is given at the large sums contributed to male education, already by comparison so richly endowed. " To one public school alone—that of Harrow—no less than £78,000 has been contributed for various purposes during the last fifty years."

The campaign opened with a meeting at St. James's Hall, Piccadilly, on May 15, 1871. Mr. Cowper Temple, M.P., took the chair, and among those present were Lord Lyttelton, the Bishop of Peterborough,[1] Mrs. Garrett Anderson, and Mr. Joshua Fitch, besides two Members of Parliament, Sir Wilfrid Lawson and Mr. Winterbotham. The Chairman said that it was now necessary to consider whether the College should be abandoned or made permanent. Lord Lyttelton declared his conviction that women had a right to the advantages of educational foundations. The Bishop of Peterborough appealed for the higher education of women as a means of improvement in the

[1] Dr. W. C. Magee, afterwards Archbishop of York, one of the most brilliant orators of his day.

home and family life. It was Mrs. Garrett Anderson who made the speech of the afternoon. The idea of the collegiate life for women, she said, was so new, and in some respects so much opposed to the ordinary conception of what was suitable, that whoever would ask for public help for the College was bound to justify the proposal. After setting forth the need of women for education as a preparation not only for any profession, but for life in general, she stated her belief that they would not be harmed by regular and steady work, on the contrary, many of the most miserable cases of nervous weakness in women were due to the want of it. On resuming her seat, as *The Times* records, she was " loudly cheered."

(Miss Davies to Mr. Tomkinson.)

May 15 [1871].

" I want to hear your impression of the Meeting in full and on reflection. If I were quite candid, I should confess that it gave me a sense of failure, but I am not sure whether it was because I was cold, and the outer chill penetrated within. The meeting did not strike me as one from which much could be expected to follow, nor that people who came sceptical would go away enthusiastic. But I believe I was not able to judge."

May 17 [1871].

" I have been seriously considering the propriety of shutting up, but it looks almost as difficult as going on.

" Mrs. Anderson thinks we want such help as Mr. Anderson could give, and writes to say that he is willing to be on the Executive and to attend regularly if we should like it, but I am to be sure and say if we don't. I am telling her the reasons that stopped us from asking him, and inviting information as to whether he could, without outraging his convictions, accept Liberal-Conservative solutions of such questions as are likely to arise in the government of the College. . . . Mrs. Anderson has just been here, full of an idea that we ought to have a meeting at the Mansion House at once. *Could* you come this evening and talk about it, or else to-morrow ? "

Mrs. Anderson felt that her husband, who was a partner in the Orient Line, would be able, with his experience of business, to give valuable help. He accordingly joined the Committee, and was asked, with Miss Davies and Mr. Tomkinson, to make enquiries as to whether a meeting could be held in the City with any prospect of success.

DECISION TO BUILD AT GIRTON

(Mrs. Russell Gurney to Miss Davies.)

May 30 [1871].

" I don't think my opinion is worth *anything* about a City meeting —you will settle it best without me. Mr. Cowper Temple tells me he means to send £100 and Mr. Heywood would give £50 if appealed to, and Russell will add £50 if it does not go *into* Cambridge. . . . Could we not in some letter make a *written* appeal to those who care for education as to whether we should or not let the scheme fall to the ground ? . . .

" I own the lukewarmness of *friends* of the scheme and the division of their sympathies are more discouraging to me than the opposition of enemies—first, the strong feeling of many in favour of Cambridge —secondly, the dislike of many with Professor Lightfoot and J. Venn to our taking the Cambridge examinations rather than those they have agreed upon for women—then the desire for the Lecture system, and boarding out at Cambridge, Canon Westcott I found strongly upheld, and he said all his spare sympathy was called out by any schemes to improve the *schools* for girls, and *till* these were improved, a College was useless.

" I own I have serious doubts whether we are a sufficiently warm-hearted *united* body to carry it on. Each one of the Committee seems to have a different view,—the Cambridge question rends us in half, yet we are neither half strong enough to do without the other."

This was a discouraging letter ; and the City meeting fell through, as it was found that there was not likely to be enough support to make it worth while. But the St. James's Hall meeting led to better results than had been expected. " About £600 has now been promised as the result of the meeting," wrote Miss Davies to Madame Bodichon on June 4. " There have been very favourable articles in the *Saturday* and the *Guardian*." The *Saturday Review* indeed showed a welcome change from the impatient and patronizing tone habitual to it in discussing anything about women. In an article upon the meeting,[1] it announced that the time had now come for taking the question of higher culture for women seriously. It was the Bishop of Peterborough's speech that occasioned this remarkable change. " The Bishop, spoke to the point, not only like an able person, but like a family man. . . . If anything will engage the heart of England in the

[1] *The Profession of an English Matron, Saturday Review*, May 20, 1871.

cause of female culture . . . it will assuredly be the Bishop's appeal that women should have the highest possible education . . . for this object in the main, that they may the better succeed in the profession of the matron." No culture, declares the reviewer, can be too high for those who are to succeed in this great profession ; and if the experiment of collegiate life for women is to be tried, " it could not be in better hands than those of the promoters of Hitchin College."

This was encouraging ; and plans were now made for an autumn campaign of meetings in the provinces. The outlook began to be more promising, and the search for a building site was resumed with energy. Hopes were entertained of a plot of sixteen acres on the Huntingdon road, belonging to Miss Philadelphia Cotton, but she declined on the ground that " a *Ladies'* College near Cambridge appears a singular project ! " Another site was found, about two miles from Cambridge, close to the village of Girton, at the junction of the Girton and Huntingdon roads. This was accepted as suitable, and Mr. Waterhouse began to prepare building plans. Miss Davies felt that things were beginning to move, and a visit to Madame Bodichon helped to raise her spirits.

(Miss Davies to Miss Anna Richardson.)
September 27, 1871.

" I have been staying with Mrs. Bodichon at her cottage in Sussex, and greatly enjoying the change and the thorough quiet. Even the physical atmosphere is so still that it is an event when the wind blows. We had a great deal of talk about the College building and garden, etc. I hope you agree with us in liking an old-fashioned useful garden with autumn and spring hardy flowers all about. I think we ought to plant a belt of trees as soon as we can round our own domain, as we are sure to want that at any rate. Mrs. Bodichon recommends Austrian pines. . . . I have been learning from Mr. Waterhouse the cost of various items, so as to judge what will reduce expense at the least sacrifice. He is pleasantly ready to listen to non-professional suggestions. I was very glad of something you said in one of your letters about its being satisfactory to hear of building. Other people are so vexatious with their ' horror of brick and mortar ' that it is pleasant to find you rejoicing in it. I only wish we could get housed and begin to turn over the leaf and pay back to the Capital fund what has been borrowed for rent and furniture and maintenance. The amount advanced is small as compared with what it is common to risk at starting, and I am quite at ease about the temporary use of the money, as the contributions of the Executive Committee alone much more than cover the sum we have borrowed. But it would be delightful to be making money upon the students instead of spending it."

Bricks and mortar were the first need at the moment, and in October a Sub-Committee on Building was appointed, consisting of Madame Bodichon, Miss Metcalfe, Mr. Tomkinson, and Miss Davies, with the addition in the following year of Lady Stanley of Alderley, who had just joined the College Committee.[1] The financial campaign planned for the autumn turned out on the whole successfully. A meeting at Leeds was followed by another at Birmingham, where Miss Davies was the principal speaker.[2] Some of the audience were inclined to be critical on the point of possible religious exclusiveness, but on the whole Miss Davies felt the meeting cheerful and encouraging. Others were held at various places, including St. Leonards, where Madame Bodichon had local influence, and Nottingham, where Miss Davies read a paper on *College Education for Women* before the Literary and Philosophical Society. The meetings had visible results, but they involved a good deal of hard and uncongenial work.

(*Miss Davies to Madame Bodichon.*)
December 20 [1871].
" Would it be possible and useful to have a drawing-room meeting a day or two after the public meeting [at St. Leonards] ? At Clifton we had the public meeting on Friday, Schoolmistresses on Saturday afternoon, a party in the evening, private visits on Sunday, and a drawing-room on Monday. And it seemed to me that all put together was none too much to dispel the thick darkness. They are forming a Local Committee to go on working, and have started a scholarship to pick up small sums. Florence Hill said she would rather contribute to that than to the building. She has become much more friendly, and altogether I felt that there was a great deal more sympathy than that dreadful day when you and I sat with all their stony faces before us and failed to move them at all."

---

[1] Minutes of the Executive Committee of Girton College, October 19, 1871, and July 1, 1872.
[2] *Birmingham Morning News*, October 30 and 31, 1871.

DECISION TO BUILD AT GIRTON

(Miss Davies to Miss Richardson.)

January 15 [1872 ?].

" I entirely sympathize in your repugnance to asking favours. I do not know anything that tires me so much, in carrying out the College, as the perpetual necessity of asking people to do something which they don't care for, and will only do, if at all, out of good-nature. Every meeting involves a series of appeals of this sort, and in most cases, I am not likely to have the opportunity of making any return for the good-nature. It is a pull upon one's pride, and it takes a great deal of care for a thing to wind one up to doing it. However, it must be done, and I go thro' a certain amount of hair shirt every day, as a matter of course, looking forward to the time when it will end. I hope this may be within a year or two."

During the year 1871 the Committee succeeded in raising about £3,000, making a total of £7,200 since the College had been set on foot. Of this nearly £2,000 had been spent at Hitchin on furniture, iron rooms, and current expenses. The site at Girton had still to be paid for, and the new building there would cost about £7,800. Money was coming in steadily, but much too slowly, and by the New Year the matter was becoming urgent. The students at Hitchin were already uncomfortably overcrowded, and more were expected to come in October. To stay there indefinitely till the sum required for building could be raised would cost too much. The rent of the house was £150 a year, the railway fares of the lecturers came to £150, and the extra cost of the time spent in travelling was at least £100 more. These expenses might perhaps have been covered if the number of students could be increased, but this was just what was impossible at Hitchin, though an increase was much to be desired on all grounds. As Miss Davies said : " While we can only take twelve students, we can scarcely speak of the College as a national institution without being laughed at."

All possible enquiry had been made for a house that would hold them, and there was none to be had, either at Hitchin, or at Cambridge. The Building Committee cut down the plans as much as possible, going so far as to dispense with a Library, for the sake of saving £650, but with all their efforts to make both ends meet, there was not enough money available to justify their entering into a building contract. Time was running short, and there was nothing for it but to try other ways of raising money. On Sir Francis Goldsmid's advice, the Committee decided to borrow on the security of a number of friends, who would each undertake to guarantee a share of the money, to be repaid when funds were forthcoming.

In order to carry this plan into effect, the College had first to be brought into legal existence, and it was accordingly determined, on Mr. Bryce's suggestion, to apply for incorporation as an Association under the Board of Trade. The statement of policy adopted in 1869 as regards the University of Cambridge was included as Clause 3 (c) in the Memorandum of Association. This led to the withdrawal of Professor Lightfoot, who felt that he could not remain on the Committee now that incorporation in the University had been officially declared to be one of their objects. " I should strongly deprecate," he wrote, " anything like a mixed University."

As regards the government of the College, it was to be in the hands of not more than thirty " members of the College," at least one-third of whom were to be women. Vacancies were to be filled by co-option except in the case of Representative Members, who were eventually to be six in number—three to be elected by the future Certificated Students of the College, and three by the Cambridge Senate, if and when it should choose so far to recognize the College. Clause 4 of the Memorandum provided that there was to be religious instruction and services " in accordance with the principles of the Church of England as by law established," but that attendance was not to be required from students by whom, or on whose behalf, objection was made in writing. This was the point round which discussion chiefly centred. Miss Davies' views were stated in a letter to Mr. Crosskey, who had raised the question at Birmingham.

(Miss Davies to Rev. W. H. Crosskey.)
November, 1871.

" At the time this clause was under discussion, we made a special point of inserting the qualifying words ' as by law established ' distinctly on the ground that this would prevent the College from being connected with the Church merely as a religious sect. . . . It seems to me that the impossibility of saying what the principles of the Church of England were, when it was disestablished, would be a great hindrance to tying up the College on this point. Interpreters would probably be driven to ask what had been the practice of the College from the beginning. The answer would be that there was no chapel [1] and no chaplain, that the ' services ' consisted in the reading by the Mistress once a day of a portion of the Scripture and some prayers selected by her from the Common Prayer Book—that the ' instruction ' consisted in Lectures given from time to time as they are wanted, on the subjects prescribed for the University Previous Examination. . . .

" Many of those whose support we most value have a strong feeling that while those who do not want religion, in the form of instruction and observances, ought not to have it forced upon them, there ought to be some security that it will not be altogether excluded. They do not care much about the religious instruction, which practically comes to very little, but they care very much for the family prayers. A large proportion of our students come from homes in which it is usual to have prayers every morning, and to have a *resident* College, with no permanent provision for anything of the sort, would alienate many of our best friends. It is, however, carefully arranged that no one shall be obliged, even by moral compulsion, to be present, e.g. the marking, at which students are expected to appear, comes *after* Prayers, not before, so that any objector might be absent, without its being at all conspicuous. I mention what may seem a trifling detail, not merely as evidence of the liberality of the present management, but because I think you will feel that in a case like this, traditions are very important, perhaps more so than the letter of the Trust Deeds. Train up an institution in the way it should go, and when it is old it will not depart from it. From this point of view, the large proportion of Unitarians (two and one Jewess) [2] on the small governing body who will be the first Trustees, also seems to me important. There is no kind of religious qualification for Mistress or Lecturers or anything else. I do not at all suppose that this explanation can be entirely satisfactory to you. It is not possible, in the nature of things, that the College can be entirely satisfactory either to strong Churchmen on the one side or to Dissenters on the other. . . . My own feeling is that in a case like this, differences which one feels to be serious may be merged, in view of the pressing necessity of diffusing knowledge. None of us can achieve this object alone, but each of us may trust that in the light of real knowledge, the true opinions, whether one's own, or somebody else's, will ultimately prevail."

---

[1] The Chapel at Girton was not built till 1902.
[2] Madame Bodichon, Mr. Heywood, and Lady Goldsmid.

Many of the Committee agreed with the views expressed in this letter ; but some, including Miss Shirreff, Mrs. Ponsonby, and Mr. Anderson, were anxious that the clause as to religious instruction and services should not be embodied in the Memorandum of Association, which could only be altered by Act of Parliament, though they were willing that it should come in among the Bye-laws, which could be altered at any time by a simple resolution of the College. " We should thus give offence to none," wrote Mr. Anderson, " and supply a Women's College that would be so far nationally acceptable, as were the Colleges for men at Cambridge when they were founded. These are now out of harmony with the national mind. It seems to me a building of the tombs of the Prophets to copy them in this matter of the Church of England." The Board of Trade itself took the same line. " I am to suggest," wrote the proper official, " either that this requirement should be transferred to the Articles or that provision should otherwise be made to enable the College to frame such rules in this respect as from time to time may be found convenient." Miss Davies however stood firm, and carried her point, though this involved the loss of Mr. Anderson, who retired from the Committee in consequence. Other members gave way, sharing the view expressed by Mrs. Anderson in a letter to her husband :

November 16 [1871].

" Not that I think the point a small one actually . . . but that it is so in comparison with the great ends that we hope the College will further. . . . It seems to me that women want that which I hope the College will in time give them so very, very much that those who can help them to it ought not to allow *any* minor disagreements to take them from the duty of allies. Of course you do not quite share this feeling, to help women is not the passion of your life as it is of mine and Miss Davies', and if you really think it more important to help Liberalism, all this argument goes for nothing."

In practice, the religious clause gave rise to no difficulty. The rule that required objection to be made in writing, when students did not wish to attend services, was not enforced with regard either to prayers or to other observances, and no kind of test has ever been imposed on any student or any member of the staff. All were and are free to attend or not, according to their pleasure. The effect of the clause has been simply, that the prayers read every morning, and the Sunday services instituted later, have been conducted according to the forms of the Church of England.[1]

In Miss Davies' mind, it was essential to the scheme that the College should aim at being received into the University of Cambridge, and that it should be definitely connected with the Established Church. She was the one member of the Committee who kept these points steadily in view, and was always on the alert to prevent any step from being taken which might lead in other directions. Her undeviating persistence and determination carried the day. As she herself said, force was gained by working at a positive programme, which could not be had if the ultimate aim were obscure. In other words, she knew definitely what she wanted, and never lost sight of it.

Another point which Miss Davies considered essential was, that all students should be required to pass an Entrance Examination before admission to the College. This too was included in the Memorandum of Association, though it was a self-denying ordinance of a serious kind. After the Entrance Examination of 1870 Miss Davies wrote to Madame Bodichon : " The Entrance Examinations reveal a terrible want of preparatory education. It is evidently a very serious bar, and must keep the College back as regards numbers. And yet it could not be made easier without admitting people quite unfit for higher teaching." The examination, besides weeding out the unfit, acted as a deterrent to candidates who were afraid even to attempt it. As Miss Davies said in her Birmingham speech, a candidate " pictures herself going through the process of first earning an unwelcome reputation for great learning by the mere fact that she desires to learn, and then going back to her friends rejected for ignorance." Nevertheless she was inexorable in insisting that no one should be admitted to the College who had not passed. Few of the Cambridge Colleges had so strict a rule on this point.

The Memorandum and Articles of Association were finally

---

[1] Services have been held in the College since 1881, when they were instituted on the initiative of the Rev. A. H. Cooke of King's College. It may be noted that candidates for admission to the College are not asked to state what denomination they belong to.

adopted on May 15, 1872. The Memorandum was signed by Lady Stanley of Alderley, Lady Rich, Madame Bodichon, Miss Davies, Mr. James Heywood, Miss Metcalfe, Mrs. (afterwards Lady) Ponsonby, Mr. Roby, and Mr. Tomkinson. The first members of the College included, in addition to the foregoing, Lady Augusta Stanley, Lady Goldsmid, Mr. James Bryce (afterwards Lord Bryce), Mr. Gorst (afterwards Sir John Gorst), Mrs. Russell Gurney, Mr. F. Seebohm, Miss Shirreff, and Mr. Sedley Taylor, making seventeen in all. An Executive Committee was appointed, with Miss Davies as Secretary. The office of Treasurer continued to be shared by Mr. Tomkinson and Mr. Seebohm.[1]

Mrs. Manning, the first Mistress, might naturally have been a member of the governing body, but she had died on April 1, 1871. Another old friend of Miss Davies' who did not live to see the College in its permanent home was Miss Anna Richardson, who died in the summer of 1872. Miss Davies had been accustomed to correspond very freely and fully with Miss Richardson, and her death meant the loss of a most faithful and sympathetic friend.

The College having acquired a legal existence, no time was lost in proceeding with the urgent financial business which was waiting to be dealt with. Arrangements for the Guarantee Fund were concluded, whereby the College was able to raise a sum of £5,000. The way was now clear for the work of building to proceed. Benslow House was let furnished for the summer holidays ; and Mr. Tomkinson, who, with Mr. Roby, carried through the negotiations for buying the land at Girton, arranged to let so much of it as was not wanted for building to a neighbouring farmer. Everything that could be thought of was done to scrape money together.

An increase in the number of students was urgently needed to fill the new building. There was as yet little to attract them in the way of scholarships. The income for a scholar had in several cases been subscribed by friends of the College, but there was no permanent provision. Even people who could afford it were often unable to see the point of spending a hundred guineas a year on their daughter's education, and in such cases a girl who succeeded in winning a Scholarship was sometimes able to

---

[1] Mr. Seebohm resigned in the following year, 1873.

make her parents feel that it was worth while to let her go to College. The Committee decided, with some reluctance, to ask a few subscribers to purchase nominations for students to enter the College.[1] An application to the Gilchrist Trustees resulted in their offering a Scholarship of £50 on the results of the London University Examination for Women to be held in May, 1873. It soon became apparent, however, that more students could not be taken at the moment, as the buildings would not be ready in time for the Michaelmas term. One last effort was made to hire a house near Cambridge—Madingley Hall—but the owner declined to let it to a Ladies' College. There was nothing to be done but to stay on at Hitchin, where fortunately the landlord, Mr. Ransom, was willing to renew the lease for another year. The move to Girton was therefore put off, and the students reassembled at Hitchin in October, 1872, with only one addition to their number.[2]

[1] Nominations were purchased by Madame Belloc, Miss Kershaw, Mr. F. Seebohm, Mr. J. H. Tuke, Mr. Heywood, Mrs. Russell Scott, Mrs. Richard Strachey (now Lady Strachey), and Mr. Tomkinson.

[2] There were three new students (E. Baker, C. L. M. Maynard, and C. M. Shorrock) ; but room had been made for two of them by the departure of Miss Slade and Miss Tidman.

EMILY DAVIES

From a photograph

CHAPTER XVI

Miss Davies as Mistress. 1872–1874

WHILE the business affairs of the College were going through a crisis, difficulties of an almost equally acute kind had arisen internally. In the spring of 1872, Mrs. Austin's health broke down, and she was obliged to leave before the end of the Lent term. Miss Davies went at once to Hitchin, but she could not stay long, and for the remainder of the term her place was taken in turn by Madame Bodichon and Lady Stanley of Alderley. " Lady Stanley was great fun," writes Miss Gibson. " We all liked her notwithstanding her sharp tongue. She was very lively and amusing, entered into the situation, and seemed to enjoy it with no formality of any kind." The difficulty was surmounted for the moment, but the apparently insoluble problem of a permanent appointment had now to be faced. The duties of the Mistress were not interesting enough to attract the " transcendent " person of Miss Davies' visions, and the moment was not a good one for making rearrangements.

(Miss Davies to Mr. Tomkinson.)

THE COLLEGE, HITCHIN,

March 25 [1872].

" There was a great deal that I wanted to talk to you about as to the position of the Mistress here. . . . It has often occurred to me that if I were dead or in some way entirely prevented from doing anything here, it might be easier to find a solution of our difficulties. If that is true, the wise thing would seem to be for me to keep away, and to leave everything in the hands of the best person we can find. I think there is less risk now than there was at first of having the College turned into a school, or the students too much individually looked after and moulded. Then the arrangement of the Lectures would probably not be difficult to an ordinarily sensible person. It requires a tolerably clear head, and a little tact, to get all the requirements of the students attended to by the Lecturers without too much interference, and I find practically that I have to talk to the students a great deal about their work and their plans. But that is just what each Mistress that we have had, would have liked to do. . . . This is one side of the question. On the other we have to remember that if the charge of the studies were given over to the Mistress, it would be distinctly giving up everything. . . . While we are here, the customs of the place would count for something, but at the critical moment of removing to Cambridge, the moulding of the College itself (which is a different thing from individuals) would be in the hands of the Mistress, tempered by the students of the period. . . . I should be much inclined to run whatever risks this might involve, if there were anyone whom we know at all well who could come. But I know no one at all, and to trust so much to a stranger would be serious. . . . Please let me have a view."

No one at all suitable for the post could be found in the short interval before the May term, and Miss Davies again took charge. The office of Mistress was not one which she desired, or for which she felt herself suited, and it was difficult for her to be constantly at Hitchin. Besides her work as Secretary, for which she had to attend Committee meetings in London, there was the building going on at Girton, which involved much correspondence and many meetings with Mr. Waterhouse and the Building Sub-Committee. There was also her work in London and at Greenwich in connection with the London School Board. She tried to think that it might be possible to get through the year during which they must remain at Hitchin with the help of members of the Committee in turn. Lady Stanley, Madame Bodichon, and Lady Rich were all approached, but in vain. " All say they can do nothing," Miss Davies wrote to Mr. Tomkinson, " but I don't incline any more to a stranger."

(*Miss Davies to Mr. Tomkinson.*)

June 10 [1872].

" Mrs. Gurney asks in her last note, ' Shall you not be *driven* into being Mistress at last ? ' I begin to think of it as inevitable. The more I consider it and realize how little I should like it, the more natural it seems to me that no one else, whom we could trust, should be willing. Some makeshift (with all its drawbacks) must be devised for the next year, as I could neither combine this with the School Board nor (properly) resign the latter. But afterwards it might be possible, though difficult. Will you tell me some time what you think ? The suggestion of something else, practicable and preferable, would be welcome."

17, CUNNINGHAM PLACE,
July 17 [1872].

" I heard at the School Board to-day that our existence is likely to be prolonged till July, 1874. This makes a great difference to me, as it postpones, practically for a year, the time at which I thought of resigning. At the same time the difficulty of getting any fit person for the College seems as great as ever. What I come to is that I had better go to Hitchin in October, and work it as well as I can with the Board. . . . As regards home, I believe Miss Crow would be here pretty constantly during my absence, and she is anxious to set me free by taking my place as far as she can. My mother quite approves, if all the Committee wish it. This is rather difficult to find out, as those who object are not likely to tell me, but no one seems to have anything else to propose. I am writing to my brother, but I am pretty sure that he will be in favour of it. . . . Will you tell me what you think ? If I take the office of Mistress, I should like to have the salary attached to it, as the School Board work involves a good deal of travelling, and taking it in the easiest ways makes a difference in time and fatigue. . . .

" We had a nice cheerful meeting yesterday, I am getting fond of Lady Rich. There is a tender kindness in her manner which with the decisiveness at the back of it is very engaging."

July 19 [1872].
" I am glad to know your mind on the Mistress question. . . .
" It is very rash of you to feel so confident that my being at the College would answer. Nothing but the impossibility of getting a really fit person would bring me to consent to my own appointment. But perhaps it is a good thing to be too much believed in."

July 25 [1872].
" Lady Stanley . . . says that if I cannot take it, we ought to get ' social position, good sense, and power of governing and conciliating.' As if we had only to ask for it ! It is odd to go on in this way after the years we have spent in hopelessly searching for any tolerably fit person. . . .

" I am anxious that the salary should not be more than £100, as tho' I could pay it back to the Capital Fund, that would not affect the Maintenance Fund, and I think it is very important to keep within our income. . . .

" I always have an impression of a millstone hanging from your neck of people depending on you for judgment, and feel (in imagination) what a weight upon one it must be to be so trusted. It makes me hesitate in so perpetually asking for advice, and *sometimes* I resist the temptation to do it."

On August 2 the Committee appointed Miss Davies as Mistress for one year from Michaelmas, 1872, and in the October term she settled down at Hitchin with thirteen students. She was looking forward eagerly to Girton, and her letters to Madame Bodichon are full of consultations on a variety of matters, such as coal cellars, tiles, material for curtains, the planting of trees, and gifts of books to the College.

(Miss Davies to Madame Bodichon.)
HITCHIN,
October 21 [1872].

" Mr. Venn told me to-day that he and Mr. Seeley had been out to Girton, and met six or eight Cambridge men who said they had all been helping to lay bricks. They had each written their name on a brick and laid it. The walls were about the height of the mantelpiece. I am trying to stir up Mr. Waterhouse about the planting."

HITCHIN,
October 23.

" Could you ask Mr. Darwin to give us his Works ? We want also the Works of Goethe and Schiller, and could take some other books. Would it be well to make a list for Lady Goldsmid ? . . . Don't you think we had better at once order the planting of the corner opposite the farm buildings ? [at Girton]. Any trees anywhere would be better than none."

Five more students [1] were now ready for the Little-go, and the time had also arrived for three of the original students—Miss Woodhead, Miss Cook, and Miss Lumsden—to attempt the Tripos. The process of applying to the examiners, successfully carried through for the Little-go in 1870, had now to be renewed,

[1] J. F. Dove, R. Aitken, E. Welsh, A. A. Bulley, and M. Kingsland. Mr. Sidgwick arranged with Miss Davies that Miss Creak of Merton Hall should take the examination with them.

and Miss Davies wrote to Mr. E. H. Morgan, the Senior Examiner for the Previous Examination, asking " the favour of their assistance in examining some of the students of this College." Meanwhile, some members of the University who were favourable to the admission of women to University examinations were preparing to bring the matter before the Senate, and Mr. Morgan therefore replied that he could not answer till after the Senate had given their decision. Mr. Gunson, of Christ's College, intended to propose a Grace authorizing the examiners in all University examinations to admit students of Girton College, and to report to the authorities on the place taken. " I feel," he wrote to Miss Davies, " that the time has come for having this question openly settled, and that the policy of shilly-shally and connivance which has hitherto prevailed is unworthy both of the University and of Girton College." This was of course very welcome. The Grace was to come before the Council of the Senate on November 18, and Miss Davies thought it " just possible that the enemy may not think it worth while to resist it." But she was too sanguine.

(*Mr. W. M. Gunson to Miss Davies.*)

November 18, 1872.

" My motion in the Council was rejected to-day by 10 votes to 6 ; so that the same unsatisfactory mode of getting your students examined will have to go on for at least two years more. The Council carefully abstained from expressing any disapproval of our Examiners examining your students in their private capacity and in a clandestine way : so that if any set of examiners agree to do what you require and to send you certificates, you can still say that your students were examined with the ' cognisance ' or rather with the ' connivance ' of the Council. I am thoroughly dissatisfied with the result, but like sensible people, we must for the present submit to inexorable necessity."

After this it was not surprising to hear from Mr. Morgan that " the Examiners whom I represent cannot under the circumstances admit students of Girton College to the Previous Examination."

It was disappointing that official admission should be flatly refused, but Miss Davies immediately set to work to try whether anything could, as before, be done unofficially. " I have to acknowledge with thanks your letter communicating the official decision of the Examiners," she wrote to Mr. Morgan. " You were good enough to say in your former letter that some of the Examiners would be willing to oblige us in their private capacities. May I ask if you can kindly arrange this for us with the Examiners ? " Mr. Morgan replied that the Girton students could not have the same papers as those set in the Previous Examination, but that if Miss Davies wished it, no doubt papers " very much of the same standard " could easily be had. Miss Davies answered that it was quite understood that the Examiners could not officially give them the papers. " We have always," she wrote, " sent to the Senate House for them half an hour after they have been given out, at which time I believe anybody that applies may have them. Taken in this way, I suppose there could be no more objection to looking over answers to this year's papers than any others. It is entirely a private matter between the College and the Examiners who may be good enough to undertake it. To have fresh papers would give the Examiners unnecessary trouble and would not be satisfactory to the College. . . . We have always reckoned upon having the use of the papers in any case, as it was not any special privilege accorded to us." It was a blow to hear in reply from Mr. Morgan that " promiscuous distribution of the papers at the entrance of the Senate House has been of late given up. . . . If we examine your students in the same papers, at the same time, we shall be taking upon ourselves the function of the Senate and deciding the point in a manner opposed to the decision of the Council." Miss Davies however was not yet beaten.

(Miss Davies to Mr. E. H. Morgan.)

HITCHIN,
November 25 [1872].

" Thank you very much for writing at once in reply to my letter. I am afraid it must be troublesome to you to have this matter on your hands at such a busy time, but you will understand that there is no one else to whom we can look to help us out of our difficulty. I was not at all aware that the practice of distributing papers half an hour after they had been given out, had been discontinued. This would, I presume, make it improper, as well as useless, for us to send to the Senate House for them, as we have done hitherto. I suppose, however, that the papers may be considered the property of the

Examiners who set them, and that at some later hour, to which we should accommodate ourselves, they might be able to send them to us.

" I quite feel the difficulty of doing anything which might have even the appearance of contravening the decision of the Council. But a member of the Council who was present when the subject was discussed assures us that the Council carefully abstained from expressing any disapproval of the Examiners acting in their private capacity, and that the decision come to upon our application in 1870 was not *reversed.* You may perhaps find it of some use to be in possession of the letter received from the Vice-Chancellor on that occasion, and I therefore enclose a copy. You will see that we have been all thro' entirely dependent on the personal kindness of the Examiners and it is to this only that we are now trusting.

" We are of course anxious that the Examination should be as nearly as possible equivalent to the Little-go, and that it should be conducted in such a way as to be above suspicion, but you must yourself be the best judge as to how far this can be managed without compromising the University. I am sure we may rely upon your making the best arrangement that you can for us, and we should like to leave it entirely in your hands. We are very sorry to be obliged to give you so much trouble."

This letter, so determined in substance, so conciliatory in tone, is but one example of a long series on the same subject, for these correspondences had to be renewed annually till the position was regularized by the Senate in 1881. This year, 1872, was a specially critical moment, on account of the adverse decision of the Senate, and a failure to secure the good offices of the Examiners would have been disastrous. Fortunately Mr. Morgan took a favourable view of the case as presented by Miss Davies. The students would be able to answer the papers set in the forthcoming Little-go if they postponed their work " till after the time at which the students of the University cease to have a sole right to them, viz., 11.30 or 12 in the morning, and 3.30 or 4 in the afternoon." A sufficient number of examiners were willing to look over the answers and report results. This was immediately accepted by Miss Davies " with many thanks for your most kind and friendly help." The five candidates all passed.

The same kind of correspondence was being carried on during the autumn of 1872 on behalf of the three Tripos candidates—

Miss Woodhead in Mathematics, and Miss Cook and Miss Lumsden in Classics. Though the Examiners were not all willing, a sufficient number consented to look over the papers " in their private capacity and without the slightest reference to their office as University examiners." The candidates prepared themselves to face the ordeal, and Lady Rich came to Hitchin to take Miss Davies' place while she went with them to Cambridge. It was a most anxious business, as Miss Lumsden's account shows :

" At last . . . the Tripos came, and to Cambridge we went under Miss Davies' chaperonage. Earlier in the same term Miss Woodhead, the first Pioneer, had taken a Second in the Mathematical Tripos, and her success encouraged us immensely.

" How well I remember the first morning at the University Arms. We settled down in our sitting-room, pen in hand, expectant of the paper, while Miss Davies knitted away steadily by the fire—I can hear the click of her needles still ! But minute after minute slipped away and still, until a whole hour had gone by, no paper came.

" Miss Davies said nothing, but she must have despaired, for she knew, though she had considerably hidden it from us, that some of the Examiners were dead against admitting us to the examination at all. For my part I grew desperate—had the Examiners at the eleventh hour refused the paper ? When at last the messenger came, he had, it appeared, been sent first to a wrong address. My nerves were all in a quiver and work was almost impossible. . . . That morning was the worst bit of the week, and it settled my class, a Third, while Miss Cook took a Second.[1] . . . The kindness of friends and two very pleasant dinner parties cheered us, however, and the ordeal came to an end at last."

There was great triumph at Hitchin when a telegram arrived with the news of their success. The students climbed on to the roof and rang the alarm bell, with such effect that the Hitchin police began to get the fire-engines ready for action. When the Mistress remonstrated, they fell back on singing *Gaudeamus igitur*, and tying three flags to the chimneys. Miss Davies wrote in delight to Miss Manning : " We have just heard that Miss Cook's translation of Aristotle was the best in the Tripos examination, and the two Examiners who looked over it are rapturous. Miss Lumsden's paper on Roman History was ' one of the prettiest shown up.' "

[1] This information was given privately by one of the examiners.

At a time when women's power to make any serious effort was generally denied, and doubt was generally felt as to girls' capacity for profiting by good teaching, it really was of great value to demonstrate that it was possible for women to pass University examinations in Honours, under the same conditions as those imposed on men. But the conditions, though nominally the same, pressed upon them much more hardly, owing to the want of previous preparation. The candidates had to learn their Tripos subjects almost from the beginning, and yet had to give up precious time to preparing for the Little-go, almost till the moment of the Tripos itself. They were behind-hand at the start, and felt keenly how much better they would be able to do if a little more time were given them.

The students appreciated the value of the recognized standard attaching to the University examinations ; they were not content to take the College Certificates for which provision had been made, because these had no such value ; yet they felt that something less exacting than the University course would be very useful for those who found it impossible to get through the work within the prescribed time. This feeling gathered strength, and in February, 1873, all the thirteen students in residence sent a memorial to the Committee, setting forth these considerations, and asking that students should be allowed to become candidates for any Tripos without passing the Previous Examination. Some of the College lecturers sent in a statement of their views, signed by Mr. E. C. Clark and six others, to members of the Committee as individuals. They considered that while the Honours Examinations might fairly suggest useful courses of study, the Previous Examination was " not only irksome but comparatively useless." The Committee, as was to be expected, declined the students' request. Suggestions for improving the " College Certificate " were of no avail, as no one cared to enter for it. The Tripos with all its difficulties was more attractive than an examination unknown in the outer world.

This rebellion against the Little-go was a source of great distress to Miss Davies, who felt that it cut at the roots of all that she was fighting for. For a moment it seemed to her almost as if the students and lecturers were in league to defeat her objects.

This feeling was dispelled by Mr. E. C. Clark, who, while adhering to his poor opinion of the Little-go, wrote to her expressing his views with great tact and kindness, and showing that he understood her position. Miss Davies in reply urged that the Little-go had the advantage of offering to inexperienced and ill prepared students an opportunity of testing their powers and tastes before deciding on their whole course. " However," she concluded, " I am not going to extol the Little-go, and will only add how entirely I believe what you are good enough to say of the personal friendliness of the Lecturers. Their unvarying cordiality and kindness have been the greatest possible comfort thro' the difficulties and dangers, external and internal, which our struggling little institution has had, and still has I am afraid, to go through."

Miss Davies' fears were freely confided to Mr. Tomkinson, whose unfailing sympathy was as usual combined with candour and plain speaking. He accused her of dividing everybody into friends and enemies, and denouncing the latter. " I am afraid that it is true that I feel very vindictive generally," she admitted. " It is the fierceness of fear. If I felt more confident, I might perhaps be more amiable." It was difficult to feel confidence when the action of both the students and the lecturers seemed to threaten the foundations of the College, and when she knew that what they asked for could be had elsewhere. At the Hall of Residence in Cambridge [1] the attractive alternatives were offered, on the one hand, of the Higher Local (an examination less exacting than a Tripos, but bearing the stamp of the University), and on the other, of the University Honours course under easier conditions as to length of residence.[2] Both these alternatives were approved by Mr. Sidgwick, and by other people of influence in the University. Miss Davies felt that a strong body of Cambridge opinion was united against her. Mr. Sedley Taylor, who was the

---

[1] Which afterwards developed into Newnham College.

[2] Before 1881 some Newnham students took Triposes after more than three years' residence. After 1881 Newnham students often took a Tripos after passing, instead of the Little-go, certain groups of the Higher Local, in which Greek and Latin were not necessarily included. This alternative was sanctioned by the University, but Girton students were not allowed by the Committee to take advantage of it.

only resident member of the University on the College Committee, was also the only member of the Committee who showed favour to the students' memorial. The Cambridge residents assumed, she wrote to Mr. Tomkinson, " that in acting upon our view, we were setting ourselves against the *University*. Like the Radicals who call themselves the nation, the so-called Liberals here seem to consider themselves the University. The fact that the majority is against them counts for nothing, as many of the majority live away from Cambridge, and it is residence here that confers infallibility. If we differ . . . we are the country clergy, the old obstructives, who stop everything that ought to be done." The prospective move to Girton seemed to her likely to add to the difficulties of the position by bringing the College into closer touch with these opponents. She felt that there was a serious danger lest the College should be deflected from its real aim, and led astray into a side path, where women's education would be organized on a separate and inferior basis. In comparison with her great object, the hardships of the Little-go seemed trifling.

(*Miss Davies to Mr. Tomkinson.*)

February 25, 1873.

" As to the Little-go, I feel strong in this way, that *as we work it*, it certainly answers a very useful purpose. . . . When our students come to us, they are very much in the dark as to both their powers and their tastes, and there is no one competent to advise. . . . Suppose that there was no Little-go they would be *obliged*, if they looked for Honours at all, to decide on one of the seven Triposes from the very beginning. . . . They would know nothing about their chances in Classics or Mathematics. The safe thing would seem to be to choose either Natural or Moral Science, probably the latter. It looks interesting and not too hard. Now it seems to me that it would be a great mistake to spend the whole of the College course on such subjects. They would be missing the exact training which women so much want, and put on to subjects quite unsuitable for immature minds, but very easy to talk about. On the other hand, the Little-go, when used and not abused, gives a steady course of discipline in work spent upon subjects which at any rate are not totally useless, and by the time they have got so far, they are in a fair position to judge both what they can do and what they like best. . . . I can quite honestly defend the Little-go from the practical point of view, as well as with reference to our cardinal principle."

The cardinal principle triumphed, and the students accepted their defeat. " Miss Davies was right," wrote Miss Lumsden many years afterwards. " Even then I felt it. I am heartily glad she carried her point. That sacrifice of the individual was thoroughly worth while." But at the moment, relations with the students were not quite easy. In any case she did not like the position of Mistress. " I don't think I am as genuinely sociable as the Mistress here ought to be," she wrote to Mr. Tomkinson. " I always said I could not be as much to them in this way as Mistress as I could as Secretary, and it is so. One cannot play with them on quite equal terms as I used to do, and maintain authority as its sole representative besides." And there was now a source of positive disagreement. She felt it unreasonable and over confident of them, in their youth and inexperience, to propose a fundamental change of policy. " I wonder what would be thought," she wrote to Madame Bodichon, " if the undergraduates of a College, including all the freshmen, took upon them to make such a ' suggestion ' as that of our students, to the Master and Fellows." " When I see such a spirit, it makes me feel terribly out of heart about our work." And to Mr. Tomkinson : " The doubt arises, is it worth while to produce such results as these ? . . . It is only a doubt, but still it weakens."

While Miss Davies felt embarrassed by the strength of her feelings, the students showed " quite their usual cordiality." Thinking of the work as it affected each of them personally, no doubt they did not realize what she felt as to a fundamental principle being at stake. Talks with the Mistress gradually produced a better understanding of her point of view. She pointed out that " as all the cultivated thought of the country is occupied in considering and discussing what is best for men, such alterations as are needed are likely to be made, but that the same attention is not given to women's education."

(Miss Davies to Mr. Tomkinson.)

" In many ways they [the students] are very pleasant, and respond with smiling faces when I am trying to compose a Time-table to meet all their wants. And all the Lecturers are pleasant, and cordial. So things might be much worse. I am begging Mrs. Bodichon to come for the two nights I shall have to be away in the week *after* Lady

Rich's time. She is so clear and firm, and at the same time so winning and bright, and they know how much she does for the College, that I think her influence is about the most useful we can have."

Madame Bodichon could not come, so Miss Davies remained at Hitchin, while her place in chaperoning a Little-go candidate to Cambridge was taken by Miss Manning. A talk with Miss Manning produced a more hopeful spirit. " Miss Manning enters into the situation here very thoroughly," Miss Davies wrote to Mr. Tomkinson. " I think her knowledge and judgment would be very useful, both on the Committee and as a visitor at Girton. She feels strongly the good that is done *on the whole*, the sort of moral influence all over the country, by such achievements as these Honours lately gained. . . . She reminds us that all great movements have had this drawback. The people concerned in them do all sorts of wrong things, but in spite of their great imperfections, the general result is good and important."

Miss Manning was elected a member of the College and of the Executive Committee in June, 1873. " It is right that you should be one of us," Miss Davies wrote to her, " having been such a good and faithful and wise friend of the College from the beginning. It will be a remembrance too of what Mrs. Manning did for us in starting, the worth of which I feel more and more as we go on."

After a brief summer holiday with Miss Manning in Normandy, Miss Davies returned to work in September, 1873, and threw herself into the task of moving the College from Hitchin to Girton. In addition to nine students from Hitchin, six new ones were expected. Miss Lumsden, who after taking her Tripos in 1872 had returned to Hitchin as Tutor, with Miss Davies as Mistress, constituted the staff. The new buildings were not yet completed, but they had somehow to be made habitable in time for the October term. Madame Bodichon, who was, as Miss Davies said, " a perfect treasure on the Building Committee," also took an active part in dealing with the details of furniture and fittings. They spent some laborious days at Girton together, arranging such things as curtains and blinds, and trying to get the windows to open properly. Madame Bodichon soon afterwards went abroad with Miss Jekyll, but Miss Davies wrote often and reported progress.

MISS DAVIES AS MISTRESS

(Miss Davies to Madame Bodichon.)

September 6 [1873].

" I went to Girton and Cambridge yesterday and had a long talk with Professor Liveing about the Natural Science studies, which ended in our deciding that our three students (Miss Kingsland, Dove and Gamble) had better attend his Professorial Lectures on Chemistry, and Professor Humphry's on Anatomy and Physiology. . . . I don't think he has had any women in his class before, but Professor Humphry had one last year. In speaking of this, it will be best to call it Physiology, as the word Anatomy may give the impression that the Lectures are different from what they are. Professor Liveing has attended them himself, and thinks that as to the subject, there is no reasonable objection to a mixed class. I should go with them at first and occasionally. I could not undertake to go always. . . . The students by attending the Lectures will come in for other privileges, such as the use of University skeletons. I have written to Professor Humphry about his Lectures. He has always been a friend of the College and is sure to be pleasant. Professor Liveing went into the matter in the kindest way, taking it up as if it was quite his business to do the best he could for our students. It is certainly a great thing to come within range of these nice friendly people. . . .

" I shall be going to Girton for the first night there on the 15th, the day you begin your travels. There will be perpetual reminders of you at Girton."

GIRTON COLLEGE,

September 25, 1873.

" It is very nice to have your address and to be able to send you word how we are getting on. I always feel sure of you, that your interest in the things we care about does not die away when you go into other spheres. . . . I enjoyed my visit to Bradford [for the meeting of the British Association]. . . . I had as fellow-guest Mr. F. Galton, the African traveller, who is delightful company. I saw a good deal too of the Alcocks of Japan, and Miss Smith of Oxford and her brother, and ended with a night at the Forsters' pretty, quiet, unpretending place on the Wharfe. You know Mrs. W. E. Forster was a Miss Arnold. I found both place and people charming.

" I came back here on Tuesday, and found happily a good deal of progress made. Mr. Waterhouse is here to-day, and he says *all* the rooms necessary for immediate use will certainly be ready. . . . The blue carpets are here and look very nice, and Mr. W. is delighted with the Japanese curtains. . . . The sitting-rooms have a border run on which matches wonderfully and is a halfpenny a yard ! It is really amusing to get things so cheap. . . . I spoke about the College at a meeting at Bradford and quite forgot to say anything about money. . . . However, I asked for support which I suppose meant the same thing."

Miss Dove describes the first arrival of the students at Girton as follows :

" As my home was in Lincolnshire, it so happened that I was the first to arrive. . . . The whole space between the building and the Huntingdon Road was full of builders' débris, heaps of bricks, empty cement-tubs, baulks of wood, heaps of mortar and sand, shavings, etc. There were no windows or doors on the ground floor, the stair-case was covered with planks, and as I entered, Miss Davies in her white shawl came flying down the stairs most kindly to receive me. She had rather an anxious look on her face, and she escorted me up to my room. . . . There were no door-posts up, no blinds or cur-tains, but there was a beautiful fire and I did not feel dismayed. Poor Miss Davies' troubles were yet to come. In another hour or two the whole of the new year arrived. . . . Miss Lumsden, I think, had come back as Classical tutor, and it fell to her lot . . . to smooth over the series of difficulties which faced the new-comers, for the cor-ridor outside our rooms was full of carpenters' benches, their tools lying about in all directions, and you had to be very careful not to sweep quantities of shavings into your room as you entered.[1] As we had only wax candles to carry about, it certainly was a mercy that the whole College was not burnt down. . . . However, we soon settled in. Miss Davies' pluck was contagious, and after a few weeks she gave a big party. Mr. Llewelyn Davies came down from London to help her. The biggest lecture-room was made to look nice, and we all ran about putting down our nicest rugs, carrying the best arm-chairs we could find, and hanging pictures, and this first festival was thoroughly enjoyed. The mornings, of course, were all devoted to work, though I found it somewhat difficult to wrestle with the in-tricacies of trigonometry with the carpenters hammering up the door-posts outside my room. . . .

" I remember being charmed and delighted on answering a tap at my door to find that my visitor was Lady Stanley of Alderley. . . . Lady Stanley sat down and enquired kindly about our work and our comforts, and left me a most delightful remembrance of herself in the form of a student's box containing compasses, etc., with an in-

---

[1] Your skirt of course touched the ground.

scription in her own handwriting on the outside. I still treasure that box."

(Miss Davies to Madame Bodichon.)

17, CUNNINGHAM PLACE, N.W.,
January 6, 1874.

" I was very glad to hear from Rachel Cook the other day that you talk steadfastly of [coming home on] March 1. I hope you will give Girton an early place among your necessary visits. . . . There are such endless things to talk to you and to consult you about which can only be done satisfactorily on the spot. You don't know how I miss you. I had got so much into the habit of looking to you for advice and help about all sorts of things that I am always feeling after it still. . . .

" We pulled thro' our first Term bravely in spite of difficulties. Many windows were wanting, and it was long before we had outer doors. To the last there was neither bell nor lock to our principal door. However, we escaped burglars, and we had no trouble from damp, which was of course the great fear. The walls have dried beautifully, and the warming apparatus works well. Altogether the building gives great satisfaction and I think the students were agreeably disappointed in the pleasantness of the situation. There are such pretty walks about, and the views are really fine at sunset time. There is no difficulty about attending Lectures at Cambridge. . . . The proximity to Cambridge, and also having Miss Lumsden, has made a great reduction in the cost of the teaching. We shall certainly have a balance of Profits to show next June, and to help towards the Capital Fund. Miss Lumsden has been most useful and very pleasant to do with. I wish we had a Mathematical Resident Tutor besides. We have not made much way in getting money lately, but are hoping to do something at Liverpool. There is to be a meeting there on the 20th, got up by the Rathbones, who seem to be very zealous. I am to stay with them, and Lady Stanley will probably go too, and Mr. Heywood, who has rich cousins there. . . .

" There is a prospect of reform at Queen's College. My brother has been made Principal, and he is aiming at getting it re-constituted on the model of University and King's, i.e. having a good <i>school</i> for girls under 18, and making them pass an Entrance Examination for admission to the <i>College</i> ; which might then be a place of advanced teaching, preparing for London University Examinations. The London University is moving a little bit. Dr. Carpenter says the Women's Examination is likely (he thinks quite certain) to be made identical with Matriculation, and he thinks this will be a step towards getting

284

Degrees. He says the feeling is decidedly growing more favourable to this than it was. It seems to me that his own is, at any rate, which is something. You may have seen that the Cambridge Women's Examination is extended to men. We have been considering whether to accept it now, and have decided to postpone it for the present. The Time-table is so arranged that the same candidate cannot take both Latin and Mathematics, which would not do at all for us. This is likely to be altered. You will have seen that we have still two women on the School Board. It is vexing to have lost Greenwich, Isa worked very hard for Miss Guest, and heard a great deal of talk —among other things, that I did not fight enough for the church and did not care for needlework but left it to an old bachelor.

" Now I think I have given you a good cram of news. We go back to Girton on the 27th. I expect there will be a great deal of receiving to do. People swarm out to see the place. Hammond [the housekeeper] heard a party in the Dining Hall one day and went to look after the spoons, and found a Bishop ! (Colonial). Lady Rich is coming on a visit."

The Liverpool meeting referred to in this letter was attended by Miss Davies, Lady Stanley, Miss Clough, and Mr. James Stuart. It was organized at the instigation of Mr. Bryce, with the general object of promoting higher education in connection with the Universities. Its results as regards Girton were most inspiriting. " The meeting was over soon after four," Miss Davies wrote to Mr. Tomkinson, " all triumphant, with promises up to £1,000, and hopes of more. The Rathbones have been angelic." It was pleasant to begin the Lent term with this piece of encouragement.

Miss Davies' delight in the growth of the College led her to see it in the gayest colours. To the Hitchin students their new abode seemed less attractive. It was comfortable for each to have her own bedroom and sitting-room, and for all to be housed under one roof ; but the bare unfinished building, standing in flat windswept fields, without trees, lawns or flower-beds, seemed in other ways a poor exchange for the old house on the hill at Hitchin, with its lovely views, and the pleasant garden sheltered by trees. Everything had an unfinished look : there were no gates, and the grounds were open to invasions of undergraduates who came in parties of half a dozen, walking together arm-in-arm. Rumour said that some of them penetrated into the College and walked along the corridors, and that two professors were seen climbing the builder's ladders and inspecting the Mistress's room through her window. The Mistress's room was not all it might have been. The chimney smoked, and the furniture was far from complete.

(*Miss Davies to Madame Bodichon.*)
GIRTON COLLEGE,
March 9 [1874].

" I did not know you meant the book case for the Mistress's room. Do you see a place for it in your mind's eye ? The carpet had arrived before Hammond [the housekeeper] left. If there are any directions about putting it down, please let me know. . . . I am sorry we cannot make the room quite nice before the show Term, but I do not think it matters very much, as there is nothing characteristic about the room. It is not a *feature*, for strangers to notice and remember."

Miss Davies did not think much about the absence of comfort in her room, though it was perhaps more of a " feature " than she realized. The College was too poor to be comfortable, and she was of necessity bent on saving every penny she could towards paying for the building. It was sometimes a trial to her when people gave what she felt to be superfluities, instead of contributing towards the general funds, as for instance when a student gave outside blinds to protect the southern windows from the sun. " One cannot of course dictate gifts," she remarked to Madame Bodichon, who was herself inclined to this kind of generosity, and was apt to produce her gifts in a characteristically informal way. We find Miss Davies writing to her in September, 1873 : " I suppose your chairs are for the *College*. If you use that vicious expression ' for you ' again, I shall keep the things for myself."

The entertainment of visitors was now a considerable addition to the labours of the Mistress. " We have many visitors," Miss Davies wrote to Madame Bodichon, " who are welcome, tho' fatiguing, coming on the top of one's regular work. Mr. Morley, M.P., came yesterday and was very pleasant." And in another letter : " There were six parties shown over the place yesterday, and more are expected to-day, besides other engagements, and work." Madame Bodichon herself came often, bringing Dr. Elizabeth Blackwell and other friends to see the College, and there were visits from Mr. and Mrs. Roby, Lady Rich, Mr. Tomkinson, Miss Manning, and Miss Davies' old friend and ally, Mr. (afterwards Sir) Joshua Fitch. " The throng of visitors has been exhausting," wrote Miss Davies to Miss Manning in the last week of the May term, " and it is not yet over, but we have been glad to see them. The Fitch's were so easy to entertain and to please that one felt that what trouble was taken was well repaid. They are delightfully good people."

The College was reaping great benefits from its removal to Girton, which made it more accessible to the University and to the world in general. Special interest was being aroused in Cambridge at this time in the higher education of women, in great part through the efforts of Mr. Sidgwick, under whose inspiration many members of the University, including some of the most Conservative, were led to be favourable to the women students. It was through his influence that the Cambridge Association for the Higher Education of Women was able to secure admission to University Lectures, in 1873, when twenty-two out of the thirty-four Professors then existing opened their courses to women. More followed later, and intercollegiate lectures also gradually became available. Though there was as yet but little in the way of laboratory accommodation in the University, women students were generously received by Professor Liveing, Professor Humphry, and Professor Michael Foster. Attendance at the science lectures had its trials, and at first the students felt it " dreadfully uncomfortable." At Professor Humphry's lectures they sat modestly at the back in a little row by themselves, sometimes with Miss Davies as chaperone ; and when a specimen of the human brain was passed round for inspection, they became aware that the undergraduates in front had all turned round to see whether this would discompose the ladies. Their quiet demeanour however had its effect, and at the end of the first term the lecturer complimented the men on their good behaviour under this trial. Professor Michael Foster's lectures in Biology were attended by Girton students, who sat in a gallery where they had their microscopes at a low window, and the demonstrator went up to help them in their seclusion. To the undergraduates the handful of women students were an eccentric novelty, and there was but little contact between them.

After the removal to Girton, a movement of a new kind arose among some of the students. The Pioneers and their friends had been in the habit of spending Sunday evenings in reading up the politics of the week, and in a general discussion. Miss Maynard now started Bible readings, to which all students were free to come. Miss Kingsland and others supported her, and gradually the circle widened. A more private gathering, the Girton Prayer Meeting,[1] was started, the members of which continued to correspond with Miss Maynard after leaving Girton. There was much religious activity in Cambridge at this time, and mission services were held by undergraduates in the villages near Cambridge, in which some of the women students would have liked to take part. This Miss Davies discouraged, but she was pleased when they visited in the parish and taught in the Sunday School, " which I think it very good of them to do," she wrote to Madame Bodichon, " instead of wandering about for long walks, or reclining on the grass these fine summer days."

Miss Davies took no part in these religious movements ; " she did not seek to guide us in even the least degree," writes Miss Maynard. Her idea was not to guide, but to leave people free to guide themselves, within the bounds of law and order. Preserving this neutral attitude, she hardly sought to make friends with the students. She was fulfilling the functions of Secretary as well as those of Mistress, and as Secretary she was obliged to think much of the external policy of the College, to keep its existence before the eye of the public, to explain its aims, to collect money, and to attract support. The two functions are so dissimilar that one person could hardly be equally well fitted to perform both. She was an admirable Secretary ; and as Mistress, she accomplished the move to Girton, and saw the College settled there on the lines of freedom and order which she desired to establish as its tradition.

There were others who, like Miss Maynard, wished for some source of what Madame Bodichon called " genial wisdom and influence " at the College. " I do wish," wrote Madame Bodichon to Miss Marks, " we had some direct moral teaching at Girton, and I do wish we could get an ideal of life infused into the students ; but there is much to be done with the eighteen years

---

[1] Twenty years later, when the Student Christian Movement was started, the Girton Prayer Meeting was given up, and its members enrolled as a branch of the S.C.M.

of life before college, and until your ideal school is started, I do not see how *we* are to do it. The College cannot do much more than give *quiet liberty* and *opportunity* and Miss Davies never had any other idea. That is a great deal, and she who has an immense love of justice for women would die to give young women what she never had herself in early life, ah, die to get it for them, though she might hate every individual. She is intense for an idea, truly disinterested and great. I do not think anyone does her justice."

CHAPTER XVII

The College Established at Girton. 1874–1882

AMONG the various grounds of objection brought forward against the higher education of women, those connected with health were specially formidable, owing to the ease with which people could be frightened into thinking that education meant over-work. In the spring of 1874 this question came into special prominence. The *Fortnightly Review* for April of that year contained an article by Dr. Maudsley, the well-known mental specialist, on *Sex in mind and in education*. Dr. Maudsley declared that in order to prepare women for their duties as wives and mothers they should receive an education specially adapted to their sex. As a bad example of the contrary, he quoted the United States, where girls received the same mental education with boys, with the result that the American woman " is physically unfit for her duties as woman." Dr. Maudsley indeed observes that the American girl takes no part in " those outdoor exercises and pursuits which are of such great benefit in ministering to bodily health " ; but he does not dwell on this ; all the stress is laid on study as the cause of ill-health.

The article as a whole placed its author (a very eminent medical man) among the ranks of those who were opposed to the higher education of women, and Miss Davies and her friends were in some anxiety as to whether and how the attack could be met.

(Madame Bodichon to Miss Davies.)

April 5 [1874].

" I have read Dr. Maudsley's article with care, and I think it will do us much harm because there is much truth in it, and because what is not true is exactly the most difficult sort of error for us as women to discuss. I wish we could find some man to answer it. I should like to see you and Mrs. Anderson. . . . Mrs. Frederic Harrison told me of this article before it came out, and it was talked of a little at the Lewes's. . . .

"The great war in France has done us infinite harm. . . . What I said to Elizabeth Garrett Anderson about our cause looking well was not exactly true. I meant to say I thought women were waking up, and trying to learn and make themselves more valuable. But I do not think we are near any success like the Suffrage. *Men* are not ready for it is what I feel. Brute force is more in the ascendant than it was four years ago."

(Miss Lumsden to Madame Bodichon.)

Friday [April 1874].

"Thank you for lending me the article. . . . It will be difficult for Mrs. Anderson to answer it without in her turn treading on people's sense of delicacy and modern refinement. . . . An answer to Dr. Maudsley seems to me given in his own Note. Climate, food, want of physical education and free outdoor games, ' *cramping dress,* martyrdom to propriety and fashion,'—are not these enough ? And the same causes are at work here, though not so ruinously. As Maclaren of the Oxford Gymnasium says somewhere, ' That horrid word *ladylike* dogs the poor girls from the nursery upwards.' . . . Would Dr. Maudsley and his friends recommend that women should learn nothing ? Of one thing I feel sure, that a vacant mind revenges itself on the body. . . . Of course I am far from denying the necessity of rest, the danger of strain. . . . But I cannot see that girls ought to be prohibited from all hard mental work because it is possible to have too much of it. There is intense and most healthy enjoyment in hard mental effort if not prolonged too much. And if this mental effort were succeeded by the thorough bracing change of physical exercise (exercise worthy of the name) the whole nature is harmoniously developed. Low spirits, aches, morbid self-consciousness, all are forgotten. Compare it with the life of an ordinary schoolgirl. Long hours of dull work in which the intelligence is only half awake, of piano practising (often twelve hours a week) in which mere execution, not real musical knowledge, is the aim, followed by a dreary walk —no change, no active exercise to stir the blood, to quicken the whole nature. It is only a marvel that English girls are as healthy as they are. . . . I don't care in the least for the ' honour and glory ' of competition with men. What I do care for is that all fields of knowledge should be freely open to women as well as to men—that fashion and absurd prejudice shall not dictate what every girl, whatever her

291

gifts and natural bent, is to learn. . . . Let no subjects be tabooed as too *hard* or as unsuitable, unfeminine. And let us have free physical development too." [1]

(*Miss Buss to Miss Davies.*)

April 13, 1874.

" I am glad you and Mrs. Anderson have talked over that article. Girton suffers largely, I believe, from the determined opposition of medical men, and as for me, I scarcely expect anything else if a medical opinion be asked, in the case of any girl. The smallest ailment always proceeds from over-brainwork ! ! ! never from neglected conditions of health, from too many parties, etc., etc."

There was a strong feeling that some reply ought to be made to Dr. Maudsley, and Mrs. Anderson's medical qualifications and knowledge of the movement for higher education made it natural for her to be the spokeswoman. Her reply appeared in the May number of the *Fortnightly*. Dr. Maudsley accused the reformers of neglecting physical training in order to stimulate mental activity, but Mrs. Anderson was able to show that this was far from being the case. " The schoolmistresses who asked that girls might share in the Oxford and Cambridge Local Examinations were the first also to introduce gymnastics, active games, daily baths, and many other hygienic reforms sorely needed in girls' schools." The London Association of Schoolmistresses, of which Miss Davies was Secretary, applied itself especially to the study of School Hygiene, and the first paper issued by them was one on *Physical Exercises and Recreation*.

While it was true, as Mrs. Anderson said, that improvement in training and education should accomplish as much for the

---

[1] Dame Louisa Lumsden did pioneer work in introducing athletics into girls' schools. " Miss Lumsden," writes Miss J. F. Dove, " who was the first Head Mistress of St. Leonard's School [St. Andrews], had been herself at school in Belgium where gymnasium dresses were worn, and the first thing we did at St. Leonard's was to turn the stables into a gymnasium, and the dresses were made from her recollections of those in Belgium. . . . College life had taught us the necessity for exercise and if possible games, and from the very first organized games were played at St. Leonard's." Mrs. Garrett Anderson, too, was an advocate of outdoor games. (*The Renaissance of Girls' Education*, by A. Zimmern, p. 152.) Cf. *Physical Training*, in the *Englishwoman's Journal*, May, 1858.

physical as for the mental development of women, it was also true that at the moment there were some dangers arising from the fact that this improvement had so far been only partially carried out. There had not yet been time for it to affect young women over school age. Physically as well as intellectually women were handicapped by insufficient training. They needed better conditions and fuller instruction with regard to health. At Girton there was a certain amount of ill-health among the students, described as " trifling but vexatious " by Miss Lumsden, who took great pains to look after them, there being no one specially told off for this duty. Madame Bodichon and Miss Metcalfe thought the matter serious ; they wanted special arrangements to be made for the care of the students' health, and thought the housekeeping needed improvement.

(Miss Davies to Madame Bodichon.)

June 12, 1874.

" I do not think that I undervalue the importance of taking care of health—only it seems to me that even quite young people can do it better for themselves, if they are taught how, than anyone else can do it for them, and that the thing to aim at is not to be constantly looking after them about every detail, but to have a generally healthy system going on, and only to put in a word now and then, and to be ready of course to advise and help and even to nurse, when any special need arises. I think that if girls of eighteen have been well trained, either at home or at school, this will be enough. We have found it so here, as a rule. But of course exceptions may come, and we must deal with them in an exceptional way, taking care that they do not suffer seriously, but not altering our whole system on their account. . . . Our College is not a place for ' young girls,' any more than the other Colleges are for young boys. It is a place for young women. . . . We must remember that the young women who come here are considered old enough to take care not only of themselves but of husbands and households and children, with very little help from anybody. The students here are a great deal to each other, and I think it is good for them that it should be so, and that they should feel a certain responsibility for each other. . . .

" I am glad that this question has been raised and discussed. I have for some time felt that some of the Committee were dissatisfied and have been harassed by it without knowing how to meet it. It seems best that the differences of view should be brought to a definite issue and there could not be a better occasion than the appointment of the Mistress for the ensuing year. I should like it to be understood that I am not ready to carry out any other ' idea ' than this which I have tried to explain and which I have had in view, more or less distinctly, from the beginning. . . . The Committee and the Mistress must not be at cross-purposes, working against each other. If they cannot work together, one or the other must go, and clearly it cannot be the Committee. Apart from this, there is another reason for my giving up. It would be an advantage in some ways to have a Mistress without home ties, who could live here all the year round. And as you know, it is not likely to be more easy to me, but rather less, as years go on, to be away from home even during term time."

The point at issue led to discussions on fundamental principles, for the question as to the students' health was a point of administration involving the general relations between the students and the Mistress. Closely connected with this were questions as to the government of the College. The position of the Mistress, and her relations to the Committee, had not been clearly established, and their exact nature had been obscured by the fact that Miss Davies had for two years combined the offices of Mistress and Secretary, in addition to being a member of the Committee. This was impossible as a permanent arrangement, and she had entered into it only as a matter of emergency. It was in fact contrary to her principles for the Mistress or any other resident official of the College to be a member of the governing body.

Among the difficulties of the moment was the fact that, so long as the College had no past, the Committee could have no past students among its members. This made a serious gap between the students and the governing body. The first few generations of students felt themselves to be pioneers and in part creators of the College, and they were inclined to be critical of an absentee Committee which met in London. They wanted their views to be represented, and were therefore anxious that a certificated student (corresponding to a graduate) should be put on the Committee at the earliest possible moment. It was natural that they should look to Miss Lumsden, who had been a leader among them from the beginning. Knowing the desires of the students, and the value of Miss Lumsden's work and experience, Miss

Metcalfe and Madame Bodichon proposed her election. But to this Miss Davies was opposed. " I think you are in much too great a hurry to get an old student put on," she wrote to Madame Bodichon. " I have the strongest objection to this movement for putting the Mistress under the control of the students, for that is what it comes to." The proposal for Miss Lumsden's election was eventually withdrawn, and in the spring of 1875 she resigned her post as Resident Tutor.

About the same time Miss Davies announced that " family circumstances would prevent her from offering herself for re-appointment " as Mistress. She had entered upon the post of Mistress almost against her will, and in spite of her reluctance to leave her mother. She had accomplished the task of moving the College to Girton, and she was feeling the effects of the very heavy work of the last few years. " I suppose I don't show illness much," she wrote to Madame Bodichon, " for it seems impossible to make people understand how worn out I am. I have often felt as if I could bear it no longer . . . and must throw it all up."

The whole subject of the Mistress's position and duties had now to be worked out by the Committee. The situation was felt to be critical. " I feel that the College is on the verge of being a great success or a great failure," wrote Miss Metcalfe to Madame Bodichon ; and Mrs. Ponsonby expressed the same view to Miss Davies. " Matters will prosper," she wrote . . . " just in proportion as the governing body act and decide wisely in the course of the next few months."

(Miss Davies to Miss Manning.)

January 3, 1875.

" I think Madame Bodichon goes too much by the temporary opinions and tastes and requirements of the existing generation of students, as e.g. she asked anxiously about the housekeeping—Are they satisfied ? when I think the question should have been, Is it satisfactory ? and are they showing a more reasonable contented spirit ? . . . I think of course that her knowledge of the students' opinions as a whole is imperfect, but apart from that, it seems to me a wrong criterion to go by.

" When shall you like to come to Girton ? You are one of the few visitors that I feel both safe and pleasant. Your society is improving, and also I want you to keep up and develop your knowledge of things on the spot. It adds greatly to your usefulness."

(Miss Davies to Madame Bodichon.)

April 22, 1875.

" Miss Buss's opinion on the question of whether the Mistress should be on the Committee has the weight of experience, as she is on her own Governing Body. An *in*experienced person would I think be almost sure to wish to be on, fancying that it would give her a better position, but it does not follow that she would really find it so. It is certain at any rate that being on the Committee does not secure the desired effect of making things easy and pleasant for the Mistress. . . .

" To put a subordinate officer on the Governing Body seems so manifestly objectionable that I should hope not many would wish for it. . . .

" We have all the sixteen [students] here now, and . . . there is a great improvement in general as to health, and as usual much vivacity. Miss Kingsland has been remarking how the liveliness at table keeps up, in spite of Miss Welsh's absence."

April 26 [1875].

" I think if a member of the College should be appointed to any office in the internal administration, she should resign her position on the Governing Body. I do not know whether you may be thinking of my own case. I should be sorry for anyone to be put in such a position as mine. . . . It would be difficult to explain all the causes of discomfort, but in planning for anyone else I am anxious that my own and other experience should be turned to account, and the post made, if possible, less wearing than it has been to me."

(Miss Davies to Miss Manning.)

May 8 [1875].

" I had a little talk with one of our lecturers yesterday about what are sufficient reasons for giving leave of absence, etc., and I fancy that a Tutor has pretty much the same difficulties and perplexities that arise here. . . . I think you cannot realize what the position of the Mistress is, when you say in that easy way that she will probably hold her own. She *must* hold her own, or go. . . . I think you do not quite see how desirable it is that the Mistress should be strong *officially*."

As regards the Mistress's relations to the students, the question of course turned largely on the nature of the duties assigned to her. So far, she had been responsible only for the domestic arrangements and discipline, and had taken no part in the educational arrangements. Such a position was wanting both in interest and in authority. Miss Davies's own experience had at last convinced her that this was so, and that some change was necessary. The Committee, after reviewing the situation, defined the position of the Mistress in such a way as to give her a position of paramount importance as regards the internal management of the College, while herself remaining outside the governing body. She was to be responsible for all educational arrangements, as well as for discipline and domestic administration. The resident lecturers were to be appointed by the Committee on her nomination. She was to report to the Committee any important change which she might think desirable, and to " confer personally " with them whenever she desired it. In practice she reported to them regularly and fully every term. The post was one involving a variety of work, and much attention to detail. The duties shared to-day among the Directors of Studies, the Junior Bursar, the Librarian, and other officials, were then all performed by the Mistress.

These arrangements were no doubt the best that were practicable while the College was small, and they continued in force with but little modification for many years. There were two non-resident officers : Mr. Tomkinson was Treasurer, and Miss Davies Secretary. She did all the work connected with the meetings of the governing body, the admission of students, and the Entrance and Scholarship examinations. The governing body had no permanent Chairman, and the continuous direction of its affairs was thus in Miss Davies' hands.

The duties of the Mistress having been defined, the post was advertised early in May, and on June 28, 1875, the Committee appointed Miss A. F. Bernard. Miss Bernard came with an introduction from her uncle Lord Lawrence, with whom she had spent some time in India during his Viceroyalty. A course of training at the Home and Colonial Institution [1]

---

[1] This institution, founded in 1836 in Gray's Inn Road, had organized a course of training for teachers in elementary and secondary schools for girls. See *Girls' Grammar Schools*, by D. R. Fearon, in the *Contemporary Review*, Vol. XI, May–August, 1869.

had given her some special preparation for her work. The appointment gave great satisfaction to Miss Davies. " I am quite delighted with Miss Bernard—herself, and her way of taking up her work," she wrote to Madame Bodichon. " She seems to me . . . a higher sort of person than we could have ventured to hope for." In order to inaugurate the new régime, she spent the first few days of the Michaelmas term at Girton. " I . . . left it on Thursday in a most cheerful and promising condition," she reported to Madame Bodichon, " Miss Bernard setting to work in good heart, and great rejoicing going on over the increase of numbers. There are 23 students in residence now."

Miss Bernard's post was one which called for high qualities. She had to evolve a definite position and status for the Mistress in relation to the students on the one hand, and the Committee on the other ; and she had to work out a system of discipline and create a tradition. To this task she brought a high sense of duty, and a power of keeping steadily on her course while co-operating readily with others. She quickly identified herself with the interests of the College, and a mutual respect and admiration governed the relations between her and Miss Davies. Already in her first term of office, plans for building an addition to the College were set on foot. " I was immensely interested in the plans," she wrote to Miss Davies, " and am filled with admiration at the largeness of your views. We feel here that we march under a stout-hearted general." With much personal distinction and charm, Miss Bernard had a cool judgment and a manner of austere dignity, which was something of a bar to intimacy with the students, though beneath it there lay a real interest in their welfare. She took pains to cultivate relations with Cambridge society ; she knew this would help the College, and she liked society for its own sake. Her position as Mistress was a solitary one owing to the absence of colleagues. At first there was only one resident lecturer, Miss Kingsland, who left in 1876, when Miss Welsh was appointed Resident Lecturer in Classics, thus entering on a long career of service to the College. In 1878 another lecturer was added, in the person of Miss C. A. Herschel ; not till 1880, when Miss C. A. Scott was appointed, were there so many as three. There was no one at hand who resembled

Miss Bernard in age and position, except Miss A. J. Clough, who as Principal of Newnham was dealing with similar problems ; and a friendship between them was soon brought about by force of circumstances.

Meanwhile, the students of the two Colleges were also being drawn together, by the pursuit of common interests. In the outer world, they were long regarded as curiosities, but at Cambridge, as one generation succeeded another, the consciousness of being pioneers soon became less acute. One of the Hitchin students, Miss Kingsland, had written :

> " Dare to be learned, dare to be blue,
> Ours is a work that no others can do."

By 1876 an American lady, Miss Minturn (who afterwards entered the College), was able to describe the students as follows :

" One feels it difficult to convey an idea of their vigorous tone without arousing in the imagination of American readers a suspicion of the ' strong-minded ' type which has become so justly odious. Perhaps one may best indicate how false such an idea of Girton students would be by dwelling on their great unconsciousness of any representative character. They never seem to regard themselves as the exponents of a cause. . . . They are simple-hearted English girls and women, doing work for its own sake, spontaneously and with pleasure."

The high spirits which Miss Davies observed at Hitchin continued at Girton, together with the intense seriousness as regards work, which came to a climax with every examination. Candidates were the recipients of much sympathy, and a custom grew up of offering them *jeux d'esprit* just before the examination, by way of keeping up their spirits. These often took the form of verses, a fashion originating at Hitchin with the offer of a prize for the best poem by a student. The most distinguished among the poets were Miss Lumsden and Miss Welsh.

In 1883 the usual routine of life at the College was broken by the performance of a Greek play—the *Electra* of Sophocles. Miss Davies was not quite inclined to approve, fearing that it would mean too much distraction from work. " You will hear from others," she wrote to Madame Bodichon, " of the Greek

Play. I am glad to find that the inroad upon the students' time was less than might have been feared, and that there was no extravagant expense on the dresses, etc. Nearly all the performers who had anything to say or sing were Classical Students, and the learning some Greek by heart was of some use for them." The dresses were made by the actors, from the cheapest materials, and the scenery was painted by Miss Sargant (now Mrs. Sargant Florence), sister to one of the students, Miss Ethel Sargant. The play was given on three nights in the October term, with remarkable success. Miss Janet Case, who played Electra, was invited to take the part of Athena in the *Eumenides*, performed by the University in 1885—the only occasion on which a woman has acted in a Greek play at Cambridge. This was an isolated instance, and for many years Girton had little to do with Cambridge, apart from lectures and examinations. Societies such as the Students' Christian Union, the Heretics, the Fabians, the Moral Sciences Club, where men and women students now meet, were growths of a later date.

For outdoor games there was at first little provision at Girton. Games were not universal even among men as they are now, and had hardly begun to be played by girls. Lady Rich planned to give a gymnasium ; her death, which occurred suddenly in 1874, prevented this, but her intention was carried out by the Committee, with the help of her cousin Mr. Tomkinson. The building was not at first fitted up for a gymnasium, but was used for racquets ; there were no other games—no hockey, cricket, or lawn tennis. There were no lawns round the College, nothing at first but a ploughed field. A beginning was made in the winter of 1874 with fencing and planting. " Mrs. Russell Gurney is going to give us ten *large* trees, such as may be sat under next summer," Miss Davies wrote to Madame Bodichon. " I am much occupied with considerations as to the planting of them, and where they should go, etc." Her thoughts were, however, necessarily fixed on finance and building, and a garden was to her a luxury which must give way to more pressing needs. In 1879 an American observer noted that the grounds were " scanty and rough. . . . There is almost nothing that is attractive in the external appearance of the establishment." [1] This state of

---

[1] Quoted in the *Cambridge Chronicle*, February 1, 1879.

things continued till 1881, when Miss Metcalfe was so much impressed by the neglected look of the place that she took the matter seriously in hand. " I am quite of your opinion," she wrote to Madame Bodichon, " that it is useless to give gifts to a garden so utterly uncared for. . . . I am certainly not tall, but the weeds are taller than I am. . . . I think the Committee are very short-sighted in leaving the garden as the last thing and doling out such scanty supplies, when I believe if it were fairly kept it might be a powerful attraction to students—and I see certain signs of the London University advantages,[1] as well as Newnham, becoming a serious rival. I cannot tell you how my heart sinks whenever I see the dismally uncared-for state of the garden front and back." Miss Metcalfe and her sister,[2] with the help of friends, got together a sum of over £400 which in 1881 was spent under her direction on improving the garden and grounds. Lawns, trees, and shrubs were established and the place soon grew more attractive and inviting.

For a long time poverty showed its traces in the interior of the College too. Madame Bodichon wanted the walls to be papered and painted. She offered to provide for the decoration of the Mistress's room and the reception room, and with the help of her friend Miss Gertrude Jekyll she chose a scheme of colouring for the work to be done throughout the building. But the cost proved more than the College could afford.

(*Miss Davies to Madame Bodichon.*)

Sunday [*July*, 1875].

" On further reflection I am much inclined to postpone the work at Girton. I quite feel as you do, that if we do anything, we had better do it all when we are about it, and in a way that will last. If it cost £300 we should have only £70 left in the Bank. I should like to keep £370, and try to add to it as fast as we can at least enough to make up the £1000 for which we are paying interest, and pay that off. It does not seem as if this work was of urgent necessity. Of course the place looks unfinished, but that is not altogether a disadvantage. It brings home to people that we have not money. When everything looks smooth and nice, it does not occur to people that it is not paid for. And for the students it is not amiss I think to

---

[1] London University had opened its degrees to women in 1878.
[2] See Biographical Index.

have a reminder that the place did not grow up of itself without any trouble. . . ."

Although no longer in residence, Miss Davies kept in the closest touch with the College. Every month she received an abstract of the household accounts from Miss Bernard, who was besides in constant correspondence with her about details of administration and discipline, arrangements for teaching and examinations, and so forth. Miss Davies was most willing to help the new Mistress, and her keen interest in the College extended to the smallest particulars. Mr. Tomkinson sometimes thought she carried her instructions too far. " If this is going to the Mistress," he commented on one of her letters, " is it not rather too much telling her exactly what to do and how to do it ? Wire-pulling from a distance." But detailed instructions were necessary at first, and Miss Bernard welcomed them. " I am really ashamed of the length of the letters that I inflict on you," she wrote to Miss Davies. " I seem to have always so much to ask you."

As Secretary, Miss Davies corresponded with all the candidates for entrance, and got to know most of them personally during the Entrance and Scholarship examinations. Frequent visits to Girton, especially during the Long Vacation terms, enabled her to follow up her acquaintance. Among the students, as she herself knew, she was generally called " the little instigator." She was an investigator too, always looking out for some student who might prove worthy of a post at the College, or might do it credit in some other way. To students who found it difficult to come owing to want of means, she was especially sympathetic, often helping them, by every means in her power, with much delicacy and generosity. Those who made friends with her found in her a very warm ally.

For some time before Miss Bernard's appointment, Miss Davies had felt that she was very tired. On April 22, 1875, she wrote to Madame Bodichon : " I am forty-five to-day—a good age for retiring into private life." But she knew that there was still much to be done for Girton. A little later she wrote to Madame Bodichon : " As to your saying the College is mine, you know that is nonsense. It has taken all of us to get so far, and it wants us all still."

It was true that the College could not have been brought into existence without zealous co-operation on the part of its founders, but Madame Bodichon felt that it was chiefly by Miss Davies' determination and energy that the work had been accomplished. Miss Davies' resignation of the Mistress-ship offered an opportunity for giving expression to this feeling, and in the autumn of 1875 Madame Bodichon and Lady Stanley began a movement for presenting a testimonial to her, towards which £1000 was promised by various members of the Committee, the idea being that some special addition should be made to the College buildings, which should bear her name. About the same time, however, the Committee decided on general grounds that the time had come for enlarging the College, and this led to complications. Miss Davies pointed out that any additional buildings must be taken in hand by the Committee as a whole, and that she as Secretary could hardly collect money for a scheme which included a testimonial to herself. At her request, therefore, Madame Bodichon and Lady Stanley withdrew their proposal of a testimonial.

Miss Davies was now settled at home in London, where she was fully occupied with the Secretaryship and other work, especially in connection with the London Schoolmistresses' Association. It was pleasant to be in London again, but she found herself unable to resume the active social life of old days. After a party at Miss Manning's house, she wrote to her hostess : " Do you know, I was so tired after your rout that it took me two days to get over it. Does not that show, both what a wretched weakling I am, and how unworthy of the privilege of attending routs ? " This led to a fixed resolution to save her strength. " I hope you will not mind my not going to your parties," she wrote to Madame Bodichon. " I have made a rule not to go anywhere, and it is awkward to make exceptions. You will wonder why I am giving up society, so I had better explain that I prefer other ways of spending my money, which is not redundant, and also I do not care to undergo the fatigue." Madame Bodichon answered sympathetically. " Mrs. Bodichon," Miss Davies reported to Miss Manning, " takes my withdrawal from society with great equanimity. She thinks nobody ought to go to parties who is tired by them. If nobody

did, parties would soon come to nothing. . . . I went to the
Rink this afternoon with my nephew and niece, and skated away.
They assured me I was getting on like anything. . . . I had
one tumble, but it did not hurt." So she was not without
amusements and interests other than Girton. Five of her six
nephews went to school at Marlborough, and their successive
careers there were a source of great interest and pleasure. Her
friends found it difficult to realize how tired she was, and invitations to take up fresh work had to be refused.

(*Miss Davies to Miss Manning.*)

June 17 [1876].
" The specific work of Secretary to the College and the Schoolmistresses, I feel bound to do, ill or well, so long as I hold the office.
I draw the line there. I don't occupy even this limited field so fully
or so efficiently as I might if I were stronger. Any extra fatigue and
worry tends to increase the nervous weakness and irritability which
already, as you often see with regret, interfere with what would be
called my ' usefulness.' . . . Having such a very small income as
mine affects the details of daily life, making it necessary to *limit* oneself in many directions if perpetual wear and tear is to be avoided.
If I felt equal to more work, I should wish not to take up public
agitations, but something that I could be paid for, so that I could contribute more towards the household expenses and make my mother's
life easier so far as that goes. See what a long egotistic preach you
have brought upon yourself ! "

In the autumn of 1876, Miss Davies had a severe attack of
illness which kept her in bed for a month. After this she decided
to resign the Secretaryship. Miss Manning thought this unnecessary and compared her to " the traitors of history." Miss
Davies replied that she was ambitious to earn such a grand title,
" but I never can, as it cannot be traitorous to take leave of things
when they have succeeded, and my three things, Local Examinations, Schoolmistresses' Association, and College, are all
flourishing. And I shall never start anything else. Heaven
forefend ! "

In the summer of 1877, Mrs. Croom Robertson was appointed
Secretary. The new Secretary was already an old acquaintance,
as she was sister to Mrs. Llewelyn Davies (Miss Davies' sister-

in-law) ; [1] Mr. Robertson was Professor of Mental Philosophy and Logic at University College, London, and had long been a supporter of the admission of women to University education and the suffrage ; he was " interested in good things," as Miss Davies told Madame Bodichon. Miss Davies exchanged the post of Secretary for that of Treasurer, which Mr. Tomkinson now resigned. She was relieved of a heavy burden of correspondence, but in other ways the change made no difference.

Not long after this, Madame Bodichon was also attacked by illness, in her case of a very serious nature. She had recently bought a house at Zennor on the north coast of Cornwall, not far from St. Ives, then a remote and little-known place. It was a little old house, solidly built of granite, and stood high above the sea, in rocky ground covered with gorse and heather. " Hardly any bit of the kingdom, I fancy, would suit you better than your neighbourhood of the Land's End," wrote George Eliot to her. " We are poor creatures, headachy and feeble, but not the less affectionate in our memories of our too far-off friend. I often see you enjoying your sunsets, and the wayside flowers." In May, 1877, Madame Bodichon went to Zennor with Madame Mario, intending to enjoy a holiday and do some painting, but she was suddenly taken seriously ill. Her old friend Dr. Reginald Thompson went to her at once, and as soon as the journey was possible he and Madame Mario brought her back to London. Before this, however, she was well enough to receive a letter from Miss Davies :

(Miss Davies to Madame Bodichon.)

June 7 [1877].

" I went to Blandford Square this morning to get some further news of you, and I was glad to have as good an account as one could hope for. I was glad too to hear that it does not hurt you to have letters, so that I may venture to send you a word just to say—tho' you know it without saying—how much we have all been thinking of you, and how much grief and sympathy has been felt since the sad news came. It is a great comfort to know that the prostration is not accompanied by pain, and that you are able to keep up your cheerfulness. One would be afraid that to anyone so active and helpful as you have been, the

---

[1] They were the daughters of Sir Charles Crompton, Judge of the King's Bench.

necessity of being still and submitting to be waited upon, would be very trying, only I know you are so good in finding out the best side of everything, that I hope you may have been able to find some good in this, and to look upon the forced idleness as a little bit, come at last, of the rest which you have earned by years of assiduous exertion. . . .

" You will be wanting, as usual, to hear if there is any news of Girton. Nothing particular has happened. . . . I think Mrs. Robertson will be a valuable Secretary. The term ends, with a sort of climax of examinations, this week. . . . I will not write more now, but I shall be sending you reports from time to time of what is going on, as I know you will like to hear."

Miss Davies was as good as her word, and wrote often, reporting details of Girton business which she knew would be interesting. By the summer of 1878, Madame Bodichon had so far recovered that Miss Davies was able to visit her again as usual at Scalands. Dr. Bodichon, who was paying his summer visit to England, was staying there, and Madame Bodichon's devoted friend Miss Marks [1] was in charge of the invalid. A year later, Miss Davies visited her again, and reported to Miss Manning that some advance had been made.

" She can paint a little most days, and walks about, but is still very much of an invalid. Miss Marks is here and fits the position admirably. . . . I have been telling Madame that this is a place to grow handsome in, and that I felt it coming on. She said it was quite true, and I was already 20 per cent. better-looking than when I came. Then it struck her that it would be a good place for the Portrait to be taken, and asked if I could come and have it done here. I said Yes, but I scarcely think it can come off, as she will have to go away when the leaves begin to fall."

" The Portrait " was Miss Davies' portrait, which was subscribed for by Girtonians. It was painted by Rudolf Lehmann, and now hangs in the hall at Girton. Madame Bodichon recovered her health to some extent ; but she was never able to go to Algiers again, which meant increasing separation from her husband, who could not winter in England, and lived principally at their house near Algiers till his death in 1886. She could not

---

[1] Miss Marks (afterwards Mrs. Ayrton) had at this time recently entered as a student at Girton, through the help of Madame Bodichon. See *Hertha Ayrton : A Memoir*, by Evelyn Sharp.

even go to Girton, which was a great sorrow to her, but she kept in touch with the College, partly through Miss Davies, partly through visits from old students, among whom she had many friends, some of whom owed their admission to Girton to her generous help. In 1882 she sold her house in Blandford Square to Mr. Llewelyn Davies, and thenceforward lived almost entirely at Scalands. Though obliged to live an invalid's life, she was able even yet to have fresh interests. She started a " night-school " for the village, which flourished for many years under the care of Mr. Ransome, a teacher who came from Hastings to superintend it. " Madame's boys "—the labourers who attended the school—were a great institution. In 1885 she ceased to be a member of the Executive Committee of Girton, but her interest in the College, and delight in hearing of it, remained as keen as ever till her death in 1891.

Up to the time of Madame Bodichon's death, Miss Davies continued to visit her at Scalands, or occasionally at Hastings, almost every year. Visits to other friends were often arranged to suit with excursions to Edinburgh, Dublin, and elsewhere, wherever there might happen to be candidates for the Girton Entrance Examination. The examination was held in London, but if there were several candidates in some rather distant place, arrangements would be made for them to be examined in that place. Miss Davies liked taking charge on these occasions ; she was glad to have the opportunity of making Girton more widely known, and enjoyed the visits involved. She was still, however, suffering from the effects of over-work, and in the autumn of 1880 she was advised by Dr. Andrew Clark that she needed rest, and more frequent change. Arrangements were accordingly made for some one to help her at home, and take charge in her absence. By this means she was enabled in the winter of 1881 to go to Italy, for the first time in her life.

(Miss Davies to Madame Bodichon.)

October 14, 1881.
" I have had a good deal of Local Examination work lately and have been struck by the lamentable neglect of Latin by girls. Out of 129 candidates only 5 take it. The rest scatter themselves over German, Zoology, Botany, and other trumpery."

October 31.

" I know you dote upon Natural Sciences. I called them trumpery on purpose to vex you. I don't dispute their utility, in their proper place, and I only make war actively against German, as taking the place of Latin. Just now I am visiting one of Professor Beesly's Latin classes at Bedford College, and am much struck by the interest and value of the teaching . . .

" It is decided to hold the Entrance Examination in March at Dublin, so I suppose I shall have to go over. But before that, I have in view a much longer and grander expedition. It is almost settled that Miss Welsh and I go together to Italy about December 19 for five or six weeks. . . . I am hoping that a real change like this may give me a start, as I seem to go on, not getting stronger, and I feel to want something reviving. . . . I have never been in Italy."

The journey was a great success, and Miss Davies returned to work feeling much refreshed. In later years she often went abroad again, visiting Italy, Switzerland, and Germany. What she liked in travelling was to see the life of the country ; she enjoyed going in trams and having meals in small popular restaurants. During a visit to Venice she was far more interested in a Labour demonstration than in Bellini or Tintoretto. Her tastes had not changed with the passage of time.

For the moment, such distant journeys were not again possible owing to increasing anxiety about Mrs. Davies, who was now over eighty, and suffering in health. After her death, which took place in 1886, Miss Davies moved from 17, Cunningham Place, where they had lived together since 1860, to rooms in Melbury Terrace, a street adjoining Blandford Square, and therefore close to her brother's house. " My rooms are quite as nice as I expected, and the servants delightful," she wrote to Miss Manning. " Dr. Watts's Divine Song, ' Not more than others I deserve,' etc., expresses my feelings." Miss Manning was the one among her old friends who was now most within reach, and her unfailing sympathy and affection were a great support to Miss Davies. In a letter on one occasion when she had to refuse an invitation from Miss Manning, she wrote, " If you were ill and really wanted me, I would fly to you on the wings of the wind—just as I should go off to Madame Bodichon at a moment's notice."

Meanwhile the division of duties as regards her work for

Girton had undergone some rearrangement. After a time Mrs. Croom Robertson found that her work as Secretary took up more time and strength than she could spare. In 1882, a new Secretary was appointed, Miss Frances Kensington, who had held a similar post at Bedford College. Mrs. Croom Robertson became Bursar ; and Miss Davies, Honorary Secretary. It is not quite clear why she did not become permanent Chairman of the Committee ; there seems to have been some feeling that it was not suitable for a woman to occupy such a position. There was no permanent Chairman, but at each meeting of the Committee some man among those present was asked to preside. Miss Davies as Honorary Secretary retained the chief direction of affairs.

CHAPTER XVIII

The Building of Girton. 1882–1904

BY 1882, after sixteen years of hard work, the College was fairly established at Girton, and the circle of its supporters was slowly increasing as each year added a few to the number of its past students. It was still, however, on a very small scale ; the number of past students had not yet reached one hundred, and the buildings contained rooms for only fifty-five students (though a few more were squeezed in), three Resident Lecturers, and the Mistress. This was a meagre provision indeed, compared with the numbers of young women all over the country to whom Miss Davies felt that the College ought to bring new life, and for whom there was very little provision elsewhere.[1] She longed before all things to bring the advantages of the College within reach of the largest possible numbers. Her first object was therefore to build rooms for students, and for this she was prepared to sacrifice almost everything else. This appears clearly from some conversations with Madame Bodichon, of which Miss Davies made a memorandum, on the occasion of a visit to Scalands in 1878. Madame Bodichon, who was making her will, told Miss Davies that she

[1] Women had been admitted to membership of London University, in 1878, but London then had no residential colleges. Newnham was founded in 1871, and Lady Margaret and Somerville in 1879. The Association for Promoting the Education of Women in Oxford had also a number of Town Students (now the Oxford Home Students) living privately under its supervision. In 1882 the women students at Oxford and Cambridge numbered in all something under 200. The movement for the foundation of provincial Universities had only just begun, at Manchester (1880) and Liverpool (1881).

intended to leave what she inherited from her father to her relations, but her savings she felt at liberty to dispose of otherwise, and she proposed accordingly to leave £10,000 to Girton.[1] She asked Miss Davies' advice in the matter, remarking that the longer she lived, the more she felt that it was not wise to insist too much on carrying out exactly some idea of one's own, but rather to leave it to a trustworthy body to judge according to the circumstances of the time. Miss Davies suggested that her views might be expressed in a letter which would not be absolutely binding, and at Madame Bodichon's request she drafted such a letter. The legacy, as it proved, was subject to no condition, and the draft was not used by Madame Bodichon, but it is interesting as giving a clear expression of Miss Davies' views. It ran as follows :

" I have placed the sum of money which I am leaving to Girton College entirely at the disposal of the College, believing that those who are managing its affairs will be in the best position for judging of its needs, according to the circumstances of the time. I wish however to express my own general view as to the application of funds under existing conditions. My feeling is that the College as it is confers immense advantages on its students. These advantages are at present limited to a very small number of women, as compared with the multitude outside. I should wish therefore that money should be expended in extending its benefits, either by adding students' rooms and other contingent accommodation or in any way that may seem more effectual, rather than in adding to the comforts and enjoyments, and even to the solid advantages already possessed."

Miss Davies's sympathies were all with " the multitude outside," and she had a generous desire to throw open the doors to as many of them as possible. She felt that the independence and power of concentration which a College training ought to give would be invaluable in its reaction on those middle-class homes where it never occurred to anyone that the daughters could want any time to themselves. " This great boon," she wrote, " the power of being alone—is perhaps the most precious distinctive feature of College life, as compared with that of an

[1] That she was able to leave so large a sum to Girton is accounted for by the fact that she made a good deal of money by the sale of her pictures.

ordinary family."¹ This distinctive feature was kept steadily in
view, and the buildings at Girton bear testimony to the far-
sighted thoroughness with which she thought out her plans.
When the first block was built, there were rooms for twenty-one
students ; the buildings now contain accommodation for about
one hundred and eighty ; yet a stranger on seeing the College
would not be able to say at once which was the oldest part of
the building. There is no sign of a modest and tentative beginning, with more ambitious later developments ; the main features
of the first plans have been preserved in each later addition.
Most of the students have both a bedroom and a sitting-room,
and the dimensions of the rooms and the corridors show no
enlargement of scale with the passage of time. It was and still
is unusual in a women's college for students to have both sitting-
room and bedroom. The American visitor who described the
College as having almost nothing attractive about its appearance,
was much impressed by this advantage, which he notes in italics :

> " *Each pupil has at Girton a room to herself* ; in the lower stories,
> *each has two rooms.* . . . A new building was projected, which I saw
> in progress, for nineteen additional students, with two lecture rooms
> and other rooms. This new building is to cost £8000 (40,000 dols.)—
> a sum for which an American college would have accommodated forty
> or fifty pupils. But it would have been by crowding them together ;
> and Girton may well forgo elegancies and even comforts for the sake
> of the health and privacy of its students."²

Privacy was the one luxury which Miss Davies desired for
the students ; and in her eyes it was not a luxury—she despised
luxuries—but a necessity.

The College, though designed on this large and necessarily
expensive scale, was managed with the severest economy, in order
that any margin of profit might go towards enlarging the buildings.
The American visitor was " especially struck with the bareness
of the walls, which are uniformly unpapered. . . . The Library
at Girton," he adds, " was as meagre as possible, mostly mere
odds and ends of books, contrasting greatly with the excellent

¹ *Home and the Higher Education*, an address delivered at the annual
meeting of the Birmingham Higher Education Association, 1878.
² *Cambridge Chronicle*, February 1, 1879.

collection at Vassar, and the admirable and costly one at Welles-
ley. The Laboratory too was inferior to theirs." The Natural
Science students at Girton suffered from not having sufficient
facilities and suitable apparatus. On receiving from a Cambridge
lecturer " an immense list of things . . . that were absolutely
necessary for the students," Miss Bernard had it cut down to
one half. The lecturer (as she reported to Miss Davies) " remarked with a sigh, that it was not what he could have wished,
but he supposed it must do." All the students felt the want
of a Library. In 1876 an opportunity for building a Library
seemed to come, through a gift of £1000 from the parents of
a girl who had intended to enter the College, but had died before
she could come into residence. The gift was intended to be
commemorative, and to be associated with some distinct portion of the building, and Miss Shirreff wrote to suggest that
" as we have long wanted a Library . . . we might fitly spend
the money on that." But Miss Davies felt that the money was
more needed for additional rooms for students and on these it
was accordingly spent.[1]

In 1875, a scheme was adopted for building eighteen sets of
students' rooms and three lecture rooms, at a cost of £5000.
A Building Committee was appointed, consisting of Miss Davies,
Madame Bodichon, and Lady Stanley ; and the wearisome task
of raising funds had to be resumed with fresh vigour. The
College had now so far won public recognition that with the
help of Lord Lawrence and others, contributions were forthcoming from some of the City Companies, including the Clothworkers [2] and Drapers, who also gave support in the shape of
Scholarships. " It looks as if we were beginning to make way
at last," Miss Davies wrote to Madame Bodichon in the summer
of 1876, when it seemed as if even the new rooms proposed
would not be enough. Meanwhile the debt on the original
buildings had not been fully paid, though the College was being

[1] A small block of rooms, projecting to the west at the junction of
the Orchard and Hospital wings, was built with this money, and was
for many years known as " the Taylor knob."
[2] The Clothworkers' Company have given Scholarships to Girton since
1874. See a notice of Sir Owen Roberts, in the *Girton Review*, Lent
Term, 1915, p. 16.

forced into expansion by the demands of candidates for admission. For many years this state of things was continually repeated, each access of numbers involving fresh struggles and expedients for raising money. It is a monotonous story of subscription lists, loans, and mortgages. The buildings were enlarged again in 1879 and in 1884. The cost of this last addition amounted to over £12,000 and was partly met by means of a gift from Madame Bodichon of £5000 subject to a charge of £250 per annum to be paid to her during her life. The College was now able to hold about eighty students, and the new rooms were quickly filled.

The extension of 1884 included not only students' rooms, but a Library, for which Lady Stanley of Alderley gave £1000. This was warmly welcomed by the students. In 1882, a letter to the first number of the *Girton Review* had suggested that students should give books towards the formation of a Library, as " the College fund for this purpose scarcely allows a dozen books to be bought in the year." This suggestion bore fruit, and the students did a great deal to provide the College with books. The new Library was a fine and dignified room, and the many empty shelves in it encouraged people to give books. Tennyson and Ruskin presented their works, and there were generous donations from some of the lecturers, and from Lady Goldsmid, Professor Croom Robertson, and others. " The generous kindness of the Dowager Lady Stanley of Alderley has now provided us with the Library which we have so long and so urgently needed," wrote a student in the *Girton Review*. " We are already beginning to wonder how we contrived to do without it in the Dark Ages before it was built." Lady Stanley was a great benefactor, and provided for many special wants. Besides the Library, she gave the Chemical Laboratory, a lodge at the front gate for the head gardener, and many lesser gifts.

In 1885, Miss Bernard, who had held the post of Mistress for nine years, resigned it on her marriage with Dr. P. W. Latham of Cambridge. It was now possible to appoint as her successor a former student of the College, Miss Welsh, who was Mistress from 1885 till 1904. She had been a Classical Scholar at Girton, and Resident Lecturer in Classics since 1876. She carried on the traditions established by Miss Bernard, and under her careful and kindly administration the College was kept more closely in touch with its past students, especially with those who were engaged in teaching. Not a year had passed since Miss Welsh's appointment, when an unexpected event made it possible to add to the College on a large scale. This was the bequest from a hitherto unknown benefactor, Miss Jane Catherine Gamble, of her residuary estate, amounting to about £19,000. Whatever the cause which may have inspired her to make this magnificent bequest, the results on the fortunes of Girton were great and immediate. A larger extension than anything hitherto undertaken was now carried out. An adjacent plot of seventeen acres of land was bought; and rooms for twenty-seven more students were built, bringing the total up to one hundred and four. There remained some acres unoccupied by buildings, and this piece of grass land was laid out by Miss Welsh as a miniature park surrounded by a walk sheltered with trees and shrubs. It is to her care and skill, and to Miss Gamble's gift, that this garden—one of the great attractions of Girton—owes its existence.

Large as Miss Gamble's legacy was, even more was soon spent, and the College was again in debt; while the increasing number of candidates for admission again created a pressing need for extension. Miss Davies had the outlines of a complete building scheme ready in her mind's eye, and in the summer of 1890 she submitted them to the Committee. To build while the College was in debt was no new thing. But this time, there were unusual difficulties to overcome. The scheme she proposed was on a magnificent scale, including, besides rooms for about forty more students, lecture rooms, a large dining-hall, new kitchens, and a Chapel. Many of the Committee felt that the financial burden would be too great, and that any money that could be raised would be better spent on improving the salaries of the staff, and the equipment of the College, than on buildings; while some—in particular Lady Stanley of Alderley—were strongly opposed to the addition of a Chapel, which in Miss Davies's mind was an essential feature. " I should be open to the compromise of doing it by a separate fund," she wrote to Miss Manning, " but if the Committee refused to include it in the plans, I should withdraw the scheme."

Miss Davies' proposals for building, seconded by Miss Manning, were rejected by the Committee in July, 1890.

(Miss Davies to Miss Manning.)

July 19, 1890.

" Thank you for your note. I do not regret having brought the subject forward again. I think it was the most reasonable course. There seems to be nothing to be done but to try when vacancies on the Committee occur to fill them better. It may be difficult to see what is best to do in carrying on the College. To cut off Scholarships might result in so reducing our number that we might have empty rooms instead of being overcrowded. . . . After the meeting, Mr. Wright [1] was talking in a friendly way to Miss Welsh, and said to me, ' You will get your way in the end '—a disagreeable way of putting it, but not meant to be so."

SCALANDS GATE.

July 25 [1890].

" I enclose a classification of the opposition. . . . The financial alarmists seemed determined not to see that having sketches of plans in our hands would not bind us to build at any particular time. . . . The Chapel looks as if it would be the greatest difficulty."

A year later, the College received a legacy of £10,000 from Madame Bodichon, who had died on June 11, 1891, after many years of ill-health. The Committee, however, were still unwilling to proceed with Miss Davies' building scheme.

October 16 [1891].

" I said [to Mrs. Croom Robertson] we were *now* in a state of stagnation, not able to move on or increase our numbers, and that no one was likely to leave or to give money while we are doing nothing with what we have. She said if people asked what we were going to do with Madame Bodichon's legacy, we could say that we should be building by and by—and that she only wanted to put it off because there would be such discussions while Lady Stanley is so much against it."

In the following year, a sum of £5000 was received by Girton under Madame Emily Pfeiffer's will, and Miss Davies hoped that the money could be used for building, but this proved impossible owing to the terms of the bequest.

(Miss Davies to Miss Manning.)

April 6, 1892.

" An unfortunate condition will . . . be attached. The money must be applied to some specific purpose, to which the name can be

---

[1] See Biographical Index.

given. Mr. Fitch said that if we wanted to build a beautiful Library it could be called Pfeiffer (Mrs. Ayrton [1] stuck in Laboratories), or to found something analogous to Fellowships, they might be called Pfeiffer. I threw out that what was wanted was a roof over the students' heads, and he said we might have a Pfeiffer wing, but it is quite evident that he would be against it, and Lady Stanley was as much opposed as ever."

April 8 [1892].
" I have decided not to propose using the Pfeiffer money for building. There would be some practical difficulty in assigning the name to a small part of what I have in view, and in any case I doubt whether the plan can be carried out at present. The *best* to be hoped is the application of the money to Scholarships, which are of course wanted. The *worst* would be a great new Hall stuck out at the end of the present building—next worst, a new Laboratory, next ' Studentships,' i.e. ' something analogous to Fellowships.' . . . I hope it may be possible to prevent it [the Hall] and the Laboratory scheme. The Studentship will I expect be irresistible."

It was decided to use the Pfeiffer money as an endowment for Scholarships and Studentships, and it was at first applied (as Miss Davies wished) only to Scholarships. Though building projects remained in abeyance, they were kept in mind ; the water supply was increased by the sinking of a new artesian well, and arrangements were made for drainage on a scale sufficient to provide for any future extension. After the death of Lady Stanley of Alderley, which occurred early in 1895, building schemes revived in full force, and in 1897 Miss Davies' plans were provisionally adopted, " to be carried out as soon as adequate contributions can be secured," as announced in the annual Report. The cost was estimated at £50,000, towards which £8,000 had been promised by subscribers, and the College had actually succeeded by means of the strictest economy in saving nearly £8,000 out of income. Two years later, the work of building was begun.

By 1902 the new buildings were complete, and the final touch was put by the inauguration of the Chapel, on May 23, in the presence of a large gathering of old students and friends of the

[1] Mrs. Ayrton was at this time an elected member of the College, representing the Certificated Students.

College. Two services were held, the preachers being Mr. Llewelyn Davies and Dr. A. H. Cooke, who had for many years conducted services at Girton on Sunday evenings. " Hucusque auxiliatus est nobis Dominus," was the text chosen by Miss Davies to be carved in the panelling over the entrance to the Chapel. To her the day was one of happiness and triumph ; her aspirations had been in great measure fulfilled ; and the Chapel was the visible expression of a fundamental article of her faith. The task of paying for the new buildings remained to be faced.

Payments on account for building, planting, and drainage had been made, amounting to £45,000. But the total bill, as often happens, was much in excess of the original estimate, and there was nothing for it but to borrow on a large scale. Miss Davies wrote in the Annual Report :

" Arrangements have been made with the Prudential Assurance Company for a loan on mortgage, not to exceed £40,000. So far, £36,500 has been drawn, and the temporary advance of £20,000 made last year by the College Bankers has been repaid. The drain on the College resources for payment of interest on borrowed money is necessarily heavy, and though additional students' fees will give some increase of income, such increase cannot suffice to relieve the College from the burden of debt. Further contributions are therefore greatly needed."

The debt was indeed crippling ; the interest on loans amounted to about £1,500 annually. In May, 1904, events to be narrated later caused Miss Davies to resign her post of Honorary Secretary, and to give up active participation in the affairs of the College. The story of the debt may however be finished here. For eleven more years the College struggled with the burden. At last the situation began to mend. In 1904 Rosalind Countess of Carlisle offered a gift of £2000, and in 1909 a vigorous financial campaign was set on foot among former students, the chief organizers being Lady Dorothy Howard [1] (Lady Carlisle's daughter), Mrs. Walter Runciman, and Miss Honor Lawrence. By dint of much hard work, the debt was in 1910 reduced to £29,000. Two years later, Mrs. Garrett Anderson and Miss Davies each gave £1,000, and in 1913 the debt came down to £24,000. A new benefactor now

[1] Now Lady Henley.

came to the rescue. Sir Alfred Yarrow most generously offered to pay half this sum, on condition that the other half should be collected by January 1, 1914.

Never was there a more timely gift, and the condition imposed seems as if framed to meet the unseen catastrophe which was approaching. By the summer of 1913 nearly £5,000 had been subscribed by past students, and with the help of generous gifts from City Companies, the necessary sum was collected just in time. On January 8, 1914, the mortgage was finally paid off, and the College released from debt, with a surplus in hand of about £1,600.

Miss Davies hoped that the Committee would at once begin on fresh building schemes; two hundred students was the number on which she had set her heart and that limit had not yet been reached. She therefore suggested that the surplus should become the starting-point of a new building fund. Other counsels however prevailed; and the money was set aside to form the nucleus of an endowment fund, which was sorely needed. The outbreak of war just seven months later put an end, for the time, to these hopes; but Girton was solvent in the face of the crisis, and was able to weather the lean years which followed.

CHAPTER XIX

Girton and the University. 1880–1897

THE buildings added to Girton in 1902 were the last to be carried through under Miss Davies' direction. The College was now able to hold 180 students; from its modest opening with only six, it had in little more than thirty years multiplied thirty-fold. When the essential framework of a college has already been provided by the benefactors of past ages, thirty years seems a short space in its history; but to those who were bringing the new foundation into existence, these years were a long period of toil and struggle and sacrifice. They were also a period of steady quiet work within the walls of Girton, which soon began to have its effect in the world outside.

The great development of women's education, in which the College was a factor, was in its full tide after 1872, when the Girls' Public Day School Company was founded. During the first fifteen years of Girton's existence, no less than twenty-eight day schools were opened in various parts of the country by that Company alone,[1] and many schools were also started by other agencies. The consequent demand for highly qualified teachers led to the establishment of a close connection between the schools and the women's colleges, by means of which University standards of work were brought to bear on the education of girls. From the schools to the colleges, there was a flow of students, who went back to the schools as teachers, eager in their turn to send pupils to the colleges. In 1875 one of the Girton pioneers, Dame Louisa Lumsden, established a school of another type, resembling the public schools for boys. St. Leonard's School,

[1] *The Jubilee Book of the Girls' Public Day School Trust*, 1873–1923, by Laurie Magnus, M.A., Vice-Chairman of the Council.

St. Andrews, was the forerunner of many others founded after its model and staffed chiefly by former students of the women's colleges. The influence of these students on the schools was quickly felt ; and there were others who carried the collegiate ideal into fresh fields. Miss Rachel Cook, for instance, who in 1874 married Mr. C. P. Scott, of the *Manchester Guardian*, established lectures and advanced classes for women in connection with Owens College, Manchester, which led eventually to the admission of women to the Victoria University. Miss Maynard (another early student of Girton) became in 1882 the first Principal of Westfield College,[1] which was definitely modelled on Girton ; and in the same year, Miss Müller and Miss Kilgour opened a Hall of Residence for Women Students in London. From Cambridge, too, came the Women's University Settlement, Southwark, the first institution of the kind for women, founded in 1887 by former students of Newnham and Girton. The colleges were beginning to exercise an influence hardly perceived by the world at large.

Meanwhile, at Cambridge, the steady and successful work of the women students was producing its impression, and at last a step was taken which gained official recognition for Girton. Provision had been made when the College was incorporated in 1872 for three members representing the University to have a share in its government ; and in 1880 action was at last taken under this clause.

(*Miss Davies to Madame Bodichon.*)

February 1, 1880.

" I went to Girton the week before last for the sake of making enquiry as to the chances of an application from the College to the Cambridge Council to appoint Representative Members. I was agreeably surprised at finding people most friendly, and I feel encouraged as to our prospects altogether. I went to see the Vice-Chancellor (Dr. Perowne), who was supposed to be unfavourable, and found him very gracious. The Master of Trinity [W. H. Thompson], who I had been told was our great enemy, expressed his willingness to make the proposal for us ! He struck out also a good idea, i.e. that the three Representatives should represent the three great branches of study, Language, Mathematics, and Natural Science, and will suggest this to the Council. There are

---

[1] Now a constituent college of London University

seventeen Members of Council, including the Vice-Chancellor, and I saw fourteen. All these seemed ready to support us, except two, who will not, I think, oppose. The remaining three, Mr. Gunson, Mr. Bonney, and Mr. Coutts Trotter, were considered so safe that it was not worth while to go to them."

The Council of the Senate elected Mr. Austen Leigh, Professor Adams, and Professor Liveing as their representatives. Professor Liveing had been a member of the College from the first, but it was of great value to have not only friends but official links to connect Girton with the University.

The position however remained precarious so long as admission to University examinations depended on the goodwill of individual examiners. An attempt to regularize it from outside was made in 1877, when Mr. Leonard Courtney brought in an amendment to the Universities of Oxford and Cambridge Bill, for enabling the University " to examine female students concurrently with male students." Mr. Courtney supported his proposals in the House of Commons with information supplied by Miss Davies as to the success with which such examinations had been carried on during the past seven years ; but public opinion was not ready, and the amendment was lost by 119 votes to 239. " We were beaten by a large majority," Mr. Courtney wrote to Miss Davies, " but I hope the discussion will do the College no harm." At Cambridge it was felt that the longer the examinations were carried on informally the better, since each year would make refusals more difficult. At the same time, occasional refusals did occur, and there was always the risk of a complete breakdown.

Such was the position of affairs when in 1880 the authorities of Girton and Newnham had their hands forced by a movement from outside. In that year a Girton student, Miss C. A. Scott, obtained a high place in the Mathematical Tripos ; the exact places of women candidates were not published, but it was privately known that she was equal to the eighth Wrangler.[1] This

---

[1] When the Mathematical lists were read in the Senate House, loud cheers for " Scott of Girton " made it impossible to hear the name of the eighth Wrangler. See *Hertha Ayrton : A Memoir*, by Evelyn Sharp.

success attracted much attention ; and Mr. and Mrs. W. S. Aldis, of Newcastle, on their own initiative, got up a memorial to the Cambridge Senate asking for the admission of women not only to examinations but to degrees. Their first idea was that the memorial would be a comparatively small affair from their own neighbourhood, but, as Mrs. Aldis wrote to Miss Bernard, " persons of influence at a distance " expressed such hearty approval and offered so much help, that the movement quickly became much larger than had been expected. " There is a good deal of alarm about it," wrote Miss Davies to Madame Bodichon, " and one feels that it ought not to have been set on foot without consulting us, but I am inclined to be hopeful about it." The Newnham authorities also felt some alarm, fearing lest a request for degrees might result in the loss of even the toleration that had so far been accorded. After a time, however, both colleges decided that since the question had been raised, they could not remain passive. The question was, what part ought they to take ?

It was clear that the petition for admission to degrees would not be granted, and Miss Davies was afraid that premature action would lead to a move for Certificates specially intended for women. She asked if the memorial could be postponed for a time, but Mrs. Aldis wrote on April 15 that it had already received more than 8000 signatures, and would be presented as soon as possible. Miss Davies explained to Mrs. Aldis that the Girton Committee felt a difficulty as to taking part in the memorial, owing to the fact of its following so immediately on the granting of their application to the Council of the Senate for the appointment of representative members. It was not a fortnight (as she told her) since these members had been summoned for the first time to a Girton meeting, and it would give the impression of excessive haste and urgency if the College were at once to come forward with a very serious and disturbing fresh proposal. As however the movement was to go forward, a statement, prepared by Miss Davies, was adopted by the Girton Committee, in which, while disclaiming all part in the memorial, the view was expressed that the experiment of University examinations for women had been sufficiently tested to justify their admission to the B.A. degree. This statement was forwarded to the Council of the Senate.

Mr. Sidgwick was convinced that it would be " harmful, and merely harmful," as he wrote to Miss Davies, to ask for degrees at this juncture. The utmost that could prudently be asked for was some measure which should give formal sanction to the examinations hitherto carried on informally. He was anxious that the two colleges should act in harmony with each other, and he urged his view upon Miss Davies, that the regularization of the existing arrangements would be a step and not a bar to the degree, and therefore a gain upon the whole. To this however she could not agree. She regarded as purely mischievous the Newnham practice of presenting candidates for Triposes who had not precisely fulfilled the University conditions, and she was determined to avoid the slightest appearance of supporting a plan which she felt was likely to lead to the establishment of a separate system for women. Formal co-operation was therefore impossible, and the Association for Promoting the Higher Education of Women in Cambridge (guided by Mr. Sidgwick) accordingly sent a statement to the Senate, to the effect that they would welcome any arrangements by which the present informal examination of women could be put on a more stable footing. The statements sent in by the two colleges did not conflict, they merely ignored each other's point of view ; this much had been agreed upon between Miss Davies and Mr. Sidgwick. " I am afraid it seems very ungracious to repudiate a common cause," she wrote to him. " One feels a want of reciprocity in our not being ready to work with you, in return for your friendly help to us, but I do not see how we can help it."

A Syndicate was appointed by the Senate early in June, 1880, to consider the question raised by the memorial, and in December it reported in favour of regularizing the admission of women to the Previous and Tripos Examinations on the same conditions as those required from members of the University, except in one respect, that the women students might, if they wished, substitute certain parts of the Higher Local for the Previous Examination, and thus escape the necessity for learning Latin and Greek. The Poll Degree examinations were to be definitely closed to women.

Though this was not what she had hoped for, Miss Davies accepted the situation and threw herself into the work of collecting support for the proposed measure. A memorial came in from 123 resident members of the Senate, asking for the formal admission of women to examinations ; and another from 560 non-resident members, promoted by Mr. Llewelyn Davies and others, asked for admission to the B.A. degree. Ten memorials were also sent in from outside bodies, including one from the London Association of Schoolmistresses, of which Miss Davies was Secretary.

(Miss Davies to Madame Bodichon.)

November 2 [1880].

" We want the Memorial [from non-resident members of the Senate] to be as largely signed as possible. Will you ask Norman Moore ? . . . There are nearly 6000 non-resident members. We are going to send applications from the Hon. Sec. to all whose addresses we can find, i.e. about 3000 clergy and 1000 lawyers and 80 doctors, but we want private help besides, as people are more likely to respond to a personal appeal from a friend. Lady Goldsmid is helping zealously. Mr. F. Galton came to a Committee meeting and was helpful and hopeful, but I am afraid the feeling at Cambridge is not at all favourable . . . I am *very* busy with this and other Memorial work."

[*February*, 1881.]

" There is to be opposition at Cambridge on the 24th. I have had a very strong letter from Professor Stuart, urging us to do all we can to send up voters. The Vice-Chancellor has declared war against us, and our friends are greatly alarmed. I am hopeful, as we have many friends at work. If we can send up 200 voters we shall be safe. I shall rely upon you for Dr. [Reginald] Thompson, and Dr. Moore."

The Vice-Chancellor, Dr. Perowne, was (as Mr. Stuart told Miss Davies) the leader of the Conservative party in Cambridge, and fundamentally opposed to the admission of women in any form. He had been very gracious the year before, when she approached him in regard to the appointment of members of the Senate on the Girton Committee. There was no objection to the appointment of representatives who would exercise a friendly influence over Girton ; but to admit Girton students to a regular footing in the University was a very different thing.

Nevertheless, through vigorous exertions on the part of friends of Girton and Newnham, when the Graces embodying the recommendations of the Syndicate came before the Senate on

February 24, they were passed by 398 votes to 32. The announcement of the numbers was followed, as a friend wrote to Miss Davies, by " loud cheers and much laughter." The Master of Emmanuel, Dr. Phear, wrote of the " remarkable demonstration in the Senate House." He was " simply amazed at the gathering, which proved how effective the appeals for support have been." " The victory just won," wrote Mr. Stuart to Miss Davies, " is indeed a magnificent one ; and I think it would be difficult to over-estimate the value it will have for women's education generally, as showing that the Senate of the University is so really in earnest about the carrying on the work it has begun. It is to my mind now a mere question of policy as to when we should take the next step." From Mrs. Garrett Anderson came a postcard : " Heartiest congratulations ! even in spite of its limitations, which probably won't live long." " I find it quite difficult to subside from my pleasure," wrote Miss Bernard, " but as you say, the thing now is to make a good use of it, of the good you and the other workers have gained."

The thing gained was not exactly what Miss Davies wanted ; but the point she most disliked—the special alternative for women in regard to the Previous Examination—was not compulsory, and she repudiated it on behalf of the Girton students, who were never allowed to avail themselves of it. This was a small matter in comparison with the step that had been gained by acquiring a definite position in relation to the University. The long series of letters which Miss Davies had had to write to each examiner, before every examination, came to an end ; there was no more anxiety as to whether the examiners would consent to act ; the successful candidates' names were at last to be published in class lists and in the University Calendar, and the University was to grant a Certificate to each woman candidate who succeeded in passing an examination in Honours. " What we gain," wrote Miss Davies to Madame Bodichon, " is that what we have been doing all along by favour, will now be secured as a right."

The existence of the College had been made secure, and the enthusiasm of victory gave rise to high hopes for the future. Admission to the University seemed likely to be carried without serious opposition, before the lapse of many years. Henceforward Miss Davies was constantly on the watch for a suitable opportunity to take the next step. At last, in 1887, a combination of causes led her to make a move. The immediate occasion was the success won in the class lists that summer by Miss A. F. Ramsay (now Mrs. Montagu Butler), then a student at Girton. Miss Ramsay was placed in the first division of the first class of the Classical Tripos, while of the men who took the same examination, none was placed higher than the second division ; an event which attracted so much public attention as to inspire a drawing by Du Maurier in *Punch*.[1] Miss Davies had already set to work in May, in anticipation of this success, to form a Committee for promoting the admission of duly qualified women to degrees. This Committee consisted largely of people living in London—Miss Davies herself, Lady Stanley of Alderley, Lady Goldsmid, Mrs. Garrett Anderson, Mr. Llewelyn Davies, and others ; with some Cambridge residents, notably Professor Liveing and Dr. Henry Jackson. Their intention was to ask the Senate for the admission of women to degrees (including the Poll Degree) on the same terms as those prescribed for men.

Dr. Sidgwick declined to join the Committee. Though he himself was, as he wrote to Miss Davies, " not opposed on principle to identity of conditions for the two sexes," he was " determined if possible to prevent the University from applying to the education of girls the pressure in the direction of classics that would inevitably be given if the present Previous Examination were made compulsory for female students preparing for Triposes." The opening of the Poll Degree to women would be " very strongly resisted " by himself and others. Moreover, he thought it too soon to reopen the question, and careful enquiry at Cambridge had convinced him that proposals of any kind for admission to degrees would be defeated. The substance of this letter was incorporated by Dr. Sidgwick in a letter published in the *Times* on July 10, in which he declared that the memorial was being promoted " against the wish of the majority of those resident members of the Senate who have hitherto supported the extension of the educational advantages of the University to women."

[1] *Honour to Agnata Frances Ramsay, Punch*, July 2, 1887—Mr. Punch politely showing Miss Ramsay into a first-class compartment " for ladies only."

This was a serious blow ; but the Committee, fortified by the support of Dr. Jackson, Professor Liveing, Mr. Archer-Hind, and other resident members of the University, resolved to proceed nevertheless. Dr. Jackson, though himself in favour of the admission of women on identical terms with men, suggested that some compromise might be effected in order to meet Dr. Sidgwick's views. " I hope you will not be shocked," he wrote to Miss Davies, " if I propose that we should treat with the malcontents on these terms—that *they* should include Poll Examinations among the examinations which entitle to degrees, and that *we* should allow their stipulation for an alternative to the Little-go. . . . If this can be arranged, I shall be very hopeful of the result."

(Miss Davies to Dr. Henry Jackson.)

July 27, 1887.

" We are I think drawing to the conclusion that it may be expedient to attempt something in the way of compromise. Before going into the matter, however, I should like to tell you, as shortly as I can, of the steps by which we have arrived at the present position. The Girton students had from time to time been asking whether something could not be done, but there seemed to be no special occasion for moving, and our idea was to wait for some striking success, such as would rouse public sympathy, and then to act. The moving cause came however in a different way. Last autumn Mrs. Fawcett gave an address in which she brought up the withholding of Cambridge degrees as a grievance. I was agreeably surprised to find anyone so closely connected with Newnham taking this line, and afterwards had a talk with Mrs. Fawcett on the subject. She said that Dr. Sidgwick would be ready to work with us for degrees if in his judgment the time was fitting, and that his policy was the same as ours, i.e. to wait for some remarkable achievement by a Girton or Newnham student, and then to turn to account the sympathy thus called forth. She said his aim from the beginning had been to get degrees and everything else for women, but added the disclosure, that it was to be on his own terms, i.e. with dissimilar conditions. This startling revelation was what set us to work. We were hoping that Miss Ramsay would gain distinction, but without counting on help of that kind, it seemed to me that the time had come for us to move. We felt that we should be in an awkward position if, a success having been won by a Newnham student, we were, while so to speak trading upon it, to be strongly opposing Dr. Sidgwick's views, and that we had better move at a time when we could take the initiative and the lead. Before any step was taken, however, we consulted Professor Liveing, and it was on his opinion that we decided at once to take action. We knew of course that it was most important to get the alliance, if possible, of both Dr. Sidgwick and Mr. G. F. Browne,[1] and we invited them to join us, first however, as you know, laying down our policy in the Resolution which was sent to you.[2] I have greatly feared a repetition this time of the former experience [of 1881], i.e. that . . . we should again be in the position of having to support his [Dr. Sidgwick's] scheme or none. Some of us cared much less for the Poll than for the identity of conditions, and were on the point of giving it up as a propitiatory offering to Dr. Sidgwick, but on the whole it was thought best to stand out for both. . . .

" You will see from what I have said, what a prominent place the principle of the ' common standard,' as we have hitherto called it, has occupied in our minds . . . Our fanaticism on this point arises perhaps chiefly from looking at it with reference to women's questions generally, as to which it has been felt to be of extreme importance to maintain the principle."

Meanwhile, news came from Mr. Archer-Hind that Dr. Sidgwick, seeing that the question would inevitably be raised, had decided to withdraw from opposition. " If," wrote Mr. Archer-Hind, " we can agree to sink the question of preliminary conditions, so far as to accept the higher local as an alternative temporarily, and pending the removal of compulsory Greek from the Little-go, I think we shall have no further opposition on his part." [3] " I am very glad," wrote Dr. Jackson, " that Dr. Sidgwick is inclined to make concessions ; for if he had stood out, our voting power would have been seriously diminished, whilst, as it is, we may hope to carry the principle, even if some details are not finally settled." In accordance, therefore, with suggestions

[1] Afterwards Bishop of Bristol.

[2] A resolution to the effect that the Committee would not support any measure admitting women to degrees on other conditions than those laid down for undergraduates generally.

[3] It must be remembered that Dr. Sidgwick took a leading part in the movement for the abolition of Compulsory Greek, which had been set on foot about seventeen years before this date and was not carried to a successful issue till 1919. Those who hoped for and expected its speedy success thought that the special treatment of women as regards Greek was a point of slight importance.

made by Dr. Jackson, the Committee for promoting the admission of women to Cambridge degrees circulated a covering letter with their memorial, stating their willingness to accept an alternative to the Little-go allowing a modern language to be substituted for Greek by women candidates. Dr. Sidgwick, on his part, was willing that the question of the admission of women to the Ordinary Degree should be raised separately, when he would be free to vote against it.

The Memorial itself asked that degrees should be granted " to all, without distinction of sex, who fulfil the prescribed conditions." Over seven hundred signatures were obtained, and other memorials were sent in ; five were in support of the admission of women, but two were against it, and it became clear that there was, as Dr. Sidgwick had foretold, an adverse majority of resident members of the Senate. In February, 1888, the Council of the Senate, by a majority of eight to seven, decided against the appointment of a Syndicate to consider the question, and there was an end of it.

The reverse was a great disappointment, and seems at first sight surprising, after the prosperous beginning of 1881. But in 1881 the women's colleges were still in the experimental stage ; they seemed to be in the nature of a provision for a few exceptional women, and it was hardly expected by the world at large that they would grow to any size or importance. By 1888 it had become clear that they were on the upward grade ; only the year before, Girton had been enlarged (by means of Miss Gamble's legacy) sufficiently to hold over a hundred students, while Newnham provided for about the same number. The admission of women to a share in the benefits of the University had become a serious question, and many who were friendly to the women's colleges thought that the system established six years previously had not yet been sufficiently proved. A suggestion was made that a separate University should be created for women, with power to grant degrees to women who passed the examinations of any University.[1] With one voice the supporters of Girton and Newnham rejected this proposal ; no one, of any party, cared to take steps to promote it ; and nothing more was heard of it for

---

[1] See *The Recollections of a Bishop* (pp. 309–11), by the Right Rev. G. Forrest Browne, lately Bishop of Bristol.

another ten years, till the question of degrees for women was again raised at Cambridge in 1897.

The movement of 1897 arose in the first instance from Newnham, in consequence of a widespread and growing opinion that women who had passed the Cambridge examinations were handicapped in their subsequent careers by the want of degrees. During the winter of 1895, two Committees were formed, one of resident members of the Senate, the other of representatives of the two women's colleges. This joint Committee included the Mistress of Girton and the Principal of Newnham, as well as Dr. Sidgwick, Dr. Jackson, and other members of the University ; its secretaries were Miss Davies and Miss Marion Kennedy, Honorary Secretary of Newnham College. Miss Davies threw herself heartily into co-operation with the representatives of Newnham, and her heart was softened towards Dr. Sidgwick when she found herself fighting beside him. Early in the proceedings, he was invited to meet her at Miss Kennedy's house, to discuss the situation. After the interview was over, she summed up her impressions to Miss Kennedy : " He certainly is a very engaging man "—an expression of real feeling on her part.

In February, 1896, a memorial was presented by 2088 members of the Senate to the Council of that body asking for the nomination of a Syndicate " to consider on what conditions and with what restrictions, if any, women should be admitted to degrees in the University." This was supported by three other memorials— one from Head Mistresses of girls' schools, one from past students of Girton and Newnham, and one forwarded by Miss Davies and Miss Kennedy. The Senate agreed to the request, but threw out the first Syndicate proposed, which included Dr. Sidgwick, Dr. Peile, Dr. Henry Jackson, and other well-known friends to the admission of women ; and a fresh Syndicate was appointed, in which opinions were more evenly divided. It was clear that a proposal for granting degrees was not likely to be carried ; and the opposition was greatly encouraged.

The Syndicate began their work by asking those who had presented memorials to produce evidence in support of their representations. Evidence was submitted by a joint Committee of past students of Girton and Newnham, showing that the lack of degrees placed women educated at Cambridge at a disadvantage,

331

since degrees were now given to women members of London University, and of all the provincial Universities. A pamphlet [1] which Miss Davies had already prepared was also sent to the Syndicate. In this pamphlet she reviews the history of the movement for the higher education of women, showing that the proposals now made, far from being hasty, sudden, and revolutionary, were based on many years of work and experience, and were by no means in advance of prevailing conditions. The request for degrees came from recognized authorities on the education of girls, who would be hardly likely to ask for anything injurious to their own cause. As to the dreaded assimilation of women's education to that of men, Miss Davies points out that, while women have been successfully pursuing courses of study originally devised for men, on the other hand, men have been encouraged to take up many studies usually considered especially feminine, such as History, Botany, Music, and Modern Languages. [2]

The women's colleges had now been in existence nearly thirty years, and during that period the range of studies at Cambridge had been greatly extended in the interests of men, entirely without reference to the interests or desires of women. It is enough here to note that Triposes had been instituted in History, Law and Modern Languages ; encouragement had been given to the studies of Economics and Philosophy ; and in the department of natural sciences, the expansion had been enormous. There was now no force in the argument that women's education would be cramped and fettered if it were assimilated to that of men. On the contrary, women had shared in the expansion which had taken place in the education of men. As Miss Davies points out in her pamphlet, the whole character of the studies in girls' schools " has been raised and strengthened by the influence of University standards," and those who cared for the education of girls were anxious for this influence to be increased and confirmed.

Before publishing her pamphlet, Miss Davies had sent it to Dr. Sidgwick, asking him to express his views on it.

[1] *Women in the Universities of England and Scotland.* Cambridge : Macmillan & Bowes, 1896.
[2] Cf. Report of the Consultative Committee of the Board of Education on *Differentiation of Curricula between the Sexes in Secondary Schools*, 1923.

GIRTON AND THE UNIVERSITY

(*Dr. Sidgwick to Miss Davies.*)

May 14 [1896].

" My wife and I have read and considered your pamphlet and I
will give you our ideas. I think the historical sketch gives very clearly
the instruction which you wish to give, and which is certainly oppor-
tune. I should of course describe somewhat differently the events
narrated on pp.17, 18, but I have no objection to make to your statement
[as to the early history of Newnham]. . . .

" The part of the pamphlet which we are disposed to criticize on the
ground of policy is pp. 26, 27 [as to the movement for degrees in 1887].
Your tone seems to me dangerously aggressive and challenging. . . .
This is what I have to say as to the substance : I add one or two minor
criticisms on the form. . . .

" You will understand that I have criticized quite frankly, thinking
you would prefer this."

Miss Davies accepted the criticisms in the spirit in which
they were offered, and altered the wording of her pamphlet in
deference to them. The agitation proceeded ; early in 1897 the
Syndicate produced a report recommending the admission of
women to titular degrees, a measure which would add to their
credit with the outside world, while in no way altering their relation to the University. The report was discussed at great length
in March. Among the speakers in its support were Dr. Sidgwick,
Dr. Jackson, Professor Maitland, the Master of Trinity (Dr.
Butler), Dr. Clark, and Mr. Berry—to mention only a few among
the friends to whom the women's colleges have reason to be
grateful. But the day was carried by the fears of those who, as
Dr. MacAlister said, felt that they were being asked to adopt a
tiger cub, on the grounds " that it is such a little one, and can't
do any harm, and won't be in the way, and will please the children
very much." On May 21 the report was rejected by 1707 votes
to 661.

In the course of the discussion, the suggestion of founding a
separate women's University was revived, and reference was made
to proposals brought forward by an Oxford Committee of which
Sir William Anson (Warden of All Souls) was Chairman, for the
co-operation of Oxford and Cambridge in promoting such a
scheme. As before, the idea was rejected by all who were actively
concerned in the education of women. Professor Maitland, in

a brilliant speech, showed that the " Bletchley Junction Academy " was a practical impossibility. Who would care to pay the expenses of getting a Royal Charter for the Women's University, and of providing an endowment for it ? Before long an opportunity arose for a full discussion of the merits of the scheme. In the Deed of Foundation of the Royal Holloway College, there was a clause expressing the founder's desire that the College should eventually seek power to confer degrees on its students. The Governors of the College arranged to hold a conference in London, with a view to eliciting the opinions of those interested in the education of women. The conference, which was presided over by Mr. James Bryce, was attended by the Governors and members of the teaching staff of Holloway College, and by representatives of the Universities of Oxford and Cambridge, of the women's colleges and girls' schools, and many others. Miss Davies, who, with Miss Welsh, attended as representing Girton, made a practical little speech, drawing attention to the lessons of experience. Queen's College, Harley Street, she said, had since 1855 granted certificates to its students, and had made little progress in comparison with Bedford College, which had sent its students in for London degree examinations. As to granting special degrees for women, " In America," she said, " this power is conferred on a great number of colleges, with the result that degrees have fallen into disrepute, and have practically no value at all." No formal vote was taken on the questions discussed ; but the sense of the conference was perfectly clear. " No one," said Mr. Bryce, in summing up the discussion, " who is concerned with the education of women as a teacher, whether a man or a woman, is in favour of having a separate University for Women." [1]

[1] *University Degrees for Women : Report of a Conference convened by the Governors of the Royal Holloway College, and held at the house of the Society of Arts, on Saturday, December* 4, 1897. (Printed for the College by Spottiswoode & Co., 1898.)

From a photograph by J. Russell & Sons

EMILY DAVIES
1906.

CHAPTER XX

Girton and Miss Davies. 1883–1904

THE defeat of the proposals for granting degrees to women in 1897 was followed by a period of material growth at Girton, accompanied by a growing divergence of opinion on the Committee. There were two main points in Miss Davies' policy which were contrary to the views held by some members of the Committee, and by an increasing number of old students. One was her disapproval of expenditure on the encouragement of post-graduate work and research ; the other was her opposition to the inclusion of the Mistress, or any member of the staff, in the governing body. Some explanation is necessary to show how both these questions became more acute as time went by.

During the last thirty years of the nineteenth century, the years in which Girton was growing up, profound changes were taking place at Cambridge. The legislation of the Statutory Commission of 1877–82 made it possible for the University to develop new ideals and methods of education. The results are described in the Report of the Royal Commission of 1919, where it is stated that " Oxford and Cambridge are totally different places from the establishments reported on in 1850–2. . . . They have advanced and are daily advancing . . . to make the whole range of modern learning and science their province." There is no need to enter here into the particulars of reorganization ; the important point is that a new spirit had entered into the University. To quote the Report of the Royal Commission again : in the present day " educational problems are considered from the point of view of the subject as well as from that of the College, and the growth and furtherance of the subject itself is

335

constantly in the minds of teachers and taught." The growth of scientific studies, which was especially remarkable at Cambridge, was one of the chief causes of this change of view. In natural sciences there was opened a new and almost unbroken field for work ; and the application of scientific methods stimulated investigation on new lines in old fields, such as Classics, Philosophy, and History. Research gradually became an essential and most important part of University life.

The staff at Girton, and many of the past students, felt the influence of the new spirit. Its reaction upon Girton was imperfect, owing to the relations, or rather want of relations, between the College and the University. Nevertheless, women students were taught by members of the University who were willing to lecture at Girton, and to admit Girton students to their lectures in Cambridge ; and the spirit which animated the teachers naturally had its effect upon the students. The standard of achievement gradually rose higher ; the earliest students had been thought absurdly ambitious when they aspired to success in a Tripos, but this success had been won, and repeated by successive generations, until from being a wonder it had become a commonplace. We have seen how quickly the colleges reacted on the schools ; before long, the schools began to react no less powerfully on the colleges, sending them pupils who had been prepared for a University course by teachers who were the equivalent of graduates. Both lecturers and students began to look beyond the Tripos as the goal of their ambitions ; post-graduate work and research became objects of desire ; the staff, and many of the past students, came to feel that the want of provision for work of this sort was keeping Girton back, and preventing it from becoming a place of real higher education, worthy of that admission to the University which (like Miss Davies) they earnestly desired.

Passages in the *Girton Review* [1] show that the need was felt so long ago as 1883. In 1885 the hope was expressed that Miss Gamble's legacy would make it possible to found Studentships.[2] Nothing, however, was done till the past students at last made

[1] *Resident Graduates, Girton Review*, December, 1883 ; letter from *L.M.*, December, 1884.
[2] *Girton Review*, December, 1885, p. 16.

a move. After a subscription dinner of old students held in 1892, a surplus of £5 remained in hand, and Miss Gertrude Jackson (then Junior Bursar at Girton) proposed that this small sum should be set aside as the nucleus of a fund for the endowment of a Studentship. This continued to be done on subsequent occasions, but the process was discouragingly slow. Four years later a petition was presented from past students to the Executive Committee of the College, asking them " to consider the possibility of establishing a Studentship for the encouragement of post-graduate work." This resulted in the offer of a Studentship of £40 per annum—the first ever offered at Girton—the money for which came from the Pfeiffer fund.[1] A great effort was now made to raise money to provide an adequate fund for a second Studentship. Past students were very generous to their College, but few among them could afford to give largely, and the fund for extending the College buildings was at this very time asking for their support, and receiving it in large measure. By July, 1897, the total sum invested for the Studentship fund amounted to only £418. Fifteen more years were to pass before the fund became substantial enough to support a student on its own account. Such slow progress was unsatisfactory, and in 1899 another fund was raised by Miss Florence Durham,[2] who collected about £200, which was spent immediately on the stipend of a research studentship held for three years only.

It was clear that past students felt increasingly that research should be encouraged at Girton, but they had neither the means nor the power to do much for this object, the majority of them having to earn their own living. The case for research was well stated by Miss Ethel Sargant,[3] in an article entitled *The Inheritance of a University*, in the *Girton Review* for the Lent term, 1901. Miss Sargant showed how the development of scientific research in the University had led to a new revival of learning. Women

---

[1] The first Pfeiffer student was an astronomer, Mrs. Walter Maunder, to whom the studentship was awarded in 1897. Since 1910 the income of the Pfeiffer fund has been applied entirely to the encouragement of post-graduate work.

[2] Now a member of the Research Staff of the Medical Research Council.

[3] See Biographical Index.

students, in their first anxiety to satisfy University tests, had neglected the pursuit of learning for its own sake, but now that the experimental stage was passed, this ought not to continue.

" The great inheritance of the Universities is the tradition of learning for learning's sake. . . . It is not enough that our graduates can point with pride to their achievements in the Finals. These may satisfy their college, but the University asks how many women trained in her schools are adding to the sum of knowledge ? "

In the following passage, Miss Sargant described what had so far been achieved by the Women's Colleges.

" Those of us who left college more than ten years ago may look round and see our fellows playing many parts in the world. We need hardly be surprised to find that in teaching, in medicine, on committees and councils, those who were leaders in the social and intellectual life of a college are still distinguished among their colleagues. . . . But we have seen more. We have seen the habit of thoroughness carried into domestic life ; homes wisely ruled, children brought up healthy in mind and body, wives their husbands' comrades, single women enjoying a happy middle age neither narrow nor dissipated on trifles. We have reason to hope that one end of University education has been attained—that the Women's Colleges train good women to become good citizens."

This much was entirely in harmony with Miss Davies' views. But Miss Sargant goes on to observe that, if this were all, the same end might have been attained by other means than University education. "Any place in which men of much the same standing mix freely with each other becomes a school of character. Universities are more than this. They bear witness to the existence of an intellectual life. . . . The standard of the whole University is raised by the presence within it of true scholars, and without them the training given to the mass of residents would not deserve the name of a liberal education."

If women were really to be admitted to the University, they too must be capable of contributing to its intellectual life. There were special difficulties in their way, but some of these could be met. Women, as Miss Sargant points out, are generally handicapped in the pursuit of learning by want of means and the claims of home ties. Most women graduates are obliged to earn their living, and the lecturers in Women's Colleges are almost the only ones who would have opportunities for research, if the way were smoothed for them by the authorities. An endowment fund might in the future be provided to enable the College to increase the numbers of its staff, so that each member of it might have leisure for research.

" For the present it would be a great step if post-graduate student-ships were attached to each Woman's College, and if the governing body cordially recognized the importance of research to its internal life. . . . It is hardly too much to say that University education for women is still on its trial. . . . When women distinguish themselves in research as they have already distinguished themselves in the class lists, the foresight of our founders will be fully justified. . . .

" The support on which I lean with confidence is the collective opinion of many women who are *de facto* or *de jure* graduates of a British University. This opinion has been repeatedly expressed, and its supporters increase in number every year. Who, indeed, should take a more vital interest in the fortunes of a Woman's College than its students past and present ? "

It was perhaps hardly surprising that Miss Davies did not feel it essential to provide for advanced work and research at Girton. Her conceptions of the University had been formed long ago ; her brother had taken the Mathematical and Classical Triposes, both in one year (as the custom was) in 1848. To her, the University education of that day remained the accepted type. Naturally she was delighted by any success or distinction achieved by past students ; but she wished to see the benefits that women were gaining through their colleges extended as widely as possible. These benefits were great ; by means of the colleges, women were enabled to work for University examinations, and to produce teachers of recognized value. Moreover, in the early days, the colleges really were the only places where women could mix freely with each other as equals, and thus gain the discipline and development of what Miss Sargant called a " school of char-acter." As was well said by Dr. Verrall, through the colleges was gained " the joy and pleasure and energy of self-development which come to women from being put in a position to be them-selves for a short time, to choose their associates and mutually to educate one another." These benefits were more essential, as he perceived, to women than to men, " because society presses upon women more hardly than it does upon men, and leaves them in ordinary circumstances less leisure and liberty to be themselves." [1]

All this was an immense advance, and the women's Colleges did much to raise the standard of women's education and life generally. For such results, no effort or sacrifice seemed too great, and in comparison with them, advanced learning and research appeared to Miss Davies of little importance. With every effort, as she held, Girton could never grow large enough for the work it had to do. But meanwhile, the provision for the higher education of women was gradually much increased by their admission to London and to the newer provincial Universities, and by the foundation of women's Colleges at Oxford and elsewhere ; yet Miss Davies still felt the overmastering need of earlier days, and her sympathies remained with " the multitude outside " for whom there was no room at Girton. Those who wanted to remain at College for more than three years seemed to her to be asking too much for themselves. Fellows and research students, even fourth-year students, would fill places which might be occupied by new-comers ; and she set her face against any expenditure on such luxuries.

By the end of the century, the past students of Girton had become a body of over five hundred women, with a corporate spirit and an interest in the College of sufficient strength to make them wish to share in directing its policy. Many of them felt that the Committee was out of touch with new developments in the University, and this feeling strengthened the wish. In 1901, a memorial from old students was presented to the governing body, asking them " to consider the advisability of adding to the number of Past Students now serving as members of the College." A reply was received to the effect that the memorial would be considered before any new member was proposed, and Miss J. F. Dove was co-opted in the following year. Nothing was done towards changing the constitution of the College with a view to admitting past students to a larger share in its government ; this remained as established in 1873, in the hands of

[1] Speech on the question of the admission of women to degrees. *Cambridge University Reporter*, March 26, 1897, pp. 786-7.

a Committee which consisted largely of members resident in London, and included a very small proportion of past students and only three members of the staff—two of whom had been sent there by the action of the certificated students, who elected them as their representatives. The electors were naturally inclined to be in sympathy with the staff, who were generally, like themselves, certificated students.

In 1870 Miss Davies had remarked that as the College grew, it would " tend more and more to be governed by the resident body, when there *is* a body, over which the Mistress will preside. But this cannot be till there *is* a body grown up in College traditions and qualified by previous training to direct the studies as well as the other departments." Thirty-one years had passed since these words were written, but Miss Davies' views had not moved in the direction indicated. On the contrary, she had always consistently opposed the admission of members of the resident staff to the governing body. Miss Welsh had been elected a member of the College and of the Executive Committee, in 1885, on her appointment as Mistress, but it was against Miss Davies' wish, and she intended to take the first opportunity that presented itself for reversing this step.

The opportunity came on Miss Welsh's resignation of the post in 1903. Miss Davies drew up a memorandum on the position, which was signed by herself and by fifteen members of the governing body, and circulated among the certificated students of the College. The memorandum states " some of the grounds on which we hold that the participation of paid officers of the College in its government . . . is inexpedient." At Girton, the Executive Committee directs the policy of the College as regards finance and buildings, appoints the staff, regulates the admission of students and the awards of Scholarships, and other matters in regard to which " practical experience and general knowledge of affairs seem to be needed." For the internal administration, it is pointed out that large powers are devolved on resident officers, who are " responsible for the disbursement of about three-fourths of the annual income of the College. Under these circumstances, the need of unbiassed criticism and investigation on occasion, seems to be obvious, and it is equally obvious that such criticism and investigation can hardly be

carried on in the presence of those whose work is under review."
Joint government by paid officers and other persons is not likely
to work well, and is generally specially guarded against, under
restrictions imposed since 1896 on corporations by the Board of
Trade. To place the government entirely in the hands of the
resident staff would not, as often supposed, be putting Girton
in a similar position to that of the colleges of the University.
These colleges are not independent of external control ; they
are corporations bound by Statutes, by which they are " safe-
guarded in all directions." Such was the substance of her
argument.

A special meeting of the Association of Certificated Students
was held in April, 1903, to consider the questions raised by the
Memorandum, and it was resolved to send a reply. This reply
made it clear that the bulk of the certificated students supported
the policy of giving the staff a larger share in the government
of the College. While not desiring that government to be placed
entirely in their hands, the view was expressed that the residents
were more intimately acquainted with the needs and interests of
the College than non-residents could be, and that it was of vital
importance to establish an intimate connection between the
governing body and the internal administration.

The question came to a practical issue soon after the appointment, in 1903, of Miss Constance Jones as Mistress. A proposal " that it is desirable that the Mistress should be a member of
the College and of the Executive Committee " was carried at a
meeting of the College by a substantial majority, and this was
followed by the election of Miss Jones as a member of both these
bodies. After much consideration, Miss Davies decided, as she
wrote to Miss Manning, that it was not " worth while to carry
on the struggle. . . . The immediate question is only one
among others. . . . It will be a relief to give up contention,
often useless and always painful." In May, 1904, she resigned
her office of Honorary Secretary and her membership of the
Executive Committee, a decision to which she adhered in spite
of a request from the Committee that she would reconsider it.
Her connection with Girton was, however, still maintained, as
she continued to be a member of the " College "—the governing
body, from which the Executive Committee was appointed.

(*Miss Davies to Miss Manning.*)

May 11 [1904].

" Except among Members of the College, there will, I imagine, be no talk about my resignation, until some such thing happens as the issue of an appeal without my name. When, or if, this arrives, I should like my friends to say somewhat vaguely that of late years the College business has been very much transferred to Cambridge (we have lost many London members, etc.), and that as it is being carried on at Cambridge it was thought suitable that Cambridge names should appear. It could be thrown in, if necessary, that I have not withdrawn from membership of the College, and my name will appear in the Report, as heretofore."

A question of principle was at issue ; but Miss Davies no longer felt " the fierceness of fear " which had animated her thirty years before.[1] She was not now fighting, as in 1873, for the life of the College. Success and experience had softened her. In spite of differences of opinion, she had confidence in the future of Girton ; she foresaw difficulties which might arise, and she made provision for meeting them in such a way as to create no unfavourable impression with regard to the College. Her interest in Girton remained as keen as ever, and she continued her annual visits during the Long Vacation term, when her relations with every one there remained perfectly friendly, as they had always been, while coloured by the deference which all at Girton felt was due to her unique position. She entered into whatever was going on, as if differences of opinion had never arisen. The defeat of her policy and her withdrawal from active work at Girton were accompanied by no loss of dignity ; on the contrary, it was shown that her devotion to the College rose above personal considerations.

The process begun in 1903, when the Committee adopted it as a principle that the Mistress should be one of its members, has since been carried much further. After an interval of suspended development, caused by the War, the College was in 1924 incorporated under a Charter, the terms of which placed its government in the hands of a body composed of the Mistress and Fellows, with a certain number of members elected from outside this body, including representatives of the University of Cambridge, and of

[1] See *ante*, Chap. XVI, p. 278.

past students of the College. The original constitution of the College had, as the years went on, become increasingly difficult to work. The first Committee was a band of pioneers establishing an entirely new institution. As the institution grew, and ceased to be a novelty, its very success made it less interesting to the world at large, and increased the difficulty of filling vacancies on the Committee. At the same time, a new class of supporters was brought into existence, in the steadily growing number of old students.

These were facts to which Miss Davies refused to yield. She was accustomed to uphold the original constitution as analogous to the system under which a public school is commonly governed by a Council of which neither the head master nor any of his assistants are members. Not seeing the necessity of provision for post-graduate work and research, she did not realize this essential difference between a college and a school ; she regarded the College chiefly as an organization for teaching. She did not see that so long as it was governed like a school, its staff would lack the kind of experience that they would need if admission were ever to be gained to membership of the University. She could not admit any force in the arguments for placing the main direction of the College in the hands of its own officers, who, while carrying on the work of teaching and administration, should aim at keeping as far as possible in touch with new developments in the University. Those who, like her, initiate a revolution and live to see its success, must often see their work turning in directions which they had neither foreseen nor desired. In defeat as in battle she showed herself, as Miss Bernard had said long ago, " a stout-hearted general "—adapting herself to the new position, and making the best of it. Her energies and affections, in all their intensity, had for more than thirty years been centred on the College ; yet after defeat and loss of power, she accepted the situation in such a way as to deprive it of bitterness, and even to make the time that followed not only endurable but pleasant.

In estimating the wisdom of Miss Davies' policy, it must be borne in mind that in order to attain efficiency, a College must attain to a reasonable size. It was found by the Royal Commission of 1919 on the Universities of Oxford and Cambridge that " large numbers of students . . . form the only security for the supply of first-rate science teachers and researchers. Only by casting the net wide can the haul be satisfactory." [1] What is here said of science is also true of other subjects. The wearisome task of collecting funds and raising buildings is a necessary preliminary to the far more attractive work of developing facilities for research. It is true that Miss Davies undervalued the importance of such facilities ; but it has needed all her determination and perseverance to bring the College up even to its present size, which is none too large for the work to be done. A smaller body would not have been strong enough to undertake the encouragement of research which is now part of its policy ; and even now, such encouragement must necessarily be kept within narrow limits so long as the College remains dependent on students' fees for the bulk of its income.

[1] *Report*, p. 34.

CHAPTER XXI

Miss Davies and Women's Suffrage
1904–1919

WHEN Miss Davies resigned her place on the Girton Committee she was by no means ready to retire from active work, although she had attained the age of seventy-four. It was a wrench to part from what had been the chief centre of her thoughts and cares for nearly forty years ; but she could still fight for the cause which was the passion of her life. She had never ceased to follow the course of the suffrage agitation with interest, though she had resolved in 1867 to abstain from working for it. Girton became more and more absorbing, and she continued to feel that it would be unwise to hamper the movement for University education by identifying herself prominently with an unpopular cause.

So far was silence carried by the pioneers of women's education, that when the Women's Suffrage Bill of 1877 was rejected it was stated in the House of Commons that none of those pioneers were in favour of the enfranchisement of women ; and the supporters of Girton and Newnham were particularly mentioned. This roused Mrs. Grey (Miss Shirreff's sister) to protest. At a suffrage meeting held to discuss the Bill, she declared that practically " all the women, who had been active in any cause for the benefit of their sex, were strong friends to the suffrage." [1] Two years later, an enquiry was made into the opinions of women eminent in literature, science, art, and in professional and philanthropic work, and the answers were collected into a pamphlet.

---

[1] *A Record of Women's Suffrage*, by Helen Blackburn, p. 144.

Naturally the declared suffragists responded, such as Miss Davies, Mrs. Garrett Anderson, Mrs. Fawcett, Madame Bodichon, and Madame Belloc ; among other contributors were educationists such as Mrs. Grey and Miss Shirreff, Miss Manning, and Miss Mary Gurney ; and women eminent in other walks of life, such as Miss Florence Nightingale, Miss Davenport Hill, Mrs. Richmond Ritchie, and Mrs. Mark Pattison. All declared themselves in favour of women's suffrage.[1]

Miss Davies however remained outside the suffrage movement, knowing that the work on which she was engaged was one of the main sources of the growing improvement in the position of women. Their admission to University and medical education, to the School Boards and the municipal franchise, and the passing of the Married Women's Property Acts, all were steps in the same direction. With the formation of the Primrose League in 1884, followed later by the Women's Liberal Federation and the Women's Liberal Unionist Association, the admission of women to an active part in political life became an acknowledged fact. While women were gaining experience and proving their value in various fields—political, professional, educational, and philanthropic—to men was given a large extension of the franchise. The Reform Act of 1884 gave the vote to agricultural labourers and other workmen, and the omission of women became more and more of an anomaly. When a women's suffrage amendment to the Reform Bill of 1884 was defeated by a large majority, Miss Davies, who was staying at Grasmere with Miss Richardson at the time, wrote to Miss Manning that she was " watching the crisis with vivid interest." At last, in 1886, a Women's Suffrage Bill passed its second reading without a division ; and though similar bills continued to be blocked by Parliamentary tactics, after that date there was always a favourable majority in the House of Commons.

By this time Girton was fairly established, and Miss Davies began to feel that she could safely engage again in the cause. In 1886 her name appears among the subscribers to the London National Society for Women's Suffrage. Three years later, she joined the Society's General Committee. In 1890, she joined

---

[1] *Opinions of Women on Women's Suffrage,* issued by the Central Committee of the National Society for Women's Suffrage, 1879.

the Executive Committee, and from that time forth was an active worker.

Miss Davies' first appearance in public on behalf of the cause was as a member of a deputation (consisting of herself, Mrs. Fawcett, Lady Goldsmid, and Miss Blackburn) to Mr. W. H. Smith, then First Lord of the Treasury, in April, 1891. The London Society for Women's Suffrage had lately adopted the plan of sending memorials to members of Parliament asking them to support their cause, and to one such petition were attached the names of seventy-seven women who had signed the petition of 1866, including Miss Davies, Madame Bodichon, Madame Belloc, and Mrs. Garrett Anderson. A few years before this, the anti-suffrage movement made its first appearance, in a protest against the proposed enfranchisement of women, published in the *Nineteenth Century*, and signed by Mrs. Humphry Ward, Mrs. Creighton,[1] and other ladies.

(Miss Davies to Miss Manning.)

May 17, 1891.

" I have been thinking of what you said yesterday on the proper method of working at the Women's Suffrage question. I think that tho', as you say, women in general do not want votes, it is fair to consider, as against the *number* of those who are indifferent, the *quality* of those who are on our side. We really have a very large proportion of the women who have thought, and done useful work. The names collected by Mrs. H. Ward and Mrs. Creighton against us were not those of the best and ablest women. As was remarked at the time, they were not distinguished women, but wives of distinguished men. This seems to me to tell in favour of its being fair to act on the assumption that the women worth listening to desire the vote. And if so, it seems to follow that they are justified in pressing their views on M.P.'s, who as a rule have no *convictions* on the subject."

(Miss Davies to Miss Manning.)

May 21, 1891.

" There was an interesting debate at Miss Toynbee's last night. There were 6 men, all of whom spoke, and about 14 ladies. Nobody was opposed, except one man who did not like the idea of women being eager politicians—but nearly every one said men would

---

[1] Subsequent experience in social work led Mrs. Creighton to change her views, and after 1906 she was a convinced and active suffragist.

be willing to give it if women wanted it, but they did not. I asked a working man if working men were for or against or did not care. He said they did not care, because women did not."

Miss Davies, being already engaged in suffrage work, was able, when she resigned her place on the Girton Committee in 1904, immediately to devote all her energies to that cause. One of her first thoughts was for Girton ; two articles were contributed by her to the *Girton Review* for 1905—*The Women's Suffrage Movement: I. Why should we care for it? II. How can we help to further it?* To rouse people to care for the question, and to stir them up to practical work—this was the task to which she addressed herself.

It was not long before fresh developments brought increased vigour together with new difficulties to the work for women's suffrage. Towards the end of 1905, the militant movement became prominent, and the sensational appearances of its supporters at meetings, and in the lobby of the House of Commons, where they made speeches, waved flags, and so forth, attracted public attention to the question to a degree hitherto unknown. At first, as Mrs. Fawcett has recorded, they suffered violence but used none ; and Miss Davies was pleased to find that a younger generation of women cared for the cause as intensely as she did, though she disapproved of their unconventional methods. She dissented strongly when, in the winter of 1906, the non-militants gave a dinner in honour of Mrs. Cobden-Sanderson and other militants who had just been released after serving a term of imprisonment for making a demonstration in the lobby of the House of Commons. A little later, Miss Davies was writing to eminent men, such as Lord Milner and Lord Robert Cecil, asking for their support, and in one of these letters we find her views expressed as follows : " The old law-abiding school of women suffragists feel it the more necessary for them to be in evidence at the present moment, as the action of the new and noisy section is apt to monopolize attention, and the whole movement is misrepresented and misunderstood." She was the first speaker on the deputation from Women's Suffrage societies to Sir Henry Campbell-Bannerman in May, 1906, when the *Daily Graphic* had a most unflattering sketch of her among its illustrations of the deputation. She was also a member of the deputation to

349

Mr. Asquith which has been amusingly described by Mrs. Fawcett in *The Women's Victory and After*.[1]

When the militants adopted aggressively violent methods, Miss Davies was greatly shocked. Her feelings were expressed in a leaflet published by the National Union of Women's Suffrage Societies, entitled *A Plea for Discrimination*. " The advocates of women's suffrage," she writes, " are finding, to their keen disappointment and regret, that friends to whom, at this critical moment, they are looking for countenance and support, are being alienated by proceedings in which they are in no way implicated. . . . I would appeal to our friends' sense of proportion, and beg them not to allow their just indignation at proceedings which are deplored by none so much as by the great body of Suffragists, to lead them to desert a cause which is none the less worthy because unworthy action has been taken in its name." She continued to work for the suffrage on the constitutional lines followed by the older societies ; she wrote leaflets, spoke at meetings, and took part in deputations with unwavering zeal and energy. On June 21, 1908, she took part in one of the huge demonstrations which became a feature of the agitation. About 15,000 women suffragists gathered on the Embankment and went in procession to the Albert Hall.[2] There were contingents representing Girton and Newnham, women graduates and writers, professional women—in fact, women of all sorts and conditions. Miss Davies joined in the procession, wearing her cap and gown as an honorary LL.D. of Glasgow, a degree which had been conferred on her in 1901. The success of the demonstration, which was strikingly well organized, was exhilarating, and she thoroughly enjoyed herself.

On the Committee of the London Society, Miss Davies' energy and ability, no less than her experience, made her a person of importance. Her power of expressing herself clearly and succinctly was especially valuable in Committee. While other people were fumbling for words, she would have all the points clear in her mind, and would draft resolutions or amendments for her opponents, rather than let the question at issue be confused. Both her enterprise in anything concerning women, and

[1] *The Women's Victory and After*, pp. 16–19.
[2] See *What I Remember*, by Dame Millicent Garrett Fawcett, p. 191.

her natural conservatism, were as strongly marked as ever. As a member of the " Organization Committee," she invented a plan of setting up local suffrage committees in the various London districts, making special efforts to induce people of social distinction to join them. Another plan which she invented was to insert advertisements in the papers drawing attention to the cause and the work that was being done for it. This was warmly taken up by younger members of the Committee, and with the advice of experts, some very striking advertisements were prepared ; but when Miss Davies saw them, she shrank in horror from such flamboyant methods, and insisted that the advertisements should be reduced to a more modest tone and scale. Difficulties such as these led to the formation of a " Public Meetings Committee " of which she was not a member ; she saw what this meant, but continued to be an active member of the other committee, where her work could have its full value. Her collaboration with the Secretary, Miss Philippa Strachey, was an especial pleasure to her ; she liked younger women, enjoyed working with them, and was very ready to discuss matters freely and listen to their views, though she usually held to her own.

Hitherto, the Women's Suffrage Bills introduced in the House of Commons had always been of a moderate and non-party character. In 1909 Mr. Geoffrey Howard and some other Liberal members brought forward a Bill for what was practically universal adult suffrage. This was most unwelcome to the older suffrage societies, and Miss Davies shared their disapproval. In July, 1910 (being then over eighty), she wrote a letter to the papers, urging that neither " the adult suffrage scare " nor the militants should be allowed to stand in the way of the enfranchisement of women. She supported the practical compromise which was found in the Conciliation Bill, which proposed to admit women (including wives) to Household Suffrage. The Women's Suffrage Societies and the Women's Liberal Federation were united in its support, and on May 5, 1911, it was passed on a second reading by a majority of 167. High hopes were roused, with corresponding disappointment and indignation, when in November Mr. Asquith announced his intention of introducing a Reform Bill which would grant what was practically adult suffrage to men, while ignoring women. Next year, when the Conciliation Bill was again introduced, it was defeated by a majority of 14, giving him a pretext for declining to include any extension of the franchise to women in his Reform Bill, which was to give votes to " citizens of full age and competent understanding." Upon this, the National Union of Women's Suffrage Societies changed their policy, and resolved that henceforth they would give their support to a member of Parliament who had the support of his party on the question, rather than to one who had not. This was, as Mrs. Fawcett writes, " in effect a declaration of war against the official Liberal party, and of support of the Labour party, which was the only party which had made women's suffrage a part of its programme." [1] This was a policy to which Miss Davies could not bring herself to subscribe ; she would not join in supporting the Labour party ; and she felt constrained to leave the London Society, to which she had belonged for about twenty-five years, and join the Conservative and Unionist Women's Franchise Association. She accepted an invitation to become a Vice-President of the Association, of which Lady Selborne was President. Miss Davies, however, was now eighty-two, and could hardly embark on fresh work.

It was not long before all thoughts of the suffrage were swept away by the war. The work done by women during the war was watched by Miss Davies with interest and pride. The suffrage societies at once turned all their powers to war work. Both the London Society and the Conservative and Unionist Women's Franchise Association began by undertaking relief work of various kinds. As the war went on, an ever-increasing demand arose for the services of women who had had a University education. Past students of the women's colleges, beginning as scrubbers in hospitals or waitresses in canteens, were found to be valuable as scientific investigators, chemists, clerks in government offices, or teachers in boys' schools. Five Girtonians who had become doctors served in France, and one in Serbia and Roumania with the Scottish Women's Hospitals for Foreign Service. These hospitals, organized by Dr. Elsie Inglis through the National Union of Women's Suffrage Societies, were perhaps the most

[1] *The Women's Victory, and After*, pp. 31, 33.

striking manifestation of women's power to help. One of the hospital units in France was financed by the students (past and present) of Girton and Newnham ; five units eventually went to Serbia. There is no need to dwell on the heroic work done in these hospitals, and on the services rendered by women generally —services which they would have been incapable of rendering before the women's movement had made it possible for them to acquire some degree of education, experience, and independence.[1]

It is unnecessary to describe the steps which led to the political enfranchisement of women in 1918. A message of " affectionate greetings and congratulations " from the Organization Committee of the London Society for Women's Suffrage, assured Miss Davies that on this great occasion her work was gratefully remembered. In 1919 she, who had been one of the first petitioners for women's suffrage, was able to record her vote in the general election. Within her lifetime the work had been accomplished.

---

[1] See *What I Remember*, by Dame Millicent Garrett Fawcett, Chaps. XXII and XXIII.

CHAPTER XXII

Conclusion

THE story of Miss Davies' public work has now been told in its main outlines. Her eager interest in life led her into various lesser undertakings, most of them auxiliary to the main object, such as the National Union of Women Workers and the Women's Local Government Society. In holiday times, she enjoyed visits to her friends; after 1889, when her brother became Vicar of Kirkby Lonsdale in Westmoreland, she generally stayed during some part of the summer with him and his family. Travelling was a great pleasure to her; she went to the North of Ireland in 1889, and spent some time there with her friends Miss Kensington and Mrs. Mylne; in later years there were journeys to Wiesbaden and Frankfort with Miss Caroline Richardson,[1] and to France and Italy, sometimes with Miss Manning, sometimes with Miss C. M. Ridding. Her manner of life in London was plain and simple in the extreme. After her mother's death, she lived in lodgings till she was seventy-two, when, feeling that it would be well to be a little more comfortable, she settled herself in a flat in Montagu Mansions, Baker Street. She took great pleasure in furnishing and decorating her new abode, going into all the details with lively interest and satisfaction, like a statesman entering upon his retirement, as one of her nephews remarked. It was a pleasure to receive her friends and relations in a house of her own.

Acknowledgments of Miss Davies' great services were not wanting during her later years. In 1901 the University of Glasgow, on the occasion of its ninth jubilee, conferred the

---

[1] Miss Anna Richardson's sister.

honorary degree of LL.D. for the first time in its history on several ladies, of whom she was one. With Miss Constance Jones (then Vice-Mistress of Girton) she went to Glasgow and was invested with the doctor's hood of red and purple. In 1912 a Committee was formed to commemorate Miss Davies' jubilee, it being then fifty years since she had come to London and definitely entered upon the work which was to be the main object of her life. The sum of 700 guineas was collected and presented to her, with an address from over 1,300 subscribers, among whom were old friends and fellow-workers, including many past students of Girton. Signatures were also appended on behalf of the Clothworkers' Company, who had from early days given generous encouragement to the education of women ; the Association of University Women Teachers, the Headmistresses' Association, and other educational bodies, as well as various suffrage societies. The money was given by Miss Davies to Girton, to be devoted to the building of additional students' rooms, whenever the financial and general condition of the College should be such as to make this possible.[1] The oldest part of the College, including that small portion which was in existence when Miss Davies was Mistress, was at this time named after her, the Emily Davies Court.

Seven years later, in 1919, another jubilee was celebrated— the jubilee of the foundation of Girton. Miss Davies was unable to be present, but an address signed by past and present students was presented to her in her own home, to which she sent a written reply. This was her last public act. For some years past she had lived in quiet retirement at Hampstead, whither she had moved on her brother's coming with his daughter to live there after leaving Kirkby Lonsdale in 1908. She accepted the limitations of old age with uncomplaining cheerfulness. " She was so rational and serene, and kindly accommodating," writes her niece, who saw her constantly during the last years, " and her good sayings and humour continued." Death came on July 13, 1921, when she was in her ninety-second year. In May, 1922,

---

[1] At the time of the presentation the College was heavily in debt, as related in Chap. XVIII ; and since the extinction of the debt, the war and subsequent troubles have so far made it impossible to proceed with the addition.

a service was held at St. Martin's-in-the-Fields, to commemorate and give thanks for her life and the work she had achieved. A scholarship has been founded at Girton in her name, and a memorial tablet placed in the Chapel ; though such memorials may seem scarcely necessary, while Girton itself stands as a visible result of her work.

CHAPTER XXIII

Postscript

MISS DAVIES' life was so closely bound up with Girton, that for the sake of completeness the story of the relations between Girton and the University of Cambridge should be carried on from 1897, where the problem was left unsolved in Chapter XVII, to the present day, when a considerable advance can be recorded.

For nearly forty years the position remained as established in 1881. The first change came in 1918, when the Representation of the People Act, in admitting women to the franchise, conferred the right of voting for the University representatives in Parliament on women who had fulfilled the conditions imposed on members of the University who were qualified to vote. To the outside world, these new voters appeared to be qualified in virtue of having had a University education ; in the University, on the other hand, they had no standing. The women's colleges were still recognized by the University only in so far as their students were admitted to honours examinations, and no further.

When the privilege of admission to examinations was first granted, in 1881, there was a great sense of relief from anxiety, and under cover of the security thus gained the newly founded colleges made steady progress. Meanwhile education was advancing in the world outside, and in the course of forty years a great change was wrought. In London and at the provincial Universities, women gained the right of admission, not only to examinations but to degrees ; and women who had taken honours at Cambridge were thus placed at a disadvantage. This disadvantage was removed in 1921, when Graces were passed by

357

the Cambridge Senate granting titles of degrees to duly qualified members of the women's colleges. This meant that such women could call themselves B.A., M.A., and so forth. These titles did not carry with them membership of the University ; but they gave the right to wear cap and gown, and they conveyed to the outer world the impression that the women holding them were really the equivalent of Cambridge graduates.

A further step was gained by Ordinances passed in March, 1923, which secured to women students at Cambridge the right of admission to University lectures and laboratories, which they had hitherto attended only by the courtesy of individual lecturers —a courtesy which might at any time be withheld. This had in fact seldom occurred during the forty years which had passed since women were admitted to examinations ; but it might occur at any time, especially as the lecture rooms were becoming more crowded with the growth of the University. It was a great advantage to the women's colleges to have their position at last made regular and secure in this respect. At the same time, women lecturers and holders of the titular M.A. degree were granted the same facilities in the University Library as were enjoyed by Masters of Arts, and women students were admitted to the Library on much the same conditions as undergraduates. This v:as a most welcome and valuable concession. The number of women students was to be limited to five hundred ; but the position was otherwise substantially improved by the concessions already mentioned.

In other respects the situation was unchanged, and the women lecturers at Girton and Newnham remained entirely outside the University. Women students, being largely taught by members of the University (as well as by women lecturers), were scarcely aware of being excluded from anything ; but the women lecturers felt increasingly the disadvantages of never being present at the discussion of University schemes of teaching and examining. They fitted in their courses of lectures with the University and intercollegiate lecture lists as best they could, after the publication of these lists at the beginning of each term. This was something more than a practical inconvenience ; it meant that the women lecturers had no share in the intellectual life of the University, and it made a great gap in their experience. A passage may be quoted from the memorial presented to the Senate in 1897 by past students of Girton and Newnham :

" While appreciating to the full the privileges accorded by the Graces of the Senate, February 24, 1881, we feel that women are without the necessary encouragement and support which status in the University confers. Since at the present time the official relation of the University to the education of women is that of an examining body only, they owe the privileges of an academic education to the courtesy of the teachers of the University. We are conscious that women do not share fully in the great benefits which the University has to bestow upon education, learning, and research."

The courtesy of University teachers had been invaluable. Without their generous encouragement and support, the women's colleges could never have carried on, or even begun, their existence. But as time went by, and the colleges enlarged the scope and improved the standard of their work, the cramping effect of exclusion from the University came more and more to be felt as a bar to efficiency by the residents of Girton and Newnham. The difficulty was again emphasized, as in the case of degrees, by comparison with London and the provincial Universities,[1] where women worked with men as colleagues, sharing in the organization of teaching, examinations, and other University business, as well as in opportunities for advanced work and research. The attractions thus offered by these Universities have tended to draw away from Cambridge some of the ablest among the women educated at Girton and Newnham.

Such was the position in 1919, when a Royal Commission was appointed to enquire into the Universities of Oxford and Cambridge. An indication as to public opinion may be seen in the

---

[1] It should be noted that the proportion of women in these Universities is much higher than at Oxford and Cambridge. At Cambridge there are two women's colleges, having a total number of 561 residents, students and staff included. There are seventeen men's colleges, besides one hostel (Selwyn), and Fitzwilliam Hall (for non-collegiate students). The numbers of men are as follows :

Undergraduates	4,356
M.A.'s, etc.	981
B.A.'s	362
Research students	125

These are the official figures for October, 1925.

fact that the women's colleges, though in the case of Cambridge not officially part of the University,[1] were included within the scope of the enquiry, and two women were appointed as members of the Commission.[2] The Report of the Commission, issued in 1922, contains the following paragraph in reference to Cambridge :

" The University has played a great part in raising and keeping up the tone of women's education in the country. . . . It would be a national disaster if the standard of women's education at Cambridge should decline. But in our opinion this result is inevitable in the coming generation if Cambridge is left, for the first time, in the position of the only University in the country where neither women students nor women teachers have the status of membership of the University, and where the teachers, however well qualified, are not eligible for posts or offices in the University, and are excluded from all share in discussions on the organization of teaching." [3]

In the Summary of Recommendations and Suggestions at the end of the Report, may be found the following :

" That women be entitled to be admitted on the same conditions as men to membership of the University, subject to the limitations summarized below, so that Cambridge may continue to be, alongside of Oxford and the other Universities of the country, a centre of the highest education for women."

The main recommendations of the Royal Commission have been embodied in new Statutes drafted by the Statutory Commission set up in 1923. Under these, the teaching of the University is to be reorganized on a new system, whereby a Faculty or Department will be established for every Tripos, with a staff of University lecturers. This staff is to include (besides Professors, Readers, and University Lecturers) Fellows of Colleges who are giving lectures or demonstrations recognized by the Board of

[1] Women were admitted to membership of the University of Oxford in 1919, before the Commission was appointed.

[2] Miss Penrose, Principal of Somerville College, and Miss B. A. Clough, at that time Vice-Principal of Newnham College. Miss B. S. Phillpotts, O.B.E. (at that time Mistress of Girton College), was a member of the subsequently appointed Statutory Commission for Cambridge ; and Miss Penrose was a member of the Oxford Statutory Commission.

[3] *Report of the Royal Commission on Oxford and Cambridge Universities*, 1922, pp. 173–4.

the Faculty, or who hold the position of Directors of Studies in a College. In this connection the term " Fellows of Colleges " includes the Fellows of Selwyn, Girton, and Newnham Colleges ; [1] and it is further laid down that " Women shall be eligible for all University teaching offices." Broadly speaking, the result will be that qualified women will become members of Faculties,[2] and will be eligible for Boards of Faculties. At a general meeting of any Faculty, which must occur at least once a year, there is to be discussion of the teaching programme, and of arrangements for teaching and research. Women will have the opportunity of hearing these discussions and sharing in them ; and any woman who may be elected to the Board of a Faculty will have a voice in the determination of the University's policy in such matters. The small numbers of the women's colleges make it unlikely that this last privilege will be exercised by more than a very few women, but the opportunity will mean much to those few ; and admission to the general meetings of the Faculties, though it will add very little to the size of those meetings, will be valuable to the women admitted. There is every reason to hope that if these changes are carried into effect, the women's colleges will be able to make good progress and to attain a higher standard of work than would otherwise be possible.

It may be added, that in accordance with the recommendations of the Royal Commission, a grant of £4,000 a year has been made to the women's colleges both at Oxford and at Cambridge, for a period of ten years, one-half of the grant being ear-marked for pensions and stipends. In this may be seen a sign of the change which has been effected since the days when desperate efforts had to be made to raise £7,000 to provide the barest necessities for the foundation of Girton. It is now an acknowledged fact that in higher education and learning, women can take their share and do work of value to the nation of which they are part.

[1] *Cambridge University Reporter*, August 8, 1924. Selwyn is not a college but a hostel.

[2] Eleven women have been offered appointments as University Lecturers and will in consequence become members of Faculties.

BIOGRAPHICAL INDEX

THE following particulars are intended as supplementary to what has been written in the foregoing pages about some of the persons concerned. Among other sources, the *Dictionary of National Biography* and Boase's *Modern English Biography* have been especially valuable.

BELLOC, MADAME (1829–1925), daughter of Joseph Parkes of Birmingham (Secretary to the Commission of 1833 on Municipal Corporations, and an active politician with Whig and Radical sympathies). Her mother was the daughter of Joseph Priestley, the famous dissenter and man of science. She married M. Belloc in 1868, and was the author of *Essays on Woman's Work* (1865), *Vignettes* (1866), *In a Walled Garden* (1895), *A Passing World* (1897), and *The Flowing Tide* (1900).

BRODIE, SIR BENJAMIN (1817–80), Professor of Chemistry at Oxford. He and his wife were friends of Madame Bodichon.

BRYCE, JAMES (1838–1922), P.C., G.C.V.O., O.M., D.C.L., LL.D., F.R.S., etc., Regius Professor of Civil Law at Oxford, 1870–93 ; Liberal M.P. 1880–1907 ; held Cabinet office in various capacities 1886–1907 ; Ambassador at Washington 1907–13 ; created Viscount Bryce 1914 ; Author of *The Holy Roman Empire*, *The American Commonwealth*, and other books. He was a Member of Girton College from 1872 till his death. See *Lord Bryce*, by Rt. Hon. H. A. L. Fisher, Warden of New College, Oxford.

CHESSAR, JANE AGNES (1835–80) was a member of the staff of the Home and Colonial Training College (then in Gray's Inn Road, now at Wood Green) from 1852 till 1866. Ill health obliged her to retire, but she continued to teach, and lectured on Elementary Physiology and Hygiene for the National Health Society. She was a member of the London School Board, 1873–5, and did much for the domestic training of girls. The J. A. Chessar Classical Scholarship at Girton was named after her by the donor, Miss Minturn.

COOK, HARRIET, daughter of Professor Cook of St. Andrews, and sister to Rachel Cook, one of the " Girton Pioneers " (afterwards Mrs. C. P. Scott).

CORNWALLIS, CAROLINE FRANCES (1786–1858), editor and in great part author of a series of *Small Books on Great Subjects*, in twenty-two volumes, of which *Philosophical Theories and Philosophical Experience* was the first. There are two articles on the legal disabilities of women by her in the *Westminster Review*, 1856 and 1857. A volume of *Selections* from her letters was published in 1864. Miss Beale, of Cheltenham, was her cousin.

COURTNEY, LEONARD HENRY (1832–1918), Fellow of St. John's College, Cambridge, held office under Mr. Gladstone 1880–4, adhered to the Liberal-Unionist Party in 1885 ; and was Chairman of Committees in the House of Commons 1886. In 1906 he was created Baron Courtney of Penwith. He was a Member of Girton College from 1876 till his death.

DICEY, EDWARD (1832–1911), a member of the staff of the *Daily Telegraph*, 1862–70 ; special correspondent in the Schleswig-Holstein War 1864 ; editor of the *Observer*, 1870–89.

DOVE, JANE FRANCES, M.A. (T.C.D.), J.P., was a student of Girton from 1871 to 1874, Headmistress of St. Leonards' School, St. Andrews, and afterwards Headmistress and founder of Wycombe Abbey School, Bucks. She was a Member of Girton College from 1902 till 1924, when she was appointed a Governor of the College under the terms of the Charter granted in that year.

FAITHFULL, EMILY (1836–95), youngest daughter of Rev. F. Faithfull, rector of Headley near Epsom, started the Victoria Printing Press in August, 1859, and was appointed Printer and Publisher in ordinary to the Queen, June 1862. She published the *Victoria Magazine*, 1863–80, and was later engaged in lecturing and various literary enterprises.

FITCH, SIR JOSHUA (1824–1903), M.A.(Lond.), was appointed an Inspector of Schools in 1863. From 1865 to 1867 he acted as Assistant Commissioner to the Schools Enquiry Commission, and afterwards held various important educational appointments. He was a member of the Senate of the University of London, and was instrumental in procuring the admission of women to London degrees. He assisted in the foundation of Girton College, and of many undertakings on behalf of women's education, such as the North of England Council for the Higher Education of Women, the Girls' Public Day School Company, the London School of Medicine for Women, the Royal Holloway College, and the Maria Grey Training College. (*Sir Joshua Fitch*, by A. L. Tilley, 1906.)

GATTY, MRS. (1803–73), author of *Parables from Nature* and other books, and editor of *Aunt Judy's Magazine*.

GOLDSMID, LOUISA, LADY (1819–1909), was the wife of Sir Francis Goldsmid, the first Jew to become a barrister, and a Member of the House of Commons. Lady Goldsmid shared her husband's public and philanthropic interests, and was a constant supporter of the movements for the education and enfranchisement of women. She was among the first Members of Girton College, to which she gave many benefactions. Some account of her may be found in an article by Miss Welsh, in the *Girton Review*, Lent Term, 1909.

GORST, SIR JOHN (1835–1911), M.P. for Cambridge 1866–8, for Chatham 1875–92, for Cambridge University 1892–1906. After holding various government offices, he was Vice-President of the Committee of Council on Education, 1895–1902. He was a Member of Girton College 1872–83.

GURNEY, EMELIA (1823–96), daughter of Rev. S. E. Batten, Assistant Master at Harrow, and wife of Russell Gurney, a charming and cultivated woman, friend of Julia Wedgwood, General Gordon, and Lord and Lady Mount Temple, at whose house, Broadlands, she attended religious conferences 1874–88.

" Her religious experiences were the very keynote of Emelia's life. . . . She loved to sit at the feet of religious and artistic teachers ; as she once said to me, ' I have an intense pleasure in being converted.' " (Letter from Caroline Stephen, in *Letters of Emelia Russell Gurney*, edited by her niece, E. M. Gurney.) She published *Letters from a Mystic of the Present Day*, and *Dante's Pilgrim's Progress*, a collection of extracts from the *Divina Commedia* with notes. In 1875 Mr. and Mrs. Gurney established a convalescent home for women at 3, Orme Square, Bayswater, and after Mr. Gurney's death she lived there (1878–96), ministering to the patients. She bought the disused burial ground in Hyde Park Place, and built a chapel there (designed by Herbert Horne and decorated by F. Shields) as a refuge for meditation and prayer. She was a Member of Girton College, 1872–96.

GURNEY, RUSSELL (1804–78), Q.C., Recorder of London 1857–78, Conservative M.P. for Southampton 1865–78, took charge of the Married Women's Property Bill in the House of Commons 1870, and of other important measures. He was a strikingly handsome man, with much sweetness and dignity of character, as well as great ability.

HAYLEY, WILLIAM (1745–1820), friend and patron of William Blake, and author of *The Triumphs of Temper* and other poems. He appears in Gibbon's *Autobiography* as offering " an elegant compliment " in verse on the publication in 1788 of the three last volumes of the *Decline and Fall of the Roman Empire*.

HERSCHEL, CONSTANCE ANN (now Lady Lubbock), daughter of Sir John Herschel and niece of Caroline Herschel, was Resident Lecturer in Natural Sciences and Mathematics at Girton, 1878–81.

HEYWOOD, JAMES (1810–97), F.R.S., M.P. for North Lancs. 1847–57, a University reformer, was debarred as a Unitarian from taking a degree at Cambridge, and was especially interested in the abolition of religious tests. An early supporter of Girton, he was a member of the College 1872–97, and he was also a supporter of women's suffrage.

HIGGS, MRS. See KINGSLAND, MARY.

HILL, MATTHEW DAVENPORT (1792–1872), brother of Sir Rowland Hill, was a member of the first reformed Parliament; Recorder of Birmingham, 1839–64; and did much to .eform the criminal law.

JACKSON, HENRY (1839–1921), O.M., Litt.D., Fellow of Trinity College, Cambridge, 1864–1921; Regius Professor of Greek, 1906–21; Vice-Master of Trinity College, 1914–19; a Member of Girton College, 1875–1921. See *Henry Jackson, O.M.*, by Dr. R. St. John Parry.

KINGSLAND, MARY (Mrs. Higgs), Resident Lecturer at Girton, 1875–6. Author of *The Master ; How to Deal with the Unemployed ;* and *Glimpses into the Abyss*, a study on vagrancy based on practical experience as a vagrant.

LYTTELTON, RT. HON. GEORGE WILLIAM (1817–76), fourth Baron Lyttelton, K.C.M.G., D.C.L., LL.D., F.R.S., was a member of the Public Schools Enquiry Commission, 1861; a member of the Schools Enquiry Commission, 1864; and chief Commissioner of endowed schools, 1869.

MANNING, CHARLOTTE (1803–71), daughter of Isaac Solly, of Leyton, Essex, married (1) 1835, Dr. William Speir; (2) 1857, Serjeant Manning (as his second wife). She was the author of *Life in Ancient India*, by Mrs. Speir, with illustrations by George Scharf, Junior, F.S.A., Smith Elder 1856; and of *Ancient and Medieval India*, by Mrs. Manning, 2 vols., 1869. A reference to this book may be found in J. S. Mill's *Letters*, II, 235. The clock in the Emily Davies Court at Girton was put up as a memorial to Mrs. Manning.

MANNING, JAMES (1781–1866), Serjeant-at-law, a very learned lawyer, assisted Lord Brougham and Lord Denman in the defence of Queen Caroline.

MARIO, MADAME. See WHITE, JESSIE MERITON.

METCALFE, FANNY, founded in 1863, with her elder sister Annie, a boarding school for girls at Highfield, Hendon, which became one of the largest and best known schools of its kind in England.

Miss Metcalfe's aim was to follow in the steps of Arnold of Rugby ; and though at that date she could not introduce the modern system of freedom and responsibility, she did secure the help of some excellent teachers, and was eager to encourage girls to continue their education after leaving school. She was a Member of Girton College, 1872–96, and of the Council of Westfield College from 1890 till her death in 1897.

MOHL, MARY (1793–1883), daughter of Charles Clark, married in 1847 Julius Mohl, the orientalist. In earlier life she was intimate with Madame Récamier, of whom she wrote a short life ; later, her own salon attracted many people of intellectual distinction, both French and English.

NORTON, CAROLINE (1808–77), grand-daughter of R. B. Sheridan, married in 1827 the Hon. G. C. Norton, who in 1836 brought an action against Lord Melbourne (then Prime Minister) for the seduction of his wife. The jury decided in favour of the defendants without leaving the box ; Mrs. Norton's innocence was established ; and she remained legally bound to her husband. Norton agreed to make her an allowance but refused to let her see their three children. Disputes about these matters kept the case before the public ; and in 1838, when Serjeant Talfourd's Infant Custody Bill was before the House of Commons, a personal attack was made on Mrs. Norton in the *British and Foreign Review*. She found that as a married woman she could not sue for libel ; only her husband could sue on her behalf. A fresh agreement with him about money matters proved no protection against further troubles. The income bequeathed to her by her father was (in accordance with the law) paid by her trustees to her husband, who also laid claim to a legacy from her mother. In 1852 he stopped her allowance, and claimed the proceeds of the literary work on which she was supporting herself. On her appealing to their agreement, he defied her to prove it, as no contract between man and wife was legally valid. The case attracted much attention, partly because of the social position of the parties, partly owing to Mrs. Norton's pamphlets, the only means open to her of defending herself. (*Life of Mrs. Norton*, by J. G. Perkins.)

PARKES, BESSIE RAYNER. See BELLOC, MADAME.

PONSONBY, MARY ELIZABETH, wife of General Sir Henry Ponsonby, and daughter of J. C. Bulteel, was Maid of Honour to Queen Victoria, 1853–61, and Extra Woman of the Bedchamber, 1895–1901. Her husband was Private Secretary to the Queen, 1870–95. She was a Member of Girton College till her death in 1916.

RICH, JULIA, LADY, daughter of Rev. James Tomkinson of Dorfold Hall, Cheshire, and cousin to Mr. H. R. Tomkinson, married Sir Henry Rich, Bt., who died in 1869. Lady Rich was a Member of Girton College from 1872 till her death in 1874.

ROBY, HENRY JOHN (1830–1915), author of *Grammar of the Latin Language*, was a Fellow and Tutor of St. John's College, Cambridge, 1853–60 ; Secretary of the Schools Enquiry Commission of 1864, and of the Endowed Schools Commission which followed ; subsequently Professor of Jurisprudence at University College, Liverpool. He was a Member of Girton College, 1872–1905. (See an article by Miss Davies in the *Girton Review*, Lent Term 1915, pp. 14–15.)

SARGANT, ETHEL (1864–1918), botanist, was fortunate in being endowed both with great intellectual powers, and with the means and leisure to use them. She was a Fellow of the Linnæan Society, and the first woman to serve on its Council ; she was also the first woman to preside over a section of the British Association (1913) ; an old student of Girton, she was elected to an honorary Life Fellowship at the College, and appointed a member of the Council. During the war she organized a Register of University Women available for work of national importance, which was afterwards taken over by the Ministry of Health. Her botanical library, which she bequeathed to the College, is at Girton. See the *Girton Review*, Lent Term, 1918, pp. 11–12.

SEELEY, SIR JOHN ROBERT (1834–95), Professor of Modern History at Cambridge, 1869–95, author of *Ecce Homo, The Expansion of England, The Life and Times of Stein*, and other books.

SEWELL, ELIZABETH (1815–1906), author of *Amy Herbert* and other stories of High Church tendency, and founder of St. Boniface School, Ventnor.

SHIRREFF, EMILY (1814–97), and her younger sister Mrs. Grey (founder of the Maria Grey Training College) became well known after 1872, as founders of the National Union for Improving the Education of Women of all Classes, out of which grew the Girls' Public Day School Company. Miss Shirreff was the author of *Intellectual Education and Its Influence on the Character and Happiness of Women* (first ed. 1858) ; and joint author with her sister of *Thoughts on Self-Culture addressed to Women* (first ed. 1850), and other books. She was one of the founders, and for many years President, of the Froebel Society. Her father was Rear-Admiral W. H. Shirreff ; her mother was the daughter of Hon. David Murray.

SIDGWICK, HENRY (1838–1900), Fellow of Trinity College, Cambridge, 1859–69 ; Knightbridge Professor of Moral Philosophy, 1883–1900 ; one of the founders of Newnham College, of which Mrs. Sidgwick was Principal from 1892 till 1910. See *Henry Sidgwick: A Memoir*, by A. Sidgwick and E. M. Sidgwick.

SOMERVILLE, MARY (1780–1872), daughter of Vice-Admiral Sir W. G. Fairfax, married in 1804 Captain Greig, and secondly, in 1812, Dr. William Somerville. She was the author of various scientific works, a passage in one of which (*The Connection of the Physical Sciences*) suggested to Professor Adams the calculations from which he deduced the orbit of Neptune. Her contributions to science were recognized by various learned bodies, including the Royal Astronomical Society, of which she was an honorary member. The *Personal Recollections of Mary Somerville*, published in 1873, reveal a delightful character. Her mathematical library was presented to Girton College, where there is also a drawing of her by Samuel Laurence.

STANLEY OF ALDERLEY, HENRIETTA MARIA, LADY (1807–95), was the wife of the second Lord Stanley of Alderley, who held government office under Lord Melbourne and Lord Palmerston. The latter said of her that she was joint-whip, with her husband, of the Whig party. After her husband's death in 1869, she took an active part in promoting the foundation of Girton College ; of the Girls' Public Day School Company ; and of the London School of Medicine for Women. She was a leading member of the Women's Liberal-Unionist Association. She was a Member of Girton College from 1872 till her death.

STEPHEN, SARAH (1816–95), was the daughter of Henry John Stephen, Serjeant-at-law. A very able woman, she was a dutiful daughter at home during her father's lifetime. After his death she engaged in social work with Miss F. P. Cobbe, Mrs. Nassau Senior, and Miss Octavia Hill, and was one of the founders of the Metropolitan Association for Befriending Young Servants.

TAYLOR, MRS. PETER, Clementia, daughter of John Doughty, and wife of P. A. Taylor (1819–91, Radical M.P. for Leicester 1862–84, and friend of Mazzini), was a prominent and active worker for Women's Suffrage. From 1860 to 1873 the Taylors lived at Aubrey House, Notting Hill, where Mrs. Taylor held fortnightly political receptions. In some outbuildings she arranged accommodation for the Aubrey Evening Institute, a club for shop girls and their friends. She was a subscriber to the fund organized by Miss Davies in 1862 in connection with efforts to obtain admission for women to University examinations. She was a friend of George Eliot's. She died in 1908. (See *Aubrey House, Kensington*, by Florence M. Gladstone, 1922.)

TAYLOR, SEDLEY (1834–1920), elected a Fellow of Trinity College, Cambridge, 1861 ; took orders 1863, relinquishing them and resigning his Fellowship some years later. He continued to reside at Trinity till the end of his life, and did much to encourage music in the University. He was President of the University Musical Society when he was an undergraduate, and again later for many years. He was interested in the co-operative movement and other social questions, and was the author of *Sound and Music* (1873), *Profit-Sharing*, and other books. For his benefactions to the Dental Institute at Cambridge he received the freedom of the borough in 1911. He was a Member of Girton College 1872–1920, and he gave an Organ Scholarship to Girton in 1910.

TAYLOR, TOM (1817–80), journalist and playwright, editor of

Punch 1874–80, author of a number of plays, including *Our American Cousin*, famous for the character of Lord Dundreary.

WEDGWOOD, JULIA (1833–1913), a daughter of Mr. Hensleigh Wedgwood, was the author of *The Moral Ideal* and *The Message of Israel*.

WELSH, ELIZABETH, Resident Classical Lecturer at Girton, 1876–84 ; Vice-Mistress, 1880–5 ; Mistress, 1885–1903 ; Member of the College, 1885–1916. Miss Welsh's insight into character, her sense of humour, and steady influence over a long period of years were of great value to the College. She was famous for her skill in writing testimonials, being able to express her opinions in such a way as to convey an extraordinarily true impression. She had the Irish gift of remembering all about her friends and acquaintances, and their friends and relations. To her judicious planning and constant care the garden and grounds at Girton owe many of their most attractive features.

WESTLAKE, JOHN (1828–1913), K.C., LL.D., Fellow of Trinity College, Cambridge, 1851–60 ; Professor of International Law, 1888–1908 ; a member of the International Court of Arbitration under the Hague Convention, 1900–6 ; author of various works on international law.

WHITE, JESSIE MERITON (1832–1906), daughter of a ship builder at Gosport, applied in 1856 " to all the London hospitals, fourteen in number," for leave to enter as a medical student, which was refused, as was also leave to take the examinations of the University of London. (See *Women and Work*, by Madame Bodichon, pp. 40–44, and Appendix.) She was afterwards correspondent of the *Daily News* in Genoa, nursed the wounded in Italy, married the Garibaldian officer Mario in 1857, and wrote *Vita di Giuseppe Garibaldi, Vita di Mazzini, Garibaldi e i suoi tempi*, and *Supplement to English Translation of Garibaldi's Memoirs*. (See *The Birth of Modern Italy : Posthumous Papers of Jessie White Mario*, edited by Duke Litta Visconti Varese.)

WRIGHT, ROBERT SAMUEL, Judge of the Queen's Bench Division of the High Court from 1891 till his death in 1904. He gave substantial help to Girton in the shape of scholarships in 1876 and 1877, and was a Member of the College, 1878–1900.

BIBLIOGRAPHY

I. Writings by Miss Emily Davies.

1860. *Letters to a Daily Paper, Newcastle-on-Tyne.

1861. *Report of the Northumberland and Durham Branch of the Society for the Promotion of the Employment of Women.

1862. *Medicine as a Profession for Women (Social Science Association).

*Female Physicians (*Englishwoman's Journal*, 1862).

1863. *The Influence of University Degrees on the Education of Women (*Victoria Magazine*, June, 1863).

Needleworkers *v.* Society (*Victoria Magazine*, August, 1863),

The Social Science Association (*Victoria Magazine*, November, 1863).

1864. *Secondary Instruction as Relating to Girls (Social Science Association).

Reasons for the Extension of the University Local Examinations to Girls.

1865. The Application of Funds to the Education of Girls (Social Science Association).

1866. The Higher Education of Women (published by Strahan).

Letters to the *Morning Post* (Women's Suffrage leaflet).

1868. *On the Influence upon Girls' Schools of External Examinations (*The London Student*).

*Some Account of a Proposed New College for Women (Social Science Association).

Special Systems of Education for Women (*The London Student*, June, 1868).

1869. The Training of the Imagination (*Contemporary Review*, reprinted for the London Schoolmistresses' Association).

1871. College Education for Women (unpublished, read before the Nottingham Literary and Philosophical Society).

1878. *Home and the Higher Education (Birmingham Higher Education Association).

1896. *Women in the Universities of England and Scotland (published by Macmillan).

1897. Speech at the Conference on University Degrees for Women, convened by the Governors of the Royal Holloway College (Report published by Spottiswoode).

1900. Some Recollections of Work with Miss Buss (*Frances Mary Buss Schools Jubilee Magazine*, April, 1900).

1905. *The Women's Suffrage Movement (two articles in the *Girton Review*).

1906. A Plea for Discrimination (Women's Suffrage leaflet).

1907–8. *Letters to *The Times* and *The Spectator* on Women's Suffrage.

1910. Thoughts on Some Questions Relating to Women.

II. WRITINGS BY MADAME BODICHON.

Note.—Madame Bodichon wrote a number of letters and short articles to the *Englishwoman's Journal* (referred to as *E.W.J.*) which are not included in this list.

1854. A Brief Summary, in Plain Language, of the most important Laws concerning Women. By Barbara Leigh Smith.
Second edition, 1856.
Third edition, by B. L. S. Bodichon, 1869.

1857. Women and Work.

1858. Algeria Considered as a Winter Residence for the English [by Dr. and Madame Bodichon]. Published at the *E.W.J.* Office.
Slavery in America. By B.[2] [Dr. and Madame Bodichon] (*E.W.J.*, Oct., 1858).
An American School (*E.W.J.*, Nov., 1858).

1860. Slave Preaching (*E.W.J.*, March, 1860).
Algiers : First Impressions. By B. L. S. B. (*E.W.J.*, Sept., 1860).
Middle Class Schools for Girls (Social Science Association) (*E.W.J.*, Nov., 1860).

1861. Slavery in the South (*E.W.J.*, Oct., Nov. and Dec., 1861).

1862. Painted Glass Windows executed by the Carmelite Nuns of Le Mans (*E.W.J.*, Jan., 1862).

1863. Of those who are the property of others, and of the great power that holds others as property (*E.W.J.*, Feb., 1863).
Cleopatra's Daughter, St. Marciana, Mama Marabout, and other Algerian Women (*E.W.J.*, Feb., 1863).

* Reprinted in *Thoughts on Some Questions Relating to Women.*

BIBLIOGRAPHY

1866. Reasons for the Enfranchisement of Women, by Mrs. Bodichon (Social Science Association). Published as a pamphlet.

1866. Objections to the Enfranchisement of Women Considered. By Mrs. Bodichon (pamphlet).

1868. Australian Forests and African Deserts (article in *Pall Mall Gazette*).

1869. Reasons For and Against the Enfranchisement of Women. By Mrs. Bodichon.
Second edition, 1872.

A number of letters from Madame Bodichon have been published in *Letters to William Allingham* (1911), and in *Hertha Ayrton : A Memoir*. By Evelyn Sharp (1926).

INDEX

Acland, Sir Thomas Dyke, 83, 85–7, 131, 136–7

Adams, Professor J. C., 250 *n*, 322

Aldis, W. S., 323

Alford, Dean, 87, 161, 172–3

Alford, Mrs., 111

Allingham, William, 47–8, 76

Anderson, Mrs. Garrett (Elizabeth Garrett), character, 3 ; first acquaintance with Miss Davies, 26 ; shares Miss Davies's interest in women's movement, 52–3 ; enters on study of medicine, 55–8 ; early education, 56 ; work at Middlesex Hospital, 58–66 ; allowed to enter for L.S.A., 66–7 ; efforts to obtain leave to matriculate at London University, 67, 72–4 ; work for L.S.A., 78–81 ; work at London Hospital, 78–9 ; application to College of Physicians refused, 79–80 ; takes Paris M.D., 80 ; declines to be called Doctor, 80 ; marriage, 80 ; opens women's dispensary, 80 ; Senior Physician of New Hospital for Women, 80 ; Dean of London School of Medicine for Women, 80

attends discussion on Local Examinations, 90 ; joins Kensington Society, 106 ; works for first Suffrage petition, 111–12 ; on Women's Suffrage Committee, 116–17 ; on London School Board, 120–7 ; attends Social Science Congresses, 135, 178 ; subscribes to Girton, 151, 173, 318 ; visits Mrs. Davies, 162 ;

member of College House Committee, 218 ; visits The College, Hitchin, 235 ; speaks at St. James's Hall meeting, 257–8 ; answers Dr. Maudsley's article, 291–2 ; member of Cambridge Degrees Committee, 327 ; supports Women's Suffrage, 347–8

Anderson, Mrs. Garrett, letters from, to Miss Davies, 53, 55, 57, 58, 59, 61–8, 79, 80, 100, 120, 326 ; to Mr. Anderson, 124, 125, 265

Anderson, Mr. J. G. S., 124, 125, 258, 265

Archer-Hind, Mr. R. D., 328, 329

Arnold, Matthew, 77, 130, 145, 189, 198

Association for promoting the Higher Education of Women in Cambridge, 247, 287, 324

Association of University Women Teachers, 355

Athenæum, 10, 102

Austen, Jane, 7, 12, 15

Austin, Mrs. (Annie Crow), 26, 53, 121, 162, 168, 172, 208, 218, 220, 236, 237, 241–3, 246, 249, 269

Ayrton, Mrs. (Hertha Marks), 48, 187, 306, 317

Barchester Towers, 14

Beale, Dorothea, 13, 84, 97, 106, 132*n*, 138, 158

Becker, Lydia, 111, 115, 119, 120

Bedford College, 13, 33, 97, 131, 134–6, 142, 146, 147, 168, 334

Belloc, Madame (Bessie Rayner Parkes), 34, 37, 41, 43, 47, 50–52, 54, 75*n*, 76, 107, 268*n*, 347–8, 363

377

INDEX

INDEX

INDEX

Glasgow, 354-5 ; Jubilee presentation to, 355 ; Jubilee of Girton, 355 ; death, 355 ; commemoration of, 356

Davies, Emily, letters from :

to Matthew Arnold, 130

to Mme. Bodichon, 108, 109, 116, 117, 138, 140, 150, 157-8, 169, 178, 193, 196, 205, 208, 210, 215, 216, 222, 249, 261, 272, 280, 282, 284, 286, 288, 293, 295, 296, 298, 299, 301, 302, 303, 305, 307, 308, 313, 321, 323, 325, 326

to Mrs. Bradley, 212

to Rev. W. H. Crosskey, 263

to Miss Jane Crow, 70, 182-4, 184-6

to Miss Elizabeth Garrett, 124

to an enquirer, 256

to George Grote, 131

to R. H. Hutton, 103-5

to Dr. Henry Jackson, 328

to Miss Adelaide Manning, 91, 102, 110-14, 117-18, 123, 161, 176, 195-6, 198, 207, 210-11, 224, 228, 236, 276, 281, 286, 295-6, 303-4, 308, 315-17, 342-3, 348

to Mrs. Manning, 211, 218, 234, 236

to Mr. E. H. Morgan, 274

to Mr. Plumptre, 146

to Miss Anna Richardson, 71, 83, 88-9, 106, 114, 118, 149, 151, 159, 162, 166-8, 174, 178, 188-92, 194, 196, 202, 204, 207, 209, 213, 216, 227, 235, 237-9, 247, 249, 260, 262

to Mr. H. J. Roby, 132, 135

to Professor Sidgwick, 251, 255

to Mr. H. R. Tomkinson, 24, 88-90, 100, 109, 121-3, 158, 164, 166, 172, 174, 195-6, 208, 226, 242-3, 254, 256, 258, 261, 267, 269-71, 278-81, 285

Davies, Emily, writings by, 29-30, 53, 74-7, 94-7, 99, 102, 116, 133, 142-5, 174-6, 251n, 261, 311-12, 332-3, 349, 350, 375-4

Davies, Henry Barton, 21, 26, 28

Davies, Rev. John, 19-22, 24, 26-7, 67

Davies, Rev. J. Llewelyn, 20, 26-8, 52, 56, 67-70, 72, 120, 132, 172, 203, 211, 214, 248, 271, 283-4, 307, 318, 325, 327, 339, 354

Davies, Mary Jane, 20-3, 27-8

Davies, Mrs. John, 20-3, 25-6, 121, 271, 308

Davies, Mrs. J. Llewelyn, 69, 70, 73, 106, 304

Davies, William Stephen, 20, 23, 25-8

De la Tour du Pin, Madame, 11

Degrees for Women, 322-6, 327-30, 331-4, 357-8

Dicey, Edward, 77, 100, 364

Disraeli, Benjamin, 14

Divorce, Act of 1857, 42

Domestic Life, 8n

Dove, Miss Jane Frances, 223, 225-6, 246n, 272n, 282-3, 292n, 340, 364

Drapers' Company, 313

Durham, Miss Florence, 337

Edinburgh Review, 41n

Education of girls, 12-13, 128-9

Education of Girls, by Dr. Hodgson, 92

Eliot, George, 13, 37, 44, 49, 54, 169-71, 173, 180-7, 196, 222, 227, 243, 305

Ellis, Mrs. William, 7, 8, 16n

Elmy, Mrs. Wolstenholme. *See* Miss Wolstenholme

Endowed Schools Act, 133

Endowments for girls' schools, 133-4, 141

English Female Artists, by Ellen Clayton, 39n

English Maiden, The, 7

Englishwoman's Journal, The, 13n, 29, 39n, 40n, 41n, 45, 50-2, 54-5, 60, 64, 73n, 75-6, 128n, 137n, 148

Englishwoman's Review, The, 39n, 52n

Essays in Defence of Women, 173-4

Examinations :

Cambridge Examinations for Women, 188-95, 217, 256

Higher Local, 194n, 278, 324

Little-go, 217, 231, 238-40, 272-5, 277-9, 324, 326-30

Previous. *See* Little-go

Senior and Junior Local, 83-102, 105, 136, 141, 188-9, 210, 304, 307

Tripos, 275-7

381

INDEX

INDEX

Little-go. *See* Examinations

Liveing, Professor G. D., 83–4, 99, 149, 190, 206–7, 213, 250n, 282, 287, 322, 327–9

Liverpool, meeting, 284–5
  Memorial against admission of girls to Local Examinations, 98–9, 102

University, 310n

Lloyd, Miss Anna, 213, 217, 219, 221, 225, 227, 232, 235

London Schoolmistresses' Association, 140, 147, 184, 292, 303–4, 325

Lubbock, Lady. *See* Herschel, Miss C. A.

Lumsden, Dame Louisa, 216, 219–20, 222–4, 227, 229, 232–3, 235, 237–40, 242, 272, 276, 280–1, 283–4, 291, 292n, 293–5, 299, 320

Lyell, Sir Charles, 159, 166

Lyttelton, Lord, 74, 90, 98, 130, 136, 150–1, 161, 176–7, 257, 367

MacAlister, Dr., 333

McArthur, Miss E. A., 111

Maitland, Professor, 333–4

Malleson,·Mrs. F. (Miss Whitehead), 35–7, 140

Maltby, Dr., 22

Manchester Assize Courts, 149, 151

Manchester meeting of Schoolmistresses, 146, 148

Manchester University, 310n, 321

Manning, Miss Adelaide, 69, 70, 106, 140, 166, 184–6, 210–11, 218–20, 234, 281, 286, 304, 315, 347, 354

Manning, Mrs. Charlotte, 69, 87, 97, 106, 113–14, 147, 165, 171, 173, 196, 204, 210–11, 218, 220, 222, 227, 233–4, 237, 267, 281, 367

Manning, H. E., Cardinal, 19, 22

Manning, Mr. Serjeant, 40, 41, 69, 367

Mario, Madame (Jessie Meriton White), 72, 305, 366, 372

Married Women's Property Act (1882), 42
  Bill (1856–7), 40–3, 69

Married Women's Property Committee, Report of, 42n
  Petitions, 41, 74

Markby, Thomas, 99, 100–1, 189, 193

Marks, Hertha. *See* Mrs. Ayrton

Martin, Mrs. Theodore (Helen Faucit), 17

Martineau, Miss Harriet, 6, 13n, 33, 42, 51

Mason, Miss Annabella, 27

Maudsley, Dr., 290–2

Maurice, Rev. F. D., 27–8, 37, 70, 73–4, 76–7, 90, 107–8, 203

Maynard, Miss C. L., 222–5, 231, 268n, 288, 321.

Memoirs of a Highland Lady, 11

Mental and Moral Dignity of Woman, The, 7

Metcalfe, Miss Fanny, 140, 196, 199n, 211, 214, 251, 261, 267, 293, 295, 301, 367

Middlesex Hospital, 58–66

Mill, John Stuart, 74, 90, 107–9, 111–14, 117–18, 121, 123, 132, 231, 246n

Milnes, R. Monckton, 41, 73

Minturn, Miss E. T., 299

Miss Mackenzie, by Anthony Trollope, 12n

Mohl, Madame, 10, 368

Morgan, Mr. E. H. 273–5.

Moulton, J. F. (Lord Justice Moulton), 230

Mrs. Caudle's Curtain Lectures, 15

Müller, Miss H., 321

Municipal Franchise opened to women, 120

Murray, Miss, 13

National Association for the Promotion of Social Science, 74–6
  Congress of 1857 (Birmingham), 128
  1860 (Glasgow), 128
  1862 (London), 74–5, 82
  Special meeting, 1864, in London, 90–2
  Congress of 1864 (York), 92–6, 129, 142
  1865 (Sheffield), 133
  1866 (Manchester), 114–15
  1868 (Birmingham), 174–9

National Indian Association, 69

National Union of Women Workers, 354

384

INDEX